24Hours
to the Postal Exam

Shannon R. Turlington
Ellen Lichtenstein

2nd Edition

THOMSON
ARCO

Australia • Canada • Mexico • Singapore • Spain • United Kingdom • United States

An ARCO Book

ARCO is a registered trademark of Thomson Learning, Inc., and is used herein under license by Peterson's.

About The Thomson Corporation and Peterson's

The Thomson Corporation, with 2002 revenues of $7.8 billion, is a global leader in providing integrated information solutions to business and professional customers. The Corporation's common shares are listed on the Toronto and New York stock exchanges (TSX: TOC; NYSE: TOC). Its learning businesses and brands serve the needs of individuals, learning institutions, corporations, and government agencies with products and services for both traditional and distributed learning. Peterson's (www.petersons.com) is a leading provider of education information and advice, with books and online resources focusing on education search, test preparation, and financial aid. Its Web site offers searchable databases and interactive tools for contacting educational institutions, online practice tests and instruction, and planning tools for securing financial aid. Peterson's serves 110 million education consumers annually.

For more information, contact Peterson's, 2000 Lenox Drive, Lawrenceville, NJ 08648; 800-338-3282; or find us on the World Wide Web at: www.petersons.com/about

ISBN 0-7689-1409-4

Printed in Canada

10 9 8 7 6 5 4 3 2 1   05 04 03

Second Edition

Contents

Part I   **Working for the United States Postal Service (USPS)**

Part II   Preparing for Test 470

Introduction

Welcome to *24 Hours to the Postal Exam*. By working your way through these pages, you'll get a fast-paced course on all the key points you need to know to score high on your United States Postal Service exam and get the job you want. In just 24 one-hour lessons, you'll review all the topics and concepts that are tested on the Postal Exam and learn powerful strategies for answering every question type.

How to Use This Book

This book was designed as a 24-hour teach-yourself training course, complete with examples, workshops, practice sessions, timed tests, and a full-length sample test. It is expected that you can complete each lesson in about an hour; however, you should work at your own pace. If you think you can complete more than one lesson in an hour, go for it! Also, if you think that you should spend more than one hour on a certain topic, spend as much time as you need.

Here is how the book is organized:

Part I: Working for the United States Postal Service (USPS)

The first section of the book gives you a quick overview of important facts you need to know about the U.S. Postal Service job market as well as the jobs covered by the standard Postal Service exam, Test 470. You'll learn:

- Where to get job information.
- How to apply for Postal Service positions.
- The basic requirements for working for the Postal Service.
- The benefits and responsibilities of Postal Service jobs.
- What to expect on test day.

Part II: Preparing for Test 470

This section of the book focuses on teaching strategies for answering the four different question types that you'll find on the Postal Service exam. First, you'll find a general overview of the test, including scoring information and general test-taking strategies.

Each chapter after that goes more in-depth into the specific question types and teaches you proven strategies for tackling them. A workshop is included for practice with each strategy. The question types include:

- Address Checking
- Memory for Addresses
- Number Series
- Following Oral Instructions

Part III: Timed and Untimed Tests

The last section of the book, starting with Hour 13 includes important test-taking practice. Each hour focuses on one of the question types with untimed practice exercises and follows up with timed tests that simulate the actual exam conditions as closely as possible. There's even a bonus hour—a full-length, timed practice exam—that's just like the real thing. Once you have finished this section, you'll be ready for your test day and will be fully prepared to get your best score on the Postal Service exam.

Special Features of This Book

The following special features are included to help highlight important concepts and information:

- A **Note** box presents interesting pieces of information related to the surrounding discussion.
- A **Tip** box offers advice or teaches you an easier way to do something.
- A **Caution** box advises you about potential problems and helps you steer clear of disaster.
- A **Make Connections** box tells you where you can find more information on a particular subject elsewhere in the book.

Part I

Working for the United States Postal Service (USPS)

Hour

HOUR 1

Finding Post Office Jobs

What You Will Learn in This Hour

In this hour, you'll be introduced to your potential employer, the United States Postal Service (USPS), and learn how you get hired for the most popular entry-level jobs. The extremely competitive nature of this hiring process demands you know as much as possible about the work and the written examination you will be required to take—Test 470. You will become a stronger candidate for the job when you have a greater understanding of the USPS and its employment procedures. Here are your goals for this hour:

- Learn key facts about USPS history and organization.
- Understand the benefits of working for the USPS.
- Find out what qualifications are needed for employment.
- Understand the USPS hiring process and how to seek out job openings.
- Learn everything you need to know about test application procedures.
- Learn about Veterans Preference.

3

About the USPS

The more you know about the postal service, the better your chances of getting hired. So here's a brief history and description of the USPS.

The United States Postal Service (USPS) is an independent agency of the United States federal government. It was created by the Postal Reorganization Act of 1970 and began operations on July 1, 1971. Previously, postal services had been carried out by the Post Office Department (POD), a branch of Congress. However, the critical need for modernizing postal operations in the 1960s brought about the creation of the new agency.

As the nation's largest civilian employer, with more than 856,000 employees, the USPS handles 41 percent of the world's mail volume, 630 million pieces every day.

Almost 85 percent of all postal workers are in jobs directly related to processing and delivering mail. This group involves postal clerks, city carriers, rural carriers, mail handlers, and truck drivers. Postmasters and supervisors make up nearly 10 percent of total employment, and maintenance workers about four percent. The remainder includes such groups as postal inspectors, guards, personnel workers, and secretaries.

Technological Innovation in Today's USPS

When you work for today's USPS, you will come in contact with many high-tech systems and procedures. The first extensive application of technology started in the late 1960s when MultiPosition Letter Machines (MPLSMs) began replacing manual mail-sorting equipment. In the early 1980s, more advanced automated technology, Optical Character Readers and Bar Code Sorters, were introduced and are now essential components in the mail processing environment. The latest technological advance is the Remote Bar Coding System (RBCS).

Tip
Remember the saying "knowledge is power"? Passing a written test is just one hurdle in the hiring process. When it comes time for your personal interview, you need to know about your potential employer. Use the information in this chapter as a stepping stone. If you have access to the Internet, go directly to the official USPS Web site (**http://www.usps. gov**) for useful information on USPS organizational history and technological growth.

1

Where the Jobs Are

The USPS operates more than 41,000 installations. Most are post offices, but some serve special purposes such as handling payroll records, supplying equipment, or maintaining vehicles.

Urban Postal Operations

Although every community receives mail service, employment is concentrated in large metropolitan areas. Post offices in New York City, Chicago, and Los Angeles employ large work forces to process huge amounts of mail for their own populations and to serve as mail-processing points for the smaller communities that surround them.

Remote Encoding Centers

The first move toward decentralizing postal operations has been the development of the RBCS at Remote Encoding Centers. These centers are being established outside the most congested population centers where land, construction, and operating expenses are far lower. The centers are becoming an important source of new postal jobs.

Advantages of Working for the USPS

If you're thinking about working for the USPS, you are not alone. Each year thousands of qualified applicants compete for USPS jobs that offer attractive salaries, a solid pension plan, and job security. Because the number of applicants for the most desired jobs—postal clerk and mail carrier—far exceeds the number of job openings, expect keen competition throughout the hiring process.

Employee Benefits

USPS employees are federal workers who enjoy the benefits offered to federal government workers. These include:

- An automatic raise at least once a year
- Regular cost-of-living adjustments
- Liberal paid vacation days (13-26), paid holidays (10), and paid sick leave days (13) each year
- Health and life insurance

- Pension plan
- Uniform allowance (if applicable)
- Credit unit availability

Strong Unions

Many postal workers belong to one of four unions:

- American Postal Workers Union, AFAL-CIO
- National Association of Letter Carriers, AFL-CIO
- National Postal Mail Handlers Union, AFL-CIO
- National Rural Letter Carriers Association

These unions have been very effective bargainers for their members.

Career Opportunities

The postal service is committed to providing career development opportunities for its employees and prefers to hire from within its own ranks before taking on new applicants.

Job Bids

If you are a postal employee in good standing and are interested in different work within the service, you may submit a written request "bid" for a job when a suitable vacancy occurs. The bidder who meets the qualifications, including exam requirements, and has the most seniority gets the job. You do not have to retake a written examination that you have already taken.

> **Tip**
> As you will learn below, the hiring process is slow, and, because the post office hires from within, you may not see an opening for the job you want for some time. Exam 470, however, covers eight different jobs. If you get hired for one job covered by the test battery, you do not have to retake the test to change positions.

Training and Promotion

You can advance to better-paying positions within the postal service by learning new skills. Training programs are available for low-skilled workers who wish to become technicians or mechanics.

Promotion to supervisory positions is possible and applicants for such jobs must pass an examination. Additional requirements for promotion may include:

- Training or education
- A satisfactory work record
- Appropriate personal characteristics such as leadership ability

If the leading candidates are equally qualified, length of service is also included.

Basic Job Requirements

Before you spend a lot of time on a job search, check to see if you can meet the minimum requirements for all USPS jobs:

- **Age Limits:** You must be at least 18 years of age at the time of appointment; however, high school graduates may begin work at 16 years of age if the job is not hazardous and does not require driving.
- **Citizenship:** You must be a U.S. citizen or be a permanent resident alien.
- **Drug Screening:** You must be willing to pass a urinalysis drug test.
- **Physical Agility Test:** You may be required to take a physical agility test depending on your job requirements.
- **Medical Review:** If you are offered employment, you will be required to pass a medical exam to see if you can physically handle the work required on your job.
- **Driver's License:** You must possess a valid driver's license and a good driving record if your work requires driving.
- **Suitable Screening:** You will be required to pass a suitability screening, including a background investigation.

> **Note**
> Because of the keen competition for clerk-carrier positions, you can expect a one- to two-year waiting period for employment after passing the required written exam. Most new hires are over age 25 and transfer from other occupations.

How to Find USPS Jobs

Finding out about USPS job openings takes some doing. You can't just sit back and wait for a classified notice in your local newspaper to appear. You have to be proactive.

Locating job openings can be done in a number of ways, including using Internet resources. Unfortunately, the USPS Web site provides no employment information.

USPS District Offices

One of the best ways to locate jobs and obtain application information is to contact the post office Customer Service District (CDC) office nearest you. You can either write or call CDC Human Resources for registration information.

CDC offices are also listed in the post office's two-volume *National Five-Digit Zip Code and Post Office Directory*. Copies of the directory are usually provided in post office lobbies.

Local Post Offices

Always check the bulletin board in your local post office for hiring information. Because hiring decisions are made at the local level, this may be a good option for applicants in rural areas. The postmaster may be able to give you helpful information.

State Employment Office

Openings are announced and posted in state employment offices. Thus, you will have to go to the office to check out job openings. If you have Internet access, you should log on to America's Job Bank (**http://www.ajb.dni.us**) for links to all state employment Web sites. In addition to job postings, you will find valuable employment information at both America's Job Bank and the state job sites to help in your job search.

Office of Personnel Management Web Site

At the OPM site (**http://www.usajobs.opm.gov**), you can search for jobs in all government agencies including the USPS. Jobs are listed nationwide, so if you've thought about relocating, here is your chance. Check this site as often as possible.

Additional Sources of Job Information

This section looks at some further possibilites on how to find information about USPS job openings.

Classified Ads

Always check your Sunday classifieds for job announcements. Once a decision has been made to open an examination, the post office will place ads in local newspapers.

Print and Online Services

The following are good sources of Federal job information:

- **Federal Employee News Digest:** This is a free service to search for government employment (**http://www.fendonline.com**).
- **Federal Job Central:** A subscription service run by the Federal Research Service (**http://www.fedjobs.com**).

Test Battery 470

This section will prepare you for Test Battery 470, the required primary test for eight popular and highly competitive entry-level jobs.

- Window or Counter Clerk
- City Carrier
- Distribution Clerk
- Flat Sorting Machine Operator
- Mail Handler
- Mail Processor
- Mark-Up Clerk, Automated
- Rural Carrier

Note
Strictly speaking, you must take Test Battery 460 to apply for rural carrier jobs. However, Exam 460 is exactly the same as Exam 470. The USPS uses different test titles for administrative purposes.

Make Connections
Full descriptions of all the above jobs are provided in Hour 2, "Jobs Covered Under Test 470."

Applying for Test 470

When an opening has been announced, you will need to apply for Test 470 within the specified application period. Do the following as quickly as possible:

1. Ask the CDC, the hiring post office, or your local post office for Form 2479 (see the sample USPS Application form). The two-section form is a bright yellow perforated card. Do *not* separate the sections.

2. Follow the instructions precisely for filling out both sections that are printed on the back of the card.

3. Fill in all required information including your name and address, birth date, telephone number, title of examination, post office location applied for, date of application, title of examination, and military service information with Veterans Preference claim.

4. Hand in or mail the completed application.

Caution
We have separated the sections of the sample form to fit the book page. Do not do this yourself.

Tip
Because applicants are scheduled for the written test in the order that applications are received, you need to take action fast. In addition, the application period may not last longer than five business days, so you need to sign up as quickly as possible.

After receiving your application, the post office will mail you the following:

- Notification of the examination date, time, and place
- Admission card portion of the application form
- Sample answer sheet for completion
- Test information, including sample questions
- Exam center admission requirements

(Front)   (Back)

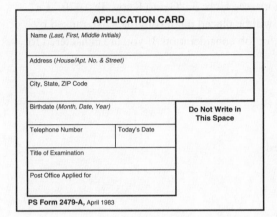

Sample Answer Sheet

You must fill in the sample answer sheet to be admitted to the testing center. Take as much time as you need to fill it in accurately and completely. At the test center, you will transfer the information on the sample answer sheet to the actual answer sheet.

Test Center Admission Requirements

You will need to bring the following four items to the test center:

- Completed sample answer sheet
- Admission card/notice
- Photo ID
- Two sharpened no. 2 pencils

> **Caution**
> Make a checklist of the above items once you are notified about the exam. You will not be admitted to the test center without any of the above.

Getting Hired

If you pass the test with a score of 70 or more (see Hour 3, "Get to Know Test 470," for complete scoring information), your name will be placed on the eligibles list, ranked by exam score. Names are selected top-down for job consideration. If you are considered for a job, you must then do the following:

- Fill out an employment application
- Pass a background investigation
- Take a personal interview
- Take a physical agility test, if required
- Pass a drug test
- Pass a medical examination

Veterans Preference

If you can take Veterans Preference, you may be able to boost your test score. By law, veterans who are disabled or who served on active duty in the Armed Forces during certain specified time periods or in military campaigns are entitled to preference over nonveterans.

In the examination process, Veterans Preference may entitle you to have either five or ten points added to your test score if you achieve a score of 70 or higher on the test. You can apply for Veterans Preference if you meet the eligibility requirements.

General Requirements

- An honorable or general discharge is necessary.
- Military retirees at the rank of major, lieutenant commander, or higher are not eligible for preference unless they are disabled.
- Guard and Reserve active duty for training purposes does not qualify for preference.

Five-Point Preference Requirements

Five points are added to the passing examination scores of veterans who served during any of the following:

- Any war (defined as a war declared by Congress)
- The period April 28, 1952, through July 1, 1995

- More than 180 consecutive days, any part of which occurred after January 31, 1955, and before October 15, 1976
- The Gulf War from August 2, 1990, through January 2, 1992
- A campaign or expedition for which a campaign medal has been authorized, including El Salvador, Grenada, Haiti, Lebanon, Panama, Somalia, Southwest Asia, and Bosnia and Herzegovina.

Ten-Point Preference Requirements

Ten points are added to the passing examination scores of the following:

- A veteran who served at any time and who (1) has a present service-connected disability, or (2) is receiving compensation, disability retirement benefits, or pension from the military or the Department of Veterans Affairs. Purple Heart recipients qualify as disabled veterans.
- An unmarried spouse of certain veterans or a spouse of a veteran unable to work because of a service-connected disability.
- A mother of a veteran who died in service or is permanently and totally disabled.

Caution
Entitlement to Veterans Preference does not guarantee a job. You must prepare for the exam as vigorously as all other applicants.

Claiming Veterans Preference

When applying for federal jobs, eligible veterans should claim preference on their application or resume. Applicants claiming ten-point preference must complete SF-15, the application for ten-point Veteran Preference.

Special Filing Procedures

Veterans may be able to file job applications after examinations have been closed:

- A veteran with a ten-point preference may file an application at any time for any position for which a nontemporary appointment has been made from a competitive list of eligibles within the past three years.
- A veteran who is unable to file for an open competitive examination because of military service may file after the closing date.

Exam Scoring

Once the five- or ten-point preference is added to a score, the applicant is ranked along with all other applicants in numerical order. Disabled veterans who have a compensable, service-connected disability of 10 percent or more, however, are placed at the top of the eligibility list.

Tip

For additional help on understanding Veterans Preference, contact these sources:

1. Use the Internet to access the Office of Personnel Management Web site (**http://www.opm.gov**).
2. Get help from a veteran representative in your State Employment Service Office.

Q&A

Q If my name is placed on the register, will I get hired?

A Not necessarily because many other factors are involved. For example, if the post office fills all the open positions before reaching your name on the list, you will not be considered for selection. In addition, you have to do well on your interview and pass the other required tests. If you fail the drug test, you will probably not be considered for selection.

Q If I had a past employment problem or was convicted of a crime, will I be automatically disqualified?

A You won't be automatically disqualified, but a troubled work record will not be looked upon favorably. Be sure that you answer all questions honestly on your job application form. The USPS will verify your work history, education, and citizenship status; contact former employers; and perform a criminal records and military check.

When you get to the interview, deal with all concerns about your background, answer all questions honestly, and show why you're the best applicant for the job.

Q How seriously should I prepare for the interview?

A Very seriously. The interview could be your make-or-break situation. Many candidates who score high on Exam 470 may be interviewed. However, the interviewer will use the job interview to determine the best candidates. You will have to prove why the USPS should hire you.

> **Tip**
> You will want to prepare seriously for your interview. At your local library or bookstore, you'll find many books with good advice about job interviews. For example, *Peterson's Insider's Guide to Finding the Perfect Job* by Robert Orndorff offers suggestions for handling difficult interview questions, dressing for the interview, behavior and etiquette, and interview follow-up procedures.

Q What is a conditional offer of employment?

A If you are judged suitable for employment based on your background investigation, personal interview, and drug and physical ability tests, then you will be made a conditional offer of employment, subject to a satisfactory medical exam. This is determined by law; a medical examination cannot be done unless you are offered employment.

The Hour in Review

1. Hour 1 shows you the benefits of working for the postal service and how to seek out employment in a competitive environment.

2. Knowing about the USPS, its history, and recent technological innovations will make you a better candidate at the job interview.

3. Use as many resources as possible to seek out entry-level jobs and expect fierce competition for any job when an examination is announced.

4. Get your application form in as early as possible. Make sure you fill it out accurately and completely.

5. Fill in your sample answer sheet carefully and have all your test admissions items ready before examination day.

6. Prepare seriously for your job interview and know how to handle questions about your past employment history.

7. Take advantage of the Veterans Preference if you qualify for it.

HOUR 2

Jobs Covered Under Test 470

What You Will Learn in This Hour

In this hour, you'll learn all about the eight entry-level jobs covered by Test 470. These positions in mail processing, distribution, and delivery form the backbone of USPS employment. You may see them as career opportunities in themselves or as entrees to other USPS jobs. Here are your goals for this hour:

- Learn about the most desired entry-level jobs: postal clerks and mail carriers.
- Understand job responsibilities.
- Learn about the working conditions you may face.
- Learn the employment outlook for post office occupations.

> **Note**
> Clerks and carriers are distinguished by the type of work they do. Postal clerks are usually classified by the mail processing function they perform, such as sorting or distributing, whereas carriers are classified by their type of route, city or rural.

Importance of Postal Clerks and Carriers

Postal clerk and carrier positions form the largest component of USPS jobs and are the most visible representatives of the USPS to the public. Currently, the postal service employs about 297,000 clerks and mail handlers and 332,000 mail carriers (48,000 of whom are rural carriers). The amount of work they perform is awesome when viewed by numbers:

- Post offices serve an average of seven million customers each day.
- More than 3.4 billion pieces of mail are delivered every week.
- Daily mail delivery and pick-up are provided for over 130 million households and businesses.

All applicants for clerk and carrier positions, as well as for several mail-processing jobs, must pass Test 470.

Window or Counter Clerk

These are the people you see behind the counter in the lobby at your local post office. If you like working with the public, this might be the right job for you.

Responsibilities

Window or counter clerks perform the following tasks:

- Selling stamps, money orders, postal stationery, and mailing envelopes or boxes
- Weighing packages to determine postage
- Checking that packages are in satisfactory condition for mailing
- Registering, certifying, and insuring mail
- Answering questions about postage rates, post office boxes, mailing restrictions, and other postal matters
- Helping customers file claims for damaged packages

> **Note**
> The size of the post office you work for can affect your job duties. As a window clerk in a large post office, your duties primarily involve the above. In a smaller post office, you will probably be required to perform some sorting functions.

Working Conditions

Window clerk positions are very desirable, but you should consider these pros and cons if you want to apply for this job:

Pros

- You will usually work in clean, well-ventilated, and well-lit buildings.
- You will have a wide variety of duties and frequent contact with the public.
- You will rarely work at night.

Cons

- You may have to deal with upset and angry customers.
- You must stand for long periods of time.
- You are held accountable for the assigned stock of stamps and postal funds.

Distribution Clerk (Including Distribution Clerk, Machine)

The majority of postal clerks are distribution clerks who sort incoming and outgoing mail in workrooms.

Responsibilities

When mail arrives at the post office, distribution clerks and mail handlers sort the mail by category: letters, parcel post, and magazine and newspapers. Distribution clerks are then responsible for:

- Feeding letters into stamp-canceling machines and canceling other mail by hand
- Separating mail into primary destination categories: local area, nearby states, distant states, and large cities
- Separating mail into secondary distribution areas

Distribution clerks sort mail using a complicated scheme that must be memorized. Distribution clerks, machine (also called letter sorting machine operators) must learn computer codes for automatic mail sorting and routing.

Working Conditions

Working conditions differ according to specific work assignments, post office size, and the amount of labor-saving machinery at the facility:

- In small post offices, you must carry heavy mail sacks regularly from one part of the building to the other and sort mail by hand.
- In large post offices, chutes and conveyors move the mail and much of the sorting is done by machine.

The pros and cons of being a distribution clerk are as follows:

Pros

- Work is primarily indoors.
- The starting salary is higher than for other postal clerks.
- Increased automation within the USPS has made this job quite secure.

Cons

- You must handle mail sacks weighing as much as 70 pounds.
- You may be on your feet all day.
- Weekend and night work is frequently required.
- Work may become very routine.
- You will work closely with other clerks, frequently under tension and the strain of meeting deadlines.

City Carrier

Once mail has been processed and sorted, it must be delivered by a mail carrier. In the cities and the suburbs, this is the job of the city carrier. Most city carriers travel planned routes delivering and collecting mail.

Responsibilities

For city carriers, each workday generally has three parts:

1. Early in the morning, carriers perform a number of tasks:

    - They arrange their mail for delivery.

    - They readdress letters to be forwarded.

    - They also take care of other details.

2. Later, carriers cover their routes on foot, by vehicle, or a combination of both:

    - On foot, they carry a heavy load of mail or push it in a cart.

    - Residential carriers cover their routes only once a day, but carriers assigned to a business district may make two trips or more.

    - Deliveries are made house to house except in large buildings, such as apartment houses, that have all the mailboxes on the first floor.

    - In addition to making deliveries, carriers collect c.o.d. fees and obtain signed receipts for registered, certified, and insured mail. If a customer is not at home, the carrier leaves a notice telling where the special mail is being held.

    - Carriers answer customer questions about postal regulations and services and provide change of address cards and other postal forms when requested.

    - Carriers also pick up letters to be mailed.

3. After completing their routes, carriers return to the post office with mail gathered from street collection boxes, homes, and businesses:

    - They turn in the mail receipts collected during the day.

    - They may separate letters and parcels for further processing by clerks.

> **Note**
> Many carriers have more specialized duties than those described. Some deliver only parcel post, while others only collect mail from street boxes and office mail chutes.

Working Conditions

The job of a carrier definitely has its pros and cons. Being outdoors for much of the workday, may or may not be very appealing to you. Here are some other aspects of the job to think about:

Pros

- If you begin work early in the morning, you will be through by early afternoon.
- You spend most of the day on your own, relatively free from direct supervision.
- You are free to work at your own pace as long as you cover your route within a specified time period.

Cons

- You will probably begin work very early in the morning, as early as 4 a.m. for routes in business districts.
- You may be required to work overtime during peak delivery times, such as before holidays.
- You will be outdoors in all kinds of weather.
- Even if you use a vehicle, you must often walk when making deliveries and lift heavy sacks of parcel post items when loading vehicles.
- You will be subject to hazards such as wet and icy roads and sidewalks.
- You will face that constant threat to mail carriers: Dogs.

Rural Carrier

Rural carriers do many of the same things as city carriers and window clerks, but their job also has certain special characteristics of its own. The working conditions are similar to that of city carriers.

Responsibilities

The workday of a rural carrier also generally has three stages, as follows:

1. First, early in the day at the post office, a rural carrier sorts and loads mail for delivery.
2. After loading, the rural carrier covers his or her route, often driving over unpaved roads and rough terrain, performing mail delivery, pickup, and other functions.
    - Most deliveries and pickups of outgoing mail are made from the car.
    - Occasionally, bulky packages must be delivered directly to the homeowner's door.
    - As necessary, rural carriers sell stamps and money orders, weigh and set charges for packages, and accept parcels, letters, and items to be registered, certified, or insured.

- Carriers answer customer questions about postal regulations and services and provide change of address cards and other postal forms when requested.

3. Finally, after returning to the post office, the rural carrier has some additional tasks to perform:

- Mail receipts and money collected during the day must be turned in.

- Postal funds and supplies taken on must be accounted for.

2

> **Note**
> Do you like to get involved in community work? Many mail carriers, city and rural, are involved in community service. In addition to their regularly scheduled duties, many carriers participate in neighborhood service programs in which they check on elderly or shut-in patrons or notify the police of any suspicious activities along their routes.

> **Caution**
> If you want to be a mail carrier, you must have a driver's license and a good driving record, and you must receive a passing grade on a road test.
> City carriers may have vehicles provided by the postal service; however, most rural carriers use their own automobiles.

Mail Handlers

Mail handlers load, unload, and move bulk mail and perform duties related to the movement and processing of mail. If you are interested in applying for this position, make sure you read the requirements for the strength and stamina test first.

Responsibilities

Mail handlers perform a variety of tasks:

- Unloading sacks of incoming mail
- Separating letters, parcel posts, magazines, and newspapers
- Transporting mail to sorting and processing centers
- Loading mail into automated letter-sorting machines
- Performing postage-canceling operations
- Rewrapping packages damaged in processing

Working Conditions

The work of a mail handler is physically demanding due to the weight of the mail that must be moved. Here are some other conditions that you would encounter in this job:

- You must spend most of your time on your feet, reaching for sacks and trays of mail or placing packages and bundles into sacks and trays.
- You may find that the work becomes extremely routine.
- You may have to work at night or on weekends.
- You may experience stress as you process large quantities of mail under tight production deadlines and quotas.

> **Note**
> The size of the post office where you work as a mail handler can determine how much heavy labor you perform. In small post offices, mail handlers use handtrucks to move heavy mail sacks from one part of the building to another. In large post offices and mail processing centers, chutes and conveyors move the mail.

Strength and Stamina Test

If you make the eligibles list for a mail handler job, you must still pass a stamina and strength test. Here is what you will have to do:

- Lift, shoulder, and carry two 70-pound sacks 15 feet—one at a time—and load them on a handtruck.
- Push the handtruck to an area containing 40-, 50-, and 60-pound sacks.
- Load these sacks on the truck.
- Unload the truck and return it to its original location.

> **Note**
> If you have a certain physical condition, you will not be permitted to take the strength and stamina test without prior approval from a physician. The conditions include hernia or rupture, back trouble, heart trouble, pregnancy, or any other condition where lifting and carrying 70 pounds could be dangerous to you. If you do take the test, you will be given special instructions at the time of testing.

Mail Processor

This job involves a variety of mail processing functions, but is not as physically demanding as the mail handler job.

Responsibilities

A mail processor performs such tasks as:

- Operating mail-processing equipment, including bar code sorters and optical bar code readers
- Troubleshooting minor equipment problems
- Collating and bundling processed mail and transferring it from one work area to another
- Hand-processing mail that cannot be handled by machines
- Loading mail into bins and onto trucks

Flat Letter Sorting Machine Operator

The work of flat letter sorting machine operators involves sorting flats (magazines, oversized envelopes, and so on) by automated machine. The work is similar to the distribution clerk, machine job, yet greater physical strength and stamina are required in this position. With automation and mechanization of post office jobs, job security is virtually assured.

Mark-Up Clerk, Automated

Mark-up clerks operate an electromechanical machine to process undeliverable mail.

Responsibilities

A mark-up clerk performs tasks such as the following:

- Entering and extracting mailing data to and from several database applications to redirect incorrectly addressed mail
- Selecting the correct program and mode for each application
- Affixing labels to mail either manually or with mechanical devices
- Preparing forms for address-correction services
- Performing other job-related tasks to support primary duties

Qualification Requirements

Applicants for the job of mark-up clerk must have fulfilled certain educational and training requirements and must also pass an alpha-numeric typing test.

Education and Training

To be considered for a mark-up clerk position, you must have completed any of the following:

- Six months of clerical or office-machine-operating experience,
- High school, or
- One full academic year (36 weeks) of business school

Your records must show that you can:

- Use reference materials and manuals
- Perform effectively under pressure
- Operate any office equipment appropriate to the position
- Work with others
- Read, understand, and apply certain regulations and procedures commonly used in processing mail undeliverable as addressed

Exam 715—Alpha-Numeric Typing Test

If you are a strong candidate for the job, you will be asked to take Exam 715 as openings occur and hiring is likely. This is not a competitive test; you just need to pass to qualify.

> **Tip**
> Although the USPS does not distribute sample questions for this test, you will find excellent suggestions for taking this test in Arco's *Postal Exams* by E.P. Steinberg (Peterson's).

Earnings

Postal service employees are paid under several separate pay schedules, depending on the duties of the job and the knowledge, experience, or skills required. Separate schedules are made for clerks and carriers. In all pay schedules, except that of executives, employees receive periodic "step" increases up to a specified maximum if their job performance is satisfactory. Published figures for 1998-1999 are as follows:

- For beginning postal clerks who operate scanning and sorting machines, base pay is $24,599 a year, rising to a maximum of $35,683 after 14 years of service.
- For window clerks, entry-level pay is $26,063; for those with 14 years of service, pay is $36,551.
- For full-time regular mail handling clerks entry-level pay ranges from $21,676 to $22,944.
- For experienced, full-time city carriers the pay average is $34,135.
- For rural carriers, base salaries average $35,000.

Employment Outlook

In the next few years, the number of postal clerk jobs is expected to grow more slowly than the average rate for all jobs, but the number of mail handler jobs is expected to grow as fast as the average. Mechanization of mail processing should allow the USPS to handle increasing amounts of mail without increases in clerical employment. Carriers will be faced, however, with an increasing volume of mail. In all areas, thousands of job openings will result as workers retire or leave their careers.

Remember, though, no matter how many postal jobs are open, the competition for each one will be fierce. To get your foot in the door, you must do well on Test 470. Once you've landed that entry-level job, you can look forward to a rewarding career in the postal service.

Q&A

Q I would like to explore other postal service jobs besides those described here. Where can I get this information?

A You can get information about many other postal jobs from *24 Hours to the Postal Service Exam*. If any of those other jobs appeal to you and you have the proper qualifications, go ahead and take the qualifying test whenever it is given (there is never a fee). If there is a long wait for the particular job you want, your best bet might be to take Test 470 and apply for a clerk or carrier job. Once you are a USPS employee in good standing, you can apply for a different job.

The Hour In Review

1. This hour provides an overview of the eight entry-level positions covered under Test 470.

2. Some jobs, such as the window clerk position, require constant interaction with the public; others, like distribution clerk, may require frequent night and weekend work.

3. If you like being outdoors, you might be well suited for a mail carrier job. You will need a driver's license for this position.

4. For mail handler positions, you should consider the physical demands of the job and the requirements of the strength and stamina test.

5. Because competition for all openings is extremely intense, you need to start preparing for Test 470 as soon as possible.

Part II

Preparing for Test 470

Hour **3**

Get to Know Test 470

What You Will Learn in This Hour

In this hour, you'll be introduced to the unusual format of Test 470 and become familiar with some basic test-taking strategies. This knowledge is essential for preventing test anxiety and answering the questions in the time allotted. If you find at first that Test 470's question types appear intimidating and complicated, this is understandable. Although the questions do not ask you to perform difficult tasks, their appearance is probably different from questions on typical, standard tests. Understanding each question type will help you overcome your fears and provide the basis for learning individual question-answering strategies in later chapters. Here are your goals for this hour:

- Become familiar with the format of Test 470 and the four types of questions you will have to answer.

- Learn the importance of adhering to testing rules and procedures, including following instructions and correctly filling in answer sheets.

- Understand basic test-taking strategies.

- Learn how the test is scored and how this affects your chances for post office employment.
- Understand the guessing "penalty" and how this affects your strategy for guessing on each test section.

Test 470 at a Glance

The four-part examination is structured as follows:

Question Type	Part Number	Number of Questions	Time Allotted
Address checking	A	95	Six minutes
Memory for addresses	B	88	Five minutes*
Number series	C	24	20 minutes
Following oral instructions	D	20-25 (varies)	25 minutes (approximately)

*Does not include the time allowed for memorizing addresses.

Tip
Test 470 is used by the postal service to evaluate job-related skills, but it is not a true test of your abilities. Don't fall into the trap of thinking you must be gifted with certain innate talents to get a high score. On the contrary, preparing for this test will definitely increase your chances for doing well on it. The four question types are extremely coachable and get easier with practice. Use your desire for getting hired as a key motivator throughout the test preparation process.

How to Answer the Different Question Types

The following questions are official Test 470 questions. They are a good introduction to each of the different question types. Note that these particular questions will not be used on any actual exam you take.

Address Checking

Part A, Address Checking, tests your attention to detail by your ability to quickly discern similarities or differences in addresses. This aptitude is important for postal clerks and carriers who must read and sort mail for daily delivery. Your task will be to decide whether two addresses are alike or different, and you are given two answer choices to choose from: (A) if the addresses are alike or (D) if the addresses are different.

Sample Questions

1.	2134 S 20th St	2134 S 20th St
2.	4608 N Warnock St	4806 N Warnock St
3.	1202 W Gerard Dr	1202 W Gerard St
4.	Chappaqua NY 10514	Chappaqua NY 10514
5.	2207 Markland Ave	2207 Markham Ave

Answers

1. The two addresses are exactly alike, so you would choose (A).

2. The second and fourth numbers of the street address are transposed in the right column, so you would choose (D).

3. The left column has "Dr" in the address; the right column has "St" so you would choose (D).

4. The two addresses are exactly alike, so you would choose (A).

5. "Markland" is the name of the avenue on the left; "Markham" is on the right. You would choose (D).

> **Note**
> In Part A, the questions themselves are not difficult. Your challenge lies in correctly completing as many questions as possible in the allotted time. Although your aim is to work accurately and quickly, you are not expected to answer all 95 questions on this part of the test.

Memory for Addresses

Part B, Memory for Addresses, tests your aptitude to sort mail speedily and accurately. Because the mail sorting function is a crucial part of postal operations, this part of the test is considered extremely important. Your first task is to memorize in five minutes the location of 25 addresses in five lettered boxes (A, B, C, D, or E). In other words, you have to know in which lettered box each address belongs. Each box contains five addresses: three are street addresses with number ranges (such as "6800-6999 Table" in Box B on the following page); two of the addresses are simple place names with no numbers (such as "Sardis" in Box C on the following page).

A	B	C	D	E
4700–5599 Table	6800–6999 Table	5600–6499 Table	6500–6799 Table	4400–4699 Table
Lismore	Kelford	Joel	Tatum	Ruskin
5600–6499 West	6500–6799 West	6800–6999 West	4400–4699 West	4700–5599 West
Hesper	Musella	Sardis	Porter	Nathan
4400–4699 Blake	5600–6499 Blake	6500–6799 Blake	4700–5599 Blake	6800–6999 Blake

Sample Questions

1. Musella
2. 4700-5599 Blake
3. 4700-5599 Table
4. Tatum
5. 4400-4699 Blake
6. Hesper
7. Kelford
8. Nathan
9. 6500-6799 Blake
10. Joel

Answers

1.   Musella is in Box B, so your answer would be (**B**).

2.   4700-5599 Blake is in Box D, so your answer would be (**D**).

3.   4700-5599 Table is in Box A so your answer would be (**A**).

4.   Tatum is in Box D, so your answer would be (**D**).

5.   4400-4699 Blake is in Box A, so your answer would be (**A**).

6.   Hesper is in Box A, so your answer would be (**A**).

7.   Kelford is in Box B, so your answer would be (**B**).

8.   Nathan is in Box E, so your answer would be (**E**).

9.   6500-6799 Blake is Box C, so your answer would be (**C**).

10. Joel is in Box C, so your answer would be (**C**).

> **Note**
> For this part of the exam, before you take the real test, you will be given three practice test sections using the same lettered boxes. As a result, you'll have more time than just five minutes to memorize the address locations. Only after you complete the practice sections will you be given the test section that counts.

> **Note**
> You might feel that Part B is the most difficult part of the test. Don't become discouraged! This question type will become easier with practice. If you have a positive attitude about your ability to learn, this may become the easiest part of the test for you. You are also not expected to finish every question in this section.

Number Series

Part C, Number Series, measures your ability to think with numbers and to see relationships between elements of a series. It tests your aptitude for working with the new generation of sorting, routing, and marking machines used in the postal service. Although this question type may be new and unfamiliar to you, the actual mathematics of number series questions is not complicated. The problems involve nothing more than simple addition, subtraction, multiplication, and division. Your task will be to determine how a series of numbers is ordered and then decide on the next two numbers in that series. You will have five answer choices to choose from.

Sample Questions

1. 1 2 3 4 5 6 7 ....(A) 1 2   (B) 5 6   (C) 8 9   (D) 4 5   (E) 7 8
2. 15 14 13 12 11 10 9 .....(A) 2 1   (B) 17 16   (C) 8 9   (D) 8 7   (E) 9
3. 20 20 21 21 22 22 23 ...(A) 23 23   (B) 23 24   (C) 19 19   (D) 22 23   (E) 21 23
4. 17 3 17 4 17 5 17 ....(A) 6 17   (B) 6 7   (C) 17 6   (D) 5 6   (E) 17 7
5. 1 2 4 5 7 8 10 ....(A) 11 12   (B) 12 14   (C) 10 13   (D) 12 13   (E) 11 13

Answers

1. The numbers in the series are increasing by 1. If the series were continued for two more numbers, it would read: 1 2 3 4 5 6 7 8 9. Therefore, the correct answer is 8 and 9, answer choice (**C**).

2. The numbers in this series are decreasing by 1. If the series were continued for two more numbers, it would read: 15 14 13 12 11 10 9 8 7. Therefore, the correct answer is 8 and 7, answer choice (**D**)

3. Each number in this series is repeated and then increased by 1. If the series were repeated for two more numbers, it would read: 20 20 21 21 22 22 23 23 24. Therefore, the correct answer is 23 and 24, answer choice (**B**).

4. This series is the number 17 separated by numbers increasing by 1, beginning with the number 3. If the series were continued for two more numbers, it would then read: 17 3 17 4 17 5 17 6 17. Therefore, the correct answer is 6 and 17, answer choice (**A**).

5. The numbers in this series are increasing by 1 (plus 1) and then by 2 (plus 2). If the series were continued for two more numbers, it would read: 1 2 4 5 7 8 10 11 13. Therefore, the correct answer is 11 and 13, answer choice (**E**).

Following Oral Instructions

Part D, Following Oral Instructions, tests your ability to follow spoken directions quickly and precisely. It will demand your total concentration because the instructions are read only once and cannot be repeated. It is important to remember that your ability to follow directions easily is a good indication of your on-the-job trainability. A high score on this part of the test will help you get hired. Your task will be to write in your test booklet and answer sheet according to directions spoken by the examiner in person or on tape. The test booklet will contain material such as the following:

Sample Questions

1. 5___
2. 1 6   4   3   7
3. D B   A   E   C

You will then have instructions read to you like:

"Line 1 has a number and a blank space beside it. In the blank space, write A as in ace. Then on the answer sheet, find number 5 and darken the letter you just wrote on the line."

"Look at line 2. Draw a line under the third number. Now look at the answer sheet, find the number under which you just drew a line and darken B as in boy."

"Look at the letters in line 3. Draw a line under the third letter in the line. Now on your answer sheet, find number 9 and darken the letter under which you drew a line."

Answers

For questions 1, 2, 3 above, you would have marked on your answer sheet 4B, 5A, and 9A.

Caution
As you have just seen from the sample questions, you will mark your answers on your answer sheet according to the instructions you are given, not in consecutive order. You will be skipping around the page and most likely will not use all the answer spaces. Be prepared for this.

> **Note**
> The best way to practice the oral instruction questions in later chapters is to have another person read the instructions to you or to tape yourself reading them. The oral instructions will be provided on separate pages so you can easily photocopy or tear them out of the book. In planning your study schedule, you should take this into account.

Test-Taking Rules and Procedures

You must not underestimate the importance of following all the rules and procedures required at the test center. This includes following all the examiner's instructions and filling in the answer sheets correctly.

Instructions from the Examiner

Instructions read by the examiner are intended to ensure that you and all the other applicants have the same fair and objective opportunity to compete in the examination. All of you are expected to perform on the same level playing field. Any infraction of the rules is considered cheating. If you cheat, your test paper will not be scored and you will not be eligible for appointment.

Do

DO pay close attention to the examiner at all times.
DO follow all instructions the examiner gives you.
DO stop working on any part of the test when told to do so.
DO review your work on a test part if you finish it before time is called.

Don't

DON'T begin working on any part of the test until told to do so.
DON'T work on any part of the test other than the one you are told to work on.
DON'T turn any pages until you are told to do so.
DON'T assume anything or do anything other than what the examiner tells you.

DO pay close attention to the examiner at all times. Although the directions and questions given in this book are modeled after recent 470 directions and questions, the postal service can change the examination format without notifying you. Listen to what the examiner says at all times. Be prepared to act immediately on any exam changes to content, question type, directions, or time limits.

DO follow all instructions the examiner gives you. If you do not understand any of the examiner's instructions, ask questions. Perhaps the acoustics in the test room are poor or the examiner's voice is too soft. You must rectify the situation to ensure you know what is required on the test. This is your right. If you do not do this, your score might suffer.

DO stop working on any part of the test when told to do so. Remember that your ability to follow instructions is considered in the hiring process. Failure to follow any direction given to you by the examiner may be grounds for disqualification, so keep a positive attitude about following instructions throughout the exam.

DO review your work on a test part if you finish it before time is called. Although you cannot go back to any previous part of the test, you have the chance to review the answers you are unsure of in the part you are currently working. Use whatever extra time you have wisely.

DON'T begin working on any part of the test until told to do so. You must play fair. All applicants must be tested under the same time constraints. Time limits and timing signals will be explained to you. Try to stay relaxed and focused during breaks between test parts. If you let your nerves get the better of you, you will not be able to concentrate on doing your best.

DON'T work on any part of the test other than the one you are told to work on. Be certain to check that you're working on the right test part immediately. Although working in the wrong section could be an inadvertent error on your part, it would not leave a favorable impression and probably put you out of the running.

DON'T turn any pages until you are told to do so. Once again, how you follow instructions is considered extremely important. Not playing by the rules is an indication you would not be a good employee. Also, corporations today look for employees who are team players. Looking out for number one says you are not team material and a poor hiring risk.

DON'T assume anything or do anything other than what the examiner tells you. This not only indicates your willingness to follow instructions but also demonstrates your ability to focus on getting the job done.

Filling in the Answer Sheet

As discussed in Hour 1, "Finding Post Office Jobs," you will be required to fill in required personal information on the sample answer sheet sent to you by the postal service to be admitted to the test center. You cannot take the test without doing this. At the center, you will be instructed to transfer the personal information you filled in on the sample answer sheet to the actual answer sheet.

Caution
Because you will have only 15 minutes to transfer the answer sheet information, check your information at home. Be certain that all the information is entered correctly in the right place. Have someone else check your work, if possible.

Entering Your Answers

Because Test 470 is machine scored, you must be careful to fill in your answer sheets clearly and accurately; instructions on entering your answers are included in the test kit sent to you by the postal service. You are also given ample opportunities to perfect your answering skills in the practice material later in this book. Keep the following in mind as you take the exam:

- Blacken your answer space firmly and completely. Poorly entered answers might not be read by the machine or may be misinterpreted.

- Mark only one answer for each question. If you mark more than one answer, you will be considered wrong even if one of the answers is correct.

- If you wish to change your answer once you have entered it, you must erase your mark completely. An incomplete erasure might be read as a second answer.

- Do not cross out any answers if you want to change them. Erase them as above. Crossed-out answers are unacceptable.

- Do not write any note in the margin of your answer sheet. The machine scoring your answers may misinterpret this.

- Answer each question in the right place. If you skip an answer space and mark a series of answers incorrectly, you must erase all your answers and properly reenter them.

> **Tip**
> You cannot afford to lose precious exam time erasing and reentering incorrectly entered answers. Therefore, as you answer each question for Parts A through C, look at its number and check that you are marking your answer in the space with the same number. If you cannot do this after each question, then remember to check yourself after every five questions. Either way, plan a strategy and stick to it.

How Test 470 Is Scored

When the exam is over, the examiner will collect your test booklet and answer sheet. Your answer sheet will be sent to the National Test Administration Center in Merrifield, Virginia, where a machine will scan your answers. Your raw score will then be calculated according to the steps described below.

Determining Raw Scores

The procedures for determining raw scores for each test part are listed in the following table.

Test Part	How Raw Scores Are Determined
Part A: Address Checking	Number of correct answers *minus* number of incorrect answers
Part B: Memory for Addresses	Number of correct answers *minus* number of incorrect answers
Part C: Number Series	Total number of correct answers
Part D: Following Oral Instructions	Total number of correct answers

> **Note**
> You should remember that questions that are not answered are not scored. And questions with more than one answer marked (even if one answer is correct) are counted as incorrect.

Converting Raw Scores to Scaled Scores

Your raw score is not your final score. The postal service takes your raw scores for each test part, combines them according to a formula of its own, and converts them to a scaled score, on a scale of 1 to 100. The entire process of conversion from raw to scaled score is confidential information.

A total scaled score of 70 is a passing score. The names of all persons with scores of 70 or more are placed on an eligibles list called the register that remains valid for two years. The register is ordered according to score rankings—the highest scores are at the top of the list. Hiring then takes place from the top of the list as vacancies occur.

Caution
Although a total scaled score of 70 is considered passing, it will probably not get you hired. Many candidates prepare rigorously for this test and strive for perfect scores. In fact, most applicants who are hired score between 90 and 100 percent.

Note
The Veterans Preference discussed in Hour 1 will be added to your score only if you have a scaled score of 70 or more. If you fail, your score cannot be brought up to a passing level by veteran's points. Your earned score plus your veteran's service points result in your final scaled score that winds up on the eligibility list.

Getting Your Score Report

The scoring process may take six to ten weeks or even longer, so be patient. The process is long, but you remain eligible for employment for two years after taking the test. If you pass the exam, you will receive notice of your scaled score. As the hiring process nears your number, you will be notified to appear for the remaining steps of the hiring process:

- Drug testing
- Psychological interview
- Physical performance tests according to the requirements of the position
- For mark-up clerk candidates, the Alpha-numeric typing test

If you fail the exam, you will not be informed of your score. You will simply be notified that you have failed and will not be considered for postal employment.

> **Caution**
> You should know that as many as 50 percent of applicants fail Test 470. This number, of course, varies per exam administration. Use this number as a reality check for setting a serious study schedule, and although this is a high failure rate, don't let it shake your confidence. Your preparation will give you better odds of getting a higher score than many of the other candidates.

General Test-Taking Strategies

Know the Directions for Each Question Type

You will be given the instructions by the postal service in your exam kit, so know them inside-out. This book also gives you the most recent directions used on Test 470. Remember, though, to listen to the examiner in case something has changed.

Skip Questions When Stumped

When you cannot answer a question for Parts A through C, skip the question and come back to it after finishing the other questions in that part of the test. Circle the question's number in your test booklet to indicate the question skipped and remember to skip the appropriate space on your answer sheet.

Don't Worry about Being Perfect

You are not expected to answer every question in Parts A and B. Don't be a perfectionist and waste time on questions you cannot answer. This can restrict the number of questions you answer, which will lower your score. Come back to the difficult questions if you have time to spare.

> **Note**
> Use the practice tests in this book to get used to the quick pace of the test and the strict time limitations for each test part. Stick to these time limitations without exception. Use a stopwatch or kitchen timer for accurate measurement. This will give you a sense of how to pace yourself on the actual test.

Know How Much Time You Have

To do well on Test 470, you must work quickly within the time limits allowed. The examiner will probably inform you at periodic intervals of how much time you have left. Check your wristwatch as a backup, but don't be a clock watcher. Your time is better spent answering the questions.

Use the Test Booklet as Scratch Paper

Particularly for number series questions, you may find it useful to make notes in the test booklet. Notes of this kind may focus your thoughts and help you to solve the question. However, don't overdo it. If you find you're spending too much time making notes, stop and try to solve the questions without them.

Understanding the "Guessing Penalty"

If you've prepared for standardized tests before, you may have heard about "guessing penalties." When there is a guessing penalty, you lose points for wrong answers. As its name implies, the guessing penalty is meant to discourage you from simply filling in answers at random in the hope that you'll get some of them right. On Test 470, there is a guessing penalty in Parts A (Address Checking) and B (Memory for Addresses). Parts C (Number Series) and D (Following Oral Instructions) have no guessing penalty.

TEST 470: GUESSING PENALTIES

Test Section	Guessing Penalty
Part A: Address Checking	When determining your raw score, the total number of incorrect answers is subtracted from the total number of correct answers.
Part B: Memory for Addresses	When determining your raw score, one-quarter of the total number of incorrect answers is subtracted from the total number of correct answers.

Should You Guess?

On Test 470, guessing can be a good or bad idea depending on which test section you are taking. The following table will help you know when and when not to guess.

Test Section	Should You Guess?	Explanation
Part A: Address Checking	No	Never guess because the guessing penalty is so severe. Filling in answers at random will likely cost you points.
Part B: Memory for Addresses	Sometimes	Here the guessing penalty is less severe, so you might want to guess if you can eliminate some of the answer boxes. Guess cautiously, however, and don't risk losing points by filling in answers at random.
Part C: Number Series	Yes	Because there's no guessing penalty in this section, always guess. You have nothing to lose.
Part D: Following Oral Instructions	Not Applicable	This question type offers no opportunity for guessing.

Q&A

Q Will a score above 90 ensure I get hired?

A There is no guarantee that any specific score will get you hired. Other steps exist in the hiring process besides the written test, but because you are ranked by score on the register, the higher your test score, the better your chance of being selected.

Q When should I begin preparing for the test?

A Start studying as soon as you decide to take the test. Although you may have several months time between sign-up and taking the test, you'll want to set up your 24-hour study schedule according to your current needs.

Q If I am not hired, can I retake the test?

A Yes. If you pass the test, your application remains effective for two years. If you are not hired within that period, however, you have to reapply and go through the entire registration process, including retaking the exam.

The Hour in Review

1.   Hour 3 provides an overview of Test 470's format and question types to help you score your best.

2.   Knowing what to expect on the actual test and learning general test-taking strategies will give you control over the testing process, relieve test anxiety, and give you a better chance of outscoring your competitors.

3.   Understanding how the test is scored is the key to knowing when and when not to guess.

HOUR 4

Address Checking—1

What You Will Learn in This Hour

In both this hour and the next, you will learn specific techniques for answering the Address Checking questions. Although this question type is probably the easiest on Test 470, it carries the stiffest penalty for guessing. Therefore, speed and accuracy will be your greatest allies in this test section. Here are your goals for this hour:

- Understand power reading techniques for answering the Address Checking questions.
- Learn how to use your hands to ensure accuracy in reading.
- Understand vocalization techniques for answering questions.
- Pick out differences in address numbers and ZIP codes.

Mini Warm-Up Quiz

The following 25-question address checking quiz will not be timed. Take it simply to familiarize yourself with this question type without worrying about time pressure. After you complete it, check your answers against the answer key below. Review the questions you answered incorrectly. Can you easily spot your mistakes?

> **DIRECTIONS:** For each question, compare the address in the left column with the address in the right column. If the two addresses are *alike* in every way, write A next to the question number. If the two addresses are *different* in any way, write D next to the question number.

1.	197 Apple Ridge Dr Nw	197 Apple Ridge Dr NW
2.	243 S Calumet Ave	234 S Calumet Ave
3.	4300 Las Pillas Rd	4300 Las Pillas Rd
4.	5551 N Summit Ave	5551 N Summit St
5.	Walden CO 80480	Waldon CO 80480
6.	2200 E Beach St	2200 E Beech St
7.	2700 Helena Way	2700 Helena Way
8.	3968 S Kingsberry Ave	3698 S Kingsbury Ave
9.	14011 Costilla Ave NE	14011 Costilla Ave SE
10.	1899 N Dearborn Dr	1899 N Dearborn Dr
11.	8911 Scranton Way	8911 Scranton Way
12.	3653 Hummingbird St	3563 Hummingbird St
13.	1397 Lewiston Pl	1297 Lewiston Pl
14.	4588 Crystal Way	4588 Crystal Rd
15.	Muscle Shoals AL 35660	Muscle Shoals AL 35660
16.	988 Larkin Johnson Ave SE	988 Larkin Johnson Ave SE
17.	5501 Greenville Blvd NE	5501 Greenview Blvd NE
18.	7133 N Baranmor Pky	7133 N Baranmor Pky
19.	10500 Montana Rd	10500 Montana Rd
20.	4769 E Fox Hollow Dr	4769 E Fox Hollow Cir

21.	Daytona Beach Fla 32016	Daytona Beach FL 32016
22.	2227 W 94th Ave	2272 W 94th Ave6399
23.	6399 E Ponce De Leon St	6399 E Ponce De Leon Ct
24.	20800 N Rainbow Pl	20800 N Rainbow Pl
25.	Hammond GA 31785	Hammond GA 31785

Answers

1.	D	11.	A	21.	D
2.	D	12.	D	22.	D
3.	A	13.	D	23.	D
4.	D	14.	D	24.	A
5.	D	15.	A	25.	A
6.	D	16.	A		
7.	A	17.	D		
8.	D	18.	A		
9.	D	19.	A		
10.	A	20.	D		

Why You Should *Not* Guess

Remember that in this test section there is a severe guessing penalty. The total number of wrong answers is subtracted from the total number of right answers. So random guessing is a bad idea; it will probably lower your score. So when time starts running out, if you're tempted to fill in answers at random, don't do it! Instead learn to master the power reading techniques that follow.

Techniques for Power Reading

Power reading means reading for speed and accuracy. This is exactly what is tested in Part A of Test 470. Address checking directions tell you to compare two addresses and mark (A) on your answer sheet if the two addresses are *alike* in any way, or mark (D) on your answer sheet if the addresses are *different* in any way. Sounds easy, doesn't it? However, you have only six minutes to answer 95 questions.

Read to Spot Differences

Read only to spot differences between the two addresses. Once you spot one, mark answer (D) and go immediately to the next question. It is pointless to look at the remainder of an address once you have found a difference. You will be amazed at how much time you can save by not reading the entire address.

Note
You are not expected to answer all 95 questions on an Address Checking question section. However, the more questions you answer correctly, the higher your score.

Use Vocalizing Techniques to Focus Your Reading

The best way to read and compare addresses is to filter out all extraneous information; read exactly what you see, not what abbreviations or numbers mean when spelled out. A good way to do this is to vocalize abbreviations and numbers by sounds as in the following examples:

- If you see "St.," read "es tee" not "street."
- If you see "NH," read "en aitch" not "New Hampshire."
- If you see "1035," read "one zero three five" not "one thousand thirty-five."

Tip
Remember to focus directly on the letters, not on the meaning. If you read "Kansas City, MO" as "Kansas City, Missouri," you are unlikely to catch the difference with "Kansas City, MD." But if you read "Kansas City, em oh," you will certainly pick up on "Kansas City, em dee."

Practice Vocalizing Techniques

Vocalizing requires constant practice to get used to, so sound out the following abbreviations and numbers:

NY	MT	10001
CA	MA	3694
OR	IL	Ct
VA	TX	Pkwy
AL	68919	Cir
HA	828	

Use Your Hands as Reading Aids

When reading long columns of addresses, it is easy to lose your place and misread an address. Therefore, it's a good idea to use your hands as reading aids.

Index Finger as Ruler or Pointer

In your writing hand, hold your pencil poised at the question number on your answer sheet. Run the index finger of your other hand under or along the addresses being compared. This will help you focus on one line at a time and keep your eyes from jumping up or down a line. By holding your place on both the question and answer sheets, you are less likely to skip a question or answer space.

Try using your index finger as a ruler or pointer and compare the following addresses. Are they alike or different?

1. 5115 Colchester Rd   5115 Calchester Rd
2. 4611 N Randall Pl   4611 N Randall Pl
3. 17045 Pascack Cir   17045 Pascack Cir
4. 3349 Palma del Mar Blvd   3346 Palma del Mar Blvd
5. 13211 E 182nd Ave   13211 E 182nd Ave
6. Francisco WY 82636   Francisco WI 82636
7. 6198 N Albritton Rd   6198 N Albretton Rd
8. 11230 Twinflower Cir   11230 Twintower Cir
9. 6191 MacDonald Station Rd   6191 MacDonald Station Rd
10. 1587 Vanderbilt Dr N   1587 Vanderbilt Dr S

Answers

1. D	5. A	9. A
2. A	6. D	10. D
3. A	7. D	
4. D	8. D	

Caution

You are not allowed to bring a ruler or any other straight-edge tool into the examination room. Therefore, using your finger as a ruler or pointer will probably become an essential part of your question-answering strategy.

Break the Address into Parts

An effective power reading technique is to break addresses into parts and read only one part at a time. In the Address Checking questions, the addresses are usually of two types:

1. Street addresses (for example, 35600 Elm St or 7 W 34th Ave)

2. City addresses (for example, Sacramento CA 89960)

Focus on one element at a time, such as the ZIP code or street name. If you narrow your focus to compare only the numbers or only the words, you are more likely to notice differences and less apt to see what you expect to see rather than what is actually printed on the page.

Try this technique with the following addresses. Are they alike or different?

1.	3993 S Freemont Ter	3993 S Freemount Ter
2.	3654 S Urbane Dr	3564 S Urbane Cir
3.	1408 Oklahoma Ave NE	1408 Oklahoma Ave NE
4.	6201 Meadowland Ln	6201 Meadowlawn Ln
5.	5799 S Rockaway Ln	15799 S Rockaway Ln
6.	3782 SE Verrazanno Bay	37872 SE Verrazanno Bay
7.	2766 N Thunderbird Ct	2766 N Thunderbird Ct
8.	2166 N Elmmorado Ct	2166 N Eldorado Ct
9.	10538 Innsbruck Ln	10538 Innsbruck Ln
10.	888 Powerville Rd	883 Powerville Rd

Answers

1.	D	5.	D	9.	A
2.	D	6.	D	10.	D
3.	A	7.	A		
4.	D	8.	D		

Read from Right to Left

This is another power reading technique that requires practice. You should use it only if you find it comfortable and can apply it consistently throughout the test section.

In the following two addresses, first focus your eyes on the terms in bold and then read the rest of the address in reverse order. Use your finger as a pointer or ruler.

Centralville, MT **08869**

17760 E Westmorland **Ave**

Now try this technique and compare the following addresses:

1.	4202 N Bainbridge Rd	4202 N Bainbridge Rd
2.	300 E Roberta Ave	3000 E Roberta Ave
3.	Quenemo KS 66528	Quenemo KS 66528
4.	13845 Donahoo St	13345 Donahoo St
5.	10466 Gertrude NE	0466 Gertrude NE
6.	2733 N 105th Ave	773 N 105th Ave
7.	3100 N Wyandotte Cir	3100 N Wyandottte Ave
8.	11796 Summerville Dr	11769 Summerville Dr
9.	Wilburnum Miss 65566	Vilburnum Miss 65566
10.	9334 Kindleberger Rd	9334 Kindleberger Rd

> **Tip**
> This technique of reading in reverse order becomes easier when you combine it with the technique of breaking the address into parts. You are scanning solely for information, not for meaning.

Answers

1.	A	5.	A	9.	D
2.	D	6.	D	10.	A
3.	A	7.	D		
4.	D	8.	D		

Reading Alternately from Left to Right and Right to Left

This technique of alternating your reading direction can be a real time-saver if you can master it.

Start by reading the first line from left to right using your finger as a pointer. When you reach the last letter in the second (right-hand) column, drop your finger to the second line and move from right to left. Try this with the following addresses.

1.	Ontarioville IL 60103	Ontarioville IL 60103
2.	4204 Bridgeton Ave	204 Bridgetown Ave
3.	31215 N Emerald Dr	31215 N Emerald Cir
4.	4601 N Perlman Ave	4201 N Perlmann Ave
5.	9898 Western Terrace	9898 Western Terrace
6.	Quickley MA 09821	Quickley ME 09821
7.	48901 Broderick Ct	4890 Broderick Ct
8.	1001 Hemstead Way	1001 Hempstead Way
9.	2199 West Pinebrook Rd	2199 West Pindebrook Rd
10.	3989 Two Bridges Hwy	3889 Two Bridges Hwy

Answers

1.	A	5.	A	9.	D
2.	D	6.	D	10.	D
3.	D	7.	D		
4.	D	8.	D		

> **Note**
> With practice, some of these power reading techniques will become second nature to you and you won't feel awkward when using them. It's up to you to determine which techniques feel most comfortable. This only comes with practice.

Differences in Numbers

Expect to find many differences in Address Checking questions, either in the street addresses or ZIP codes. Numbers can be missing, reversed, or replaced.

Differences in the Number of Digits

Can you quickly tell if the two numbers contain the same number of digits? Take the following quick test.

Answer (A) if the two numbers are exactly alike, (D) if the two numbers are different in any way. Write your answer next to the question number.

1.	2003	2003
2.	75864	75864
3.	7300	730
4.	50105	5016
5.	2184	2184
6.	8789	8789
7.	36001	3601
8.	1112	1112
9.	89900	8990
10.	07035	07035

Answers

1.	A	5.	A	9.	D
2.	A	6.	A	10.	A
3.	D	7.	D		
4.	D	8.	A		

Differences in Order of Digits

Can you quickly tell if two numbers have the same digits but are in different order? In Address Checking questions, you can expect to find some numbers in reverse order. In the following exercise, answer **(A)** if the ordering is the same, **(D)** if the ordering is different. Write your answer next to the question number.

1.	7516	7561
2.	80302	80302
3.	19832	18932
4.	6186	6186
5.	54601	54610
6.	6609	6609
7.	10910	10190
8.	11178	11178
9.	49988	49898
10.	1633	1633

Answers

1.	D	5.	D	9.	D
2.	A	6.	A	10.	A
3.	D	7.	D		
4.	A	8.	A		

Substitution of One Digit for Another

Can you quickly tell if one number is different from another by a single digit? In the following exercise, answer (A) if the digits are the same in every way or (D) if one digit is different. Write your answer next to the question number.

1.	16830	16830
2.	94936	94636
3.	3287	3285
4.	54216	54216
5.	32341	33341
6.	9987	9989
7.	1664	1664
8.	82089	82089
9.	3939	3936
10.	4248	4248

Answers

1.	A	5.	D	9.	D
2.	D	6.	D	10.	A
3.	D	7.	A		
4.	A	8.	A		

4

Finding Differences in Numbers
Practice Exercise

DIRECTIONS: In the following set of practice questions, all differences are in the numbers. Work quickly, focusing only on the numbers. You may find any of the three types of differences just described.

Write **(A)** if the two addresses are *alike* in every way, **(D)** if they are *different* in any way. Write in your answer next to the question number.

Tip
If you feel confident, you should also apply the precision reading techniques you learned earlier in this hour.

1.	3685 Brite Ave	3865 Brite Ave
2.	Ware MA 08215	Ware MA 08215
3.	4001 Webster Rd	401 Webster Rd
4.	9789 Bell Rd	9786 Bell Rd
5.	Scarsdale NY 10583	Scarsdale NY 10583
6.	1482 Grand Blvd	1482 Grand Blvd
7.	Milwaukee WI 53202	Milwaukee WI 52302
8.	3542 W 48th St	3542 W 84th St
9.	9461 Hansen St	9561 Hansen St
10.	32322 Florence Pkwy	3232 Florence Pkwy
11.	Portland OR 97208	Portland OR 99208
12.	3999 Thompson Dr	3999 Thompson Dr
13.	1672 Sutton Pl	1972 Sutton Pl
14.	Omaha NE 68127	Omaha NE 68127
15.	1473 S 96th St	1743 S 96th St

16.	34225 Geary St	3425 Geary St
17.	Dallas TX 75234	Dallas TX 75234
18.	4094 Horchow Rd	4904 Horchow Rd
19.	San Francisco CA 94108	San Francisco CA 94108
20.	1410 Broadway	141 Broadway
21.	424 Fifth Ave	4240 Fifth Ave
22.	Westport CT 06880	Westport CT 06880
23.	932 Wilton Rd	1923 Wilton Rd
24.	2052 Victoria Sta	2502 Victoria Sta
25.	1982 Carlton Pl	1982 Carlton Pl

Answers

1.	D	11.	D	21.	D
2.	A	12.	A	22.	A
3.	D	13.	D	23.	D
4.	D	14.	A	24.	D
5.	A	15.	D	25.	A
6.	A	16.	D		
7.	D	17.	A		
8.	D	18.	D		
9.	D	19.	A		
10.	D	20.	D		

Self-Evaluation

Ask yourself the following questions:

- Were you able to focus on the numbers?
- Were you able to spot the differences quickly?
- Could you make a rapid decision when there was no difference?

If you got any of the above questions wrong, check to see why.

The Hour in Review

1. In this hour, you learned how different power reading techniques can help you answer Address Checking questions quickly and accurately.

2. Strategies such as using your index finger as a pointer or reading from right to left can be combined or used separately to maximize power reading techniques.

3. Focusing on the numbers in Address Checking questions can help you quickly spot differences in digit number and order.

Hour **5**

Address Checking—2

What You Will Learn in This Hour

In this hour, we'll explore more specific techniques for answering the Address Checking questions. You will gain knowledge to help you answer these test questions quickly and precisely. Here are your goals for this hour:

- Review the many types of abbreviations you can expect on the examination.
- Understand differences in address names caused by spelling errors.
- Learn different strategies for detecting differences in address names.
- Take a full-length address checking exercise to evaluate your strengths and weaknesses.

Mini Warm-Up Quiz

To get started, take this untimed mini-quiz to reacquaint yourself with the format of the Address Checking questions. After you complete it, check your answers against the answer key that follows. Review the questions you answered incorrectly. Can you easily spot your mistakes?

> **DIRECTIONS:** For each question, compare the address in the left column with the address in the right column. If the two addresses are *alike* in every way, write **(A)** next to the question number. If the two addresses are *different* in any way, write **(D)** next to the question number.

1.	9392 Northrup Ave	9392 Northrop Ave
2.	11736 Flemington Rd	11736 Flemington Rd
3.	3878 Flammang Dr	3878 Flammang Dr
4.	2101 Johnstontown Way	2101 Johnstontown Way
5.	1177 Ghentwoodrow St	1177 Ghentwoodrow Ct
6.	888 Mohegan Ct	888 Mohegan Ct
7.	3205 N Rastetter Ave	3205 N Rastetter Ave
8.	1144 Yellowsands Dr NE	1144 Yellowsands Dr Nw
9.	3197 Clerkenwell Ct	3197 Clerkenwell Ct
10.	3021 Pemaquid Way	3210 Pemaquid way
11.	1398 Angelina Rd	1398 Angelino Rd
12.	4331 NW Zoeller Ave	4881 NW Zoeller Ave
13.	1805 Jeassamine Ln	1805 Jassamine Ln
14.	14411 Bellemeade Ave	14411 Bellemeade Ave
15.	Noquochoke MA 02790	Noguochoke MA 02790
16.	11601 Hagamann Cir	11601 Hagamann Ct
17.	1594 S Frontage St	1594 S Frontage Ave
18.	37099 Oliphant Ln	37909 Oliphant Ln
19.	2248 Avonsdalea Cir NW	2248 Avonsdale Cir NE
20.	1733 Norlander Dr SE	1733 Norlander Dr Sw
21.	15469 W Oxalida Dr	15469 W Oxalido Dr
22.	4192 E Commonwealth Ave	4192 E Commonwealth Ave
23.	Kingsfield, Maine 04947	Kingsfield, Maine 04947
24.	246 East Ramsdell Rd	246 East Ramsdale Rd
25.	8456 Vina del Maro Blvd	8456 Vina del Maro Blvd

Answers

1.	D	11.	D	21.	D
2.	A	12.	D	22.	A
3.	A	13.	D	23.	A
4.	A	14.	A	24.	D
5.	D	15.	D	25.	A
6.	A	16.	D		
7.	A	17.	D		
8.	D	18.	D		
9.	A	19.	D		
10.	D	20.	D		

Differences in Abbreviations

In Address Checking questions, you will encounter many different types of standard abbreviations—state, address, and compass. You'll find that it's quite easy to misread these abbreviations when comparing addresses in columns. Reading for differences between abbreviations requires the same power reading techniques you used in the last hour to spot differences between numbers. Here's a recap of those techniques:

Do

DO read only to spot for differences. Nothing else about the addresses should concern you.

DO vocalize or sound out the information you read. This way you will read what you see, not what you expect to see.

DO use hands as reading aids. Keep track of your place on the answer sheet with your pencil and use the index finger of your other hand as a ruler or pointer.

DO break the address into parts to focus on one element at a time.

DO read from right to left or in alternate directions on alternate lines to speed your reading.

Don't

DON'T read more than you have to. Once you have found a difference in a question, go on to the next question.

DON'T use any technique you find distracting. Reading from right to left may not be easy for you to do.

Familiarize Yourself with Standard and Nonstandard Abbreviations

It pays to be prepared. On this part of the test, you may encounter some abbreviations you have not seen before.

Note
Do not memorize the following abbreviations. They are presented to show you how easy it is to mistake one abbreviation for another when you are working quickly. Remember your task on this test section is to spot differences, *not* to read for meaning.

State and Territory Abbreviations

You should be familiar with conventional abbreviations as well as the two-letter capitalized abbreviations used with ZIP codes.

Alabama	Ala.	AL
Alaska	n/a	AK
American Samoa	Amer. Samoa	AS
Arizona	Ariz.	AZ
Arkansas	Ark.	AR
California	Calif.	CA
Colorado	Colo.	CO
Connecticut	Conn.	CT
Delaware	Del.	DE
District of Columbia	D.C.	DC
Florida	Fla.	FL
Georgia	Ga.	GA
Guam	n/a	GU
Hawaii	n/a	HI
Idaho	n/a	ID
Illinois	Ill.	IL
Indiana	Ind.	IN
Iowa	n/a	IA

Kansas	Kans.	KS
Kentucky	Ky.	KY
Louisiana	La.	LA
Maine	n/a	ME
Maryland	Md.	MD
Massachusetts	Mass.	MA
Michigan	Mich.	MI
Minnesota	Minn.	MN
Mississippi	Miss.	MS
Missouri	Mo.	MO
Montana	Mont.	MT
Nebraska	Nebr.	NE
Nevada	Nev.	NV
New Hampshire	N.H.	NH
New Jersey	N.J.	NJ
New Mexico	N. Mex.	NM
New York	N.Y.	NY
North Carolina	N.C.	NC
North Dakota	N.Dak.	ND
Ohio	n/a	OH
Oklahoma	Okla.	OK
Oregon	Oreg.	OR
Pennsylvania	Pa.	PA
Puerto Rico	P.R.	PR
Rhode Island	R.I.	RI
South Carolina	S.C.	SC
S.Dakota	S.Dak.	SD
Tennessee	Tenn.	TN
Texas	Tex.	TX
Utah	n/a	UT
Vermont	Vt.	VT
Virginia	Va.	VA
Virgin Islands	V.I.	VI
Washington	Wash.	WA
West Virginia	W.Va.	WV
Wisconsin	Wis.	WI
Wyoming	Wyo.	WY

5

Address Abbreviations

In your career as a postal worker, you will encounter many standard and nonstandard address abbreviations. The list below is a sampling of some of the more popular abbreviations. How many of them are familiar to you?

Annex	Anx	Northeast	NE
Apartment	Apt	Northwest	NW
Avenue	Ave	Park	Pk
Boulevard	Blvd	Parkway	Pky or Pkwy
Building	Bldg	Place	Pl
Canyon	Cyn	Plaza	Plz
Causeway	Cswy	Point	Pt
Circle	Cir	Road	Rd
Court	Ct	Room	Rm
Crescent	Crst	Route	Rte
East	E	South	S
Drive	Dr	Southeast	SE
Expressway	Expy	Southwest	SW
Fort	Ft	Square	Sq
Green	Gr	Street	St
Highway	Hwy	Summit	Smt
Island	Isl	Terrace	Ter or Terr
Junction	Jct	Turpike	Tkpe
Knolls	Knls	Trail	Trl
Lane	La or Ln	Way	Wy
Mountain	Mtn	West	W
North	N		

Tip

With abbreviations, it makes sense to sound them out as you see them. If you didn't apply this power reading technique when reading the above lists, go back now and reread them. Vocalize the sounds as you learned to do in the previous hour. This will prevent your mistaking Pk for Pt or Sq. for St.

Practice Finding Differences in Abbreviations

DIRECTIONS: In the following set of practice questions, all differences are in the abbreviations. Work quickly, focusing only on the abbreviations. Write **(A)** if the two addresses are alike in every way, **(D)** if they are different in any way. Write your answer next to the question number.

1.	3238 NW 3rd St	3238 NE 3rd St
2.	7865 Harkness Blvd	7865 Harkness Blvd
3.	Seattle WA 98102	Seattle WY 981012
4.	342 Madison Ave	342 Madison St
5.	723 Broadway E	723 Broadway E
6.	4731 W 88th Dr	4731 W 88th Rd
7.	Boiceville NY12412	Boiceville NY 12412
8.	9021 Rodeo Dr	9021 Rodeo Drive
9.	2093 Post St	2093 Post Rd
10.	New Orleans LA 70153	New Orleans LA 70153
11.	5332 SW Bombay St	5332 SW Bombay St
12.	416 Wellington Pkwy	416 Wellington Hwy
13.	2096 Garden Ter	2096 Garden Terr
14.	3220 W Grant Ave	3220 W Grant Ave
15.	Charlotte VT 05445	Charlotte VA 05445
16.	4415 Oriental Blvd	4415 Oriental Blvd
17.	6876 Raffles Rd	6876 Raffles Road
18.	891 S Hotel Hwy	891 E Hotel Hwy
19.	9500 London Br	9500 London Br
20.	24A Motcomb St	24A Motcomb St
21.	801 S Erleigh Ln	801 S Erleigh La
22.	839 Casco St	839 Casco St
23.	Freeport ME 04033	Freeport NE 04033
24.	3535 Island Pky	3535 Island Pkwy
25.	2186 Missouri Ave NE	2186 Missouri Ave NW

5

Answers

1.	D	11.	A	21.	D
2.	A	12.	D	22.	A
3.	D	13.	D	23.	D
4.	D	14.	A	24.	D
5.	A	15.	D	25.	D
6.	D	16.	A		
7.	A	17.	D		
8.	D	18.	D		
9.	D	19.	A		
10.	A	20.	A		

Differences in Address Names

You can expect to find many sorts of differences in the street and city names in the Address Checking section. You have to apply your power reading techniques to spot them. Remember to read what you see, not what you expect to see.

> **Tip**
> You may want to adjust your method of vocalization when checking for differences in address names. Instead of vocalizing the words by sound, spell them out. This will be easier when encountering long, exotic, and unfamiliar names.

Similar but Different Words

One tricky category of address differences consists of addresses that are pronounced the same but spelled differently. Here is a quick exercise with this type of item. Next to each pair, write A if the addresses are alike in every way, or D if they differ in any way.

1.	Brookfield	Brookville
2.	Wayland	Wayland
3.	Harrisburg	Harrisberg
4.	Spring	Springs
5.	Glastonberry	Glastonbury
6.	Hamburgh	Hamberg
7.	Riverdale	Riverdell
8.	Beech	Beach
9.	Fairmount	Fairmount
10.	Montboro	Montborough

Answers

1.	D	5.	D	9.	A
2.	A	6.	D	10.	D
3.	D	7.	D		
4.	D	8.	D		

Letter Doublings, Reversals, and Plain Old-Fashioned Spelling Errors

When comparing addresses, check for the following:

- Is the spelling exactly the same?
- Are the same letters doubled?
- Is a letter dropped?
- Are two letters reversed?

Now try this quick exercise, checking for the differences just mentioned. Next to each item, write (A) if the addresses are alike in every way or (D) if they differ in any way.

1.	Manchester Cove	Manchester Cave
2.	Torrington	Torington
3.	Brayton	Brayton
4.	Collegiate	Collegaite
5.	Weston	Wetson
6.	Depford	Deptford
7.	Rangeley	Rangeley
8.	Whitfield	Whitefield
9.	West Newfield	West Newfield
10.	Temple	Tempel

Answers

1.	D	5.	D	9.	A
2.	D	6.	D	10.	D
3.	A	7.	A		
4.	D	8.	D		

Practice Finding Differences in Address Names

> **DIRECTIONS:** In the following set of practice questions, all differences are in the address names. Work quickly, focusing only on the names. You may find any of the three types of differences just described. Write **(A)** if the two addresses are *alike* in every way, **(D)** if they are *different* in any way. Write your answer next to the question number.

1.	5254 Shaeffer St	5254 Schaeffer St
2.	8003 Sheraton Wy	8003 Sheraton Wy
3.	1937 Cordelia Terr	1937 Cordelia Terr
4.	392 Kauai Hwy	392 Kauaui Hwy
5.	7500 Preferred Rd	7500 Preffered Rd
6.	Natick MA 01760	Natick MA 01760
7.	727 Stickbridge Rd	727 Stockbridge Rd
8.	294 Friend St	294 Freind St
9.	4550 Munching St	4550 Munchkin St
10.	Gt Barrington MA 02130	Gt Barnington MA 02130
11.	7070 Baltic Wy	7070 Baltic Wy
12.	889 Safari St	889 Seafari St
13.	Irvington NY 10533	Irvington NY 10533
14.	475 Ghirardelli Sq	475 Ghirardelli Sq
15.	Sea Island GA 31561	Sea Inland GA 31561
16.	8486 Massachusetts Tpke	8486 Massachusetts Tpke
17.	6874 Cloister St	6874 Cloister St
18.	292 Westminster MI	292 Westminister MI
19.	Providence RI 02903	Providence RI 02903
20.	Arundel ME 04046	Anurdel ME 04046
21.	1000 Cadiz St	1000 Cadiz St
22.	821 Calphalon Wy	821 Caphalon Wy
23.	Oakland CA 94604	Oakland CA 94604
24.	371 Himalaya St	371 Himalaya St
25.	1053 Columbus Cir	1053 Columbia Cir

Answers

1.	D	11.	A	21.	A
2.	A	12.	D	22.	D
3.	A	13.	A	23.	A
4.	D	14.	A	24.	A
5.	D	15.	D	25.	D
6.	A	16.	A		
7.	D	17.	A		
8.	D	18.	D		
9.	D	19.	A		
10.	D	20.	D		

Address Checking Practice Exercise

The following practice exercise tests the address checking techniques you learned in this and the previous hour. Take this exercise as follows:

1. Proceed through the test at a steady pace.
2. Try not to reread a single address as you mark your answer.
3. Use the power reading techniques you are most comfortable with in answering the questions.
4. When you finish, check your answers against the answer key.
5. Fill in the self-evaluation chart to see what kinds of errors you made.
6. Based on your results, review the sections in this and the previous hour where you need the most practice.

5

> **DIRECTIONS:** For each question, compare the address in the left column with the address in the right column. If the two addresses are *alike* in every way, write **(A)** next to the question number. If the two addresses are *different* in any way, write **(D)** next to the question number.

1.	8690 W 134th St	8960 W 134th St
2.	1912 Berkshire Rd	1912 Berkshire Wy
3.	5331 W Professor St	5331 W Proffesor St
4.	Philadelphia PA 19124	Philadelphia PN 19124
5.	7450 Gaguenay St	7450 Saguenay St
6.	8650 Christy St	8650 Christey St

7.	Lumberville PA 18933	Lumberville PA 1998333
8.	114 Alabama Ave NW	114 Alabama Av NW
9.	1756 Waterford St	1756 Waterville St
10.	2214 Wister Wy	2214 Wister Wy
11.	2974 Repplier Rd	2974 Repplier Dr
12.	Essex CT 06426	Essex CT 06426
13.	7676 N Bourbon St	7616 N Bourbon St
14.	2762 Rosengarten Wy	2762 Rosengarden Wy
15.	239 Windell Ave	239 Windell Ave
16.	4667 Edgeworth Rd	4677 Edgeworth Rd
17.	2661 Kennel St Se	2661 Kennel St Sw
18.	Alamo TX 78516	Alamo TX 78516
19.	3709 Columbine St	3709 Columbine St
20.	9699 W 14th St	9699 W 14th Rd
21.	2207 Markland Ave	2207 Markham Ave
22.	Los Angeles CA 90013	Los Angeles CA 90018
23.	4608 N Warnock St	4806 N Warnock St
24.	7718 S Summer St	7718 S Sumner St
25.	New York NY 10016	New York NY 10016
26.	4514 Ft Hamilton Pk	4514 Ft Hamilton Pk
27.	5701 Kosciusko St	5701 Koscusko St
28.	5422 Evergreen St	4522 Evergreen St
29.	Gainsville FL 43611	Gainsville FL 32611
30.	5018 Church St	5018 Church Ave
31.	1079 N Blake St	1097 N Blake St
32.	8072 W 20th Rd	80702 W 20th Dr
33.	Onoro ME 04473	Orono ME 04473
34.	2175 Kimbell Rd	2175 Kimball Rd
35.	1243 Mermaid St	1243 Mermaid St
36.	4904 SW 134th St	4904 SW 134th St
37.	1094 Hancock St	1049 Hancock St
38.	Des Moines IA 50311	Des Moines IA 50311
39.	4832 S Rinaldi Rd	48323 S Rinaldo Rd
40.	2015 Dorchester Rd	2015 Dorchester Rd
41.	5216 Woodbine St	5216 Woodburn St
42.	Boulder CO 80302	Boulder CA 80302
43.	4739 N Marion St	479 N Marion St
44.	3720 Nautilus Wy	3270 Nautilus Way
45.	3636 Gramercy Pk	3636 Gramercy Pk
46.	757 Johnson Ave	757 Johnston Ave

47.	3045 Brighton 12th St	3045 Brighton 12th St
48.	237 Ovington Ave	237 Ovington Ave
49.	Kalamazoo MI 49007	Kalamazoo MI 49007
50.	Lissoula MT 59812	Missoula MS59812
51.	Stillwater OK 74704	Stillwater OK 47404
52.	47446 Empire Blvd	4746 Empire Bldg
53.	6321 St Johns Pl	6321 St Johns Pl
54.	2242 Vanderbilt Ave	2242 Vanderbilt Ave
55.	542 Ditmas Blvd	542 Ditmars Blvd
56.	4603 W Argyle Rd	4603 W Argyle Rd
57.	653 Knickerbocker Ave NE	653 Knickerbocker Ave NE
58.	3651 Midwood Terr	3651 Midwood Terr
59.	Chapel Hill NC 27514	Chaple Hill NC 27514
60.	3217 Vernon Pl NW	3217 Vernon Dr NW
61.	1094 Rednor Pkwy	1049 Rednor Pkwy
62.	986 S Doughty Blvd	986 S Douty Blvd
63.	Lincoln NE 68508	Lincoln NE 65808
64.	1517 LaSalle Ave	1517 LaSalle Ave
65.	3857 S Morris St	3857 S Morriss St
66.	6104 Saunders Expy	614 Saunders Expy
67.	2541 Appleton St	2541 Appleton Rd
68.	Washington DC 20052	Washington DC 20052
69.	6439 Kessler Blvd S	6439 Kessler Blvd S
70.	4786 Catalina Dr	4786 Catalana Dr
71.	132 E Hampton Pkwy	1322 E Hampton Pkwy
72.	1066 Goethe Sq S	1066 Geothe Sq S
73.	1118 Jerriman Wy	1218 Jerriman Wy
74.	5798 Grand Central Pkwy	57998 Grand Central Pkwy
75.	Delaware OH 43015	Delaware OK 43015
76.	Corvallis OR 973313	Corvallis OR 97331
77.	4231 Keating Ave N	4231 Keating Av N
78.	5689 Central Pk Pl	5869 Central Pk Pl
79.	1108 Lyndhurst Dr	1108 Lyndhurst Dr
80.	842 Chambers Ct	842 Chamber Ct
81.	Athens OH 45701	Athens GA 45701
82.	Tulsa OK 74171	Tulsa OK 71471
83.	6892 Beech Grove Ave	6892 Beech Grove Ave
84.	2939 E Division St	2929 W Division St
85.	1554 Pitkin Ave	1554 Pitkin Ave

5

86.	905 St Edwards Plz	950 St Edwards Plz
87.	1906 W 152nd St	1906 W 152nd St
88.	3466 Glenmore Ave	3466 Glenville Ave
89.	Middlebury VT 05753	Middleberry VT 05753
90.	Evanston IL 60201	Evanston IN 60201
91.	9401 W McDonald Ave	9401 W MacDonald Ave
92.	55527 Albermarle Rd	5527 Albermarle Rd
93.	9055 Carter Dr	9055 Carter Dr
94.	Greenvale NY 11548	Greenvale NY 11458
95.	1149 Cherry Gr S	1149 Cherry Gr S

Answers

1. D	25. A	49. A	73. D
2. D	26. A	50. D	74. D
3. D	27. D	51. D	75. D
4. D	28. D	52. D	76. D
5. D	29. D	53. A	77. D
6. D	30. D	54. A	78. D
7. D	31. D	55. D	79. A
8. D	32. D	56. A	80. D
9. D	33. D	57. A	81. D
10. A	34. D	58. A	82. D
11. D	35. A	59. D	83. A
12. A	36. A	60. D	84. D
13. D	37. D	61. D	85. A
14. D	38. A	62. D	86. D
15. A	39. D	63. D	87. A
16. D	40. A	64. A	88. D
17. D	41. D	65. D	89. D
18. A	42. D	66. D	90. D
19. A	43. D	67. D	91. D
20. D	44. D	68. A	92. D
21. D	45. A	69. A	93. A
22. D	46. D	70. D	94. D
23. D	47. A	71. D	95. A
24. D	48. A	72. D	

5

Self-Evaluation

Type of Difference	Question Number	Number of Questions You Missed
Difference in Numbers	1, 7, 13, 16, 22, 23, 28, 31, 37, 43, 47, 51, 61, 63, 66, 71, 73, 78, 82, 86, 94	
Difference in Abbreviations	4, 8, 11, 17, 20, 30, 32, 42, 44, 50, 52, 60, 67, 75, 77, 81, 84, 90, 93	
Difference in Address Names	3, 6, 9, 14, 21, 24, 27, 33, 34, 39, 41, 46, 55, 59, 62, 65, 70, 72, 80, 88, 89, 91	
No Difference	2, 5, 10, 12, 15, 18, 19, 25, 26, 29, 35, 36, 38, 40, 45, 48, 49, 53, 54, 56, 57, 58, 64, 68, 69, 74, 76, 79, 83, 85, 87, 92, 95	

The Hour in Review

In this hour, you have:

1. Learned many of the standard and nonstandard abbreviations found in mailing addresses.

2. Understood the differences in address names found in Address Checking questions.

3. Applied power reading techniques to discover differences in abbreviations and address names.

4. Taken a full-length practice exercise to evaluate your ability to answer Address Checking questions.

Hour 6

Memory for Addresses—1

What You Will Learn in This Hour

Memory for Addresses" is often considered the most difficult part of the test. You'll find, however, that the questions look harder than they really are. In this hour, you'll be introduced to strategies for answering the Memory for Addresses questions and will learn how to approach this part of the test with confidence. Practice will help you get a higher test score. Here are your goals for this hour:

- Take a mini-warm-up test with the official sample set of addresses.
- Learn a step-by-step approach for answering the Memory for Addresses questions.
- Understand a basic strategy for memorizing single name locations.
- Learn the trick for memorizing number spans.

Mini Warm-Up Quiz

The following 10-question mini-quiz using the official set of sample questions will introduce you to this question type.

DIRECTIONS: The five boxes below are labeled A, B, C, D, and E. In each box are five addresses; three are street addresses with number ranges and two are unnumbered place names. The position of an address within a box is not important. You need only remember the letter of the box in which the address is found. After memorizing the addresses, cover the boxes up and answer the questions. Take as much time as you need to answer the questions.

A	B	C	D	E
4700–5599 Table	6800–6999 Table	5600–6499 Table	6500–6799 Table	4400–4699 Table
Lismore	Kelford	Joel	Tatum	Ruskin
5600–6499 West	6500–6799 West	6800–6999 West	4400–4699 West	4700–5599 West
Hesper	Musella	Sardis	Porter	Nathan
4400–4699 Blake	5600–6499 Blake	6500–6799 Blake	4700–5599 Blake	6800–6999 Blake

DIRECTIONS: For each of the following addresses, select the letter of the box in which one address is found. Then write the letter next to the question number.

1. Sardis
2. 4700-5599 Table
3. 4700-5599 Blake
4. Porter
5. 4400-4699 West
6. Tatum
7. Hesper
8. Musella
9. 6500-6799 West
10. Ruskin

Answers

1. C
2. A
3. D
4. D
5. D
6. D
7. A
8. B
9. B
10. E

Testing Memory

Memorizing is a special skill, simple for some people but a chore for most. If you are one of the lucky ones with a good visual memory—that is, if you can look at a page and remember not only what was on the page but how the page looked—you should have found the above quiz easy. Odds are, however, you found the quiz a pretty daunting task.

What the Test Asks You to Do

The actual test requires you to answer up to 88 questions in five minutes without referring back to the original boxes. You are, however, given extensive unscored pretest practice with these boxes to help you memorize what's in each box. The practice sets are as follows:

1. Sample set: a short set of questions in which you are allowed to refer to the original boxes

2. Practice I: 88 questions in which you are allowed to look at the original boxes

3. Practice II: 88 questions in which you are not allowed to look at the original boxes

4. Practice III: 88 questions in which you are allowed to look at the original boxes

> **Tip**
> This extensive pretest practice works in your favor. It gives you time to memorize the address locations using the techniques described in this hour and the next hour. The practice sets turn what looks like a very difficult exercise into one you can master.

6

Memorization Techniques

Specific memorization techniques can help you master memory for address questions. But before you start to work on memorizing, decide whether you want to memorize the contents of all five boxes or just four. How can you skip a box? Once you have thoroughly memorized the contents of four boxes, any name or number that you cannot place automatically may be assigned to the fifth box. Should you do this? This depends on your level of comfort with the practice material that follows.

Use the following five-step Action Plan to tackle the Memory for Addresses questions.

1. Decide in advance whether you're willing to consider memorizing just four of the five boxes.

2. Zero in on the single names listed in the boxes.

3. If you find all the single names equally easy to learn, eliminate Box E.

4. If the names in one particular box give you more trouble than the others, choose that box to skip.

5. When you learn the number span/name combinations, skip the same box so that all the unknowns can be assigned to that box when you are answering questions.

Tip
Although all items must be memorized in their correct boxes, the order of the items within the boxes is irrelevant. This means you can memorize from the top down or from the bottom up, and you do not need to be consistent in the order in which you memorize the names from one box to the next. Memorize the addresses in the order you find easiest.

Memorize Single Names First

Take a good look at the five boxes. You will note that in each box there are two single names and three sets of number spans with names. Single names tend to be easier to memorize than the name/number span combinations, so your first order of business is to first memorize the single names.

A	B	C	D	E
Lismore Hesper	Kelford Musella	Joel Sardis	Tatum Porter	Ruskin Nathan

Combine Name Pairs into Key Words

The best way to learn the single names and memorize their location is to combine each pair of words into a key word that is easy to remember and then memorize those key words from left to right. The key words can be real or imaginary; the important thing is that you can easily remember them.

With the above names, you could combine them as follows:

Box A = HeLi

Box B = MuKe

Box C = JoS

Box D = TaP

Box E = RuNt

When doing this, you can skip the pair you find most difficult to combine or combine all five pairs. The choice is yours.

Practice Making Key Words

Using the same names as above, create two new key words per lettered box:

Box A: _____		_____
Box B: _____		_____
Box C: _____		_____
Box D: _____		_____
Box E: _____		_____

Take Advantage of Word Associations

Key words are easier to remember if you can associate them with some idea or mental picture. For example, "HeLi" might remind you of "heliport" or "TaP" might bring tap dancing to mind. Use these images to fix the key words in your mind.

6

Memorize Key Word Locations

Once you have developed your key words, memorize them from left to right. This will make the location of each word easier to recall under the time pressure of the test. To memorize the words, say them to yourself and keep repeating them.

> **Tip**
> Vocalize. Vocalize. Vocalize. All combining of words must be done in your head. You are not permitted to write down anything during this part of the test on memorizing addresses. Vocalizing the key words in order from left to right will help you stay on track.

Use the Name Pairs to Make up Sentences or Phrases

An alternate technique for memorizing single names is to make up a sentence or phrase using both names in a box, and then associate that sentence or phrase with the letter of the box. This technique has its limitations. Under the time constraints of the exam, it may be difficult to create meaningful phrases or sentences with the unfamiliar names listed in the boxes. Using the names in the above boxes, you can come up with sentences or phrases like these:

- Box C = Joel is at the <u>C</u>omfortable Sardis house.
- Box E = Nathan Ruskin lives <u>E</u>ast of here.

Can you think of a sentence for each box?

Box A: _____

Box B: _____

Box C: _____

Box D: _____

Box E: _____

> **Caution**
> Use one or the other of these two memorization techniques for single names, but don't try to use both. That would be too confusing under the time pressure of Test 470. Making up key words is quicker than creating sentences. And you have ample practice time on the actual test to master 10 names and locations.

Practice Memorizing Single Names

Now it's your turn to apply the techniques you've learned in a practice exercise. After you have finished memorizing which names belong in each box, cover the boxes and answer the questions. Write your answer next to the question number. This exercise is not timed.

A	B	C	D	E
Lismore Hesper	Kelford Musella	Joel Sardis	Tatum Porter	Ruskin Nathan

1.	Sardis	11.	Nathan	21.	Porter
2.	Ruskin	12.	Porter	22.	Musella
3.	Lismore	13.	Joel	23.	Kelford
4.	Tatum	14.	Tatum	24.	Ruskin
5.	Nathan	15.	Ruskin	25.	Tatum
6.	Porter	16.	Hesper		
7.	Hesper	17.	Sardis		
8.	Kelford	18.	Nathan		
9.	Lismore	19.	Joel		
10.	Musella	20.	Lismore		

Answers

1.	C	11.	E	21.	D
2.	E	12.	D	22.	B
3.	A	13.	C	23.	B
4.	D	14.	D	24.	E
5.	E	15.	E	25.	D
6.	D	16.	A		
7.	A	17.	C		
8.	B	18.	E		
9.	A	19.	C		
10.	B	20.	A		

6

Focus on Number Span/Name Addresses

Look again at the five sample lettered boxes. This time, focus on the numbered street addresses (the addresses with number spans or number ranges before them). You will find, in most cases, five different number spans paired with three street names:

A	B	C	D	E
4700–5599 Table	6800–6999 Table	5600–6499 Table	6500–6799 Table	4400–4699 Table
5600–6499 West	6500–6799 West	6800–6999 West	4400–4699 West	4700–5599 West
4400–4699 Blake	5600–6499 Blake	6500–6799 Blake	4700–5599 Blake	6800–6999 Blake

In other words, each street name has the same five number spans:

Street Names	Associated Number Spans
Table	4400-4699, 4700-5599, 5600-6499,6500-6799, and 6800-6999
West	4400-4699, 4700-5599, 5600-6499, 6500-6799, and 6800-6999
Blake	4400-4699, 4700-5599, 5600-6499, 6500-6799, and 6800-6999

Note
The fact that the number spans are repeated does not make your job any easier. Count them: You have 15 (12 if you opt to discard a box) separate addresses to remember, not five, because each number span is paired with three different names in three different locations. This makes your task a bit more daunting than memorizing single names.

Caution
Remember if you skipped a box when learning the single names, you must skip the same box when memorizing numbered addresses. Although some combinations may be easier to learn than others, it would be far too confusing to skip one box for names and another for numbered addresses.

Shorten the Numbers to Simplify Your Memorization Task

Your memorization task can be made easier by shortening the numbers in each address. You can do this because each of the five number spans has a different two-digit beginning. In the number spans in the sample boxes, these two-digit combinations are 44, 47, 56, 65, and 68. Drop the remaining numbers and the sample boxes look like this:

A	B	C	D	E
47 Table	68 Table	56 Table	65 Table	44 Table
56 West	65 West	68 West	44 West	47 West
44 Blake	56 Blake	65 Blake	47 Blake	68 Blake

Memorize Number Span/Name Locations

Once you've simplified the addresses mentally, you still have to memorize box locations. To do this, create a personalized memory scheme one box at a time. Try different methods of associating numbered addresses with box locations to find the one that works best for you. Here are some suggestions:

Method	Examples
Associate the numbered address with initials that combine both the letter of the box with the first letter of the street address	47 Table AT, 56 West AW, 44 Blake BA, 68 Table BuT, 65 West BoW, 56 Blake BuB
Simply memorize the address by adding the box letter to the numbered address	47 A Table or 47 TableA, 56 A West or 56 WestA, 44 A Blake or 44 BlakeA, 68 B Table or 68 TableB, 65 B West or 65 WestB, 56 B Blake or 56 Blake B
Associate the address with the sound of the letter location	cee 56 Blake, 47 Table ee

6

> **Tip**
> You do not have to use the same method in each box; you just have to create a system that you can learn quickly and remember without any possible confusion.

Practice Memorizing Number Span/Name Combinations

DIRECTIONS: Using the official sample set of numbered addresses below, learn the number/name combinations and their locations. Then cover the boxes and try the untimed exercise below. Write your answer next to the question number.

A	B	C	D	E
47 Table	68 Table	56 Table	65 Table	44 Table
56 West	65 West	68 West	44 West	47 West
44 Blake	56 Blake	65 Blake	47 Blake	68 Blake

1.	6500-6799 West	11.	4400-4699 Blake	21.	4700-5599 West
2.	6800-6999 Blake	12.	4700-5599 Table	22.	6500-6799 Table
3.	4400-4699 West	13.	6800-6999 West	23.	6500-6799 Blake
4.	5600-6499 Table	14.	6500-6799 West	24.	6500-6799 West
5.	6500-6799 Blake	15.	4400-4699 Table	25.	6800-6999 Blake
6.	4700-5599 Table	16.	6800-6999 Blake		
7.	5600-6499 West	17.	5600-6499 Blake		
8.	4700-5599 Blake	18.	6800-6999 Table		
9.	6800-6999 Table	19.	5600-6499 West		
10.	6800-6999 West	20.	5600-6499 Table		

Answers

1.	B	11.	A	21.	E
2.	E	12.	A	22.	D
3.	D	13.	C	23.	C
4.	C	14.	B	24.	B
5.	C	15.	E	25.	E
6.	A	16.	E		
7.	A	17.	B		
8.	D	18.	B		
9.	B	19.	A		
10.	C	20.	C		

Memory for Addresses Practice Exercise

Now that you have learned different ways to memorize the box locations of the single names and the number span/name combinations, you must put together all you have learned and answer questions that combine both address types. This is what you'll have to do on the actual test. This practice exercise will use the official sample questions and will not be timed.

DIRECTIONS: The five boxes below are labeled A, B, C, D, and E. In each box are five addresses; three are street addresses with number ranges and two are unnumbered place names. The position of an address within a box is not important. You need only remember the letter of the box where the address is found. After memorizing the addresses, cover the boxes up and answer the questions. Take as much time as you need to answer the questions.

A	B	C	D	E
4700–5599 Table	6800–6999 Table	5600–6499 Table	6500–6799 Table	4400–4699 Table
Lismore	Kelford	Joel	Tatum	Ruskin
5600–6499 West	6500–6799 West	6800–6999 West	4400–4699 West	4700–5599 West
Hesper	Musella	Sardis	Porter	Nathan
4400–4699 Blake	5600–6499 Blake	6500–6799 Blake	4700–5599 Blake	6800–6999 Blake

DIRECTIONS: For each of the following addresses, select the letter of the box in which each address is found. Write the letter next to the question number.

1. 4400-4699 West
2. Nathan
3. 4400-4699 Table
4. 6500-6799 Blake
5. 5600-6499 Blake
6. Joel
7. Hesper
8. 4700-5599 Table
9. 6800-6999 West
10. Kelford
11. Musella
12. Ruskin
13. 6500-6799 Table
14. 5600-6499 West
15. 4400-4699 Blake
16. Nathan
17. 6500-6799 Blake
18. 4700-5599 West
19. Tatum
20. 6800-6999 Table
21. 4400-4699 Table
22. Joel
23. 6500-6799 West
24. 6800-6999 West
25. 6800-6999 Blake
26. 5600-6499 Blake
27. Ruskin
28. Sardis
29. 4400-4699 Blake
30. 5600-6499 West
31. Lismore
32. 6500-6799 Table
33. 4700-5599 West
34. Musella
35. 6500-6799 Blake
36. 6800-6999 Table
37. 4700-5599 Table
38. 6800-6999 West
39. Joel
40. Porter
41. Hesper
42. 5600-6499 Table
43. Nathan
44. 4400-4699 West
45. 6500-6799 West
46. Kelford
47. 5600-6499 Blake
48. 6800-6999 Blake
49. 5600-6499 West
50. 6500-6799 Table

6

Answers

1.	D	18.	E	35.	C
2.	E	19.	D	36.	B
3.	E	20.	B	37.	A
4.	C	21.	E	38.	C
5.	B	22.	C	39.	C
6.	C	23.	B	40.	D
7.	A	24.	C	41.	A
8.	A	25.	E	42.	C
9.	C	26.	B	43.	E
10.	B	27.	E	44.	D
11.	B	28.	C	45.	B
12.	E	29.	A	46.	B
13.	D	30.	A	47.	B
14.	A	31.	A	48.	E
15.	A	32.	D	49.	A
16.	E	33.	E	50.	D
17.	C	34.	B		

The Hour in Review

In this hour, you learned a systematic approach for answering the Memory for Addresses questions, Part B on Test 470.

1. Memorize single names first. Do this by combining them into key words or by using them in made-up phrases or sentences.

2. Next, memorize address/number span combinations. Shorten each number span to two digits, and then create a personalized memory scheme to associate each numbered address with the proper box.

3. Use all these techniques together to master the Memory for Addresses questions.

HOUR 7

Memory for Addresses—2

What You Will Learn in This Hour

In the previous hour, you learned that answering the Memory for Addresses questions involves a dual and complex strategy that can be mastered only with practice. You have to be able to memorize both single names and number span/name combinations to do well on this part of the test. In this hour and the next hour, you'll practice with step-by-step exercises to learn this strategy. Here are your goals for this hour:

- Get ready for the practice exercise by understanding its goals.

- Apply the memorization techniques you learned in the last hour to a new set of boxes.

- Complete the practice exercise at an unhurried pace but within the one-hour limit.

- Evaluate your work on the practice exercise.

Preparing for the Practice Exercise

The Memory for Addresses practice exercise that you'll take in this hour gives you the opportunity to apply the techniques that you learned in Hour 6, "Memory for Addresses—1." The right mindset will help you benefit the most from the practice exercise, so keep the following in mind:

- Concentrate only on learning the addresses in this exercise.
- Follow the steps given; they are based on extensive analysis working with this question type.
- Don't look at the official sample addresses in Hour 6, but if you need to, you can refer back to the Notes, Tips, and Cautions in that hour.
- Take the practice exercise at your own pace, but complete it within one hour.
- Use Set 1 to reinforce your mastery of the address locations.
- Evaluate your work as described after Set 2.

Caution
If you finish the practice exercise in less than one hour, do not go ahead and try the practice exercise in Hour 8, "Memory for Addresses—3." You can review the Tips, Notes, and Cautions given in Hour 6, but don't clutter your memory with items, locations, or key words that interfere with your learning this hour's practice exercise.

Memory for Addresses Practice Exercise

The practice exercise contains two sets of questions based on the following five lettered boxes:

A	B	C	D	E
3200–3499 Apple Gray 3500–3599 Hills Book 2900–3199 Leaf	1000–2199 Apple Fish 2200–2899 Hills Trace 3200–3499 Leaf	3500–3599 Apple Arden 3200–3499 Hills Paris 1000–2199 Leaf	2200–2899 Apple Stewart 2900–3199 Hills Narrows 3500–3599 Leaf	2900–3199 Apple Hard 1000–2199 Hills Inman 2200–2899 Leaf

Begin by devising memory schemes for the single names and the number span/name combinations. Then answer the questions in Set 1, referring back to the boxes if necessary. Answer Set 2 strictly from memory.

Memorize Single Names

Zero in on the single names right away. Think of a good combination for each pair of words and write this key word directly under the box, as shown in the following table. Under box A, you might write GraB or BoG; under Box B, FiT; under box C, PArdon; under Box D, StuN or NeST; under Box E, HI. Of course, you could also come up with key words that are meaningful to you.

A	B	C	D	E
Gray Book GRaB or BoG or other	Fish Trace FiT or other	Arden Paris PArdon or other	Stewart Narrows StuN or NeSt or other	Hard Inman HI or other

You can also try the alternate memorization technique of creating a sentence from the two words. For example, under Box C, you could write, "Arden went to See (C) Paris." Remember to use the technique that best enables you to memorize the single names quickly and accurately.

> **Tip**
> Don't discard any boxes in this practice exercise. Memorizing the single names in every box will give you more practice.

7

Shorten the Number Spans

Cross out the numbers from 00 to the end of each number span to shorten them, leaving only the essential material to be memorized, as shown in the following table:

A	B	C	D	E
32~~00–3499~~ Apple Gray	10~~00–2199~~ Apple Fish	35~~00–3599~~ Apple Arden	22~~00–2899~~ Apple Stewart	29~~00–3199~~ Apple Hard
35~~00–3599~~ Hills Book	22~~00–2899~~ Hills Trace	32~~00–3499~~ Hills Paris	29~~00–3199~~ Hills Narrows	10~~00–2199~~ Hills Inman
29~~00–3199~~ Leaf GRaB or BoG or other	32~~00–3499~~ Leaf FiT or other	10~~00–2199~~ Leaf PArdon or other	35~~00–3599~~ Leaf StuN or NeSt or other	22~~00–2899~~ Leaf HI or other

> **Caution**
> On the actual test, you can't write anything down during the time allowed for memorization. This practice exercise is designed to help you develop your memorization skills. With practice and patience, you won't need to cross out material or write down key words.

Memorize Number Span/Name Combinations

Devise a personalized method for remembering the number span/name combinations for each box. You don't need to use the same method for each box. In this step, you'll learn the number span/name combinations listed in the following table:

A	B	C	D	E
32 Apple	10 Apple	35 Apple	22 Apple	29 Apple
35 Hills	22 Hills	32 Hills	29 Hills	10 Hills
29 Leaf	32 Leaf	10 Leaf	35 Leaf	22 Leaf

Take the Practice Sets

DIRECTIONS: Complete the two practice sets. For Set 1, you can refer back to the boxes. You must answer Set 2 solely from memory. Write your answer next to the question number.

Practice Set 1

1. 2200-2899 Hills	11. 2900-3199 Leaf	21. 3500-3599 Leaf
2. 3500-3599 Leaf	12. Trace	22. 3500-3599 Apple
3. Stewart	13. Hard	23. 2200-2899 Apple
4. 3200-3499 Apple	14. Arden	24. Fish
5. 3200-3499 Hills	15. 2200-2899 Hills	25. Book
6. 2200-2899 Apple	16. 1000-2199 Hills	26. 2900-3199 Apple
7. Inman	17. 1000-2199 Apple	27. 2900-3199 Hills
8. Gray	18. Narrows	28. 1000-2199 Leaf
9. 3500-3599 Hills	19. 3200-3499 Leaf	29. 2200-2899 Hills
10. 2200-2899 Leaf	20. Paris	30. 3200-3499 Apple
31. Gray	51. 3200-3499 Hills	71. 2900-3199 Apple
32. Trace	52. 2900-3199 Apple	72. 1000-2199 Apple
33. Arden	53. 2200-2899 Leaf	73. Fish
34. 3200-3499 Hills	54. Gray	74. Gray
35. Narrows	55. Narrows	75. 2200-2899 Leaf
36. Hard	56. Hard	76. 3500-3599 Apple
37. 2900-3199 Leaf	57. 3200-3499 Apple	77. 2200-2899 Hills
38. 2200-2899 Hills	58. 1000-2199 Hills	78. Stewart
39. 3500-3599 Apple	59. 1000-2199 Leaf	79. Hard
40. 2900-3199 Hills	60. Inman	80. 3500-3599 Hills
41. 2200-2899 Leaf	61. Book	81. 2200-2899 Apple
42. Inman	62. 3500-3599 Hills	82. Paris
43. Stewart	63. 2900-3199 Hills	83. 3500-3599 Leaf
44. Paris	64. 3500-3599 Apple	84. 2900-3199 Leaf
45. 3500-3599 Hills	65. 3500-3599 Leaf	85. Gray
46. 1000-2199 Apple	66. Trace	86. 2900-3199 Hills
47. Fish	67. Paris	87. Inman
48. Book	68. 2200-2899 Apple	88. 3500-3599 Apple
49. 3200-3499 Leaf	69. 2900-3199 Leaf	
50. 2200-2899 Apple	70. Narrows	

7

Practice Set 2

1. 2200-2899 Leaf
2. Narrows
3. 3200-3499 Hills
4. Fish
5. 3200-3499 Apple
6. 2900-3199 Leaf
7. Trace
8. Stewart
9. 2900-3199 Apple
10. 3500-3599 Apple

11. 1000-2199 Leaf
12. Hard
13. 1000-2199 Hills
14. 3500-3599 Leaf
15. 1000-2199 Apple
16. Gray
17. Arden
18. 2200-2899 Hills
19. 3200-3499 Hills
20. Paris

21. Book
22. 3500-3599 Hills
23. 3500-3599 Apple
24. Inman
25. 2200-2899 Apple
26. 2900-3199 Leaf
27. 2900-3199 Apple
28. 3200-3499 Hills
29. Arden
30. Gray

31. 1000-2199 Apple
32. 3500-3599 Leaf
33. 2200-2899 Leaf
34. 3500-3599 Apple
35. Trace
36. Stewart
37. Inman
38. 3500-3599 Hills
39. 2900-3199 Hills
40. 2200-2899 Hills
41. 2200-2899 Apple
42. Hard
43. Fish
44. 3500-3599 Leaf
45. 3200-3499 Hills
46. 3200-3499 Apple
47. 3200-3499 Leaf
48. Narrows
49. Paris
50. 1000-2199 Apple

51. 2900-3199 Hills
52. 3500-3599 Leaf
53. 2200-2899 Apple
54. Book
55. Stewart
56. 3500-3599 Hills
57. 2900-3199 Leaf
58. 1000-2199 Hills
59. 1000-2199 Leaf
60. Fish
61. Hard
62. 3200-3499 Hills
63. 3200-3499 Leaf
64. 2200-2899 Leaf
65. Arden
66. Inman
67. 2900-3199 Apple
68. 1000-2199 Apple
69. 2900-3199 Hills
70. 3500-3599 Hills

71. 2900-3199 Leaf
72. Paris
73. Book
74. Hard
75. Gray
76. 3200-3499 Leaf
77. 3200-3499 Apple
78. 1000-2199 Hills
79. 2200-2899 Hills
80. Stewart
81. Fish
82. 2200-2899 Apple
83. 2900-3199 Leaf
84. 2900-3199 Hills
85. Book
86. Trace
87. 3500-3599 Leaf
88. 2900-3199 Apple

Answers

Practice Set 1

1.	B	11.	A	21.	D
2.	D	12.	B	22.	C
3.	D	13.	E	23.	D
4.	A	14.	C	24.	B
5.	C	15.	B	25.	A
6.	D	16.	E	26.	E
7.	E	17.	B	27.	D
8.	A	18.	D	28.	C
9.	A	19.	B	29.	B
10.	E	20.	C	30.	A
31.	A	51.	C	71.	E
32.	B	52.	E	72.	B
33.	C	53.	E	73.	B
34.	C	54.	A	74.	A
35.	D	55.	D	75.	E
36.	E	56.	E	76.	C
37.	A	57.	A	77.	B
38.	B	58.	E	78.	D
39.	C	59.	C	79.	E
40.	D	60.	E	80.	A
41.	E	61.	A	81.	D
42.	E	62.	A	82.	C
43.	D	63.	D	83.	D
44.	C	64.	C	84.	A
45.	A	65.	D	85.	A
46.	B	66.	B	86.	D
47.	B	67.	C	87.	E
48.	A	68.	D	88.	C
49.	B	69.	A		
50.	D	70.	D		

7

Practice Set 2

1.	E	11.	C	21.	A
2.	D	12.	E	22.	A
3.	C	13.	E	23.	C
4.	B	14.	D	24.	E
5.	A	15.	B	25.	D
6.	A	16.	A	26.	A
7.	B	17.	C	27.	E
8.	D	18.	B	28.	C
9.	E	19.	C	29.	C
10.	C	20.	C	30.	A
31.	B	51.	D	71.	A
32.	D	52.	D	72.	C
33.	E	53.	D	73.	A
34.	C	54.	A	74.	E
35.	B	55.	D	75.	A
36.	D	56.	A	76.	B
37.	E	57.	A	77.	A
38.	A	58.	E	78.	E
39.	D	59.	C	79.	B
40.	B	60.	B	80.	D
41.	D	61.	E	81.	B
42.	E	62.	C	82.	D
43.	B	63.	B	83.	A
44.	D	64.	E	84.	D
45.	C	65.	C	85.	A
46.	A	66.	E	86.	B
47.	B	67.	E	87.	D
48.	D	68.	B	88.	E
49.	C	69.	D		
50.	B	70.	A		

Evaluate Your Mistakes

To evaluate your mistakes in Set 2, ask yourself the following questions:

- Did you miss any single names?
- Which names gave you the most trouble?
- What other key words or sentences could you have used?
- How many number span/name combinations did you get wrong?
- Could you have devised a better memory scheme for the number span/name combinations?

Retake Set 2 if you need additional practice.

The Hour in Review

1. The step-by-step practice exercise reinforces the complex memorization strategy for answering the Memory for Addresses questions that you learned in Hour 6.

2. To prevent information overload, only complete one Memory for Addresses practice exercise per hour.

3. Don't bring old baggage to a new exercise; forget all the addresses and key words for the official sample questions.

7

HOUR **8**

Memory for Addresses—3

What You Will Learn in This Hour

In the last hour, you applied the three-step memorization technique to Memory for Addresses questions in a practice exercise. In this hour, you'll do another step-by-step practice exercise to help make this strategy second nature. By now, you have begun to develop skill at combining names into key words and remembering the key words and their locations. You have also begun to devise a system for remembering the locations of number span/name combinations. As you work through this next practice exercise, you'll gain even more confidence in your abilities. By the end of this hour, you should feel confident that you can memorize addresses and place them in appropriate boxes. Here are your goals for this hour:

- Get ready for the practice exercise with a short review.
- Use the three-step memorization process on a new set of boxes that are different than the practice exercise in Hour 7, "Memory for Addresses—2," and the official sample set.
- Complete the practice exercise at an unhurried pace but within a one-hour limit.
- Evaluate your work on the practice exercise.

Preparing for the Practice Exercise

This practice exercise reinforces the memorization technique that you learned in Hour 6, "Memory for Addresses—1." Keep the following points in mind when practicing memorizing addresses:

Do

DO use the memorization technique that works best for you when memorizing single names—either the key word technique or the sentence technique.

DO go with your instincts when creating key words or sentences. The key words or sentences don't have to make sense; they only need to be easy for you to memorize.

Don't

DON'T use both the key word and sentence techniques at the same time; this will only confuse you.

DON'T use the sentence method if you have to struggle to create meaningful sentences. On the actual test, you'll be creating them in your head and you'll want to keep them simple.

Memory for Addresses Practice Exercise

The practice exercise contains two sets of questions based on the following five lettered boxes:

A	B	C	D	E
8800–9399 Rose	7000–7599 Rose	7600–8199 Rose	6300–6999 Rose	8200–8799 Rose
Gateway	Palace	Rainbow	Ocean	Grove
7000–7599 Dawn	6300–6999 Dawn	8200–8799 Dawn	8800–9399 Dawn	7600–8199 Dawn
Cottage	Hammer	Anna	Apricot	Birch
7600–8199 King	8200–8799 King	6300–6999 King	7000–7599 King	8800–9399 King

Begin by devising memory schemes for the single names and the number span/name combinations. After memorizing them to your own satisfaction, answer the questions in Practice Set 1, referring back to the boxes if necessary. Answer the questions in Practice Set 2 strictly from memory.

> **Tip**
> In this exercise, you can discard one box when memorizing addresses. If you choose to skip a box, mark an X across it so that you won't pay attention on its contents while you're busy memorizing.

Memorize Single Names

Think of a good combination word for each pair of single names and write this key word directly under the box, as shown in the following table. Under Box A, you might write CoG; under Box B, HaP; under Box C, AnRa; under Box D, AprO; under Box E, BiG. You can also try the alternate memorization technique of creating a sentence from the two words. For example, under Box E write "A Grove of Birch trees is East of here."

A	B	C	D	E
Gateway Cottage CoG or other	Palace Hammer HaP or other	Rainbow Anna AnRa or other	Ocean Apricot AprO or other	Grove Birch BiG or other

Shorten the Number Spans

Cross out the numbers from 00 to the end of each number span, leaving only the essential material to be memorized, as shown in the following table:

A	B	C	D	E
8800-9300 Rose Gateway 7000-7500 Dawn Cottage 7600-8100 King CoG or other	7000-7500 Rose Palace 6300-6000 Dawn Hammer 8200-8700 King HaP or other	7600-8100 Rose Rainbow 8200-8700 Dawn Anna 6300-6000 King AnRa or other	6300-6000 Rose Ocean 8800-9300 Dawn Apricot 7000-7500 King AprO or other	8200-8700 Rose Grove 7600-8100 Dawn Birch 8800-9300 King BiG or other

Memorize Number Span/Name Combinations

Devise a personalized method for remembering the number span/name combinations for each box listed in the following table (you don't need to use the same method for each box):

A	B	C	D	E
88 Rose 70 Dawn 76 King	70 Rose 63 Dawn 82 King	76 Rose 82 Dawn 63 King	63 Rose 88 Dawn 70 King	82 Rose 76 Dawn 88 King

Take the Practice Sets

DIRECTIONS: Complete the two practice sets. For Set 1, you can refer back to the boxes, but you must answer the questions in Set 2 solely from memory. Write your answer next to the question number. Work at your own pace. There is no time limit for this practice exercise, but you should complete it in less than an hour.

Practice Set 1

1.	6300-6999 Dawn	16.	8800-9399 Dawn	31.	Cottage
2.	7000-7599 King	17.	8200-8799 Rose	32.	7600-8199 King
3.	7000-7599 Rose	18.	Gateway	33.	7600-8199 Rose
4.	Cottage	19.	Palace	34.	8800-9399 Dawn
5.	Ocean	20.	8200-8799 King	35.	7600-8199 Rose
6.	7600-8199 King	21.	8800-8399 King	36.	Grove
7.	8200-8799 Dawn	22.	Apricot	37.	Ocean
8.	7600-8199 Dawn	23.	7000-7599 Dawn	38.	8800-9399 King
9.	Grove	24.	8800-9399 Rose	39.	8200-8799 Rose
10.	Anna	25.	Birch	40.	Palace
11.	Rainbow	26.	6300-6999 King	41.	8800-9399 Rose
12.	7600-8199 Rose	27.	7000-7599 Rose	42.	8200-8799 Dawn
13.	7600-8199 King	28.	7600-8199 Dawn	43.	6300-6999 Dawn
14.	Hammer	29.	Rainbow	44.	Anna
15.	6300-6999 Rose	30.	Hammer	45.	Gateway
46.	7000-7599 King	61.	6300-6999 Dawn	76.	Cottage
47.	8200-8799 King	62.	7600-8199 Rose	77.	Palace
48.	Apricot	63.	6300-6999 Rose	78.	7600-8199 Rose
49.	7000-7599 Dawn	64.	7000-7599 King	79.	8800-9399 King
50.	Birch	65.	Grove	80.	7000-7599 Dawn
51.	6300-6999 Rose	66.	Apricot	81.	8800-9399 Rose
52.	6300-6999 King	67.	7600-8199 Dawn	82.	Hammer
53.	8800-9399 Rose	68.	8200-8799 Rose	83.	6300-6999 King
54.	8200-8799 Dawn	69.	8800-9399 Dawn	84.	Rainbow
55.	8800-8399 King	70.	7000-7599 Dawn	85.	Grove
56.	Birch	71.	Anna	86.	8800-9399 Dawn
57.	Ocean	72.	Rainbow	87.	7000-7599 Rose
58.	Hammer	73.	8200-8799 King	88.	7000-7599 King
59.	Gateway	74.	6300-6999 King		
60.	7600-8199 King	75.	7000-7599 Rose		

Practice Set 2

1. 8200-8799 Rose	16. Birch	31. Hammer
2. Ocean	17. Gateway	32. Gateway
3. 8200-8799 Dawn	18. 7600-8199 Rose	33. 7000-7599 Dawn
4. Hammer	19. 6300-6999 Rose	34. 7600-8199 Rose
5. 7600-8199 King	20. Anna	35. 7000-7599 Rose
6. Cottage	21. 6300-6999 King	36. Palace
7. 7000-7599 Rose	22. 6300-6999 Dawn	37. Apricot
8. 6300-6999 Dawn	23. 8800-9399 Rose	38. Cottage
9. Grove	24. 8800-9399 Dawn	39. 6300-6999 Rose
10. Palace	25. 8200-8799 Rose	40. 7600-8199 Dawn
11. 8800-9399 Rose	26. Birch	41. 8200-8799 Dawn
12. 7000-7599 Dawn	27. Grove	42. Anna
13. 7600-8199 Dawn	28. 7600-8199 King	43. Ocean
14. 8200-8799 King	29. 7000-7599 King	44. 8200-8799 King
15. 7000-7599 King	30. Rainbow	45. 8800-9399 King
46. 7000-7599 Rose	61. 7000-7599 Rose	76. Cottage
47. 8800-9399 Dawn	62. 8200-8799 Dawn	77. 8200-8799 Rose
48. Gateway	63. 7600-8199 King	78. 8200-8799 King
49. 6300-6999 King	64. 8800-9399 King	79. 7000-7599 Rose
50. Rainbow	65. Anna	80. Apricot
51. 8800-9399 Rose	66. Palace	81. 6300-6999 Rose
52. 6300-6999 Dawn	67. 6300-6999 Rose	82. 7000-7599 King
53. 7000-7599 King	68. 7600-8199 Rose	83. 6300-6999 Dawn
54. 8200-8799 Rose	69. 7600-8199 Dawn	84. Anna
55. 8200-8799 King	70. 7000-7599 Dawn	85. Palace
56. 8800-9399 Dawn	71. Ocean	86. 7600-8199 Dawn
57. Grove	72. Rainbow	87. 7600-8199 Rose
58. Birch	73. Gateway	88. 8200-8799 King
59. Hammer	74. 6300-6999 King	
60. Apricot	75. 6300-6999 Dawn	

Answers

Practice Set 1

1.	B	16.	D	31.	A
2.	D	17.	E	32.	A
3.	B	18.	A	33.	C
4.	A	19.	B	34.	D
5.	D	20.	B	35.	C
6.	A	21.	E	36.	E
7.	C	22.	D	37.	D
8.	E	23.	A	38.	E
9.	E	24.	A	39.	E
10.	C	25.	E	40.	B
11.	C	26.	C	41.	A
12.	C	27.	B	42.	C
13.	A	28.	E	43.	B
14.	B	29.	C	44.	C
15.	D	30.	B	45.	A
46.	D	61.	B	76.	A
47.	B	62.	C	77.	B
48.	D	63.	D	78.	C
49.	A	64.	D	79.	E
50.	E	65.	E	80.	A
51.	D	66.	D	81.	A
52.	C	67.	E	82.	B
53.	A	68.	E	83.	C
54.	C	69.	D	84.	C
55.	E	70.	A	85.	E
56.	E	71.	C	86.	D
57.	D	72.	C	87.	B
58.	B	73.	B	88.	D
59.	A	74.	C		
60.	A	75.	B		

Practice Set 2

1.	E	16.	E	31.	B		
2.	D	17.	A	32.	A		
3.	C	18.	C	33.	A		
4.	B	19.	D	34.	C		
5.	A	20.	C	35.	B		
6.	A	21.	C	36.	B		
7.	B	22.	B	37.	D		
8.	B	23.	A	38.	A		
9.	E	24.	D	39.	D		
10.	B	25.	E	40.	E		
11.	A	26.	E	41.	C		
12.	A	27.	E	42.	C		
13.	E	28.	A	43.	D		
14.	B	29.	D	44.	B		
15.	D	30.	C	45.	E		
46.	B	61.	B	76.	A		
47.	D	62.	C	77.	E		
48.	A	63.	A	78.	B		
49.	C	64.	E	79.	B		
50.	C	65.	C	80.	D		
51.	A	66.	B	81.	D		
52.	B	67.	D	82.	D		
53.	D	68.	C	83.	B		
54.	E	69.	E	84.	C		
55.	B	70.	A	85.	B		
56.	D	71.	D	86.	E		
57.	E	72.	C	87.	C		
58.	E	73.	A	88.	B		
59.	B	74.	C				
60.	D	75.	B				

Evaluate Your Mistakes

Evaluate your mistakes in Set 2 by answering the following questions:

- Did you miss any single names in Set 2?
- Which names gave you the most trouble?
- Could you have devised a better memory scheme for the number span/name combinations?

Take this time to write out additional number schemes for problem boxes. Retake Set 2 if you think you need additional practice. If you retake Set 2, discard a different box (if you did this) to see the effect.

The Hour in Review

1. This second practice exercise helped you master the memorization strategy for answering Memory for Addresses questions.

2. Again, you should forget the addresses and key words for the official sample questions and previous practice exercise and concentrate on memorizing this new set of addresses.

3. With practice, you will be able to do this complex strategy in your head on the real test.

Hour 9

Number Series—1

What You Will Learn in This Hour

In this hour and the next, you'll learn strategies for completing the Number Series questions, the only part of Test 470 that measures your ability to work with numbers. Don't let these problems intimidate you; they involve nothing more than simple addition, subtraction, multiplication, and division. Many of the questions can be solved quickly and you won't be penalized for guessing, unlike in the previous two parts of Test 470. Here are your goals for this hour:

- Learn basic techniques for tackling the Number Series portion of Test 470.

- Understand the number patterns found in Number Series questions.

- Learn a three-part strategy for solving Number Series questions.

- Complete a practice exercise to test what you have learned.

Mini Warm-Up Quiz

The following 10-question number series quiz will familiarize you with this question type. Take it at your own pace and don't worry about the time. The correct answers follow the quiz.

DIRECTIONS: Each question contains a series of numbers that follows a definite pattern. Determine what the pattern is and then decide what the next two numbers in the series would be if the order were continued. Circle the letter of the correct answer.

1. 21 21 19 17 17 15 13...(A) 11 11   (B) 13 11   (C) 11 9   (D) 9 7   (E) 13 13
2. 23 22 20 19 16 15 11...(A) 6 5   (B) 10 9   (C) 6 1   (D) 10 6   (E) 10 5
3. 5 6 8 9 11 12 14...   (A) 15 16   (B) 16 17   (C) 15 17   (D) 16 18   (E) 17 19
4. 7 10 8 13 16 8 19...   (A) 22 8   (B) 8 22   (C) 20 21   (D) 22 25   (E) 8 25
5. 1 35 2 34 3 33 4...   (A) 4 5   (B) 32 31   (C) 32 5   (D) 5 32   (E) 31 6
6. 75 75 72 72 69 69 66...(A) 66 66   (B) 66 68   (C) 63 63   (D) 66 63   (E) 63 60
7. 12 16 21 27 31 36 42...(A) 48 56   (B) 44 48   (C) 48 52   (D) 46 52   (E) 46 51
8. 22 24 12 26 28 12 30...(A) 12 32   (B) 32 34   (C) 32 12   (D) 12 12   (E) 32 36
9. 5 70 10 68 15 66 20... (A) 25 64   (B) 64 25   (C) 24 63   (D) 25 30   (E) 64 62
10. 13 22 32 43 55 68 82...(A) 97 113 (B) 100 115 (C) 96 110 (D) 95 105 (E) 99 112

Answers and Explanations

1. **(B)** The pattern of this series is to repeat the number, subtract 2, and subtract 2 again; repeat the number, subtract 2, and subtract 2 again; and so on. Following the pattern, the series should continue as follows: 13 11 9 9 7 5 5 3 1 1.

2. **(E)** The pattern of this series is to subtract 1, subtract 2; subtract 1, subtract 3; subtract 1, subtract 4; subtract 1, subtract 5; and so on. Therefore, the next two numbers are 11 − 1 = 10 and 10 − 5 = 5.

3. **(C)** The pattern of this series is to add 1, add 2; add 1, add 2; add 1, add 2; and so on. The next two numbers are 14 + 1 = 15 and 15 + 2 = 17.

4. **(A)** First notice that the number 8 repeats after each two numbers. If you disregard the 8s, you can see that each number increases by 3, so you can choose (A)

as the correct answer because $19 + 3 = 22$, and the two numbers 19 and 22 are then followed by 8.

5. **(C)** This series is actually two alternating series. One series, beginning with 1, increases by 1. The alternating series begins with 35 and decreases by 1. The correct answer is (C) because the next number in the decreasing series is 32 and the next number in the increasing series is 5.

6. **(D)** The pattern established in this series is to repeat the number, subtract 3; repeat the number, subtract 3; and so on. To continue the series, repeat 66 and then subtract 3 to get 63.

7. **(E)** The pattern is to add 4, add 5, add 6, repeating over and over. The next two numbers are $42 + 4 = 46$ and $46 + 5 = 51$.

8. **(C)** The basic pattern is to add 2. The series can be read 22, 24, 26, 28, 30, 32, and so on. The number 12, however, is repeated after each two numbers of the series. To continue the series, add 2 to 30 to get 32; after 30 and 32, you must insert the number 12.

9. **(B)** In this problem, two distinct series alternate with each other. The first series is ascending by a factor of 5; it reads 10, 15, 20, and so on. The alternating series is descending by a factor of 2; it reads 70, 68, 66, and so on. At the point where you must continue the series, the next number is a member of the descending series, so it must be 64. Following that number must be the next number of the ascending series, 25.

10. **(A)** The numbers are large, but the progression is simple between each number in the series: add 9, add 10, add 11, add 12, add 13, add 14, and so on. Continue the series to find $82 + 15 = 97$ and $97 + 16 = 113$.

> **Note**
> The questions in the mini-test were at many difficulty levels, just like on the actual test. By the end of Hour 10, "Number Series—2," you should be able to easily complete all the difficulty levels of the Number Series questions. Complex questions won't appear intimidating once you know what you're looking for.

Techniques for Solving Number Series Questions

Use the following basic techniques to answer the Number Series questions:

Do

DO write directly in the test booklet. You are allowed to do so on this part of the test; you'll learn question-marking techniques in this hour and the next.

DO keep track of time. This is essential for your guessing strategy. The allotted test time is 20 minutes.

DO answer the easier questions first. An easy question is worth just as much as a difficult one.

DO randomly guess if you're running out of time. There's no penalty for guessing!

Don't

DON'T read the answer choices before figuring out the pattern and determining the next two numbers in the series.

DON'T spend too much time, no more than two minutes, on any one question. If you get bogged down, skip the question and come back later. Be careful to skip that number on your answer sheet as well!

Tip
If you have to randomly guess, make all your guesses the same letter. This may, by the law of averages, give you a better chance of guessing correctly.

Classifiying Number Series Patterns

The Number Series questions can be classified according to the number of patterns within a series, as either a series with one pattern or a series with two or more patterns. Determining how many patterns are present in a number series is the first step in solving the problem.

Finding One-Pattern Series

In number series with one pattern, look for the following kinds of patterns:

- Simple ascending or descending numbers where the same number is added to or subtracted from each number in the series
- Alternating ascending or descending numbers where two different numbers are alternately added to and/or subtracted from each number in the series
- Simple or alternating multiplication or division
- Simple repetition where one or more numbers in the series are repeated immediately before or after the arithmetic operations
- Repetition of a number pattern by itself
- An unusual pattern

> **Tip**
> Although rare, multiplication and division number series have appeared on Test 470. Look for multiplication or division if the series makes no sense in terms of addition or subtraction. They should be easy to spot because they usually involve larger numbers.

Finding Two-Pattern Series

In number series with two or more patterns, look for the following kinds of patterns:

- A random number (not one of the numbers in the series) repeated in a one-pattern series
- Two or more distinct, alternating patterns of addition and/or subtraction
- Two or more alternating patterns plus a repeating, random number
- Two or more alternating patterns of multiplication and/or division
- An unusual alternating pattern or combination of number arrangements

> **Make Connections**
> You'll learn how to find and solve alternating and unusual number series patterns in Hour 10.

Tackling Number Series Questions

The Number Series questions measure your ability to analyze a series of numbers and see the relationships between them, or their patterns. Once you've determined the pattern, you can supply the next two numbers in the series. You must be flexible enough in your thinking so that if the first pattern you try doesn't work, you can shift gears and try a different pattern.

Use the following strategy to approach the Number Series questions:

1. Try to determine the pattern by simple inspection of the numbers.
2. If you can't see the pattern, sound out the series to try to "hear" the pattern.
3. If you still can't determine the pattern, mark the differences between numbers in the series in your test booklet.

Solve at a Glance

The first step in solving a Number Series question is to inspect the series. Simple patterns may be immediately obvious.

For example, the pattern of the following number series should be clear right away: 1 2 3 1 2 3 1. The sequence 1 2 3 is repeated, so the next two numbers in the series must be 2 and 3.

You'll often be able to instantly recognize the pattern of a simple series of ascending or descending numbers, such as the following: 20 21 22 23 24 25. You should easily see that each number increases by one. Thus, the next two numbers are 26 and 27.

You might also quickly recognize a combination of these two kinds of number series: A random number repeated in an ascending or descending series, such as the following: 1 2 15 3 4 15 5. The number 15 appears after each set of two numbers. The next two numbers in this series must be 6 and 15.

> **Tip**
> Repeating, random numbers are often easy to spot. When you first inspect a number series, always check if one of the numbers is repeated.

Test Yourself

DIRECTIONS: You should be able to answer the following Number Series questions by simple inspection. Circle the letter of the correct answer.

1. 12 10 13 10 14 10 15...   (A) 15 10   (B) 10 15   (C) 10 16   (D) 10 10   (E) 15 16
2. 20 40 60 20 40 60 20...   (A) 20 40   (B) 40 60   (C) 60 40   (D) 60 20   (E) 60 40
3. 9 2 9 4 9 6 9...   (A) 9 9   (B) 9 8   (C) 8 10   (D) 10 8   (E) 8 9
4. 5 8 5 8 5 8 5...   (A) 8 5   (B) 5 8   (C) 5 5   (D) 5 6   (E) 8 8
5. 10 9 8 7 6 5 4...   (A) 4 3   (B) 4 2   (C) 3 2   (D) 5 6   (E) 2 1

Answers and Explanations

1. **(C)** This is a simple plus 1 series with the number 10 repeated after each step.
2. **(B)** The sequence 20 40 60 is repeated. No arithmetic is involved.
3. **(E)** This is a simple plus 2 series with the number 9 repeated before each member of the series.
4. **(A)** In this series, the sequence 5 8 is repeated.
5. **(C)** This is a simple minus 1 series.

Vocalize for Meaning

Your ear is often more adept than your eye, so by reading the number series aloud, you may be able to "hear" a pattern of numbers more easily than you can see it. Follow these steps:

1. If you don't spot a pattern immediately, read the series to yourself.
2. If you still can't find the pattern, read the series again. Accent the printed numbers and whisper the missing intervening numbers.
3. If the pattern still isn't apparent, arrange the numbers within the series in order into groups of two or three.
4. After grouping, try accenting the last or the first number in each group to sound out the pattern.

Test this technique by reading the following series aloud: 2 4 6 8 10 12 14. You should hear that the next two numbers are 16 and 18.

Now try a more complicated series: 31 32 33 33 34 35 35. Break this series into groups of three: 31 32 33; 33 34 35; 35. This should help you realize that the series consists of groups of three numbers in plus 1 ascending order. Each group begins by repeating the last number in the previous group. Therefore, the next two numbers of the series are 36 and 37.

Test Yourself

> **DIRECTIONS:** You may be able to answer the next five Number Series questions by simple inspection. If you can't, sound them out. Circle the letter of the correct answer.

1. 1 2 5 6 9 10 13...   (A) 15 17   (B) 14 15   (C) 14 16   (D) 15 16   (E) 14 17
2. 2 3 4 4 5 6 6...   (A) 4 5   (B) 5 6   (C) 7 8   (D) 6 8   (E) 9 10
3. 10 10 11 11 12 12 13... (A) 13 14   (B) 14 15   (C) 13 15   (D) 14 16   (E) 12 13
4. 1 2 3 2 2 3 3 2 3...   (A) 2 3   (B) 3 2   (C) 3 4   (D) 4 2   (E) 4 3
5. 10 9 8 8 7 6 6...   (A) 7 6   (B) 5 4   (C) 4 5   (D) 7 8   (E) 8 9

Answers and Explanations

1. **(E)** Read aloud (softly):

   The next number to read aloud is 14, to be followed by a whispered 15, 16, and then aloud again 17.

2. **(C)** If you arrange the numbers in groups of three and read them aloud, accenting the last number of each group, you should see that each group begins by repeating the last number of the previous group.

3. **(A)** If you arrange the numbers in groups of two and accent the second number of each group, you'll see that each number is repeated and then increased by 1. The smaller group size makes this question slightly more confusing than question 2.

4. **(D)** In this series, the rhythm (a waltz tempo) emerges when you accent the first number in each group of three: **1** 2 3; **2** 2 3; **3** 2 3. The numbers 2 and 3 are repeated in this simple plus-1 series.

5. **(B)** By arranging the numbers in groups of three and accenting the first number of each group, you should see that the first number of each descending group begins by repeating the last number of the preceding group.

Mark the Difference

If you can't see or hear the pattern, you can usually find the pattern by marking the difference between each number in your test booklet. As you read from left to right, indicate the degree and direction of change between each number as follows:

For the number series: 10 14 19 25 32

You would write: $10 \;^{+4} 14 \;^{+5} 19 \;^{+6} 25 \;^{+7} 32$

Most series are either ascending (plus) or descending (minus), or a combination of both. First try marking the number series in terms of addition (+) or subtraction (–). If you can't find the pattern, try multiplication (×) and division (÷).

Caution
When using this strategy, don't get so caught up in writing in your test booklet that you forget to mark your answer sheet. Only the answer sheet will be scored, not the exam booklet. Also, never waste exam time erasing what you've written in your exam booklet once you've determined the correct answer.

Test Yourself

> **DIRECTIONS:** In this set of practice questions, mark the differences between the numbers to establish the pattern if you can't see the pattern. Continue the pattern to determine the next two numbers of the series, and circle the correct answer.

1. 9 10 12 15 19 24 30…   (A) 35 40   (B) 36 42   (C) 30 36   (D) 30 37   (E) 37 45
2. 35 34 31 30 27 26 23…   (A) 22 19   (B) 22 20   (C) 23 22   (D) 20 19   (E) 20 17
3. 16 21 19 24 22 27 25…   (A) 28 30   (B) 30 28   (C) 29 24   (D) 30 27   (E) 26 29
4. 48 44 40 36 32 28 24…   (A) 22 20   (B) 24 22   (C) 23 22   (D) 20 18   (E) 20 16
5. 20 30 39 47 54 60 65…   (A) 70 75   (B) 68 70   (C) 69 72   (D) 66 67   (E) 68 71

Answers and Explanations

1. **(E)** $9 \;^{+1}\; 10 \;^{+2}\; 12 \;^{+3}\; 15 \;^{+4}\; 19 \;^{+5}\; 24 \;^{+6}\; 30 \;^{+7}\; 37 \;^{+8}\; 45$
2. **(A)** $35 \;^{-1}\; 34 \;^{-3}\; 31 \;^{-1}\; 30 \;^{-3}\; 27 \;^{-1}\; 26 \;^{-3}\; 23 \;^{-1}\; 22 \;^{-3}\; 19$
3. **(B)** $16 \;^{+5}\; 21 \;^{-2}\; 19 \;^{+5}\; 24 \;^{-2}\; 22 \;^{+5}\; 27 \;^{-2}\; 25 \;^{+5}\; 30 \;^{-2}\; 28$
4. **(E)** $48 \;^{-4}\; 44 \;^{-4}\; 40 \;^{-4}\; 36 \;^{-4}\; 32 \;^{-4}\; 28 \;^{-4}\; 24 \;^{-4}\; 20 \;^{-4}\; 16$
5. **(C)** $20 \;^{+10}\; 30 \;^{+9}\; 39 \;^{+8}\; 47 \;^{+7}\; 54 \;^{+6}\; 60 \;^{+5}\; 65 \;^{+4}\; 69 \;^{+3}\; 72$

Number Series Practice Exercise

You should be able to answer the following Number Series questions based on what you've learned so far. Take this practice exercise at your own pace and try using all the techniques you learned in this hour. When you're finished, check your answers against the answer key immediately following the practice exercise.

DIRECTIONS: Each question contains a series of numbers that follows a definite pattern. Determine what the pattern is and then decide what the next two numbers in the series would be if the order were continued. Circle the letter of the correct answer.

1. 8 9 10 8 9 10 8...   (A) 8 9   (B) 9 10   (C) 9 8   (D) 10 8   (E) 8 10
2. 16 16 15 15 14 14 13...   (A) 12 13   (B) 14 13   (C) 12 11   (D) 12 10   (E) 13 12
3. 2 6 10 2 14 18 2...   (A) 2 22   (B) 2 26   (C) 22 26   (D) 22 2   (E) 26 2
4. 30 28 27 25 24 22 21...   (A) 21 20   (B) 19 18   (C) 20 19   (D) 20 18   (E) 21 21
5. 25 25 22 22 19 19 16...   (A) 18 18   (B) 16 16   (C) 16 13   (D) 15 15   (E) 15 13
6. 9 17 24 30 35 39 42...   (A) 43 44   (B) 44 46   (C) 44 45   (D) 45 49   (E) 46 50
7. 28 31 34 37 40 43 46...   (A) 49 52   (B) 47 49   (C) 50 54   (D) 49 53   (E) 51 55
8. 17 17 24 24 31 31 38...   (A) 38 39   (B) 38 17   (C) 38 45   (D) 38 44   (E) 39 50
9. 87 83 79 75 71 67 63...   (A) 62 61   (B) 63 59   (C) 60 56   (D) 59 55   (E) 59 54
10. 8 9 11 14 18 23 29...   (A) 35 45   (B) 32 33   (C) 38 48   (D) 34 40   (E) 36 44
11. 4 8 12 16 20 24...   (A) 26 28   (B) 28 30   (C) 30 28   (D) 28 32   (E) 28 29
12. 3 4 1 3 4 1 3...   (A) 4 1   (B) 4 5   (C) 4 3   (D) 1 2   (E) 4 4

Answers and Explanations

1.   **(B)** The series is simply a repetition of the sequence 8 9 10.

2.   **(E)** Each number is repeated and then decreased by 1.

3.   **(C)** The pattern is to add 4 and then repeat the number 2.

4.   **(B)** This pattern is not so easy to spot. If you mark the difference between each number, you can see that this is an alternating descending series with the following pattern: subtract 2, subtract 1; subtract 2, subtract 1; and so on.

5.   **(C)** The pattern is to repeat, subtract 3; repeat, subtract 3; repeat, subtract 3; and so on.

6.   **(C)** The rule of this series is add 8, add 7, add 6, add 5, add 4, add 3, add 2, and so on.

7.   **(A)** This is a simple add 3 series.

8.   **(C)** Each number is repeated and then increased by 7.

9.   **(D)** This is a simple add 4 series.

10. **(E)** The rule of this series is add 1, add 2, add 3, add 4, add 5, add 6, add 7, add 8, and so on.

11. **(D)** This is a simple add 4 series.

12. **(A)** This series is simply a repetition of the sequence 3 4 1.

The Hour In Review

1.   In the Number Series portion of Test 470, you should write directly in your test booklet, keep careful track of time, and guess when you aren't sure about a question.

2.   The Number Series questions can be classified as a series with one pattern or a series with two or more patterns.

3.   When solving a Number Series question, first look for obvious patterns. You should be able to answer many questions at a glance.

4.   If you can't spot an obvious pattern, sound out the series to try to "hear" the pattern.

5.   When you can't see or hear the pattern, mark the differences between numbers in the series.

HOUR **10**

Number Series—2

What You Will Learn in This Hour

In this hour, you'll learn additional techniques for solving the Number Series questions as well as review the strategies that you learned in Hour 9, "Number Series—1." You'll also take a full-length practice exercise to test your understanding of the material. Here are your goals for this hour:

- Learn how to find repeating and random numbers in a number series.
- Use diagramming techniques to figure out alternating patterns.
- Look for unusual patterns when you can't figure out any other pattern.
- Understand the complete strategy for tackling the Number Series questions.

Mini Warm-Up Quiz

Take the following untimed quiz to review what you learned in Hour 9 as well as preview some goals of this hour's lesson.

DIRECTIONS: Each question contains a series of numbers that follows some definite pattern. Determine the pattern they follow and then decide what the next two numbers in the series would be. Circle the letter of the correct answer.

1. 23 23 25 23 28 23 32…   (A) 32 37   (B) 23 37   (C) 32 23   (D) 37 23   (E) 23 36
2. 40 35 31 30 25 21 20 15…(A) 10 6   (B) 14 9   (C) 14 10   (D) 11 7   (E) 11 10
3. 98 24 92 28 86 32 80…   (A) 74 36   (B) 26 84   (C) 38 84   (D) 36 75   (E) 36 74
4. 17 17 28 28 40 40 53…   (A) 53 66   (B) 53 53   (C) 66 66   (D) 53 67   (E) 67 67
5. 19 15 10 19 15 10 19…   (A) 15 10   (B) 10 15   (C) 19 15   (D) 19 10   (E) 15 19
6. 21 24 29 32 37 40 45…   (A) 50 55   (B) 48 51   (C) 50 53   (D) 48 53   (E) 48 55
7. 51 51 30 47 47 30 43…   (A) 43 43   (B) 30 30   (C) 43 30   (D) 30 39   (E) 43 39
8. 8 16 9 18 11 22 15…   (A)30 23   (B) 12 25   (C) 25 13   (D) 12 44   (E) 30 20
9. 32 25 86 32 25 86 32…   (A) 32 25   (B) 32 86   (C) 86 25   (D) 26 87   (E) 25 86
10. 75 65 56 48 41 35 30…   (A) 27 23   (B) 26 23   (C) 29 28   (D) 25 20   (E) 26 22

Answers and Explanations

1. (B) The pattern of this series is plus 2, plus 3, plus 4, plus 5, and so on with the number 23 repeating after each step. Don't be confused by what appears to be an initial repetition of the number 23. It's coincidental that the series begins with the same number that is used repetitively throughout the series.

2. (E) The pattern of this series is subtract 5, subtract 4, subtract 1; subtract 5, subtract 4, subtract 1; subtract 5, subtract 4, subtract 1; and so on. Therefore, the next two numbers are 15 − 4 = 11 and 11 − 1 = 10.

3. (E) Two alternating patterns are in this number series. The first is a minus 6 series: 98, 92, 86, 80, 74, and so on. The second is a plus 4 series: 24, 28, 32, 36, and so on.

4. (D) The rule of this series is to repeat the number, add 11, repeat the number, add 12, repeat the number, add 13, repeat the number, add 14, and so on.

5. (A) The sequence 19 15 10 is repeated to make up the series.

6. (D) When you mark the differences between the numbers of the series, the pattern that emerges is plus 3, plus 5; plus 3, plus 5; plus 3, plus 5; and so on. The next two numbers in the series are 45 + 3 = 48 and 48 + 5 = 53.

7. (C) If you look carefully, you'll see that the number 30 is repeated after every two numbers. Ignoring 30 for a moment, the pattern for the remaining numbers is to repeat the number, subtract 4; repeat the number, subtract 4; repeat the number, subtract 4; and so on. To continue the series, you must repeat the number 43; then, because the number 30 appears after each set of two numbers, you must insert the number 30. If the series were to continue, the next few numbers would be 39, 39, 30, and 35.

8. (A) At first glance, this problem seems unsolvable. You may need to try more than one approach before figuring out the pattern. This is one of the few number series that uses multiplication. Here it is used in an alternating series. The pattern is to multiply 2, subtract 7; multiply 2, subtract 7; multiply 2, subtract 7; and so on. The next two numbers in the series are 15 × 2 = 30 and 30 − 7 = 23.

9. (E) In this series, the sequence 32 25 86 is repeated.

10. (B) The pattern is subtract 10, subtract 9, subtract 8, subtract 7, subtract 6, subtract 5, and so on. The next two numbers in the series are 30 − 4 = 26 and 26 − 3 = 23.

10

> **Tip**
> There's not one way to work out a Number Series problem. Don't become discouraged if you can't see a pattern initially; you can always try a different approach.

Finding Repeating and Random Numbers

Repeating and random number patterns may not always be obvious. Marking up the question in your test booklet will help figure out the pattern. To indicate a repeated number, write an 'r' between the numbers; to indicate a random number, circle it. You'll often use this technique in conjunction with the technique of marking differences between numbers.

Caution
When deciding on the answer, avoid common pitfalls. Always remember the point in the pattern where the repeating or random number should be inserted. Also don't repeat a number in the wrong spot or repeat it too many times.

Test Yourself

DIRECTIONS: Solve the following Number Series questions. Indicate repeated numbers by writing "r" and circle random numbers.

1. 10 13 13 16 16 19 19…   (A) 19 19   (B) 19 22   (C) 22 22   (D) 22 25   (E) 22 24
2. 2 4 25 8 16 25 32…   (A) 32 35   (B) 25 64   (C) 48 25   (D) 25 48   (E) 64 25
3. 80 80 75 75 70 70 65…   (A) 65 60   (B) 65 65   (C) 60 60   (D) 60 55   (E) 55 55
4. 35 35 32 30 30 27 25…   (A) 22 20   (B) 25 25   (C) 22 22   (D) 25 22   (E) 25 23
5. 76 70 12 65 61 12 58…   (A) 55 12   (B) 56 12   (C) 12 54   (D) 12 55   (E) 54 51

Answers and Explanations

r = repetition; circle should indicate a random number repeated periodically

1. (C) $10 ^{+3} 13 ^{r} 13 ^{+3} 16 ^{r} 16 ^{+3} 19 ^{r} 19 ^{+3} 22 ^{r} 22$
2. (E) $2 ^{×2} 4 ^{×2}$ ⟨25⟩ $8 ^{×2} 16 ^{×2}$⟨25⟩$32 ^{×2} 64 ^{×2}$⟨25⟩… $128 ^{×2}$
3. (A) $80 ^{r} 80 ^{-5} 75 ^{r} 75 ^{-5} 70 ^{r} 70 ^{-5} 65 ^{r} 65 ^{-5} 60$
4. (D) $35 ^{r} 35 ^{-3} 32 ^{-2} 30 ^{r} 30 ^{-3} 27 ^{-2} 25 ^{r} 25 ^{-3} 22$
5. (B) $76 ^{-6} 70 ^{-5}$⟨12⟩$65^{-4} 61 ^{-3}$⟨12⟩$58 ^{-2} 56 ^{-1}$⟨12⟩… 55

Finding Alternating Series and Unusual Progressions

You need to be flexible when solving Number Series questions and look at the numbers from different perspectives. This will help you solve more difficult questions, such as those with alternating series or with unusual number patterns.

Solving Alternating Series

If you can't determine the pattern of a number series by inspection, vocalizing, marking differences, and noting repetitive patterns, the next step is to look for two or more alternating series. Usually, the two series have totally distinct patterns. By marking differences between numbers, you should be able to figure out the pattern, as shown in the following example:

$$
\begin{array}{c}
\overset{-6}{}\quad\overset{-5}{}\quad\overset{-4}{}\quad\overset{-3}{} \\
38\quad 15\quad 32\quad 17\quad 27\quad 19\quad 23\quad 21\quad 20 \\
\underset{+2}{}\quad\underset{+2}{}\quad\underset{+2}{}
\end{array}
$$

Solving Unusual Progressions

Sometimes you just have to look at the number series from a different angle to figure it out. Are numbers within a series formed by combining the numbers that precede them? Is there an unusual arrangement that does not involve arithmetic?

Look at the following number series:

   1 1 2 3 5 8 13

In this series, each number is the sum of the two previous numbers: $1 + 1 = 2$; $1 + 2 = 3$; $2 + 3 = 5$; $5 + 8 = 13$; and so on. Therefore, the next two numbers in the series are $8 + 13 = 21$ and $13 + 21 = 34$.

Try another example:

   1 2 2 3 3 3 4

In this series, each number appears as often as its name implies: one 1, two 2s, three 3s, and so forth. Therefore, the next two numbers are 4 and 4.

Here's another unusual number series:

   2 0 0 2 1 2 2 2 4

This series is made up of nine numbers to make the progression clearer: $2 \times 0 = 0$; $2 \times 1 = 2$; $2 \times 2 = 4$; and so on. The series would continue like this: 2 3 6 ($2 \times 3 = 6$) 2 4 8 ($2 \times 4 = 8$).

Note
The Number Series questions test your aptitude for working with sorting, routing, and marking machines. You have to be able to think on your feet to get hired. With practice, you should be prepared for most types of Number Series questions, but don't be thrown by the unexpected.

Test Yourself

DIRECTIONS: Answer the following Number Series questions. Use diagramming when appropriate. Circle the letter of the correct answer.

1. 3 2 5 2 7 2 9...   (A) 11 13   (B) 9 2   (C) 2 11   (D) 11 2   (E) 2 13

2. 90 83 92 86 94 89 96...(A) 92 98   (B) 98 100 (C) 90 90   (D) 98 92 (E) 98 99

3. 80 12 40 17 20 22 10...(A) 25 15   (B) 15 25   (C) 24 5   (D) 25 5   (E) 27 5

4. 5 6 20 21 34 35 47...   (A) 48 49   (B) 48 59   (C) 48 36   (D) 36 48 (E) 48 55

5. 91 19 92 29 93 39 94...(A) 49 95   (B) 49 50   (C) 94 95   (D) 95 49 (E) 95 96

6. 5 3 10 33 15 333 20... (A) 33 25   (B) 25 333 (C) 25 30   (D) 25 3   (E)3333 25

Answers and Explanations

1. **(C)** $3 + 2 = 5 + 2 = 7 + 2 = 9 + 2 = 11$

    or

    $3 \overset{+2}{} \;②\; 5 \overset{+2}{} \;②\; 7 \overset{+2}{} \;②\; 9 \overset{+2}{} \;②\; 11$

2. **(A)**
$$
\begin{array}{ccccccccc}
& \overbrace{}^{+2} & & \overbrace{}^{+2} & & \overbrace{}^{+2} & & \overbrace{}^{+2} & \\
90 & 83 & 92 & 86 & 94 & 89 & 96 & 92 & 98 \\
& & \underbrace{}_{+3} & & \underbrace{}_{+3} & & \underbrace{}_{+3} & &
\end{array}
$$

3. **(E)**
$$
\begin{array}{ccccccccc}
& \overbrace{}^{\div 2} & & \overbrace{}^{\div 2} & & \overbrace{}^{\div 2} & & \overbrace{}^{\div 2} & \\
80 & 12 & 40 & 17 & 20 & 22 & 10 & 27 & 5 \\
& & \underbrace{}_{+5} & & \underbrace{}_{+5} & & \underbrace{}_{+5} & &
\end{array}
$$

4. **(B)**
$$
\begin{array}{ccccccccc}
& \overbrace{}^{+15} & & \overbrace{}^{+14} & & \overbrace{}^{+13} & & \overbrace{}^{+12} & \\
5 & 6 & 20 & 21 & 34 & 35 & 47 & 48 & 59 \\
& & \underbrace{}_{+15} & & \underbrace{}_{+14} & & \underbrace{}_{+13} & &
\end{array}
$$

5. **(A)** This is a simple plus 1 series with a repetitive twist. Each number in the series is repeated in reverse before addition. Can you see it?

6. **(E)** This series contains another unusual pattern, a variation of the one in question 5. In this pattern, a random number is repeated before the plus 5 addition: first one 3, then two 3s, then three 3s, and so on. The next number must be four 3s. The answer is **(E)** 3333 25.

Analyzing Number Series Questions

You now know a variety of techniques to apply to the Number Series questions on the actual test. With practice, you'll be able to remember all of them or perhaps adapt some of them to suit you better. Use the following plan as a checklist when solving the Number Series questions that you'll find throughout the rest of this book:

1. Look for an obvious pattern and repetitive numbers. Can you solve the question at a glance?

2. Sound out the series; if necessary, group the numbers and sound them out again.

3. Mark the differences between numbers.

4. If you still haven't found the pattern, mark repeated and random numbers.

5. Look for two alternating series and for uncommon or unusual types of progressions.

Number Series Practice Exercise

The following practice exercise tests all the techniques that you've learned from this hour and the previous one. This isn't a strictly timed test, but you should allow yourself no more than 20 minutes. You may find it helpful to write the technique that you used next to the question, so you can pinpoint weaknesses when checking your answers. The answer key and explanations immediately follow the practice exercise.

DIRECTIONS: For each question, there is a series of numbers at the left that follows a definite pattern and five sets of two numbers each at the right. Look at the numbers in the left-hand series and determine the pattern they follow. Then decide what the next two numbers in the series would be if the same order were continued. Circle the letter of the correct answer.

---

1. 12 26 15 26 18 26 21...   (A) 21 24   (B) 24 26   (C) 21 26   (D) 26 24   (E) 26 25
2. 72 67 69 64 66 61 63...   (A) 58 60   (B) 65 62   (C) 60 58   (D) 65 60   (E) 60 65
3. 81 10 29 81 10 29 81...   (A) 29 10   (B) 81 29   (C) 10 29   (D) 81 10   (E) 29 81
4. 91 91 90 88 85 81 76...   (A) 71 66   (B) 70 64   (C) 75 74   (D) 70 65   (E) 70 63
5. 22 44 29 37 36 30 43...   (A) 50 23   (B) 23 50   (C) 53 40   (D) 40 53   (E) 50 57
6. 0 1 1 0 2 2 0...   (A) 0 0   (B) 0 3   (C) 3 3   (D) 3 4   (E) 2 3
7. 32 34 36 34 36 38 36...   (A) 34 32   (B) 36 34   (C) 36 38   (D) 38 40   (E) 38 36
8. 26 36 36 46 46 56 56...   (A) 66 66   (B) 56 66   (C) 57 57   (D) 46 56   (E) 26 66
9. 64 63 61 58 57 55 52...   (A) 51 50   (B) 52 49   (C) 50 58   (D) 50 47   (E) 51 49
10. 4 6 8 7 6 8 10 9 8...   (A) 7 9   (B) 11 12   (C) 12 14   (D) 7 10   (E) 10 12
11. 57 57 52 47 47 42 37... (A) 32 32   (B) 37 32   (C) 37 37   (D) 32 27   (E) 27 27
12. 13 26 14 25 16 23 19... (A) 20 21   (B) 20 22   (C) 20 23   (D) 20 24   (E) 22 25
13. 15 27 39 51 63 75 87... (A) 97 112 (B) 99 111 (C) 88 99   (D) 89 99   (E) 90 99
14. 2 0 2 2 2 4 2 6 2 8...   (A) 2 2   (B) 2 8   (C) 2 10   (D) 2 12   (E) 2 16
15. 19 18 18 17 17 17 16... (A) 16 16   (B) 16 15   (C) 15 15   (D) 15 14   (E) 16 17
16. 55 53 44 51 49 44 47... (A) 45 43   (B) 46 45   (C) 46 44   (D) 44 44   (E) 45 44
17. 100 81 64 49 36 25 16... (A) 8 4   (B) 8 2   (C) 9 5   (D) 9 4   (E) 9 3
18. 2 2 4 6 8 18 16...   (A) 32 64   (B) 32 28   (C) 54 32   (D) 32 54   (E) 54 30
19. 47 43 52 48 57 53 62... (A) 58 54   (B) 67 58   (C) 71 67   (D) 58 67   (E) 49 58
20. 38 38 53 48 48 63 58... (A) 58 58   (B) 58 73   (C) 73 73   (D) 58 68   (E) 73 83
21. 12 14 16 13 15 17 14... (A) 17 15   (B) 15 18   (C) 17 19   (D) 15 16   (E) 16 18
22. 30 30 30 37 37 37 30... (A) 30 30   (B) 30 37   (C) 37 37   (D) 37 30   (E) 31 31
23. 75 52 69 56 63 59 57... (A) 58 62   (B) 55 65   (C) 51 61   (D) 61 51   (E) 63 55
24. 176 88 88 44 44 22 22... (A) 22 11   (B) 11 11   (C) 11 10   (D) 11 5   (E) 22 10

Answers and Explanations

1.   **(D)**   12 $^{+3}$(26)15 $^{+3}$(26)18 $^{+3}$(26)21 $^{+3}$(26)24

2.   **(A)**   You can read this as a minus 5, plus 2 series:

72 $^{-5}$ 67 $^{+2}$ 69 $^{-5}$ 64 $^{+2}$ 66 $^{-5}$ 61 $^{+2}$ 63 $^{-5}$ 58 $^{+2}$ 60

Or you can read it as two alternating minus 3 series:

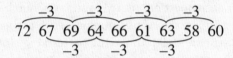

3.   **(C)**   You should see by inspection that the sequence 81 10 29 is repeated.

4.   **(E)**   91 $^{-0}$ 91 $^{-1}$ 90 $^{-2}$ 88 $^{-3}$ 85 $^{-4}$ 81 $^{-5}$ 76 $^{-6}$ 70 $^{-7}$ 63

5.   **(B)**
$$\begin{array}{ccccccccc} & \overbrace{}^{+7} & & \overbrace{}^{+7} & & \overbrace{}^{+7} & & \overbrace{}^{+7} & \\ 22 & 44 & 29 & 37 & 36 & 30 & 43 & 23 & 50 \\ & & \underbrace{}_{-7} & & \underbrace{}_{-7} & & \underbrace{}_{-7} & & \end{array}$$

6.   **(C)**   The number 0 is inserted after each repeating number of a simple plus-1 and repeat series:

(0)1 ^{r} 1 $^{+}$(0)2 ^{r} 2 $^{+}$(0)3 ^{r} 3

7.   **(D)**   Arrange the numbers in groups of three. Each succeeding group of three begins with a number that is two more than the first number of the preceding group. Within each group the pattern is plus 2, plus 2.

8.   **(A)**   26 $^{+10}$ 36 ^{r} 36 $^{+10}$ 46 ^{r} 46 $^{+10}$ 56 ^{r} 56 $^{+10}$ 66 ^{r} 66

9.   **(E)**   The pattern is to subtract 1, subtract 2, subtract 3; subtract 1, subtract 2, subtract 3; and so on.

10.   **(E)**   The given series is longer than most to help you establish the extra long pattern: plus 2, plus 2, subtract 1, subtract 1; plus 2, plus 2, subtract 1, subtract 1; and so on.

11.   **(B)**   57 ^{r} 57 $^{-5}$ 52 $^{-5}$ 47 ^{r} 47 $^{-5}$ 42 $^{-5}$ 37 ^{r} 37 $^{-5}$ 32

12.   **(C)**
$$\begin{array}{ccccccccc} & \overbrace{}^{+1} & & \overbrace{}^{+2} & & \overbrace{}^{+3} & & \overbrace{}^{+4} & \\ 13 & 26 & 14 & 25 & 16 & 23 & 19 & 20 & 23 \\ & & \underbrace{}_{-1} & & \underbrace{}_{-2} & & \underbrace{}_{-3} & & \end{array}$$

13.   **(B)**   This is a simple plus-12 series.

14.   **(C)**   The digit 2 intervenes before each number of a simple +2 series.

$$②\,0\,{}^{+2}②\,2\,{}^{+2}②\,4\,{}^{+2}②\,6\,{}^{+2}②\,8\,{}^{+2}②\,10$$

15.   **(A)**   Each number is repeated once more than the number before it. Nineteen appears only once, 18 twice, 17 three times and, if the series were extended, 16 would appear four times.

16.   **(E)**   This is a minus 2 series with the number 44 appearing after every two numbers.

17.   **(D)**   The series consists of the squares of numbers 10 to 2 in descending order.

18.   **(C)**

$$\overbrace{}^{}\;\overbrace{2\;4}^{\times2}\;\overbrace{6\;8}^{\times2}\;\overbrace{18\;16}^{\times2}\;\overbrace{54\;32}^{\times2}$$

$$2\;\underbrace{2\;4}_{\times3}\;\underbrace{6\;8}_{\times3}\;\underbrace{18\;16}_{\times3}\;54\;32$$

19.   **(D)**   The rule of this series is to subtract 4, add 9; subtract 4, add 9; and so on.

20.   **(B)** $38\,{}^{r}38\,{}^{+15}53\,{}^{-5}48\,{}^{r}48\,{}^{+15}63\,{}^{-5}58\,{}^{r}58\,{}^{+15}73$

You can also see this series as two alternating plus 10 patterns with the numbers ending in 8 repeated.

21.   **(E)**   Arrange the numbers into groups of three. Each plus 2 group begins one step up from the previous group.

22.   **(A)**   This series is nothing more than the number 30 repeated three times and the number 37 repeated three times. Because you have no further clues, you must assume that the series continues with the number 30 repeated three times.

23.   **(D)**

$$75\;\overbrace{52\;69}^{-6}\;\overbrace{56\;63}^{-6}\;\overbrace{59\;57}^{-6}\;\overbrace{61\;51}^{-6}$$

$$75\;52\;\underbrace{69\;56}_{+4}\;63\;\underbrace{59}_{+3}\;57\;\underbrace{61}_{+2}\;51$$

24.   **(B)**   The pattern is divide by 2 and repeat the number.

$$176\,{}^{\div2}88\,{}^{r}88\,{}^{\div2}44\,{}^{r}44\,{}^{\div2}22\,{}^{r}22\,{}^{\div2}11\,{}^{r}11$$

Evaluate Your Mistakes

First, check which techniques you used on the questions that you answered incorrectly. Then ask yourself the following questions to determine which techniques you need to practice more often:

- Did you miss any series with just one pattern? If so, do you know why?
- Did you have problems with alternating series?
- Did you diagram the question? Could you have diagrammed the question better?
- Which techniques worked best for you?

Review those techniques that you think need improvement.

The Hour in Review

1. When answering the Number Series questions, mark repeated and random numbers.

2. Use diagrams to make sense of alternating series patterns.

3. If the number series doesn't seem to fit into any category, look at it from an entirely new angle. Unusual patterns are sometimes included on the test.

4. Perform the same step-by-step analysis on all the Number Series questions.

Hour **11**

Following Oral Instructions—1

What You Will Learn in This Hour

This hour introduces you to the format of Part D of Test 470, "Following Oral Instructions." Because the unique format of this portion of the exam presents additional study challenges, the review strategy is different than that in previous hours. Here are your goals for this hour:

- Understand how the "Following Oral Instructions" portion of the test is structured.
- Discover how to complete the practice exercises.
- Complete an oral instructions practice exercise.

Understanding the Oral Instructions Questions

To perform well on the test and in order to simulate the test experience in this book, you must be familiar with the three components of the Oral Instructions questions:

- The worksheet, which has numbered lines with shapes and blanks to fill in
- The standard answer sheet
- The oral instructions, which specify what to mark on the worksheet and how to darken the answer sheet

Sample Exercise

The following is a sample worksheet and answer sheet:

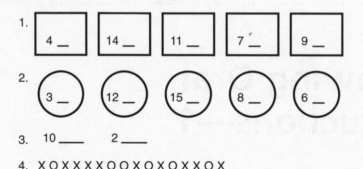

For the sample worksheet, you may be read the following oral instructions:

Look at line 1 on the worksheet. (Pause slightly.) Write a D as in dog in the fourth box. (Pause two seconds.) Now, on your answer sheet, find the number in that box and darken space D as in dog for that number. (Pause five seconds.)

Look at line 2. The number in each circle is the number of employees in a post office. In the circle holding the largest number of employees, write a B as in baker. (Pause two seconds.) Now, on your answer sheet, darken the space for the number-letter combination that is in the circle you just wrote in. (Pause five seconds.)

Look at line 3 on the worksheet. (Pause slightly.) Write the letter C on the blank next to the right-hand number. (Pause two seconds.) Now, on your answer sheet, find the number beside which you just wrote and darken space C. (Pause five seconds.)

Look at line 3 again. (Pause slightly.) Write the letter B as in baker on the blank next to the left-hand number. (Pause two seconds.) Now, on your answer sheet, find the number beside which you just wrote and darken space B as in baker. (Pause five seconds.)

Look at line 4 on your worksheet. (Pause slightly.) Draw a line under every "X" in the line. (Pause five seconds.) Count the number of lines that you have drawn, divide by 2, and write that number at the end of the line. (Pause five seconds.) Now, on your answer sheet, find that number and darken space C. (Pause five seconds.)

Answers

The correctly filled-in worksheet looks like this:

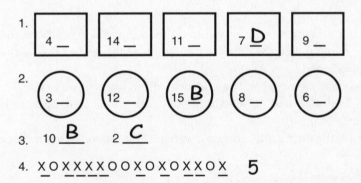

As you can see, completing the worksheet is an integral part of this section of the test and must be filled in to answer the questions correctly. The more practice you have listening to instructions and marking up worksheets and answer sheets, the better you'll perform on the actual test.

Completing the Practice Exercises

At the test, the instructions will either be read by the examiner or be given on tape. Because you have to listen and concentrate, you must be able to hear clearly. In the testing room, there will be a short practice session before the actual testing on each part of the exam. This practice session will allow you to get used to the reader's voice (live or recorded), talking speed, diction, and accent.

> **Tip**
> If the reader's voice or the tape is too low for you to hear the instructions clearly or if there are any other problems, speak up before the actual testing begins. You're entitled to optimum testing conditions.

So how can you simulate testing conditions when you practice? The best solution is to have another person read the material to you as you complete the practice exercises. If not, you should record the instructions or have another person record them for you before you take the exercises. Whichever method you choose, follow these guidelines:

Do

DO read the oral instructions at a normal conversational speed (approximately 80 words per minute). Use the practice paragraph at the end of this section to adjust your reading speed.

DO read as clearly as possible. The oral instructions will tell you to say "B as in baker" when B is indicated and "D as in dog" when D is indicated, because both letters sound alike.

DO pause for the time indicated. Use a watch with a second hand to check your time.

Don't

DON'T repeat any instructions. You can read the instructions only once.

DON'T read the material in parentheses aloud. These are your cues for pausing while reading.

> **Tip**
> If you tape the instructions, try to record as much of the instructions in advance
> as you can. At this time, you should concentrate on taping the instructions in
> this hour and the next. Set aside time later to tape the remaining oral instruc-
> tions in Hours 22 through 24 and the Bonus Hour. When taping, identify each
> set of oral instructions by page number before you begin reading the instruc-
> tions to avoid confusion.

The following paragraph should take exactly one minute to read.

> Look at line 20 on your worksheet. (Pause slightly.) There are two circles and two boxes
> of different sizes with numbers in them. If 7 is less than 3 and if 2 is smaller than 4, write
> a C in the larger circle. Otherwise, write B as in baker in the smaller box. (Pause 10
> seconds.) Now on your answer sheet, darken the space for the number-letter combination
> in the box or circle. (Pause five seconds.)

11

Oral Instructions Practice Exercise

This full-length exercise will familiarize you with the Oral Instructions test's style of questions. You'll need approximately 25 minutes to complete this exercise if you read and/or tape the instructions as directed in the previous section. But don't worry about time at this point; instead, concentrate on listening to and acting on the instructions.

Answer Sheet

1. Ⓐ Ⓑ Ⓒ Ⓓ Ⓔ	23. Ⓐ Ⓑ Ⓒ Ⓓ Ⓔ	45. Ⓐ Ⓑ Ⓒ Ⓓ Ⓔ	67. Ⓐ Ⓑ Ⓒ Ⓓ Ⓔ
2. Ⓐ Ⓑ Ⓒ Ⓓ Ⓔ	24. Ⓐ Ⓑ Ⓒ Ⓓ Ⓔ	46. Ⓐ Ⓑ Ⓒ Ⓓ Ⓔ	68. Ⓐ Ⓑ Ⓒ Ⓓ Ⓔ
3. Ⓐ Ⓑ Ⓒ Ⓓ Ⓔ	25. Ⓐ Ⓑ Ⓒ Ⓓ Ⓔ	47. Ⓐ Ⓑ Ⓒ Ⓓ Ⓔ	69. Ⓐ Ⓑ Ⓒ Ⓓ Ⓔ
4. Ⓐ Ⓑ Ⓒ Ⓓ Ⓔ	26. Ⓐ Ⓑ Ⓒ Ⓓ Ⓔ	48. Ⓐ Ⓑ Ⓒ Ⓓ Ⓔ	70. Ⓐ Ⓑ Ⓒ Ⓓ Ⓔ
5. Ⓐ Ⓑ Ⓒ Ⓓ Ⓔ	27. Ⓐ Ⓑ Ⓒ Ⓓ Ⓔ	49. Ⓐ Ⓑ Ⓒ Ⓓ Ⓔ	71. Ⓐ Ⓑ Ⓒ Ⓓ Ⓔ
6. Ⓐ Ⓑ Ⓒ Ⓓ Ⓔ	28. Ⓐ Ⓑ Ⓒ Ⓓ Ⓔ	50. Ⓐ Ⓑ Ⓒ Ⓓ Ⓔ	72. Ⓐ Ⓑ Ⓒ Ⓓ Ⓔ
7. Ⓐ Ⓑ Ⓒ Ⓓ Ⓔ	29. Ⓐ Ⓑ Ⓒ Ⓓ Ⓔ	51. Ⓐ Ⓑ Ⓒ Ⓓ Ⓔ	73. Ⓐ Ⓑ Ⓒ Ⓓ Ⓔ
8. Ⓐ Ⓑ Ⓒ Ⓓ Ⓔ	30. Ⓐ Ⓑ Ⓒ Ⓓ Ⓔ	52. Ⓐ Ⓑ Ⓒ Ⓓ Ⓔ	74. Ⓐ Ⓑ Ⓒ Ⓓ Ⓔ
9. Ⓐ Ⓑ Ⓒ Ⓓ Ⓔ	31. Ⓐ Ⓑ Ⓒ Ⓓ Ⓔ	53. Ⓐ Ⓑ Ⓒ Ⓓ Ⓔ	75. Ⓐ Ⓑ Ⓒ Ⓓ Ⓔ
10. Ⓐ Ⓑ Ⓒ Ⓓ Ⓔ	32. Ⓐ Ⓑ Ⓒ Ⓓ Ⓔ	54. Ⓐ Ⓑ Ⓒ Ⓓ Ⓔ	76. Ⓐ Ⓑ Ⓒ Ⓓ Ⓔ
11. Ⓐ Ⓑ Ⓒ Ⓓ Ⓔ	33. Ⓐ Ⓑ Ⓒ Ⓓ Ⓔ	55. Ⓐ Ⓑ Ⓒ Ⓓ Ⓔ	77. Ⓐ Ⓑ Ⓒ Ⓓ Ⓔ
12. Ⓐ Ⓑ Ⓒ Ⓓ Ⓔ	34. Ⓐ Ⓑ Ⓒ Ⓓ Ⓔ	56. Ⓐ Ⓑ Ⓒ Ⓓ Ⓔ	78. Ⓐ Ⓑ Ⓒ Ⓓ Ⓔ
13. Ⓐ Ⓑ Ⓒ Ⓓ Ⓔ	35. Ⓐ Ⓑ Ⓒ Ⓓ Ⓔ	57. Ⓐ Ⓑ Ⓒ Ⓓ Ⓔ	79. Ⓐ Ⓑ Ⓒ Ⓓ Ⓔ
14. Ⓐ Ⓑ Ⓒ Ⓓ Ⓔ	36. Ⓐ Ⓑ Ⓒ Ⓓ Ⓔ	58. Ⓐ Ⓑ Ⓒ Ⓓ Ⓔ	80. Ⓐ Ⓑ Ⓒ Ⓓ Ⓔ
15. Ⓐ Ⓑ Ⓒ Ⓓ Ⓔ	37. Ⓐ Ⓑ Ⓒ Ⓓ Ⓔ	59. Ⓐ Ⓑ Ⓒ Ⓓ Ⓔ	81. Ⓐ Ⓑ Ⓒ Ⓓ Ⓔ
16. Ⓐ Ⓑ Ⓒ Ⓓ Ⓔ	38. Ⓐ Ⓑ Ⓒ Ⓓ Ⓔ	60. Ⓐ Ⓑ Ⓒ Ⓓ Ⓔ	82. Ⓐ Ⓑ Ⓒ Ⓓ Ⓔ
17. Ⓐ Ⓑ Ⓒ Ⓓ Ⓔ	39. Ⓐ Ⓑ Ⓒ Ⓓ Ⓔ	61. Ⓐ Ⓑ Ⓒ Ⓓ Ⓔ	83. Ⓐ Ⓑ Ⓒ Ⓓ Ⓔ
18. Ⓐ Ⓑ Ⓒ Ⓓ Ⓔ	40. Ⓐ Ⓑ Ⓒ Ⓓ Ⓔ	62. Ⓐ Ⓑ Ⓒ Ⓓ Ⓔ	84. Ⓐ Ⓑ Ⓒ Ⓓ Ⓔ
19. Ⓐ Ⓑ Ⓒ Ⓓ Ⓔ	41. Ⓐ Ⓑ Ⓒ Ⓓ Ⓔ	63. Ⓐ Ⓑ Ⓒ Ⓓ Ⓔ	85. Ⓐ Ⓑ Ⓒ Ⓓ Ⓔ
20. Ⓐ Ⓑ Ⓒ Ⓓ Ⓔ	42. Ⓐ Ⓑ Ⓒ Ⓓ Ⓔ	64. Ⓐ Ⓑ Ⓒ Ⓓ Ⓔ	86. Ⓐ Ⓑ Ⓒ Ⓓ Ⓔ
21. Ⓐ Ⓑ Ⓒ Ⓓ Ⓔ	43. Ⓐ Ⓑ Ⓒ Ⓓ Ⓔ	65. Ⓐ Ⓑ Ⓒ Ⓓ Ⓔ	87. Ⓐ Ⓑ Ⓒ Ⓓ Ⓔ
22. Ⓐ Ⓑ Ⓒ Ⓓ Ⓔ	44. Ⓐ Ⓑ Ⓒ Ⓓ Ⓔ	66. Ⓐ Ⓑ Ⓒ Ⓓ Ⓔ	88. Ⓐ Ⓑ Ⓒ Ⓓ Ⓔ

11

Worksheet

> **DIRECTIONS:** Listen carefully to the instructions read to you and mark each item on the following worksheet as directed. Then complete each question by marking the answer sheet on the previous page as directed. For each answer, you will darken the answer sheet for a number-letter combination.

1.   A   B   B   D   C   D   E   D

2.   24   12   17   11   14   20

3.

41 __   62 __   18 __   27 __   73 __   10 __

4.   ___ B   ___ D   ___ C   ___ E   ___ A

5.   76   14   67   46   11   74

6.   ___ A   ___ E   ___ B   ___ C   ___ D

7.   9 __   46 __   34 __   LETTER   PARCEL

8.   G   G   G   G   G   G   G   G

9.

79 __   46 __   32 __

11

10.

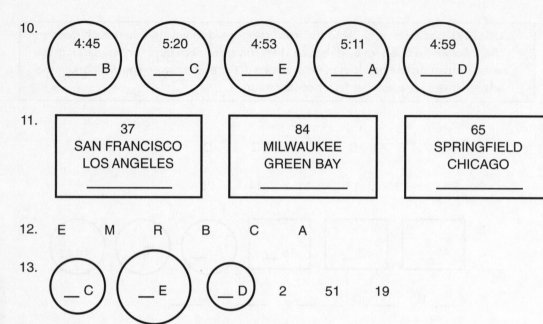

10. (circles)
4:45 ___ B   5:20 ___ C   4:53 ___ E   5:11 ___ A   4:59 ___ D

11.

| 37 SAN FRANCISCO LOS ANGELES _____ | 84 MILWAUKEE GREEN BAY _____ | 65 SPRINGFIELD CHICAGO _____ |

12.   E   M   R   B   C   A

13.   _C   _E   _D   2   51   19

14.   34 _   18 _   71 _   81 _

15.   42   68   87   20   12   36

16.   8 (star)   14 (triangle)   6 (square)   24 (circle)

17.   J   J   J   L   L   L   J   L   J   J

18.   41   38   62   59   44   40   54

19.   _ C   _ A   _ D

Directions and Sample Questions

Listening to Instructions: When you are ready to try these sample questions, give the following instructions to a friend and have the friend read them aloud to you at the rate of 80 words per minute. Do not read them to yourself. Your friend will need a watch with a second hand. Listen carefully and do exactly what your friend tells you to do with the worksheet and answer sheet. Your friend will tell you some things to do with each item on the worksheet. After each set of instructions, your friend will give you time to mark your answer by darkening a circle on the sample answer sheet. Since B and D sound very much alike, your friend will say "B as in baker" when he or she means B and "D as in dog" when he or she means D.

Before proceeding further, tear out the worksheet on pages 141 and 142. Then hand this book to your friend.

To the Person Who Is to Read the Instructions: The instructions are to be read at the rate of 80 words per minute. Do not read aloud the material that is in parentheses. Do not repeat any instructions.

Oral Instructions

Instructions to be read (the words in parentheses should not be read aloud):

On the actual job, you will have to listen to instructions and then do what you have been told. In this test, I will read instructions to you. Try to understand them as I read them; I cannot repeat them. Once we begin, you may not ask any questions until the end of the test.

On the job, you won't have to deal with pictures, numbers, and letters like those on the test, but you will have to listen to instructions and follow them. We are using this test to see how well you can follow instructions.

You are to mark your worksheet according to the instructions that I'll read to you. After each set of instructions, I'll give you time to record your answers on the separate answer sheet.

The actual test begins now.

Look at line 1 on your worksheet. (Pause slightly.) Circle the seventh letter on line 1. (Pause five seconds.) Now, on your answer sheet, find number 83 and darken the space for the letter you just circled. (Pause five seconds.)

Look at line 2 on your worksheet. (Pause slightly.) Draw a line under all the odd numbers between 12 and 20. (Pause five seconds.) Now, on your answer sheet, darken space B as in baker for all the numbers under which you drew a line. (Pause five seconds.)

Look at line 2 again. (Pause slightly.) Find the number that is two times another number on line 2 and circle it. (Pause five seconds.) Now, on your answer sheet, darken space A for the number you just circled. (Pause five seconds.)

Look at line 3 on your worksheet. (Pause slightly.) Write the letter C in the middle box. (Pause two seconds.) Now, on your answer sheet, darken the space for the number-letter combination in the figure you just wrote in. (Pause five seconds.)

Look at line 3 again. (Pause slightly.) Write the letter D as in dog in the left-hand circle. (Pause two seconds.) Now, on your answer sheet, darken the space for the number-letter combination in the figure you just wrote in. (Pause five seconds.)

Look at line 4 on your worksheet. (Pause slightly.) If first class mail costs more than bulk rate mail, write the number 22 on the third line; if not, write the number 19 on the fourth line. (Pause five seconds.) Now, on your answer sheet, darken the space for the number-letter combination on the line you just wrote on. (Pause five seconds.)

Look at line 4 again. (Pause slightly.) Write the number 31 on the second line from the left. (Pause two seconds.) Now, on your answer sheet, darken the space for the number-letter combination on the line on which you just wrote. (Pause five seconds.)

Look at line 5 on your worksheet. (Pause slightly.) Find the highest number on line 5 and draw a line under the number. (Pause two seconds.) Now, on your answer sheet, find the number under which you just drew a line and darken space E for that number. (Pause five seconds.)

Look at line 5 again. (Pause slightly.) Find the lowest number on line 5 and draw two lines under the number. (Pause two seconds.) Now, on your answer sheet, find the number under which you just drew two lines and darken space A for that number. (Pause five seconds.)

Look at line 6 on your worksheet. (Pause slightly.) Write the number 57 in the figure that differs from the others on line 6. (Pause two seconds.) Now, on your answer sheet, darken the number-letter combination that is in the figure in which you just wrote. (Pause five seconds.)

Look at line 7 on your worksheet. (Pause slightly.) Write the second letter of the second word in the first box. (Pause five seconds.) Write the fifth letter of the first word in the third box. (Pause five seconds.) Write the fourth letter of the second word in the second box. (Pause five seconds.) Now, on your answer sheet, darken the number-letter combinations in all three boxes. (Pause 15 seconds.)

Look at line 8 on your worksheet. (Pause slightly.) Count the number of Gs on line 8 and divide this number by 2. Write that number at the end of the line. (Pause five seconds.)

Now, on your answer sheet, darken space D as in dog for the number you wrote at the end of line 8. (Pause five seconds.)

Look at line 9 on your worksheet. (Pause slightly.) Write the letter B as in baker in the middle-sized circle. (Pause two seconds.) Now, on your answer sheet, darken the space for the number-letter combination in the circle in which you just wrote. (Pause five seconds.)

Look at line 10 on your worksheet. (Pause slightly.) The time in each circle represents the last scheduled pickup of the day from a street letterbox. Find the circle with the earliest pickup time and write the last two figures of that time on the line in the circle. (Pause 10 seconds.) Now, on your answer sheet, darken the space for the number-letter combination in the circle you just wrote in. (Pause five seconds.)

Look at line 10 again. (Pause slightly.) Find the circle with the latest pickup time and write the last two figures of that time on the line in the circle. (Pause 10 seconds.) Now, on your answer sheet, darken the space for the number-letter combination in the circle in which you just wrote. (Pause five seconds.)

Look at line 11 on your worksheet. (Pause slightly.) Mail directed for San Francisco and Los Angeles is to be placed in box 37; mail for Milwaukee and Green Bay in box 84; mail for Springfield and Chicago in box 65. Find the box for mail being sent to Green Bay and write the letter A in the box. (Pause two seconds.) Now, on your answer sheet, darken the number-letter combination for the box you just wrote in. (Pause five seconds.)

Look at line 11 again. (Pause slightly.) Mr. Green lives in Springfield. Find the box in which to put Mr. Green's mail and write E on the line. (Pause two seconds.) Now, on your answer sheet, darken the space for the number-letter combination in the box in which you just wrote. (Pause five seconds.)

Look at line 12 on your worksheet. (Pause slightly.) Find the letter on line 12 that is not in the word CREAM and draw a line under the letter. (Pause two seconds.) Now, on your answer sheet, find number 38 and darken the space for the letter under which you just drew a line. (Pause five seconds.)

Look at line 13 on your worksheet. (Pause slightly.) Write the smallest number in the largest circle. (Pause two seconds.) Write the largest number in the left-hand circle. (Pause two seconds.) Now, on your answer sheet, darken the number-letter combinations that are in the circles in which you just wrote. (Pause 10 seconds.)

Look at line 14 on your worksheet. (Pause slightly.) If there are 36 inches in a foot, write B as in baker in the first box; if not, write D as in dog in the third box. (Pause five seconds.) Now, on your answer sheet, darken the number-letter combination that is in the box in which you just wrote. (Pause five seconds.)

Look at line 14 again. (Pause slightly.) Find the box that contains a number in the teens and write B as in baker in that box. (Pause two seconds.) Now, on your answer sheet, darken the number-letter combination that is in the box in which you just wrote. (Pause five seconds.)

Look at line 15 on your worksheet. (Pause slightly.) Circle the only number on line 15 that is not divisible by 2. (Pause two seconds.) Now, on your answer sheet, darken space A for the number you circled. (Pause five seconds.)

Look at line 16 on your worksheet. (Pause slightly.) If the number in the circle is greater than the number in the box, write the letter E in the box; if not, write the letter E in the circle. (Pause five seconds.) Now, on your answer sheet, darken the number-letter combination that is in the figure in which you just wrote. (Pause five seconds.)

Look at line 16 again. (Pause slightly.) If the number in the triangle is smaller than the number in the figure directly to its left, write the letter A in the triangle; if not, write the letter C in the triangle. (Pause five seconds.) Now, on your answer sheet, darken the number-letter combination that is in the figure you just wrote in. (Pause five seconds.)

Look at line 17 on your worksheet. (Pause slightly.) Count the number of Js on line 17, multiply this number by five, and write that number at the end of the line. (Pause five seconds.) Now, on your answer sheet, find the number you just wrote at the end of the line and darken space C for that number. (Pause five seconds.)

Look at line 18 on your worksheet. (Pause slightly.) Draw one line under the number that is at the middle of line 18. (Pause five seconds.) Now, on your answer sheet, darken space B as in baker for the number under which you just drew a line. (Pause five seconds.)

Look at line 18 again. (Pause slightly.) Draw two lines under each odd number that falls between 35 and 45. (Pause 10 seconds.) Now, on your answer sheet, darken space D as in dog for each number under which you drew two lines. (Pause five seconds.)

Look at line 19 on your worksheet. (Pause slightly.) Next to the last letter on line 19, write the first number you hear: 53, 18, 6, 75. (Pause two seconds.) Now, on your answer sheet, darken the space for the number-letter combination you just wrote. (Pause five seconds.)

Answers

Correctly Completed Answer Sheet

1. Ⓐ Ⓑ Ⓒ Ⓓ Ⓔ
2. Ⓐ Ⓑ Ⓒ Ⓓ ●
3. Ⓐ Ⓑ Ⓒ Ⓓ Ⓔ
4. Ⓐ Ⓑ Ⓒ ● Ⓔ
5. Ⓐ Ⓑ Ⓒ Ⓓ Ⓔ
6. Ⓐ Ⓑ Ⓒ Ⓓ ●
7. Ⓐ Ⓑ Ⓒ Ⓓ Ⓔ
8. Ⓐ Ⓑ Ⓒ Ⓓ Ⓔ
9. ● Ⓑ Ⓒ Ⓓ Ⓔ
10. Ⓐ Ⓑ Ⓒ Ⓓ Ⓔ
11. ● Ⓑ Ⓒ Ⓓ Ⓔ
12. Ⓐ Ⓑ Ⓒ Ⓓ Ⓔ
13. Ⓐ Ⓑ Ⓒ Ⓓ Ⓔ
14. Ⓐ Ⓑ ● Ⓓ Ⓔ
15. Ⓐ Ⓑ Ⓒ Ⓓ Ⓔ
16. Ⓐ Ⓑ Ⓒ Ⓓ Ⓔ
17. Ⓐ ● Ⓒ Ⓓ Ⓔ
18. Ⓐ ● Ⓒ Ⓓ Ⓔ
19. Ⓐ Ⓑ Ⓒ Ⓓ Ⓔ
20. Ⓐ Ⓑ ● Ⓓ Ⓔ
21. Ⓐ Ⓑ Ⓒ Ⓓ Ⓔ
22. Ⓐ Ⓑ ● Ⓓ Ⓔ

23. Ⓐ Ⓑ Ⓒ Ⓓ Ⓔ
24. ● Ⓑ Ⓒ Ⓓ Ⓔ
25. Ⓐ Ⓑ Ⓒ Ⓓ Ⓔ
26. Ⓐ Ⓑ Ⓒ Ⓓ Ⓔ
27. Ⓐ Ⓑ Ⓒ ● Ⓔ
28. Ⓐ Ⓑ Ⓒ Ⓓ Ⓔ
29. Ⓐ Ⓑ Ⓒ Ⓓ Ⓔ
30. Ⓐ Ⓑ ● Ⓓ Ⓔ
31. Ⓐ Ⓑ Ⓒ ● Ⓔ
32. Ⓐ Ⓑ Ⓒ Ⓓ Ⓔ
33. Ⓐ Ⓑ Ⓒ Ⓓ Ⓔ
34. Ⓐ Ⓑ Ⓒ Ⓓ ●
35. Ⓐ Ⓑ Ⓒ Ⓓ Ⓔ
36. Ⓐ Ⓑ Ⓒ Ⓓ Ⓔ
37. Ⓐ Ⓑ Ⓒ Ⓓ Ⓔ
38. Ⓐ ● Ⓒ Ⓓ Ⓔ
39. Ⓐ Ⓑ Ⓒ Ⓓ Ⓔ
40. Ⓐ Ⓑ Ⓒ Ⓓ Ⓔ
41. Ⓐ Ⓑ Ⓒ ● Ⓔ
42. Ⓐ Ⓑ Ⓒ Ⓓ Ⓔ
43. Ⓐ Ⓑ Ⓒ Ⓓ Ⓔ
44. Ⓐ Ⓑ Ⓒ Ⓓ Ⓔ

45. Ⓐ ● Ⓒ Ⓓ Ⓔ
46. Ⓐ Ⓑ ● Ⓓ Ⓔ
47. Ⓐ Ⓑ Ⓒ Ⓓ Ⓔ
48. Ⓐ Ⓑ Ⓒ Ⓓ Ⓔ
49. Ⓐ Ⓑ Ⓒ Ⓓ Ⓔ
50. Ⓐ Ⓑ Ⓒ Ⓓ Ⓔ
51. Ⓐ Ⓑ ● Ⓓ Ⓔ
52. Ⓐ Ⓑ Ⓒ Ⓓ Ⓔ
53. Ⓐ Ⓑ Ⓒ ● Ⓔ
54. Ⓐ Ⓑ Ⓒ Ⓓ Ⓔ
55. Ⓐ Ⓑ Ⓒ Ⓓ Ⓔ
56. Ⓐ Ⓑ Ⓒ Ⓓ Ⓔ
57. Ⓐ ● Ⓒ Ⓓ Ⓔ
58. Ⓐ Ⓑ Ⓒ Ⓓ Ⓔ
59. Ⓐ ● Ⓒ Ⓓ Ⓔ
60. Ⓐ Ⓑ Ⓒ Ⓓ Ⓔ
61. Ⓐ Ⓑ Ⓒ Ⓓ Ⓔ
62. Ⓐ Ⓑ ● Ⓓ Ⓔ
63. Ⓐ Ⓑ Ⓒ Ⓓ Ⓔ
64. Ⓐ Ⓑ Ⓒ Ⓓ Ⓔ
65. Ⓐ Ⓑ Ⓒ Ⓓ ●
66. Ⓐ Ⓑ Ⓒ Ⓓ Ⓔ

67. Ⓐ Ⓑ Ⓒ Ⓓ Ⓔ
68. Ⓐ Ⓑ Ⓒ Ⓓ Ⓔ
69. Ⓐ Ⓑ Ⓒ Ⓓ Ⓔ
70. Ⓐ Ⓑ Ⓒ Ⓓ Ⓔ
71. Ⓐ Ⓑ Ⓒ ● Ⓔ
72. Ⓐ Ⓑ Ⓒ Ⓓ Ⓔ
73. Ⓐ Ⓑ Ⓒ Ⓓ Ⓔ
74. Ⓐ Ⓑ Ⓒ Ⓓ Ⓔ
75. Ⓐ Ⓑ Ⓒ Ⓓ Ⓔ
76. Ⓐ Ⓑ Ⓒ Ⓓ ●
77. Ⓐ Ⓑ Ⓒ Ⓓ Ⓔ
78. Ⓐ Ⓑ Ⓒ Ⓓ Ⓔ
79. Ⓐ ● Ⓒ Ⓓ Ⓔ
80. Ⓐ Ⓑ Ⓒ Ⓓ Ⓔ
81. Ⓐ Ⓑ Ⓒ Ⓓ Ⓔ
82. Ⓐ Ⓑ Ⓒ Ⓓ Ⓔ
83. Ⓐ Ⓑ Ⓒ Ⓓ ●
84. ● Ⓑ Ⓒ Ⓓ Ⓔ
85. Ⓐ Ⓑ Ⓒ Ⓓ Ⓔ
86. Ⓐ Ⓑ Ⓒ Ⓓ Ⓔ
87. ● Ⓑ Ⓒ Ⓓ Ⓔ
88. Ⓐ Ⓑ Ⓒ Ⓓ Ⓔ

11

Correctly Completed Worksheet

1.   A   B   B   D   C   D   (E)   D

2.   (24)   12   17   11   14   20

3. | 41 __ | | 62 _C_ | | 18 __ | | 27 _D_ | 73 __ | 10 __ |

4.   __ B   _31_ D   _22_ C   __ E   __ A

5.   76   14   67   46   11   74

6.   (__ A)   (__ E)   △57 B   (__ C)   (__ D)

7. | 9 _A_ | | 46 _C_ | | 34 _E_ | LETTER   PARCEL

8.   G   G   G   G   G   G   G   G   4

9.   (79 _B_)   (46 __)   (32 __)

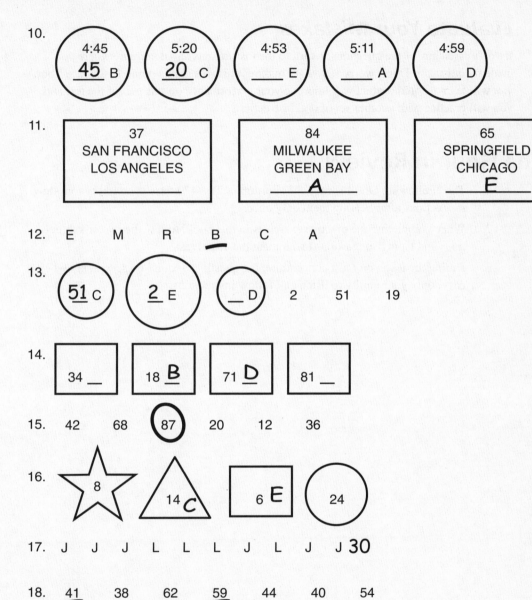

10.

4:45
45 B

5:20
20 C

4:53
___ E

5:11
___ A

4:59
___ D

11.

| 37 SAN FRANCISCO LOS ANGELES _____ | 84 MILWAUKEE GREEN BAY *A* | 65 SPRINGFIELD CHICAGO *E* |

12.   E   M   R   B   C   A

13.   **51** C   **2** E   __ D   2   51   19

14.   34 __   18 **B**   71 **D**   81 __

15.   42   68   87   20   12   36

16.   (star) 8   (triangle) 14 *C*   (square) 6 **E**   (circle) 24

17.   J   J   J   L   L   L   J   L   J   J **30**

18.   41   38   62   59   44   40   54

19.   __ C   __ A   **53** D

Evaluate Your Mistakes

If you missed any of the questions, return to the instructions and determine where you made the mistakes. Don't worry if you are making mistakes at this point. In the next hour, you will learn techniques that will improve your performance on this part of the test and you will practice with another set of oral instructions.

The Hour in Review

1. The "Following Oral Instructions" portion of Test 470 tests your ability to follow instructions after hearing them only once.

2. When completing the practice exercises in this book, follow the reader's directions and taping suggestions to simulate the actual test.

3. During the test, you must concentrate; the questions require no special knowledge, only your ability to listen and follow instructions.

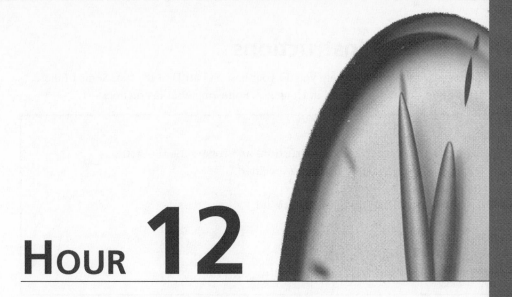

HOUR **12**

Following Oral Instructions—2

What You Will Learn in This Hour

In this hour, you will learn more question-answering techniques for doing well on the Following Oral Instructions test. These techniques will sharpen your listening skills, focus your attention on what the examiner says, and help you quickly carry out instructions.

Remember, the United States Postal Service is looking for employees who have these skills. A high score on this section will help you in the hiring process. Here are your goals for this hour:

- Understand why carefully listening to the instructions is essential.
- Learn how to listen for two-step instructions.
- Understand how to use your worksheet as a memory aid.
- Learn strategies that improve your performance on the questions.
- Learn the best way to guess on this part of the test
- Take another practice exercise to test what you have learned

How to Follow Instructions

The following techniques will help you do your best on Part D of the test. Some of these overlap with techniques presented in Hour 11, "Following Oral Instructions—1."

Do

DO pay close attention to all the instructions and follow them exactly.

DO mark your answer sheet exactly as specified.

DO work from left to right.

DO write in your worksheet as a memory aid.

Don't

DON'T waste time changing answers.

DON'T make assumptions on two-step instructions.

Pay Attention to the Instructions

You must not let your concentration waver if you are to follow through on all the instructions. Remember, the instructions will not be repeated, so you have to take immediate action and not let your mind wander.

Examples

If the reader says, "Look at line 1," then look at that line. Place your pencil at the beginning of that line and listen.

If the reader says, "Find the smallest number on line 3 and draw one line under that number," immediately turn your attention to line 3 and search out the lowest number.

Mark Your Answer Sheet as Directed

You also must never stop listening to the instructions because you will not mark your answers in a consecutive order on your answer sheet. You will skip around the page filling in answers in the order specified. In fact, you will not use all the answer spaces; blanks are acceptable and, in fact, are required.

Work from Left to Right

It is extremely important that you work, read, and count from left to right unless you are told otherwise in this section of the exam. Thus, the "fourth letter" is the fourth letter from the left, and the "sixth X" is the sixth letter from the left. Of course, if the instructions should refer to the "second circle from the right," you must follow the instructions precisely and do what you are told to do.

Don't Waste Time Changing Answers

If you are about to enter an answer on your answer sheet and find you have already darkened that space, don't make a change. Your best bet is probably to leave the mark that is already there and wait for the next instruction. You may darken only one space for each number, and the time you spend changing an answer may cause you to miss the beginning of the next question.

Caution
If you spot two answer spaces already blackened for a number on your answer sheet, should you erase one of them? Erase it if you can do it in a split second without getting flustered or losing your place. You must avoid getting distracted and falling behind on the instructions.

Listen Carefully to Two-Step Instructions

12

Some instructions are complicated and will have two parts. Don't assume that you know what to do without listening to all the steps.

1. When you hear the word "if," or the combinations "if . . . and" or "if . . . or," be especially alert.

2. Listen carefully for the choices you may be asked to make.

3. Only act when you understand what the choices involve.

Example

"If January comes before June and Monday comes after Wednesday, write the letter E in the left-hand box; if not, write the letter A in the right-hand circle."

Analysis

In this example, you would work as follows:

1. Listen for the choices to be presented to you.

2. January comes before June, so the first part of the statement is true.

3. Put your pencil in the left-hand box, but do not write until you have heard the other half of the statement.

4. Monday does not come after Wednesday, so the second part of the sentence is false.

5. You would ignore the directive to write the letter E in the left-hand box because the word "and" requires both statements to be true.

6. You would write the letter A in the right-hand circle because one of the statements is false.

Use Your Worksheet as a Memory Aid

Because you are permitted to write on your worksheet, use the worksheet to write down learning aids, but don't let these additional notations interfere with the markings you are told to enter. This technique can be useful when working with a number series or performing simple numerical calculations.

Example

In the first box, write the smallest of these numbers: 52, 41, 13, 29, 60.

Analysis

For the above instruction:

1. Write the list of numbers lightly in the margin of the worksheet.

2. Circle the smallest of the numbers.

3. Write the smallest number in the box as directed.

4. As soon as you have finished, draw a line through the number series.

Caution
Always remember to draw a line through your worksheet notes as soon as you've finished with them. This will avoid confusion if you encounter similar instructions later in the test.

Tackling Oral Instructions Questions

The post office considers your ability to follow instructions crucial for job success. There-fore, you must succeed on this section to do well on the exam. Although this portion is not difficult, you must be able to listen carefully and act upon the instructions to succeed. The following guidelines, many of which have already been discussed, will help you:

Do

DO pay close attention to all of the instructions and follow them exactly.
DO mark your answer sheet exactly as specified.
DO work from left to right.
DO write in your worksheet as a memory aid.
DO guess if you need to.

Don't

DON'T waste time changing answers.
DON'T make assumptions on two-step instructions.

DO pay close attention to all of the instructions and follow them exactly. Even if the instructions seem incorrect, do exactly as you are told; that is what you're being tested on.

DO mark your answer sheet exactly as specified. This is particularly important because you won't be marking answers in order on the answer sheet. Instead, you'll skip around the page, filling in answers in the order specified by the instructions.

DO work from left to right. It's extremely important that you work, read, and count from left to right unless you are told not to in the instructions.

DO write in your worksheet as a memory aid. Use the ability to write on your worksheet to your advantage by jotting down additional notations.

DO guess if you need to. There is no penalty for guessing on Part D.

DON'T waste time changing answers. If you're about to enter an answer on your answer sheet and find that you have already darkened that circle, don't make a change. Your best bet is to leave the mark that is already there and wait for the next instruction.

DON'T make assumptions on two-step instructions. Some instructions are complicated and have two parts. Don't assume that you know what to do without listening to all the steps.

12

Guessing on Part D

Now that we've reviewed the techniques you should use, there is still one strategy to discuss, and that is guessing. There is no penalty for guessing on Part D and the official instructions encourage you to guess if you're unsure of an answer. We agree, but not for the entire test section.

As you've learned from the above, you will not be marking your answer sheet in order. Guessing early in the section will probably cause you to fill in boxes that you may have to fill in later, which will only confuse you, so guess only during the latter part of the test.

Oral Instructions Practice Exercise

When completing the following practice exercise, try using the question-answering techniques that you learned in this hour and the previous hour. Remember the Dos and Don'ts, and above all else, keep concentrating.

You will need approximately 25 minutes to complete this exercise if you read and/or tape the instructions as directed. However, don't obsess about the time; instead, concentrate on listening to and acting on the instructions as they are read aloud to you. Turn the page to find the worksheet and answer sheet for this exercise.

Practice Exercise

The oral instructions for this practice exercise start on page 159.

The completed answer sheet is on page 163.

Answer Sheet

1. Ⓐ Ⓑ Ⓒ Ⓓ Ⓔ   23. Ⓐ Ⓑ Ⓒ Ⓓ Ⓔ   45. Ⓐ Ⓑ Ⓒ Ⓓ Ⓔ   67. Ⓐ Ⓑ Ⓒ Ⓓ Ⓔ

2. Ⓐ Ⓑ Ⓒ Ⓓ Ⓔ   24. Ⓐ Ⓑ Ⓒ Ⓓ Ⓔ   46. Ⓐ Ⓑ Ⓒ Ⓓ Ⓔ   68. Ⓐ Ⓑ Ⓒ Ⓓ Ⓔ

3. Ⓐ Ⓑ Ⓒ Ⓓ Ⓔ   25. Ⓐ Ⓑ Ⓒ Ⓓ Ⓔ   47. Ⓐ Ⓑ Ⓒ Ⓓ Ⓔ   69. Ⓐ Ⓑ Ⓒ Ⓓ Ⓔ

4. Ⓐ Ⓑ Ⓒ Ⓓ Ⓔ   26. Ⓐ Ⓑ Ⓒ Ⓓ Ⓔ   48. Ⓐ Ⓑ Ⓒ Ⓓ Ⓔ   70. Ⓐ Ⓑ Ⓒ Ⓓ Ⓔ

5. Ⓐ Ⓑ Ⓒ Ⓓ Ⓔ   27. Ⓐ Ⓑ Ⓒ Ⓓ Ⓔ   49. Ⓐ Ⓑ Ⓒ Ⓓ Ⓔ   71. Ⓐ Ⓑ Ⓒ Ⓓ Ⓔ

6. Ⓐ Ⓑ Ⓒ Ⓓ Ⓔ   28. Ⓐ Ⓑ Ⓒ Ⓓ Ⓔ   50. Ⓐ Ⓑ Ⓒ Ⓓ Ⓔ   72. Ⓐ Ⓑ Ⓒ Ⓓ Ⓔ

7. Ⓐ Ⓑ Ⓒ Ⓓ Ⓔ   29. Ⓐ Ⓑ Ⓒ Ⓓ Ⓔ   51. Ⓐ Ⓑ Ⓒ Ⓓ Ⓔ   73. Ⓐ Ⓑ Ⓒ Ⓓ Ⓔ

8. Ⓐ Ⓑ Ⓒ Ⓓ Ⓔ   30. Ⓐ Ⓑ Ⓒ Ⓓ Ⓔ   52. Ⓐ Ⓑ Ⓒ Ⓓ Ⓔ   74. Ⓐ Ⓑ Ⓒ Ⓓ Ⓔ

9. Ⓐ Ⓑ Ⓒ Ⓓ Ⓔ   31. Ⓐ Ⓑ Ⓒ Ⓓ Ⓔ   53. Ⓐ Ⓑ Ⓒ Ⓓ Ⓔ   75. Ⓐ Ⓑ Ⓒ Ⓓ Ⓔ

10. Ⓐ Ⓑ Ⓒ Ⓓ Ⓔ   32. Ⓐ Ⓑ Ⓒ Ⓓ Ⓔ   54. Ⓐ Ⓑ Ⓒ Ⓓ Ⓔ   76. Ⓐ Ⓑ Ⓒ Ⓓ Ⓔ

11. Ⓐ Ⓑ Ⓒ Ⓓ Ⓔ   33. Ⓐ Ⓑ Ⓒ Ⓓ Ⓔ   55. Ⓐ Ⓑ Ⓒ Ⓓ Ⓔ   77. Ⓐ Ⓑ Ⓒ Ⓓ Ⓔ

12. Ⓐ Ⓑ Ⓒ Ⓓ Ⓔ   34. Ⓐ Ⓑ Ⓒ Ⓓ Ⓔ   56. Ⓐ Ⓑ Ⓒ Ⓓ Ⓔ   78. Ⓐ Ⓑ Ⓒ Ⓓ Ⓔ

13. Ⓐ Ⓑ Ⓒ Ⓓ Ⓔ   35. Ⓐ Ⓑ Ⓒ Ⓓ Ⓔ   57. Ⓐ Ⓑ Ⓒ Ⓓ Ⓔ   79. Ⓐ Ⓑ Ⓒ Ⓓ Ⓔ

14. Ⓐ Ⓑ Ⓒ Ⓓ Ⓔ   36. Ⓐ Ⓑ Ⓒ Ⓓ Ⓔ   58. Ⓐ Ⓑ Ⓒ Ⓓ Ⓔ   80. Ⓐ Ⓑ Ⓒ Ⓓ Ⓔ

15. Ⓐ Ⓑ Ⓒ Ⓓ Ⓔ   37. Ⓐ Ⓑ Ⓒ Ⓓ Ⓔ   59. Ⓐ Ⓑ Ⓒ Ⓓ Ⓔ   81. Ⓐ Ⓑ Ⓒ Ⓓ Ⓔ

16. Ⓐ Ⓑ Ⓒ Ⓓ Ⓔ   38. Ⓐ Ⓑ Ⓒ Ⓓ Ⓔ   60. Ⓐ Ⓑ Ⓒ Ⓓ Ⓔ   82. Ⓐ Ⓑ Ⓒ Ⓓ Ⓔ

17. Ⓐ Ⓑ Ⓒ Ⓓ Ⓔ   39. Ⓐ Ⓑ Ⓒ Ⓓ Ⓔ   61. Ⓐ Ⓑ Ⓒ Ⓓ Ⓔ   83. Ⓐ Ⓑ Ⓒ Ⓓ Ⓔ

18. Ⓐ Ⓑ Ⓒ Ⓓ Ⓔ   40. Ⓐ Ⓑ Ⓒ Ⓓ Ⓔ   62. Ⓐ Ⓑ Ⓒ Ⓓ Ⓔ   84. Ⓐ Ⓑ Ⓒ Ⓓ Ⓔ

19. Ⓐ Ⓑ Ⓒ Ⓓ Ⓔ   41. Ⓐ Ⓑ Ⓒ Ⓓ Ⓔ   63. Ⓐ Ⓑ Ⓒ Ⓓ Ⓔ   85. Ⓐ Ⓑ Ⓒ Ⓓ Ⓔ

20. Ⓐ Ⓑ Ⓒ Ⓓ Ⓔ   42. Ⓐ Ⓑ Ⓒ Ⓓ Ⓔ   64. Ⓐ Ⓑ Ⓒ Ⓓ Ⓔ   86. Ⓐ Ⓑ Ⓒ Ⓓ Ⓔ

21. Ⓐ Ⓑ Ⓒ Ⓓ Ⓔ   43. Ⓐ Ⓑ Ⓒ Ⓓ Ⓔ   65. Ⓐ Ⓑ Ⓒ Ⓓ Ⓔ   87. Ⓐ Ⓑ Ⓒ Ⓓ Ⓔ

22. Ⓐ Ⓑ Ⓒ Ⓓ Ⓔ   44. Ⓐ Ⓑ Ⓒ Ⓓ Ⓔ   66. Ⓐ Ⓑ Ⓒ Ⓓ Ⓔ   88. Ⓐ Ⓑ Ⓒ Ⓓ Ⓔ

12

Worksheet

DIRECTIONS: Listen carefully to the instructions and mark each item on this worksheet as directed. Then complete each question by marking the answer sheet as directed. For each answer, you will darken the answer sheet with a number-letter combination.

1.   13   23   2   19   6

2.   E   B   D   E   C   A   B

3.
| 30 __ | 18 __ | 5 __ | 14 __ | 7 __ |

4.
26 __   16 __   23 __   23 __   27 __

5.
| 63 __ | 16 __ | 78 __ | 48 __ |

6.   12 ____   5 ____   22 ____

7.   14 __   1 __   36 __   7 __   19 __

8.   26 ____   86 ____

12

9. 57   63   11   78   90   32   45   70   69

10. 16   30   13   25   10   14   23   26   19

11.
9:12 __ A   9:28 __ B   9:24 __ C   9:11 __ D   9:32 __ E

12.
47 __   10 __   26 __   8 __   25 __

13.
__ A   __ B   __ C   __ D   __ E

14.
3 __   32 __   45 __   10 __

15.
72 __   81 __   49 __   ABLE   EASY   DESK

16. X X O X O O O X O X X O X X

17.
22 __   3 __   21 __   28 __

15.
21 __   38 __   29 __   31 __

19. __ A   __ C   __ E

Directions and Sample Questions

Listening to Instructions: When you are ready to try these sample questions, give the following instructions to a friend and have the friend read them aloud to you at the rate of 80 words per minute. Do not read them to yourself. Your friend will need a watch with a second hand. Listen carefully and do exactly what your friend tells you to do with the worksheet and answer sheet. Your friend will tell you some things to do with each item on the worksheet. After each set of instructions, your friend will give you time to mark your answer by darkening a circle on the sample answer sheet. Since B and D sound very much alike, your friend will say "B as in baker" when he or she means B and "D as in dog" when he or she means D.

Before proceeding further, tear out the worksheet on pages 159 and 160. Then hand this book to your friend.

To the Person Who Is to Read the Instructions: The instructions are to be read at the rate of 80 words per minute. Do not read aloud the material that is in parentheses. Do not repeat any instructions.

Oral Instructions

Instructions to be read (the words in parentheses should *not* be read aloud):

On the job, you will have to listen to directions and do what you have been told. In this oral exam, I will read some instructions to you. Listen carefully because they will not be repeated. Once we begin, you cannot ask any questions until the end of the test.

On the job, you won't have to deal with pictures, numbers, and letters like those you will see in this test, but you will have to listen to instructions and follow them. We are using this test to see how well you can follow instructions.

You are to mark your test booklet according to the instructions that I'll read to you. After each set of instructions, I'll give you time to record your answers on the separate answer sheet.

The actual test begins now.

Look at line 1 on the worksheet. (Pause slightly.) Draw a line under the fourth number in the line. (Pause two seconds.) Now, on your answer sheet, find the number under which you just drew the line and darken space A for that number. (Pause five seconds.)

Look at the letters in line 2 on the worksheet. (Pause slightly.) Draw a line under the fifth letter in the line. Now, on your answer sheet, find number 59 (pause two seconds) and darken the space for the letter under which you drew a line. (Pause five seconds.)

Look at the letters in line 2 on the worksheet again. (Pause slightly.) Now draw two lines under the third letter in the line. (Pause two seconds.) Now, on your answer sheet, find number 65 (pause two seconds) and darken the space for the letter under which you drew two lines. (Pause five seconds.)

Look at line 3 on the worksheet. (Pause slightly.) Write an E in the last box. (Pause two seconds.) Now, on your answer sheet, find the number in that box and darken space E for that number. (Pause five seconds.)

Now look at line 3 again. (Pause slightly.) Write an A in the first box. (Pause two seconds.) Now, on your answer sheet, find the number in that box and darken space A for that number. (Pause five seconds.)

Look at line 4. The number in each circle is the number of packages in a mail sack. In the circle for the sack holding the largest number of packages, write a B as in baker. (Pause two seconds.) Now, on your answer sheet, darken the space for the number-letter combination that is in the circle you just wrote in. (Pause five seconds.)

Look at line 4 again. In the circle for the sack holding the smallest number of packages, write an E. (Pause two seconds.) Now, on your answer sheet, darken the space for the number-letter combination that is in the circle you just wrote in. (Pause five seconds.)

Look at the drawings on line 5 on the worksheet. The four boxes are trucks for carrying mail. (Pause slightly.) The truck with the highest number is to be loaded first. Write B as in baker on the line beside the highest number. (Pause two seconds.) Now, on your answer sheet, darken the space for the number-letter combination that is in the box you just wrote in. (Pause five seconds.)

Look at line 6 on the worksheet. (Pause slightly.) Next to the middle number, write the letter D as in dog. (Pause two seconds.) Now, on your answer sheet, find the space beside the number that you wrote and darken space D as in dog. (Pause five seconds.)

Look at the five circles in line 7 on the worksheet. Write B as in baker on the blank in the second circle. (Pause two seconds.) Now, on your answer sheet, darken the space for the number-letter combination that is in the circle you just wrote in. (Pause five seconds.)

Now take the worksheet again and write C on the blank in the third circle on line 7. (Pause two seconds.) Now, on your answer sheet, darken the space for the number-letter combination that is in the circle in which you just wrote. (Pause five seconds.)

Now look at line 8 on the worksheet. (Pause slightly.) Write an A on the line next to the right-hand number. (Pause two seconds.) Now, on your answer sheet, find the space for the number which you wrote beside and darken box A. (Pause five seconds.)

Look at line 9 on the worksheet. (Pause slightly.) Draw a line under every number that is more than 60 but less than 70. (Pause 12 seconds.) Now, on your answer sheet, for each number that you drew a line under, darken space C. (Pause 25 seconds.)

Look at line 10 on the worksheet. (Pause slightly.) Draw a line under every number that is more than five and less than 15. (Pause 10 seconds.) Now, on your answer sheet, for each number that you drew a line under, darken space D as in dog. (Pause 25 seconds.)

Look at line 11 on the worksheet. (Pause slightly.) In each circle, there is a time when the mail must leave. In the circle for the latest time, write on the line the last two figures of the time. (Pause five seconds.) Now, on your answer sheet, darken the space for the number-letter combination that is in the circle you just wrote in. (Pause five seconds.)

Look at the five boxes in line 12 on your worksheet. (Pause slightly.) If 6 is less than 3, put an E in the fourth box. (Pause slightly.) If 6 is not less than 3, put a B as in baker in the first box. (Pause 10 seconds.) Now, on your answer sheet, darken the space for the number-letter combination that is in the box you just wrote in. (Pause five seconds.)

Now look at line 13 on the worksheet. (Pause slightly.) There are five circles and each one has a letter. (Pause slightly.) In the second circle, write the answer to this question: Which of the following numbers is smallest: 72, 51, 88, 71, 58? (Pause 10 seconds.) Now, on your answer sheet, darken the space for the number-letter combination that is in the circle you just wrote in. (Pause five seconds.) In the third circle on the same line, write 28. (Pause two seconds.) Now, on your answer sheet, darken the space for the number-letter combination that is in the circle you just wrote in. (Pause five seconds.) In the fourth circle, do nothing. In the fifth circle, write the answer to this question: How many months are there in a year? (Pause five seconds.) Now, on your answer sheet, darken the space for the number-letter combination that is in the circle you just wrote in. (Pause five seconds.)

Look at line 14 on your worksheet. (Pause slightly.) There are two circles and two boxes of different sizes with numbers in them. (Pause slightly.) If 2 is smaller than 4 and if 7 is less than 3, write A in the larger circle. (Pause slightly.) Otherwise, write B as in baker in the smaller box. (Pause 10 seconds.) Now, on your answer sheet, darken the space for the number-letter combination in the box or circle in which you just wrote. (Pause five seconds.)

Look at the boxes and words in line 15 on the worksheet. (Pause slightly.) Write the second letter of the first word in the third box. (Pause five seconds.) Write the first letter of the second word in the first box. (Pause five seconds.) Write the first letter of the third word in the second box. (Pause five seconds.) Now, on your answer sheet, darken the spaces for the number-letter combinations that are in the three boxes you just wrote in. (Pause 15 seconds.)

12

Look at line 16 on the worksheet. (Pause slightly.) Draw a line under every 0 in the line. (Pause five seconds.) Count the number of lines that you have drawn, subtract 2, and write that number at the end of the line. (Pause five seconds.) Now, on your answer sheet, find that number and darken space D as in dog for that number. (Pause five seconds.)

Look at line 17 on the worksheet. (Pause slightly.) If the number in the left-hand circle is smaller than the number in the right-hand circle, add 2 to the number in the left-hand circle, and change the number in that circle to this number. (Pause eight seconds.) Then write B as in baker next to the new number. (Pause slightly.) Next, write E beside the number in the smaller box. (Pause three seconds.) Then, on your answer sheet, darken the spaces for the number-letter combinations that are in the box and circle you just wrote in. (Pause five seconds.)

Look at line 18 on the worksheet. (Pause slightly.) If October comes before September, write A in the box with the smallest number. (Pause slightly.) If it does not, write C in the box with the largest number. (Pause 10 seconds.) Now, on your answer sheet, darken the space for the number-letter combination that is in the box you just wrote in. (Pause five seconds.)

Look at line 19 on the worksheet. (Pause slightly.) On the line beside the second letter, write the highest of these numbers: 12, 56, 42, 39, 8. (Pause two seconds.) Now, on your answer sheet, darken the space of the number-letter combination you just wrote. (Pause five seconds.)

Answers

Correctly Completed Answer Sheet

1. Ⓐ ● Ⓒ Ⓓ Ⓔ	23. Ⓐ Ⓑ Ⓒ Ⓓ Ⓔ	45. Ⓐ ● Ⓒ Ⓓ Ⓔ	67. Ⓐ Ⓑ Ⓒ Ⓓ Ⓔ
2. Ⓐ Ⓑ Ⓒ Ⓓ Ⓔ	24. Ⓐ ● Ⓒ Ⓓ Ⓔ	46. Ⓐ Ⓑ Ⓒ Ⓓ Ⓔ	68. Ⓐ Ⓑ Ⓒ Ⓓ Ⓔ
3. Ⓐ Ⓑ Ⓒ Ⓓ ●	25. Ⓐ Ⓑ Ⓒ Ⓓ Ⓔ	47. Ⓐ ● Ⓒ Ⓓ Ⓔ	69. Ⓐ Ⓑ ● Ⓓ Ⓔ
4. Ⓐ Ⓑ Ⓒ ● Ⓔ	26. Ⓐ Ⓑ Ⓒ Ⓓ Ⓔ	48. Ⓐ Ⓑ Ⓒ Ⓓ Ⓔ	70. Ⓐ Ⓑ Ⓒ Ⓓ Ⓔ
5. Ⓐ Ⓑ Ⓒ ● Ⓔ	27. Ⓐ ● Ⓒ Ⓓ Ⓔ	49. Ⓐ ● Ⓒ Ⓓ Ⓔ	71. Ⓐ Ⓑ Ⓒ Ⓓ Ⓔ
6. Ⓐ Ⓑ Ⓒ Ⓓ Ⓔ	28. Ⓐ Ⓑ ● Ⓓ Ⓔ	50. Ⓐ Ⓑ Ⓒ Ⓓ Ⓔ	72. Ⓐ Ⓑ Ⓒ Ⓓ ●
7. Ⓐ Ⓑ Ⓒ Ⓓ ●	29. Ⓐ Ⓑ Ⓒ Ⓓ Ⓔ	51. Ⓐ ● Ⓒ Ⓓ Ⓔ	73. Ⓐ Ⓑ Ⓒ Ⓓ Ⓔ
8. Ⓐ Ⓑ Ⓒ Ⓓ Ⓔ	30. ● Ⓑ Ⓒ Ⓓ Ⓔ	52. Ⓐ Ⓑ Ⓒ Ⓓ Ⓔ	74. Ⓐ Ⓑ Ⓒ Ⓓ Ⓔ
9. Ⓐ Ⓑ Ⓒ Ⓓ Ⓔ	31. Ⓐ Ⓑ Ⓒ Ⓓ Ⓔ	53. Ⓐ Ⓑ Ⓒ Ⓓ Ⓔ	75. Ⓐ Ⓑ Ⓒ Ⓓ Ⓔ
10. Ⓐ Ⓑ Ⓒ ● Ⓔ	32. Ⓐ Ⓑ Ⓒ Ⓓ ●	54. Ⓐ Ⓑ Ⓒ Ⓓ Ⓔ	76. Ⓐ Ⓑ Ⓒ Ⓓ Ⓔ
11. Ⓐ Ⓑ Ⓒ Ⓓ Ⓔ	33. Ⓐ Ⓑ Ⓒ Ⓓ Ⓔ	55. Ⓐ Ⓑ Ⓒ Ⓓ Ⓔ	77. Ⓐ Ⓑ Ⓒ Ⓓ Ⓔ
12. Ⓐ Ⓑ Ⓒ Ⓓ ●	34. Ⓐ Ⓑ Ⓒ Ⓓ Ⓔ	56. Ⓐ Ⓑ ● Ⓓ Ⓔ	78. Ⓐ ● Ⓒ Ⓓ Ⓔ
13. Ⓐ Ⓑ Ⓒ ● Ⓔ	35. Ⓐ Ⓑ Ⓒ Ⓓ Ⓔ	57. Ⓐ Ⓑ Ⓒ Ⓓ Ⓔ	79. Ⓐ Ⓑ Ⓒ Ⓓ Ⓔ
14. Ⓐ Ⓑ Ⓒ ● Ⓔ	36. Ⓐ Ⓑ ● Ⓓ Ⓔ	58. Ⓐ Ⓑ Ⓒ Ⓓ Ⓔ	80. Ⓐ Ⓑ Ⓒ Ⓓ Ⓔ
15. Ⓐ Ⓑ Ⓒ Ⓓ Ⓔ	37. Ⓐ Ⓑ Ⓒ Ⓓ Ⓔ	59. Ⓐ Ⓑ ● Ⓓ Ⓔ	81. Ⓐ Ⓑ Ⓒ ● Ⓔ
16. Ⓐ Ⓑ Ⓒ Ⓓ ●	38. Ⓐ Ⓑ ● Ⓓ Ⓔ	60. Ⓐ Ⓑ Ⓒ Ⓓ Ⓔ	82. Ⓐ Ⓑ Ⓒ Ⓓ Ⓔ
17. Ⓐ Ⓑ Ⓒ Ⓓ Ⓔ	39. Ⓐ Ⓑ Ⓒ Ⓓ Ⓔ	61. Ⓐ Ⓑ Ⓒ Ⓓ Ⓔ	83. Ⓐ Ⓑ Ⓒ Ⓓ Ⓔ
18. Ⓐ Ⓑ Ⓒ Ⓓ Ⓔ	40. Ⓐ Ⓑ Ⓒ Ⓓ Ⓔ	62. Ⓐ Ⓑ Ⓒ Ⓓ Ⓔ	84. Ⓐ Ⓑ Ⓒ Ⓓ Ⓔ
19. ● Ⓑ Ⓒ Ⓓ Ⓔ	41. Ⓐ Ⓑ Ⓒ Ⓓ Ⓔ	63. Ⓐ Ⓑ ● Ⓓ Ⓔ	85. Ⓐ Ⓑ Ⓒ Ⓓ Ⓔ
20. Ⓐ Ⓑ Ⓒ Ⓓ Ⓔ	42. Ⓐ Ⓑ Ⓒ Ⓓ Ⓔ	64. Ⓐ Ⓑ Ⓒ Ⓓ Ⓔ	86. ● Ⓑ Ⓒ Ⓓ Ⓔ
21. Ⓐ Ⓑ Ⓒ Ⓓ Ⓔ	43. Ⓐ Ⓑ Ⓒ Ⓓ Ⓔ	65. Ⓐ Ⓑ Ⓒ ● Ⓔ	87. Ⓐ Ⓑ Ⓒ Ⓓ Ⓔ
22. Ⓐ Ⓑ Ⓒ Ⓓ Ⓔ	44. Ⓐ Ⓑ Ⓒ Ⓓ Ⓔ	66. Ⓐ Ⓑ Ⓒ Ⓓ Ⓔ	88. Ⓐ Ⓑ Ⓒ Ⓓ Ⓔ

12

Correctly Completed Worksheet

1. 13   23   2   <u>19</u>   6

2. E   B   <u>D</u>   E   <u>C</u>   A   B

3. | 30 <u>A</u> | 18 __ | 5 __ | 14 __ | 7 <u>E</u> |

4. 26 __   16 <u>E</u>   23 __   23 __   27 <u>B</u>

5. 63 __   16 __   78 <u>B</u>   48 __

6. 12 ____   5 <u>D</u>   22 ____

7. 14 __   1 <u>B</u>   36 <u>C</u>   7 __   19 __

8. 26 ____   86 <u>A</u>

9. 57   <u>63</u>   11   78   90   32   45   70   <u>69</u>

10. 16   30   <u>13</u>   25   <u>10</u>   <u>14</u>   23   26   19

11. 9:12 __ A   9:28 __ B   9:24 __ C   9:11 __ D   9:32 <u>32</u>E

12.

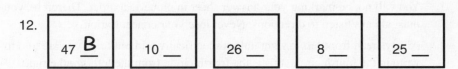

13.

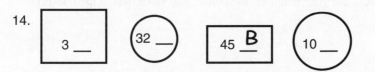

14.

15.

ABLE   EASY   DESK

16. X X O X O O O X O X X O X X **4**

17.

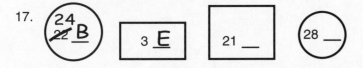

15.

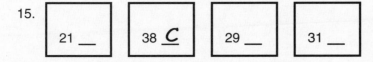

19. __ A   **56** C   __ E

The Hour in Review

In this hour, you learned the best question-answering strategies for answering the Oral Instruction questions.

1. You will not be marking your answer sheet in numerical order. Therefore, you must always listen to directions. Never lose your concentration.

2. Always read from left to right unless specifically told not to. If you are told to write in the fourth circle, this is the fourth circle from the left, *not* the right.

3. Be especially alert for two-step instructions that include the words "if," "if . . . and," or "if . . . or." When you encounter these complicated instructions, don't act prematurely. Just follow the instructions one step at a time.

4. You can also use your worksheet for calculations or other notations. Just remember to cross out your notations as soon as you've answered the question.

Part III

Timed and Untimed Tests

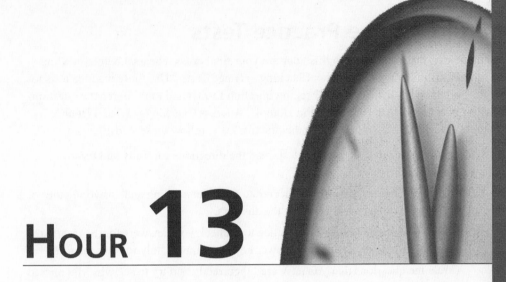

HOUR **13**

Address Checking—
Untimed Tests

What You Will Learn in This Hour

In this hour, you'll hone your skills for answering Address Checking questions by taking three practice tests at your own pace. These tests are the same length as the Address Checking portion of the actual Test 470. Here are your goals for this hour:

- Understand your goals for taking the untimed practice tests.
- Complete each of the three Address Checking practice tests in less than 20 minutes.
- Review the previous lessons on Address Checking if needed.

Preparing for the Practice Tests

The three tests that you'll take in this hour are your final dress rehearsal before tackling the timed tests in Hour 14, "Address Checking—Timed Tests." Use these practice tests to get comfortable with the Address Checking question format and to reinforce the question-answering strategies that you learned in Hour 4, "Address Checking—1," and Hour 5, "Address Checking—2." When taking the practice tests, follow these steps:

1. Before you start each practice test, read the directions carefully and try to memorize them.

2. Complete each test in order. Concentrate on understanding and answering the questions, not on quickly finding the answers.

3. Before moving on to the next practice test, check your answers for the test that you just completed against the answer key that immediately follows the test.

4. Circle the questions that you answered incorrectly and try to see why you missed them.

5. If you have time after finishing all three tests, retake the tests you found most difficult.

Make Connections

If you feel you need more review on the strategies for tackling Address Checking questions after completing any of the practice tests, turn back to Hours 4 and 5.

Tip

If you memorize the directions for the "Memory for Addresses" portion of Test 470 during this hour, you won't have to waste time rereading the directions in the timed tests in Hour 14, in the Bonus Hour examination, or on the actual test.

Practice Test 1

DIRECTIONS: For each question, compare the address in the left column with the address in the right column. If the two addresses are *alike* in every way, write A next to the question number. If the two addresses are *different* in any way, write D next to the question number.

1.	...462 Midland Ave	462 Midland Ave
2.	...2319 Sherry Dr	3219 Sherry Dr
3.	...1015 Kimball Ave	1015 Kimball Av
4.	...Wappinger Falls NY 12590	Wappinger Falls NY 12590
5.	...1255 North Ave	1225 North Ave
6.	...1826 Tibbets Rd	1826 Tibetts Rd
7.	...603 N Division St	603 N Division St
8.	...2304 Manhattan Ave	2034 Manhattan Ave
9.	...Worcester MA 01610	Worcester ME 01610
10.	...1186 Vernon Drive	1186 Vernon Drive
11.	...209 Peter Bont Rd	209 Peter Bent Rd
12.	...Miamia Beach FL 33139	Miamia Beach Fl 33193
13.	...1100 West Ave	1100 East Ave
14.	...2063 Winyah Ter	2036 Winyah Ter
15.	...3483 Suncrest Ave	3483 Suncrest Dr
16.	...234 Rochambeau Rd	234 Roshambeau Rd
17.	...306 N Terrace Blvd	306 N Terrace Blvd
18.	...1632 Paine St	1632 Pain St
19.	...Palm Springs Ca 92262	Palm Spring CA 92262
20.	...286 Marietta Ave	286 Marrietta Ave
21.	...2445 Pigott Rd	2445 Pigott Rd
22.	...2204 PineBrook Blvd	2204 Pinebrook Blvd
23.	...Buffalo NY 42113	Buffulo NY 42113
24.	...487 Warburton Ave	487 Warburton Ave
25.	...9386 North St	9386 North Ave

13

26.	…2272 Glandale Rd	2772 Glandale Rd
27.	…9236 Puritan Dr	9236 Puritan Pl
28.	…Watertown MA 02172	Watertown MA 02172
29.	…7803 Kendale Ave	7803 Kendall Ave
30.	…1362 Colonial Pkwy	1362 Colonial Pkwy
31.	…115 Rolling Hills Rd	115 Rolling Hills Rd
32.	…218 Rockledge Rd	2181 Rockledge Rd
33.	…8346 N Broadway	8346 W Broadway
34.	…West Chester PA 19380	West Chester PA 19830
35.	…9224 Highland Way	9244 Highland Way
36.	…8383 Mamaroneck Ave	8383 Mamaroneck Ave
37.	…276 Furnace Dock Rd	276 Furnace Dock Rd
38.	…4137 Lockerman St	4137 Lockermann St
39.	…532 Broadhollow Rd	532 Broadhollow Rd
40.	…Sunrise FL 33313	Sunrise FL 33133
41.	…148 Cortlandt Rd	148 Cortland Rd
42.	…5951 W Hartsdale Rd	5951 W Hartsdale Ave
43.	…5231 Alta Vista Cir	5321 Alta Vista Cir
44.	…6459 Chippewa Rd	6459 Chippewa Rd
45.	…1171 S Highland Rd	1771 S Highland Rd
46.	…Dover DE 19901	Dover DL 19901
47.	…2363 Old Farm Ln	2363 Old Farm Ln
48.	…1001 Hemingway Dr	1001 Hemmingway Dr
49.	…1555 Morningside Ave	1555 Mourningside Ave
50.	…Purchase NY 10577	Purchase NY 10577

51.	...1189 E 9th St	1189 E 9th St
52.	...168 Old Lyme Rd	186 Old Lyme Rd
53.	...106 Notingham Rd	106 Nottingham Rd
54.	...1428 Midland Ave	1428 Midland Ave
55.	...Elmhurst NY 11373	Elmherst NY 11373
56.	...1450 East Chester Pike	1450 East Chester Pike
57.	...3357 NW Main St	3357 NE Main St
58.	...5062 Marion Ave	5062 Marian Ave
59.	...1890 NE 3rd St	1980 NE 3rd St
60.	...Wilmington DE 19810	Wilmington DE 19810
61.	...1075 Central Parke West	1075 Central Park West
62.	...672 Bacon Hill Rd	672 Beacon Hill Rd
63.	...1725 W 17th St	1725 W 17th St
64.	...Bronxville NY 10708	Bronxville NJ 10708
65.	...2066 Old Wilmot Rd	2066 Old Wilmont Rd
66.	...3333 S State St	3333 S State St
67.	...1483 Meritoria Dr	1438 Meritoria Dr
68.	...2327 E 23rd St	2327 E 23rd St
69.	...Baltimore MD 21215	Baltimore MD 21215
70.	...137 Clarence rd	137 Claremont Rd
71.	...3516 N Ely Ave	3516 N Ely Ave
72.	...111 Beechwood St	1111 Beechwood St
73.	...143 N Hayward Ave	143 N Hayward Ave
74.	...Miami Beach FL 33179	Miami FL 33179
75.	...6430 Spring Mill Rd	6340 Spring Mill Rd

13

76.	…1416 87th Ave	1416 78th Ave
77.	…4204 S Lexington Ave	4204 Lexington Ave
78.	…3601 Clarks Lane	3601 Clark Lane
79.	…Indianapolis IN 46260	Indianapolis IN 46260
80.	…4256 Fairfield Ave	4256 Fairfield Ave
81.	…Jamaica NY 11435	Jamiaca NY 11435
82.	…1809 83rd St	1809 83rd St
83.	…3288 Page Ct	3288 Paige Ct
84.	…2436 S Broadway	2436 S Broadway
85.	…6309 The Green	6309 The Green
86.	…Kew Gardens NY 11415	Kew Garden NY 11415
87.	…4370 W 158th St	4370 W 158th St
88.	…4263 3rd Ave	4623 3rd Ave
89.	…1737 Fisher Ave	1737 Fischer Ave
90.	…Bronx NY 10475	Bronx NY 10475
91.	…5148 West End Ave	5184 West End Ave
92.	…1011 Ocean Ave	1011 Ocean Ave
93.	…1593 Webster Dr	1593 Webster Dr
94.	…Darien CT 06820	Darien CT 06820
95.	…1626 E 115th St	1662 E 115th St

Answers

1.	A	26.	D	51.	A
2.	D	27.	D	52.	D
3.	D	28.	A	53.	D
4.	A	29.	D	54.	A
5.	D	30.	A	55.	D
6.	D	31.	A	56.	A
7.	A	32.	D	57.	D
8.	D	33.	D	58.	D
9.	D	34.	D	59.	D
10.	A	35.	D	60.	A
11.	D	36.	A	61.	D
12.	D	37.	A	62.	D
13.	D	38.	D	63.	A
14.	D	39.	A	64.	D
15.	D	40.	D	65.	D
16.	D	41.	D	66.	A
17.	A	42.	D	67.	D
18.	D	43.	D	68.	D
19.	D	44.	A	69.	A
20.	D	45.	D	70.	D
21.	A	46.	D	71.	A
22.	D	47.	A	72.	D
23.	D	48.	D	73.	A
24.	A	49.	D	74.	D
25.	D	50.	A	75.	D
76.	D	83.	D	90.	A
77.	D	84.	A	91.	D
78.	D	85.	A	92.	A
79.	A	86.	D	93.	A
80.	A	87.	A	94.	A
81.	D	88.	D	95.	D
82.	A	89.	D		

Practice Test 2

> **DIRECTIONS:** For each question, compare the address in the left column with the address in the right column. If the two addresses are *alike* in every way, write A next to the question number. If the two addresses are *different* in any way, write D next to the question number.

1.	...7399 NW Candleworth Dr	7399 NW Candleworth Dr
2.	...New Castle AL 35119	New Castle AL 35119
3.	...2098 NE Catalpa Ln	2098 NW Catalpa Ln
4.	...17001 NE Rappaix Court	17001 NE Rappaix Court
5.	...10091 NE Larryvale Rd	10091 NE Larryville Rd
6.	...2896 NE Wallaston Way	2896 NE Walleston Way
7.	...Timonium MD 21093	Timanium MD 21093
8.	...7749 NW Barracuda Cove Ct	7749 NW Barracuda Cove Ct
9.	...6099 NW Atterbury Rd	6099 NW Atterbury Dr
10.	...2198 NE Springs St	2198 NW Springs St
11.	...6089 SE Flintshire Rd	6089 SW Flintshire Rd
12.	...13111 SE Throgmorton Ct	13111 SE Throgmorton Ct
13.	...Estacada OR 97023	Estacada OK 97023
14.	...5301 NE Monocacy Cir	5301 NE Monocacy Ct
15.	...6066 NW Schissler Ave	6606 NW Schissler Ave
16.	...1915 NE Chapletowne Cir	1915 NE Chapeltowne Cir
17.	...4505 NE Reisterstown Plaza	4505 NE Reisterstown Plaza
18.	...3399 NW Ivydene Ter	3399 NW Ivydene Trl
19.	...8605 Commanche Ave	8605 Commanche Ave
20.	...Winnemucca NV 89445	Winnemocca NV 89445
21.	...467 SE Chatterleigh Cir	467 SE Chatterleigh Cir
22.	...3300 SE Golupski Rd	3300 SE Golpski Rd
23.	...4884 NW Farmvale Ave	4884 NW Farmdale Ave
24.	...Kalamazoo MI 49009	Kalamazoo MI 49009
25.	...11676 SE Harryweiss Rd	11676 SE Harrywise Rd

26.	...4395 Auchentoroly Ter	4395 Auchentoroly Ter
27.	...11321 NE Pageland Rd	11321 NE Pageland Rd
28.	...2488 Jeannett Ave	2488 Jeannett Ave
29.	...1900 Gilford Ter	1900 Gulford Ter
30.	...5177 NE Bridgehampton Dr	5177 NE Bridgehampton Dr
31.	...7333 Martingale Ave	7333 Martingale Ave
32.	...11577 Delagrange Way	11571 Delagrange Way
33.	...13852 NE 68th Ave	13852 NE 86th Ave
34.	...11736 NE Uffington Rd	17736 NE Uffington Rd
35.	...21199 NW Huntington Ave	21199 NW Huntingdon Ave
36.	...Merriweather NY 11548	Merriweather NY 11548
37.	...11001 NE Cedarcrest Rd	11001 NE Cedarchest Rd
38.	...3569 NE Tazewell Rd	3569 NE Tazewell Rd
39.	...5297 Popperdam Creek	5297 Pepperdam Creek
40.	...2288 Dundawan Rd	2288 Dundawan Rd
41.	...17299 Rhuddlan Rd	17299 Rhuddlan Rd
42.	...37719 Underwood Ct	37719 Underwood Cir
43.	...22700 S Strathdale Rd	22700 S Strathdale Rd
44.	...Homeworth OH 44634	Homeworth OH 46434
45.	...3727 NW Ayleshire Rd	3727 NE Ayleshire Rd
46.	...4585 E Englemeade Ave	4585 E Englemeade Ave
47.	...37741 NE Jacqueline Ln	34771 NE Jacqueline Ln
48.	...3800 N Grinnalds Ave	3800 N Grinnalds St
49.	...10990 NE Kennicott Rd	10990 NE Kenningcott Rd
50.	...Vanderpool TX 78885	Vanderpool TX 78885

13

51. …11799 NE Brattel Rd   11799 NE Brattle Rd

52. …2196 Leadenhall Court   2196 Leadenhall Court

53. …Albuquerque NM 87109   Albuquerque NM 81709

54. …3789 Featherstone Ln   8789 Featherstone Ln

55. …18076 Martinque Rd   18076 Martinque Ct

56. …60111 Debonair Ct   6011 Debonair Ct

57. …4131 NE Tussock Rd   4131 NE Tussock Road

58. …299 Susquehanna Ave E   299 Susquehanna Ave W

59. …53116 NE T Avenue   53116 NE T Avenue

60. …16917 Saint Elmo Ave   16917 Saint Almo Ave

61. …10401 Olde Georgetown Rd SE 10401 Old Georgetown Rd SE

62. …7550 Wisconsin Ave   7550 Wisconsin St

63. …8054 Aberdeen Rd   8054 Aberdeen Rd

64. …Wheelersburg KY 41473   Wheelersburg KY 41473

65. …3138 Edgemere Ave   3138 Edgemore Ave

66. …11595 Heathcliff Dr   11595 Heathcliff Dr

67. …13531 N Keutel Rd   13531 N Kratel Rd

68. …7585 Breezewick Cir   78575 Breezewick Cir

69. …15530 NE Jimrowe Cir   15530 NE Jimrowe Ct

70. …2001 Quantico Way   2001 Guantico Way

71. …8899 Randolph Springs Pl   8899 Rudolph Springs Pl

72. …4010 Oakleigh Beach Rd   4010 Oakleigh Beach Rd

73. …3977 McTeague Ave   3977 McTeague Ave

74. …13827 N Lavington Pl   13827 N Lavingston Pl

75. …17390 Youngstown Ave NE   17390 Youngstown Ave SE

76.	…15999 Brookview Ave	15999 Brookview Ave
77.	…12733 NE 88th Ave	1273 NE 88th Ave
78.	…PO Box 34001	PO Box 34007
79.	…Selinsgrove PA 17870	Selingrove PA 17870
80.	…3425 Chelmareford Trl	3245 Chelmareford Trl
81.	…6080 Knickerbocker Cir	6080 Knickerbocker Dr
82.	…1700 Alconbury Rd	1700 Alconbury Rd
83.	…2620 Winnettka St	2620 Winnettka St
84.	…2367 Essextowne Cir	2367 Essextowne Cir
85.	…3588 Investment Pl	3588 Investment Pl
86.	…11888 Margarette Ave	11888 Margaretta Ave
87.	…4756 Ridervale Rd	4756 Riderview Rd
88.	…16491 Zeppelin Ave	16491 Zepperlin Ave
89.	…10195 Highway 210 N	10195 Highway 201 N
90.	…11811 Vailthorn Ln	11181 Vailthorn Ln
91.	…7299 E 41st St	7299 W 41st St
92.	…PO Box 30399	PO Box 30399
93.	…4710 Bethesda Ave N	4710 Bethesda Blvd N
94.	…Waynesboro MS 39367	Waynesboro MN 39367
95.	…99 NW M Street	99 NW M Street

13

Answers

1.	A	34.	D	67.	D
2.	A	35.	D	68.	D
3.	D	36.	A	69.	D
4.	A	37.	D	70.	D
5.	D	38.	A	71.	D
6.	D	39.	D	72.	A
7.	D	40.	A	73.	A
8.	A	41.	A	74.	D
9.	D	42.	D	75.	D
10.	D	43.	A	76.	A
11.	D	44.	D	77.	D
12.	A	45.	D	78.	D
13.	D	46.	A	79.	D
14.	D	47.	D	80.	D
15.	D	48.	D	81.	D
16.	D	49.	D	82.	A
17.	A	50.	A	83.	A
18.	D	51.	D	84.	A
19.	A	52.	A	85.	A
20.	D	53.	D	86.	D
21.	A	54.	D	87.	D
22.	D	55.	D	88.	D
23.	D	56.	D	89.	D
24.	A	57.	D	90.	D
25.	D	58.	D	91.	D
26.	A	59.	A	92.	A
27.	A	60.	D	93.	D
28.	A	61.	D	94.	D
29.	D	62.	D	95.	A
30.	A	63.	A		
31.	A	64.	A		
32.	D	65.	D		
33.	D	66.	A		

Practice Test 3

DIRECTIONS: For each question, compare the address in the left column with the address in the right column. If the two addresses are *alike* in every way, write A next to the question number. If the two addresses are *different* in any way, write D next to the question number.

1.	…14319 Edmund Park	14319 Edmound Park
2.	…34038 Princeton Rd	34038 Princetown Rd
3.	…578 George Washington Blvd	5788 George Washington Blvd
4.	…222390 W Paramus Rd	22390 E Paramus Rd
5.	…3300 W 11th Ave	3300 W 11th Ave
6.	…Calumet NY 14424	Calumet NY 14424
7.	…18450 Tanglewood Park	18450 Tangelwood Park
8.	…46325 Ceder Dr	46235 Cedar Dr
9.	…43961 Hathway Ave	43691 Hathway Ave
10.	…11236 Piermont Ln	11236 Piermount Ln
11.	…14002 Phelps Gardens	1402 Phelps Gardens
12.	…31335 Cloverdell Dr	31335 Cloverdale Dr
13.	…12305 NE Iris Ave	12305 NE Iris Ave
14.	…1608 Ackerman Rd	1608 Ackerman Rd
15.	…Canterbury VA 23480	Canterberry VA 23480
16.	…38001 E Catalpa Cir	38001 E Catalpa Ct
17.	…13872 E Kennedy Rd	13872 E Kennedy Rd
18.	…23531 Dryden Ave NE	23531 Dryden Ave NW
19.	…44615 Arrowhead Trl	44615 Arrowhead Trl
20.	…633 N Wiedeman Pl	633 N Wiedeman Pl
21.	…24609 Bergen Ter	24609 Bergen Park
22.	…11001 N Mayer Ave	10001 N Mayer Ave
23.	…35617 Shafer Blvd	35716 Shafer Blvd
24.	…98 South Christie Rd	98 South Christie Rd
25.	…19615 Midland Park	19615 Midland Pky

13

26.	…13444 Kenwood Way	13444 Kenwood Way
27.	…16567 Marsellus Rd	16567 Marsellos Rd
28.	…14726 N Falcon Park	14726 S Falcon Park
29.	…5071 E Anna Dr	5071 E Anna Dr
30.	…5304 SE Melba St	5304 SE Melba St
31.	…Victory PR 00802	Victory PR 00802
32.	…89925 Northgate Cir	89925 Northgate Dr
33.	…31011 Van Riper Park A	31011 Van Riper Park B
34.	…12306 Winding Rd	12306 Winding St
35.	…1991 McKinley Rd	1991 MacKinley Rd
36.	…34201 W Zanoni Ave	34201 W Zanoni Ave
37.	…11367 Werimus Ln	11367 Weirimus Ln
38.	…41235 N Adams Ave	41235 N Addams Ave
39.	…21003 NE Vernal Wood Blvd	21003 NE Vernal Woods Blvd
40.	…55450 S Anderson Dr	55440 S Anderson Dr
41.	…22100 College Rd	22100 College Rd
42.	…4434 N Crabtree Pl	4434 N Crabtree Ln
43.	…12807 Cleenput Pky	12087 Cleanput Pky
44.	…21756 Shetland Dr	21756 Shetland Dr
45.	…Shepherd MI 49964	Shepperd MI 49964
46.	…16735 De Burg Ln	16735 De Berg Ln
47.	…1329 La Place Ave	1329 La Place Ave
48.	…10154 Oakdene Rd	10154 Oakdene Rd
49.	…9867 NE Virgil Ct	9867 NE Virgil Ct
50.	…16089 Mansfield Cir	16089 Mansfield Dr

51.	...12196 SE Perryland Pl	12196 SE Perryland Pl
52.	...7800 SE Nielsen Way	7800 SE Nielsen Way
53.	...30697 Horseshoe Dr	30997 Horseshoe Dr
54.	...2200 Wakalee Rd	2200 Wakalea Rd
55.	...9901 Winterburn Dr	9901 Winterburn Dr
56.	...4201 Cadmus Ln	4201 Cadmus Ln
57.	...1366 Van Winkele Ave NE	1366 Van Winkle Ave NE
58.	...6377 Andover Ct NE	6377 Andover Cir NE
59.	...12397 Summer Ln NW	12397 Sumner Ln NW
60.	...4400 Donnybrook Ave SE	4400 Donnybrook Ave SE
61.	...5263 Whelah W	5263 Whelah W
62.	...7567 Vista Terra Dr NW	7567 Vista Terra Dr NW
63.	...1190 Rodgers Dr SE	1190 Rogers Dr SE
64.	...1107 NE Katherine Cir	1107 NE Katherine Cir
65.	...11300 Lincoln Central Ave	11300 Lincoln Center Ave
66.	...11205 James Hanson Cir	11205 Hamson Cir
67.	...3388 Campbell Ave	3388 Campbell St
68.	...4056 Lindbergh Ln NW	4056 Lindbergh Ln SW
69.	...Stratton OH 45624	Stratton OH 45642
70.	...1257 McLester Ave	1257 McLeister Ave
71.	...2697 Clemency Ave NW	2697 Clemency Ave NW
72.	...3401 East Gertrude Rd	3401 East Gertrude Rd
73.	...801 Krakow Ln	801 Krakow Ln
74.	...9795 NE 19th Avenue	9795 NW 19th Avenue
75.	...PO Box 32001	PO Box 32081

13

76.	...11299 Carsam Ct SE	11929 Carsame Ct SE
77.	...1800 Haviland Ave NW	1800 Haviland St NW
78.	...25011 Fabyan Pl NW	25011 Fabian Pl NW
79.	...5700 Torbush Pky NW	5700 Torbush Pky NW
80.	...999 Tip Top Ave SE	999 Tip Top Ave SW
81.	...1166 Colfax Ave SE	1166 Colfax Ave SE
82.	...7766 Buchanan Trl	7766 Buchanan Trl
83.	...Fort Dentton WA 98494	Fort Denton WA 98494
84.	...1155 Burchfiled Cir NW	1155 Birchfield Cir NW
85.	...3477 Winfield Ave NE	3477 Winfield St NE
86.	...25501 Dewitt Ct SE	2501 Dewitt Ct SE
87.	...33089 Hemlock St NW	33909 Hemlock St NW
88.	...5500 Aberdeen Dr NW	5500 Aberdeen Cir NW
89.	...2203 Warwick Pl SE	2203 Warwick Pl NE
90.	...11449 Ramapo Ter	11449 Ramapo Ter
91.	...9903 Georgetown Rd S	9903 Georgetown Rd S
92.	...13468 Rutgers Ave	13486 Rutgers Ave
93.	...Arnet AK 99681	Arnet AR 99681
94.	...500 Nomahagen Church Rd	500 Nomahegan Church Rd
95.	...3577 Watchung Ct NW	3577 Watchung St NW

Answers

1.	D	34.	D	67.	D
2.	D	35.	D	68.	D
3.	D	36.	A	69.	D
4.	D	37.	D	70.	D
5.	A	38.	D	71.	A
6.	A	39.	D	72.	A
7.	D	40.	D	73.	A
8.	D	41.	A	74.	D
9.	D	42.	D	75.	D
10.	D	43.	D	76.	D
11.	D	44.	A	77.	D
12.	D	45.	D	78.	D
13.	A	46.	D	79.	A
14.	A	47.	A	80.	D
15.	D	48.	A	81.	A
16.	D	49.	A	82.	A
17.	A	50.	D	83.	D
18.	D	51.	A	84.	D
19.	A	52.	A	85.	D
20.	A	53.	D	86.	D
21.	D	54.	D	87.	D
22.	D	55.	A	88.	D
23.	D	56.	A	89.	D
24.	A	57.	D	90.	A
25.	D	58.	D	91.	A
26.	A	59.	D	92.	D
27.	D	60.	A	93.	D
28.	D	61.	A	94.	D
29.	A	62.	A	95.	D
30.	A	63.	D		
31.	A	64.	A		
32.	D	65.	D		
33.	D	66.	D		

13

The Hour in Review

1. In this hour, you took three practice Address Checking tests to reinforce the techniques that you learned for answering this question type.

2. These untimed practice tests will prepare you for the timed tests that follow in the next hour.

3. Use the practice tests to pinpoint any weaknesses you still have with this question type and then review the appropriate materials.

HOUR **14**

Address Checking— Timed Tests

What You Will Learn in This Hour

In this hour, you'll use the techniques that you've learned to take three timed Address Checking tests. These tests will help you get used to working under the timed conditions of the actual test. Here are your goals for this hour:

- Understand your goals for taking the timed practice tests.
- Complete three practice Address Checking tests under timed exam conditions.
- Check your answers, determine your raw score, and determine if you need to review.

Preparing for the Timed Practice Tests

This hour provides your first real chance to answer Address Checking questions under the time constraints of the actual test. You should concentrate on answering the questions accurately while working quickly, using all the techniques that you've learned so far. To get the most benefit from this practice, follow these steps:

1. Choose a workspace that is quiet, well-lit, clean, and uncluttered.

2. Use a stopwatch to accurately time each test.

3. Start the first test at a convenient time and stop exactly when the six minutes are up.

4. Give yourself at least a five-minute breather between each test. You can use this nontest time to skim through the material in Hour 4, "Address Checking—1," and Hour 5, "Address Checking—2," if needed, or just take a break.

5. Complete all three tests before checking your answers against the answer keys provided. Circle all the questions that you missed.

6. Calculate your raw score for each test.

7. Determine where your scores fall on the self-evaluation chart; if you receive less than an excellent score on any test, review Hours 4 and 5.

8. Retake the appropriate tests to see your improvement.

Remember, don't get discouraged if you can't answer all 95 questions in six minutes. You're not expected to.

Tip
Try taking the tests in this hour without rereading the directions in order not to waste time. However, if you can't remember the directions, review them to avoid hurting your score.

Practice Test 1

DIRECTIONS: For each question, compare the address in the left column with the address in the right column. If the two addresses are *alike* in every way, write A next to the question number. If the two addresses are *different* in any way, write D next to the question number. You will have six minutes to complete the test.

1.	...1897 Smicksburg Rd	1897 Smithsburg Rd
2.	...3609 E Paseo Aldeano	3909 E Paseo Aldeano
3.	...11787 Ornamental Ln	1787 Ornamental Ln
4.	...1096 Camino Grande E	1096 Camino Grande E
5.	...2544 E Radcliff Ave	2544 E Redcliff Ave
6.	...5796 E Narragansett Dr	5796 E Narragasett Dr
7.	...12475 Ebbtide Way W	12475 Ebbtide Way W
8.	...14396 N Via Armando	14396 S Via Armando
9.	...2155 S Del Giorgio Rd	2155 S Del Giorgio Rd
10.	...16550 Bainbridge Cir	16505 Bainbridge Cir
11.	...1826 Milneburg Rd	1826 Milneburg St
12.	...Eureka KS 67045	Eureka KY 67045
13.	...4010 Glenaddie Ave	4010 Glenaddie Ave
14.	...13501 Stratford Rd	13501 Standford Rd
15.	...3296 W 64th St	3296 E 64th St
16.	...2201 Tennessee Cir	2201 Tennessee Cir
17.	...1502 Avenue M NE	1502 Avenue N NE
18.	...1096 SE Longrone Dr	1096 SE Longrone Dr
19.	...1267 Darthmouth Ct	1267 Darthmont Ct
20.	...825 Ophanage Rd	825 Ophanage Rd
21.	...1754 Golden Springs Rd	1754 Golden Springs Road
22.	...1015 Tallwoods Ln	1015 Tallwoods Ln
23.	...1097 Lambada Dr	1097 Lambadd Dr
24.	...Vredenburgh AL 36481	Verdenburgh AL 36481
25.	...1800 Monticello Ave	1800 Monticello Ave
26.	...1723 Yellowbird Ln	1723 Yellowbird Ct
27.	...700 Valca Materials Rd	700 Valca Materials Rd
28.	...1569 Ladywood Ln N	1569 Ladywood Ln W

14

29.	...3256 Interurban Dr	3256 Interurban Dr
30.	...1507 Haughton Cir	1507 Haughton Ct
31.	...8971 Robertson Ave	8971 Robinson Ave
32.	...3801 NE 49th Street	3801 NW 49th Street
33.	...4102 Chalkville Rd	4102 Chalkview Rd
34.	...1709 Ingersoll Cir	1709 Ingersoll Cir
35.	...6800 N Nantucket Ln	6800 N Nantucket Ln
36.	...12401 Tarrymore Dr	12401 Terrymore Dr
37.	...1097 Huntsville Ave	1097 Huntsville Ave
38.	...3566 Lornaridge Pl	3566 Lornaridge Pl
39.	...2039 Klondike Ave SW	2039 Klondie Ave SW
40.	...3267 Mayland Ln	3267 Maryland Ln
41.	...12956 Strawberry Ln	12596 Strawberry Ln
42.	...De Armanville AL 36257	De Armanville AL 36257
43.	...6015 Anniston Dr	6015 Anneston Dr
44.	...1525 E 90th St	1525 E 90th St
45.	...1299 Chappaque Rd	1266 Chappaque Rd
46.	...2156 Juliette Dr	2156 Juliaetta Dr
47.	...999 N Hollingsworth St	999 S Hollingsworth St
48.	...16901 Odum Crest Ln	19601 Odum Crest Ln
49.	...9787 Zellmark Dr	9787 Zealmark Dr
50.	...11103 NE Feasell Ave	11103 NE Feasell Ave
51.	...51121 N Mattison Rd	51121 S Mattison Rd
52.	...8326 Blackjack Ln	8326 Blackjack Blvd
53.	...18765 Lagarde Ave	18765 Lagrande Ave
54.	...11297 Gallatin Ln	11297 Gallatin Ln
55.	...Wormleysburg PA 17043	Wormleysburg PA 17043
56.	...22371 N Sprague Ave	22371 S Sprague Ave
57.	...15014 Warrior River Rd	15014 Warrior River Rd
58.	...45721 Hueytown Plaza	45721 Hueytowne Plaza
59.	...8973 Tedescki Dr	8793 Tedescki Dr
60.	...12995 Raimond Muscoda Pl	12995 Raimont Muscoda Pl
61.	...Phippsburg CO 80469	Phippsburg CA 80469
62.	...52003 W 49th Ave	52003 W 46th Ave
63.	...17201 Zenobia Cir	17210 Zenobia Cir

64.	...4800 Garrison Cir	4800 Garrison Dr
65.	...Los Angeles CA 90070	Los Angeles CA 90076
66.	...14798 W 62nd Ave	14198 W 62nd Ave
67.	...7191 E Eldridge Way	7191 E Eldridge Way
68.	...1279 S Quintard Dr	1279 S Guintard Dr
69.	...21899 Dellwood Ave	21899 Dillwood Ave
70.	...7191 Zenophone Cir	7191 Zenohone Cir
71.	...4301 Los Encinos Way	4301 Los Encinas Way
72.	...19700 Ostronic Dr NW	19700 Ostronic Dr NE
73.	...23291 Van Velsire Dr	23219 Van Velsire Dr
74.	...547 Paradise Valley Rd	547 Paradise Valley Ct
75.	...23167 Saltillo Ave	23167 Santillo Ave
76.	...43001 Mourning Dove Way	43001 Mourning Dove Way
77.	...21183 Declaration Ave	21183 Declaration Ave
78.	...10799 Via Sierra Ramal Ave	10799 Via Sierra Ramel Ave
79.	...16567 Hermosillia Ct	16597 Hermosillia Ct
80.	...Villamont VA 24178	Villamont VA 24178
81.	...18794 Villaboso Ave	18794 Villeboso Ave
82.	...24136 Ranthom Ave	24136 Ranthon Ave
83.	...13489 Golondrina Pl	13489 Golondrina St
84.	...6598 Adamsville Ave	6598 Adamsville Ave
85.	...12641 Indals Pl NE	12641 Indals Pl NW
86.	...19701 SE 2nd Avenue	19701 NE 2nd Avenue
87.	...22754 Cachalote Ln	22754 Cachalott Ln
88.	...12341 Kingfisher Rd	12341 Kingsfisher Rd
89.	...24168 Lorenzana Dr	24168 Lorenzano Dr
90.	...32480 Blackfriar Rd	32480 Blackfriar Rd
91.	...16355 Wheeler Dr	16355 Wheelen Dr
92.	...5100 Magna Carta Rd	5100 Magna Certa Rd
93.	...2341 N Federalist Pl	2341 N Federalist Pl
94.	...22200 Timpangos Rd	22200 Timpangos Rd
95.	...19704 Calderon Rd	19704 Calderon Rd

14

Practice Test 2

DIRECTIONS: For each question, compare the address in the left column with the address in the right column. If the two addresses are *alike* in every way, write A next to the question number. If the two addresses are *different* in any way, write D next to the question number. You will have six minutes to complete the test.

1.	…4623 Grand Concourse	4623 Grand Concourse
2.	…6179 Ridgecroft Rd	6719 Ridgecroft Rd
3.	…5291 Hanover Cir	5291 Hangover Cir
4.	…2333 Palmer Ave	233 Palmer Ave
5.	…1859 SE 148th St	1859 SE 148th St
6.	…Dowagiac MI 49047	Dowagiac MI 49047
7.	…4147 Wykagyl Terr	4147 Wykagyl Terr
8.	…1504 N 10th Ave	1504 N 10th St
9.	…2967 Montross Ave	2967 Montrose Ave
10.	…Chicago IL 60601	Chicago IL 60601
11.	…2073 Defoe Ct	2073 Defoe Ct
12.	…2433 Westchester Plz	2343 Westchester Plz
13.	…6094 Carpenter Ave	6094 Charpenter Ave
14.	…5677 Bolman Twrs	5677 Bolman Twrs
15.	…Chappaqua NY 10514	Chappaqua NY 10541
16.	…3428 Constantine Ave	3248 Constantine Ave
17.	…847 S 147th Rd	847 S 147th Rd
18.	…6676 Harwood Ct	6676 Hardwood Ct
19.	…3486 Mosholu Pky	3486 Mosholu Pkwy
20.	…Mindenmines MO 64769	Mindenmines MO 64679
21.	…816 Oscawana Lake Rd	816 Ocsawana Lake Rd
22.	…9159 Battle Hill Rd	9195 Battle Hill Rd
23.	…7558 Winston Ln	7558 Winston Ln
24.	…3856 W 385th St	3856 W 386th St
25.	…3679 W Alpine Pl	3679 W Alpine Pl
26.	…Hartford CT 06115	Hartford CN 06115
27.	…6103 Locust Hill Wy	6013 Locust Hill Wy

28.	...4941 Annrock Dr	4941 Annrock Dr
29.	...2018 N St Andrews Pl	2018 N St Andrews Pl
30.	...8111 Drewville Rd	8111 Drewsville Rd
31.	...463 Peaceable Hill Rd	463 Peaceable Hill Rd
32.	...Biloxi MS 39532	Biloxi MS 39532
33.	...3743 Point Dr S	3734 Point Dr S
34.	...5665 Barnington Rd	5665 Barnington Rd
35.	...2246 E Sheldrake Ave	2246 W Sheldrake Ave
36.	...1443 Bloomingdale Rd	1443 Bloomingdales Rd
37.	...2064 Chalford Ln	2064 Chalford Ln
38.	...McMinnville OR 97128	McMinville OR 97128
39.	...6160 Shadybrook Ln	6160 Shadybrook Ln
40.	...2947 E Lake Blvd	2947 E Lake Blvd
41.	...3907 Evergreen Row	3907 Evergreen Row
42.	...2192 SE Hotel Dr	2192 SE Hotel Dr
43.	...8844 Fremont St	8844 Fremont Rd
44.	...8487 Wolfshead Rd	8487 Wolfshead Rd
45.	...Anamosa IA 52205	Anamoosa IA 52205
46.	...4055 Katonah Ave	4055 Katonah Ave
47.	...1977 Buckingham Apts	1979 Buckingham Apts
48.	...983 W 139th Way	983 W 139th Wy
49.	...7822 Bayliss Ln	7822 Bayliss Ln
50.	...8937 Banksville Rd	8937 Banksville Rd
51.	...4759 Strathmore Rd	4579 Strathmore Rd
52.	...2221 E Main St	221 E Main St
53.	...South Orange NJ 07079	South Orange NJ 07079
54.	...4586 Sylvia Wy	4586 Sylvan Wy
55.	...6335 Soundview Ave	6335 SoundView Ave
56.	...3743 Popham Rd	3743 Poppam Rd
57.	...2845 Brookfield Dr	2485 Brookfield Dr
58.	...3845 Fort Slocum Rd	3845 Fort Slocum St
59.	...9268 Jochum Ave	9268 Jochum Ave
60.	...Bloomington MN 55437	Bloomington MN 54537
61.	...6903 S 184th St	6903 S 184th St

14

62.	...7486 Rossmor Rd	7486 Rosemor Rd
63.	...4176 Whitlockville Rd	4176 Whitlockville Wy
64.	...4286 Megquire Ln	4286 Megquire Ln
65.	...6270 Tamarock Rd	6270 Tammarock Rd
66.	...3630 Bulkley Mnr	3630 Bulkley Mnr
67.	...7158 Scarswold Apts	7185 Scarswold Apts
68.	...Brooklyn NY 11218	Brooklyn NY 11128
69.	...9598 Prince Edward Rd	9598 Prince Edward Rd
70.	...8439 S 145th St	8439 S 154th St
71.	...9795 Shady Glen Ct	9795 Shady Grove Ct
72.	...7614 Ganung St	7614 Ganung St
73.	...Teaneck NJ 07666	Teaneck NH 07666
74.	...6359 Dempster Rd	6359 Dumpster Rd
75.	...1065 Colchester Hl	1065 Colchester Hl
76.	...5381 Phillipse Pl	5381 Philipse Pl
77.	...6484 Rochester Terr	6484 Rochester Terr
78.	...2956 Quinin St	2956 Quinin St
79.	...Tarzana CA 91356	Tarzana CA 91536
80.	...7558 Winston Ln	7558 Whinston Ln
81.	...1862 W 293rd St	1862 W 393rd St
82.	...8534 S Huntington Ave	8534 N Huntington Ave
83.	...9070 Wild Oaks Vlg	9070 Wild Oakes Vlg
84.	...4860 Smadbeck Ave	4680 Smadbeck Ave
85.	...8596 E Commonwealth Ave	8596 E Commonwealth Ave
86.	...Ridgefield NJ 07657	Ridgefield NJ 07657
87.	...1478 Charter Cir	1478 W Charter Cir
88.	...3963 Priscilla Ave	3963 Pricsilla Ave
89.	...4897 Winding Ln	4897 Winding Ln
90.	...847 Windmill Terr	847 Windmill Terr
91.	...1662 Wixon St W	1662 Wixon St W
92.	...West Hartford CT 06107	West Hartford CT 06107
93.	...6494 Rochelle Terr	9464 Rochelle Terr
94.	...4228 Pocantico Rd	4228 Pocantico Rd
95.	...1783 S 486th Ave	1783 S 486th Ave

Practice Test 3

DIRECTIONS: For each question, compare the address in the left column with the address in the right column. If the two addresses are *alike* in every way, write A next to the question number. If the two addresses are *different* in any way, write D next to the question number. You will have six minutes to complete the test.

1.	…1038 Nutgrove St	1038 Nutgrove St
2.	…4830 Schroeder Ave	4380 Schroeder Ave
3.	…2343 Martine Ave	2343 Martini Ave
4.	…Winkelman AZ 85292	Winkelman AZ 85292
5.	…298 Chatterton Pky	298 Chatterton Pky
6.	…3798 Hillandale Ave	3798 Hillanddale Ave
7.	…7683 Fountain Pl	7863 Fountain Pl
8.	…1862 W 164th St	1864 W 164th St
9.	…Scarborough NY 10510	Scarbourough NY 10510
10.	…1734 N Highland Ave	1734 W Highland Ave
11.	…1385 Queens Blvd	1385 Queens Blvd
12.	…6742 Mendota Ave	6742 Mendota Ave
13.	…8496 E 245th St	8496 E 254th St
14.	…2010 Wyndcliff Rd	2010 Wyndecliff Rd
15.	…4098 Gramatan Ave	4098 Gramatan Ave
16.	…Denver CO 80236	Denver CO 80236
17.	…3778 N Broadway	3778 N Broadway
18.	…532 Broadhollow Rd	532 Broadhollow Rd
19.	…1386 Carriage House Ln	1386 Carriage House Ln
20.	…3284 S 10th St	2384 S 10th St
21.	…2666 Dunwoodie Rd	266 Dunwoodie Rd
22.	…Pontiac MI 48054	Pontiac MI 48054
23.	…1080 Nine Acres Ln	1080 Nine Acres Ln
24.	…2699 Quaker Church Rd	2669 Quaker Church Rd
25.	…7232 S 45th Ave	7232 S 45th Ave
26.	…1588 Grand Boulevard	1588 Grand Boulevard
27.	…2093 S Waverly Rd	2093 S Waverley Rd

14

28.	...Las Vegas NV 89112	Las Vegas NM 89112
29.	...116 Cottage Pl Gdns	116 Cottage Pl Gdns
30.	...1203 E Lakeview Ave	1203 E Lakeside Ave
31.	...3446 E Westchester Ave	3446 E Westchester Ave
32.	...7482 Horseshoe Hill Rd	7482 Horseshoe Hill Rd
33.	...Waimanalo HI 96795	Waimanale HI 96795
34.	...9138 McGuire Ave	9138 MacGuire Ave
35.	...7438 Meadway	7348 Meadway
36.	...2510 Maryland Ave NW	2510 Maryland Ave NW
37.	...1085 S 83rd Rd	1085 S 83rd Rd
38.	...5232 Maplewood Wy	523 Maplewood Wy
39.	...Kansas City MO 64108	Kansas City MO 61408
40.	...1063 Valentine Ln	1063 Valentine Ln
41.	...1066 Furnace Dock Rd	1606 Furnace Dock Rd
42.	...2121 Rosedale Rd	2121 Rosedale Rd
43.	...1396 Orawapum St	1396 Orawampum St
44.	...3004 Palisade Ave	3004 Palisades Ave
45.	...1776 Independence St	1776 Independence St
46.	...Canton OH 44707	Canton OH 44707
47.	...1515 Geoga Cir	1515 Geogia Cir
48.	...1583 Central Ave	1583 Central Ave
49.	...4096 Valley Terr	4096 Valley Terr
50.	...2075 Boston Post Rd	2075 Boston Post Rd
51.	...1016 Frost Ln	1016 Frost La
52.	...2186 Ashford Ave	2186 Ashford Ave
53.	...Battle Mountain NV 89820	Battle Mountain NV 89820
54.	...6634 Weber Pl	6634 Webber Pl
55.	...6832 Halycon Terr	6832 Halcyon Terr
56.	...198 Gedney Esplnde	198 Gedney Esplnde
57.	...8954 Horsechestnut Rd	8954 Horsechestnut Rd
58.	...1926 S 283rd Wy	1926 S 283rd Wy
59.	...Hartsdale NY 10530	Hartsdale NY 15030
60.	...1569 Ritchy Pl	1569 Ritchy Pl
61.	...423 S Columbia Ave	423 S Colombia Ave

62.	...2466 Linette Ct	2466 Linnette Ct
63.	...2970 Rockledge Ave	2970 Rockridge Ave
64.	...5764 Guion Blvd	5764 Guion Blvd
65.	...6976 SW 5th Ave	6976 SE 5th Ave
66.	...Milwaukie OR 97222	Milwaukee OR 97222
67.	...2243 Hudson View Ests	2234 Hudson View Ests
68	...7743 S 3rd Ave	7743 S 3rd Ave
69.	...2869 Romaine Ave	2869 Romaine Ave
70.	...2943 Windermere Dr	2943 Windemere Dr
71.	...5117 Balmoral Crsnt	5117 Balmoral Crsnt
72.	...3797 Wappanocca Ave	3797 Wappannocca Ave
73.	...Arkabutla MS 38602	Arkabutla MS 38602
74.	...2275 Greenway Terr	2275 Greenaway Terr
75.	...7153 Taymil Rd	7153 Taymil Rd
76.	...3864 W 248th St	3864 W 284th St
77.	...2032 Central Park S	2023 Central Park S
78.	...1803 Pinewood Rd	1803 Pineywood Rd
79.	...New York NY 10023	New York NY 10023
80.	...1555 E 19th St	1555 E 19th St
81.	...3402 Comer Cir	3402 Comer Ct
82.	...9416 Lakeshore Dr	9416 Lakeshore Dr
83.	...1576 Kimball Ave	1576 Kimbell Ave
84.	...2015 W 51st Ln	2015 W 51st Ln
85.	...Silver Springs NV 89429	Silver Springs NV 89429
86.	...2354 N Washington St	2354 N Washington St
87.	...8528 Convent Pl	8258 Convent Pl
88.	...1911 Downer Ave	1911 Downer Ave
89.	...6108 Woodstock Rd	6108 Woodstock St
90.	...Akron OH 44308	Akron OK 44308
91.	...4548 College Pt Ave	4548 College Pk Ave
92.	...8194 Great Oak Ln	8194 Great Oak Ln
93.	...280 SW Collins Ave	280 SW Collins Ave
94.	...8276 Abbott Mews	8726 Abbott Mews
95.	...4717 Deerfield Blvd	4717 Deerfield Blvd

14

Answers

Practice Test 1

1.	D	34.	A	67.	A
2.	D	35.	A	68.	D
3.	D	36.	D	69.	D
4.	A	37.	A	70.	D
5.	D	38.	A	71.	D
6.	D	39.	D	72.	D
7.	A	40.	D	73.	D
8.	D	41.	D	74.	D
9.	A	42.	A	75.	D
10.	D	43.	D	76.	A
11.	D	44.	A	77.	A
12.	D	45.	D	78.	D
13.	A	46.	D	79.	D
14.	D	47.	D	80.	A
15.	D	48.	D	81.	D
16.	A	49.	D	82.	D
17.	D	50.	A	83.	D
18.	A	51.	D	84.	A
19.	D	52.	D	85.	D
20.	A	53.	D	86.	D
21.	D	54.	A	87.	D
22.	A	55.	A	88.	D
23.	D	56.	D	89.	D
24.	D	57.	A	90.	A
25.	A	58.	D	91.	D
26.	D	59.	D	92.	D
27.	A	60.	D	93.	A
28.	D	61.	D	94.	A
29.	A	62.	D	95.	A
30.	D	63.	D		
31.	D	64.	D		
32.	D	65.	D		
33.	D	66.	D		

Determine Your Raw Score

Practice Test 1: Your score on Address Checking is based on the number of questions you answered correctly minus the number of questions you answered incorrectly:

1. Enter number of right answers: _____

2. Enter number of wrong answers: _____

3. Subtract number wrong from number right: _____

Raw Score = _____

14

Practice Test 2

1.	A	34.	A	67.	D
2.	D	35.	D	68.	D
3.	D	36.	D	69.	A
4.	D	37.	A	70.	D
5.	A	38.	D	71.	D
6.	A	39.	A	72.	A
7.	A	40.	A	73.	D
8.	D	41.	A	74.	D
9.	D	42.	A	75.	A
10.	A	43.	D	76.	D
11.	A	44.	A	77.	A
12.	D	45.	D	78.	A
13.	D	46.	A	79.	D
14.	A	47.	D	80.	D
15.	D	48.	D	81.	D
16.	D	49.	A	82.	D
17.	A	50.	A	83.	D
18.	D	51.	D	84.	D
19.	D	52.	D	85.	A
20.	D	53.	A	86.	A
21.	D	54.	D	87.	D
22.	D	55.	D	88.	D
23.	A	56.	D	89.	A
24.	D	57.	D	90.	A
25.	A	58.	D	91.	A
26.	D	59.	A	92.	A
27.	D	60.	D	93.	D
28.	A	61.	A	94.	A
29.	A	62.	D	95.	A
30.	D	63.	D		
31.	A	64.	A		
32.	A	65.	D		
33.	D	66.	A		

Determine Your Raw Score

Practice Test 2: Your score on Address Checking is based on the number of questions you answered correctly minus the number of questions you answered incorrectly:

1.   Enter number of right answers: _____

2.   Enter number of wrong answers: _____

3.   Subtract number wrong from number right: _____

Raw Score =   _____

14

Practice Test 3

1.	A	34.	D	67.	D
2.	D	35.	D	68.	A
3.	D	36.	A	69.	A
4.	A	37.	A	70.	D
5.	A	38.	D	71.	A
6.	D	39.	D	72.	D
7.	D	40.	A	73.	A
8.	D	41.	D	74.	D
9.	D	42.	A	75.	A
10.	D	43.	D	76.	D
11.	A	44.	D	77.	D
12.	A	45.	A	78.	D
13.	D	46.	A	79.	A
14.	D	47.	D	80.	A
15.	A	48.	A	81.	D
16.	A	49.	A	82.	A
17.	A	50.	A	83.	D
18.	A	51.	D	84.	A
19.	A	52.	A	85.	A
20.	D	53.	A	86.	A
21.	D	54.	D	87.	D
22.	A	55.	D	88.	A
23.	A	56.	A	89.	D
24.	D	57.	A	90.	D
25.	A	58.	A	91.	D
26.	A	59.	D	92.	A
27.	D	60.	A	93.	A
28.	D	61.	D	94.	D
29.	A	62.	D	95.	A
30.	D	63.	D		
31.	A	64.	A		
32.	A	65.	D		
33.	D	66.	D		

Determine Your Raw Score

Practice Test 3: Your score on Address Checking is based on the number of questions you answered correctly minus the number of questions you answered incorrectly:

1.   Enter number of right answers: _____

2.   Enter number of wrong answers: _____

3.   Subtract number wrong from number right: _____

                                 Raw Score =   _____

14

Evaluate Yourself

For each practice test, determine where your raw score falls on the following scale. If you scored less than excellent on any test, review all the appropriate study materials in Hours 4 and 5, and then retake the tests where you need improvement.

IF your raw score is between	THEN your work is
80-95	Excellent
65-79	Good
50-64	Average
35-49	Fair
1-34	Poor

The Hour in Review

1. In this hour, you took three Address Checking practice tests that simulate the timed conditions of Test 470.

2. These timed tests are intended to give you practice with answering Address Checking questions accurately while working quickly.

3. If you didn't perform your best on any of these tests, you should review the Address Checking lessons and retake the tests for additional practice.

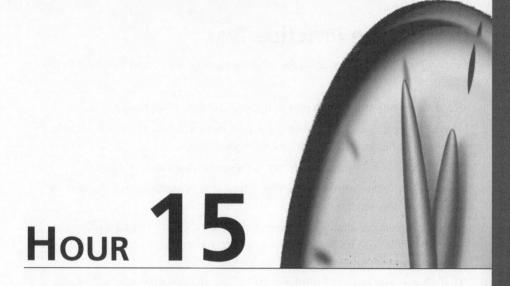

Hour **15**

Memory for Addresses— Untimed Test 1

What You Will Learn in This Hour

In this hour and the next, you'll practice the Memory for Addresses strategies that you've learned by completing two full-length practice exercises. These untimed practice tests will familiarize you with the format of the Memory for Addresses portion of Test 470 and help you perfect the memorization strategies used to answer these types of questions. Here are your goals for this hour:

- Understand your goals for taking the untimed practice tests.
- Complete the first untimed practice test within the one-hour limit.
- Review the memorization strategies for answering Memory for Addresses questions if needed.

Preparing for the Practice Test

Follow these steps to benefit most from the untimed practice tests that you'll take in this hour and the next:

1. Read the directions for each part of the exercise before beginning.

2. Use the sample questions to determine your memorization strategies, including whether or not you will memorize four or five boxes.

3. Use Practice Sets I through III to perfect these memorization strategies.

4. After finishing the entire practice test, check your answers against the answer keys that follow the test.

5. Circle the questions that you answered incorrectly and try to find a pattern in your mistakes. Also look at the questions that you got right and determine which memorization techniques worked best for you.

6. If you have time and need further study, review the memorization techniques in Hours 6 through 8.

Tip
On the actual test, you aren't allowed to write down anything during the time allowed for memorization, so you must complete this exercise without making any notes.

Practice Test

This exercise is done in the same format as the actual test. Although untimed, you should complete the practice test in less than an hour.

Sample Questions

DIRECTIONS: You have to memorize the locations (A, B, C, D, or E) of the 25 addresses in the five lettered boxes below. Indicate your answers by writing your answer (letter) next to the question number. First study the locations of the addresses. Then cover the boxes and answer the sample questions. You may look back at the boxes if you cannot yet mark the address locations from memory.

A	B	C	D	E
8100–8399 Test	6800–6999 Test	7600–8099 Test	8400–8699 Test	7000–7599 Test
Pigeon	Vampire	Octopus	Ghost	Lever
7600–8099 City	7000–7599 City	8100–8399 City	6800–6999 City	8400–8699 City
Webb	Yak	Fleet	Hammer	Nougat
6800–6999 Mark	8400–8699 Mark	7000–7599 Mark	7600–8099 Mark	8100–8399 Mark

1. 7000-7599 Test
2. Octopus
3. Nougat
4. 8100-8399 Mark
5. 7000-7599 City

6. 8100-8399 City
7. Pigeon
8. 6800-6999 Mark
9. Vampire
10. Yak

11. 8400-8699 Test
12. 7600-8099 City
13. 7000-7599 Mark
14. Hammer

Answers

1. E
2. C
3. E
4. E
5. B

6. C
7. A
8. A
9. B
10. B

11. D
12. A
13. C
14. D

Practice Set 1

DIRECTIONS: The five boxes below are labeled A, B, C, D, and E. In each box are five addresses; three are street addresses with number ranges and two are unnumbered place names. The position of an address within a box is not important. You need only remember the letter of the box in which the address is found.

A	B	C	D	E
8100–8399 Test	6800–6999 Test	7600–8099 Test	8400–8699 Test	7000–7599 Test
Pigeon	Vampire	Octopus	Ghost	Lever
7600–8099 City	7000–7599 City	8100–8399 City	6800–6999 City	8400–8699 City
Webb	Yak	Fleet	Hammer	Nougat
6800–6999 Mark	8400–8699 Mark	7000–7599 Mark	7600–8099 Mark	8100–8399 Mark

DIRECTIONS: Indicate your answers by writing the answer (letter) next to the question number. Try to do this without looking at the boxes. However, if you get stuck, you may refer to the boxes.

1. 6800-6999 Test
2. 7000-7599 City
3. 8100-8399 Mark
4. Octopus
5. Webb
6. 7000-7599 Test
7. Nougat
8. 7600-8099 Mark
9. 7000-7599 City
10. Fleet
11. Hammer
12. 7000-7599 Mark
13. 7600-8099 City
14. 8400-8699 Test
15. 8400-8699 Mark
16. 7600-8099 City
17. Vampire
18. Lever
19. Ghost

20. 6800-6999 Mark
21. 8100-8399 City
22. 8400-8699 City
23. 8400-8699 Mark
24. Pigeon
25. Fleet
26. 8400-8699 Test
27. 7000-7599 Mark
28. 6800-6999 Test
29. 7600-8099 City
30. Yak
31. Nougat
32. 8100-8399 Test
33. 7000-7599 Test
34. Lever
35. 7000-7599 City
36. 7600-8099 Mark
37. Octopus
38. Webb

39. Hammer
40. 8100-8399 Mark
41. 7600-8099 Test
42. 6800-6999 City
43. 7600-8099 Test
44. Fleet
45. 6800-6999 Mark
46. 8100-8399 City
47. 8400-8699 City
48. 8400-8699 Mark
49. Yak
50. Vampire
51. 7000-7599 Test
52. 8100-8399 Mark
53. 8100-8399 Test
54. Ghost
55. Fleet
56. 6800-6999 Mark
57. 7000-7599 Mark

15

58. 7000-7599 City	71. Nougat
59. Lever	72. 7600-8099 Test
60. Octopus	73. 8400-8699 City
61. 7600-8099 Test	74. 8400-8699 Mark
62. 8400-8699 Test	75. 8100-8399 Test
63. 7600-8099 City	76. 7000-7599 City
64. Hammer	77. 7000-7599 Mark
65. Pigeon	78. Hammer
66. 7600-8099 Mark	79. Lever
67. 6800-6999 City	80. Pigeon
68. 6800-6999 Test	81. 7600-8099 Test
69. 8100-8399 City	82. 7000-7599 Test
70. Webb	83. 8100-8399 Mark

84. Vampire
85. Fleet
86. 7600-8099 City
87. 6800-6999 Mark
88. 8400-8699 City

Practice Set 2

DIRECTIONS: The next 88 questions are for practice. This time, however, you must *not* look at the boxes while answering the questions. You must rely only on memory.

1. 7000-7599 Mark
2. 6800-6999 City
3. 6800-6999 Test
4. Pigeon
5. Nougat
6. 8400-8699 Test
7. 7000-7599 City
8. 6800-6999 Mark
9. Hammer
10. Ghost
11. 7600-8099 City
12. 8100-8399 Mark
13. 7600-8099 Mark
14. 7600-8099 Test
15. Octopus
16. Webb
17. 8100-8399 City
18. 8400-8699 City
19. 6800-6999 Mark
20. Fleet
21. Lever
22. Yak
23. 8100-8399 Test
24. 7000-7599 Test
25. Vampire
26. Octopus
27. 6800-6999 Test
28. 6800-6999 City
29. 6800-6999 Mark
30. Lever

31. Nougat
32. 7000-7599 City
33. 8100-8399 Mark
34. 8100-8399 City
35. 8100-8399 Test
36. 8400-8699 Mark
37. Yak
38. Webb
39. 7600-8099 Test
40. 7000-7599 Mark
41. Fleet
42. 8400-8699 City
43. 7600-8099 City
44. 8400-8699 Test
45. Pigeon
46. Ghost
47. Hammer
48. 7600-8099 Mark
49. 7000-7599 Test
50. 8100-8399 Mark
51. 6800-6999 City
52. 7600-8099 Test
53. Lever
54. Hammer
55. 8100-8399 Test
56. 7000-7599 City
57. 7000-7599 Mark
58. Pigeon
59. Vampire
60. 8100-8399 City

61. 7600-8099 City
62. 7000-7599 Test
63. 6800-6999 Mark
64. Nougat
65. Yak
66. Webb
67. 8400-8699 Mark
68. 7600-8099 Mark
69. 8400-8699 City
70. 6800-6999 Test
71. Ghost
72. Octopus
73. Fleet
74. 8400-8699 Test
75. 7600-8099 Test
76. 6800-6999 Mark
77. 7600-8099 City
78. Nougat
79. Webb
80. 6800-6999 City
81. 6800-6999 Test
82. 7600-8099 Mark
83. Vampire
84. Octopus
85. 7000-7599 Test
86. 8100-8399 City
87. 6800-6999 Mark
88. 8100-8399 Test

Practice Set 3

> **DIRECTIONS:** The same addresses from the previous sets are repeated in the box below, with each address in the same box as the original set. Study the locations again. Do your best to memorize the letter of the box in which each address is located. This is your last chance to see the boxes.

A	B	C	D	E
8100–8399 Test	6800–6999 Test	7600–8099 Test	8400–8699 Test	7000–7599 Test
Pigeon	Vampire	Octopus	Ghost	Lever
7600–8099 City	7000–7599 City	8100–8399 City	6800–6999 City	8400–8699 City
Webb	Yak	Fleet	Hammer	Nougat
6800–6999 Mark	8400–8699 Mark	7000–7599 Mark	7600–8099 Mark	8100–8399 Mark

> **DIRECTIONS:** This is your last practice set. Mark the location of each of the 88 addresses by writing the answer (letter) next to the question. Do *not* look back at the boxes.

1. Fleet
2. Lever
3. 8400-8699 Test
4. 7000-7599 City
5. 6800-6999 Mark
6. Vampire
7. Pigeon
8. 8100-8399 Test
9. 8100-8399 Mark
10. 7000-7599 Test
11. 8100-8399 City
12. Octopus
13. Ghost
14. Yak
15. 6800-6999 City
16. 6800-6999 Test
17. 7600-8099 Mark
18. 7600-8099 City
19. Hammer

20. Nougat
21. 8400-8699 Mark
22. 8400-8699 City
23. 8400-8699 Test
24. 7000-7599 Mark
25. Octopus
26. Fleet
27. 8100-8399 City
28. 8100-8399 Test
29. 7000-7599 City
30. 7000-7599 Test
31. 8100-8399 Test
32. 7000-7599 City
33. 7000-7599 Mark
34. Nougat
35. Ghost
36. 6800-6999 City
37. 7000-7599 Test
38. 8100-8399 Mark

39. Pigeon
40. Webb
41. 7600-8099 City
42. 8100-8399 City
43. 8400-8699 Mark
44. Fleet
45. Vampire
46. 6800-6999 Test
47. 6800-6999 Mark
48. 7600-8099 Mark
49. Hammer
50. Yak
51. 8400-8699 City
52. 8400-8699 Test
53. 7600-8099 Test
54. Lever
55. Octopus
56. 7000-7599 Test
57. 7000-7599 Mark

58. 7000-7599 City
59. 8100-8399 Test
60. Vampire
61. 8100-8399 City
62. Hammer
63. 8100-8399 Mark
64. 7000-7599 Test
65. Ghost
66. Yak
67. 6800-6999 Mark
68. 7600-8099 City

69. Octopus
70. Fleet
71. 8400-8699 City
72. 7000-7599 Mark
73. 7600-8099 Test
74. 7600-8099 Mark
75. 6800-6999 City
76. 6800-6999 Test
77. Webb
78. Pigeon
79. Lever

80. 8400-8699 Test
81. 8400-8699 Mark
82. Nougat
83. 8400-8699 City
84. 7000-7599 City
85. 7000-7599 Test
86. Hammer
87. 6800-6999 Mark
88. Yak

Memory for Addresses

DIRECTIONS: Indicate the location (A, B, C, D, or E) of each of the 88 addresses below by writing the answer (letter) next to the question. You are *not* permitted to look at the boxes. Work from memory as quickly and as accurately as you can.

15

1. 8400-8699 Test
2. 7000-7599 City
3. 8400-8699 Mark
4. Nougat
5. Pigeon
6. 6800-6999 Test
7. 8100-8399 Test
8. 8400-8699 City
9. 7000-7599 Mark
10. Ghost
11. Hammer
12. Vampire
13. 7600-8099 City
14. 7600-8099 Mark
15. 6800-6999 Mark
16. Octopus
17. Yak
18. 7600-8099 Test
19. 7000-7599 Test
20. 8400-8699 City
21. 8100-8399 Mark
22. Vampire
23. Lever
24. 7600-8099 Test
25. 7600-8099 City
26. 8100-8399 Mark
27. Webb
28. Ghost
29. 6800-6999 Mark
30. 7000-7599 Test

31. 8100-8399 City
32. 8400-8699 City
33. Pigeon
34. Yak
35. 7600-8099 Mark
36. 8400-8699 Mark
37. 8100-8399 Test
38. 6800-6999 City
39. Octopus
40. Hammer
41. Nougat
42. 7000-7599 City
43. 6800-6999 Test
44. 7600-8099 Mark
45. Nougat
46. 8400-8699 City
47. 6800-6999 Mark
48. 7600-8099 Test
49. 7000-7599 City
50. Ghost
51. Fleet
52. Yak
53. 7000-7599 Test
54. 8100-8399 City
55. 7600-8099 City
56. Pigeon
57. Octopus
58. 6800-6999 City
59. 8400-8699 Mark
60. 8100-8399 Mark

61. 8100-8399 Test
62. Webb
63. Hammer
64. 8400-8699 Test
65. 7000-7599 Mark
66. 8100-8399 City
67. Lever
68. Vampire
69. 8100-8399 Test
70. 8400-8699 City
71. 7000-7599 Test
72. 6800-6999 Mark
73. 8100-8399 City
74. 6800-6999 City
75. Yak
76. Nougat
77. Fleet
78. 6800-6999 Test
79. 7000-7599 Mark
80. 7000-7599 City
81. 8100-8399 Test
82. 8100-8399 Mark
83. Pigeon
84. Lever
85. Hammer
86. 8400-8699 Test
87. 8400-8699 Mark
88. 7600-8099 City

Answers

Practice Set 1

1.	B	31.	E	61.	C
2.	B	32.	A	62.	D
3.	E	33.	E	63.	A
4.	C	34.	E	64.	D
5.	A	35.	B	65.	A
6.	E	36.	D	66.	D
7.	E	37.	C	67.	D
8.	D	38.	A	68.	B
9.	B	39.	D	69.	C
10.	C	40.	E	70.	A
11.	D	41.	C	71.	E
12.	C	42.	D	72.	C
13.	A	43.	C	73.	E
14.	D	44.	C	74.	B
15.	B	45.	A	75.	A
16.	A	46.	C	76.	B
17.	B	47.	E	77.	C
18.	E	48.	B	78.	D
19.	D	49.	B	79.	E
20.	A	50.	B	80.	A
21.	C	51.	E	81.	C
22.	E	52.	E	82.	E
23.	B	53.	A	83.	E
24.	A	54.	D	84.	B
25.	C	55.	C	85.	C
26.	D	56.	A	86.	A
27.	C	57.	C	87.	A
28.	B	58.	B	88.	E
29.	A	59.	E		
30.	B	60.	C		

Practice Set 2

1.	C	31.	E	61.	A
2.	D	32.	B	62.	E
3.	B	33.	E	63.	A
4.	A	34.	C	64.	E
5.	E	35.	A	65.	B
6.	D	36.	B	66.	A
7.	B	37.	B	67.	B
8.	A	38.	A	68.	D
9.	D	39.	C	69.	E
10.	D	40.	C	70.	B
11.	A	41.	C	71.	D
12.	D	42.	E	72.	C
13.	C	43.	A	73.	C
14.	C	44.	D	74.	D
15.	A	45.	A	75.	C
16.	C	46.	D	76.	A
17.	E	47.	D	77.	A
18.	A	48.	D	78.	E
19.	C	49.	E	79.	A
20.	E	50.	E	80.	D
21.	E	51.	D	81.	B
22.	B	52.	C	82.	D
23.	A	53.	E	83.	B
24.	E	54.	D	84.	C
25.	B	55.	A	85.	E
26.	C	56.	B	86.	C
27.	B	57.	C	87.	A
28.	D	58.	A	88.	A
29.	A	59.	B		
30.	E	60.	C		

15

Practice Set 3

1.	C	31.	A	61.	C
2.	E	32.	B	62.	D
3.	D	33.	C	63.	E
4.	B	34.	E	64.	E
5.	A	35.	D	65.	D
6.	B	36.	D	66.	B
7.	A	37.	E	67.	A
8.	A	38.	E	68.	A
9.	E	39.	A	69.	C
10.	E	40.	A	70.	C
11.	C	41.	A	71.	E
12.	C	42.	C	72.	C
13.	D	43.	B	73.	C
14.	B	44.	C	74.	D
15.	D	45.	B	75.	D
16.	B	46.	B	76.	B
17.	D	47.	A	77.	A
18.	A	48.	D	78.	A
19.	D	49.	D	79.	E
20.	E	50.	B	80.	D
21.	B	51.	E	81.	B
22.	E	52.	D	82.	E
23.	D	53.	C	83.	E
24.	C	54.	E	84.	B
25.	C	55.	C	85.	E
26.	C	56.	E	86.	D
27.	C	57.	C	87.	A
28.	A	58.	B	88.	B
29.	B	59.	A		
30.	E	60.	B		

Memory for Addresses

1. D	32. E	63. D
2. B	33. A	64. D
3. B	34. B	65. C
4. E	35. D	66. C
5. A	36. B	67. E
6. B	37. A	68. B
7. A	38. D	69. A
8. E	39. C	70. E
9. C	40. D	71. E
10. D	41. E	72. A
11. D	42. B	73. C
12. B	43. B	74. D
13. A	44. D	75. B
14. D	45. E	76. E
15. A	46. E	77. C
16. C	47. A	78. B
17. B	48. C	79. C
18. C	49. B	80. B
19. E	50. D	81. A
20. E	51. C	82. E
21. E	52. B	83. A
22. B	53. E	84. E
23. E	54. C	85. D
24. C	55. A	86. D
25. A	56. A	87. B
26. E	57. C	88. A
27. A	58. D	
28. D	59. B	
29. A	60. E	
30. E	61. A	
31. C	62. A	

15

The Hour in Review

1. In this hour, you took an untimed Memory for Addresses test to practice the complex memorization strategies that you need to answer these questions.

2. This practice test is intended to familiarize you with the format of the Memory for Address portion of Test 470.

3. When checking your answers, determine which memorization strategies worked best for you and which need further review.

HOUR **16**

Memory for Addresses— Untimed Test 2

What You Will Learn in This Hour

In this hour, you'll take a second full-length, untimed Memory for Addresses test to strengthen your memorization skills. At the end of this hour, you should be ready to take the actual test under timed conditions. Here are your goals for this hour:

- Review tips for strengthening your memorization techniques and performing well on the second untimed test.
- Complete the practice test at your own pace, but within the one-hour limit.
- Determine which areas need further review before proceeding to the timed tests.

Improving Your Performance

When you took the first untimed practice test in Hour 15, "Memory for Addresses—Untimed Test 1," you should have been concentrating on reviewing and developing your memorization strategies. Now that you've had some practice with the format of the Memory for Addresses questions, use this second untimed practice exercise to improve your performance. Concentrate on the following areas:

Do

DO decide on your memorization strategies when you answer the sample questions, including whether you'll memorize four or five boxes.

DO use the three practice sets to perfect these strategies and revise them if you find weaknesses.

DO try to find a pattern in your mistakes when you check your answers.

DO review the memorization techniques that caused you the most trouble in Hours 6 through 8.

Don't

DON'T waste time rereading the directions. Just go straight to the boxes in the sample questions.

DON'T look back at the boxes when the instructions tell you not to.

DON'T make notes. Memorize the addresses in your head, just as you will do on the practice timed tests and the actual exam.

Practice Test

This exercise is in the same format as the actual test. Although untimed, you should complete the practice test in less than an hour.

Sample Questions

DIRECTIONS: You will have to memorize the locations (A, B, C, D, or E) of the 25 addresses in the five lettered boxes below. Indicate your answers by writing your answer (letter) next to the question number. First study the locations of the addresses. Then cover the boxes and answer the sample questions. You may look back at the boxes if you cannot mark the address locations from memory.

A	B	C	D	E
2500–2999 Mist	3600–3899 Mist	1400–1899 Mist	1900–2499 Mist	3000–3599 Mist
Glen	Season	Anchor	Cupola	Jester
1400–1899 Tank	2500–2999 Tank	3600–3899 Tank	3000–3599 Tank	1900–2499 Tank
Tarot	Howard	Bongo	Gibbon	Lattice
3600–3899 Kite	1900–2499 Kite	3000–3599 Kite	2500–2999 Kite	1400–1899 Kite

1. 3000-3599 Kite
2. 1900-2499 Mist
3. Cupola
4. 1400-1899 Kite
5. Howard

6. 1900-2499 Tank
7. 1900-2499 Kite
8. Tarot
9. 2500-2999 Tank
10. 1400-1899 Tank

11. 1400-1899 Mist
12. Jester
13. Lattice
14. 2500-2999 Mist

Answers

1. C
2. D
3. D
4. E
5. B

6. E
7. B
8. A
9. B
10. A

11. C
12. E
13. E
14. A

Practice Set 1

DIRECTIONS: The five boxes below are labeled A, B, C, D, and E. In each box are five addresses; three are street addresses with number ranges and two are unnumbered place names. The position of an address within a box is not important. You need only remember the letter of the box in which the address is found.

A	B	C	D	E
2500–2999 Mist	3600–3899 Mist	1400–1899 Mist	1900–2499 Mist	3000–3599 Mist
Glen	Season	Anchor	Cupola	Jester
1400–1899 Tank	2500–2999 Tank	3600–3899 Tank	3000–3599 Tank	1900–2499 Tank
Tarot	Howard	Bongo	Gibbon	Lattice
3600–3899 Kite	1900–2499 Kite	3000–3599 Kite	2500–2999 Kite	1400–1899 Kite

DIRECTIONS: Indicate your answers by writing in the answer (letter) next to the question number. Try to do this without looking at the boxes. However, if you get stuck, you may refer to the boxes.

1. 2500-2999 Mist
2. 3000-3599 Tank
3. Season
4. Lattice
5. 1400-1899 Kite
6. 3600-3899 Tank
7. 3000-3599 Mist
8. 1400-1899 Tank
9. Anchor
10. Glen
11. 1900-2499 Mist
12. 2500-2999 Tank
13. 2500-2999 Kite
14. Gibbon
15. 3600-3899 Kite
16. 1900-2499 Tank
17. Cupola
18. Bongo

19. 1400-1899 Mist
20. 1900-2499 Tank
21. 3600-3899 Kite
22. 2500-2999 Tank
23. Tarot
24. Jester
25. 3600-3899 Mist
26. 2500-2999 Kite
27. 3600-3899 Tank
28. Howard
29. Season
30. 1900-2499 Kite
31. 1900-2499 Mist
32. 3000-3599 Kite
33. Glen
34. Lattice
35. 1400-1899 Kite
36. 1400-1899 Tank

37. 2500-2999 Mist
38. 3000-3599 Mist
39. Anchor
40. Gibbon
41. 3000-3599 Tank
42. 3600-3899 Mist
43. 3000-3599 Tank
44. 3600-3899 Kite
45. 1900-2499 Tank
46. 2500-2999 Kite
47. Howard
48. Jester
49. 2500-2999 Mist
50. 3600-3899 Kite
51. 1400-1899 Mist
52. 1400-1899 Kite
53. Cupola
54. Bongo

55. Gibbon
56. 2500-2999 Tank
57. 1900-2499 Tank
58. Tarot
59. 1900-2499 Mist
60. 3600-3899 Tank
61. 3000-3599 Mist
62. Glen
63. Anchor
64. Season
65. 1900-2499 Kite
66. 3000-3599 Kite

67. 3600-3899 Mist
68. 1400-1899 Tank
69. 3000-3599 Tank
70. Lattice
71. 3600-3899 Kite
72. 1900-2499 Mist
73. 2500-2999 Tank
74. 3600-3899 Tank
75. 2500-2999 Mist
76. 1400-1899 Kite
77. Bongo
78. Gibbon

79. 3000-3599 Mist
80. 1400-1899 Kite
81. 3600-3899 Tank
82. Tarot
83. Lattice
84. Howard
85. 1900-2499 Mist
86. 1900-2499 Kite
87. 2500-2999 Tank
88. 3600-3899 Mist

16

Practice Set 2

DIRECTIONS: The next 88 questions are for practice, but this time you *cannot* look at the boxes while answering the questions. You must rely only on memory.

1. 1400-1899 Mist
2. 3000-3599 Kite
3. 1900-2499 Tank
4. 1400-1899 Tank
5. Howard
6. Gibbon
7. 3600-3899 Mist
8. 2500-2999 Kite
9. 1400-1899 Kite
10. Lattice
11. Jester
12. 2500-2999 Mist
13. 3600-3899 Tank
14. 3000-3599 Mist
15. 3000-3599 Tank
16. Cupola
17. Tarot
18. Bongo
19. 1900-2499 Kite
20. 3600-3899 Kite
21. Anchor
22. Season
23. 1900-2499 Mist
24. 2500-2999 Tank
25. Glen
26. 3000-3599 Mist
27. 3000-3599 Tank
28. 3000-3599 Kite
29. Jester
30. Gibbon

31. 2500-2999 Mist
32. 2500-2999 Tank
33. 1400-1899 Mist
34. Tarot
35. Glen
36. Anchor
37. 1400-1899 Kite
38. 3600-3899 Tank
39. 3600-3899 Kite
40. 1900-2499 Mist
41. 1400-1899 Tank
42. Bongo
43. Cupola
44. Season
45. Howard
46. 1900-2499 Tank
47. 1900-2499 Kite
48. 2500-2999 Kite
49. 3600-3899 Mist
50. 3600-3899 Tank
51. 2500-2999 Kite
52. 3000-3599 Mist
53. 3600-3899 Kite
54. Cupola
55. Lattice
56. Season
57. 1400-1899 Mist
58. 3000-3599 Kite
59. Anchor
60. Gibbon

61. 1900-2499 Tank
62. 1400-1899 Tank
63. 2500-2999 Mist
64. 1400-1899 Kite
65. Glen
66. Tarot
67. 1900-2499 Mist
68. 2500-2999 Tank
69. 3000-3599 Tank
70. Jester
71. Howard
72. Bongo
73. 1900-2499 Kite
74. 3600-3899 Tank
75. 1400-1899 Kite
76. 2500-2999 Mist
77. Cupola
78. Season
79. 1900-2499 Kite
80. 1900-2499 Mist
81. 1900-2499 Tank
82. 1400-1899 Tank
83. Lattice
84. Anchor
85. 3600-3899 Mist
86. 2500-2999 Kite
87. 3000-3599 Kite
88. 3000-3599 Mist

Practice Set 3

> **DIRECTIONS:** The same addresses from the previous set are repeated in the table below. Study the locations again. Do your best to memorize the letter of the box in which each address is located. This is your last chance to see the boxes.

A	B	C	D	E
2500–2999 Mist	3600–3899 Mist	1400–1899 Mist	1900–2499 Mist	3000–3599 Mist
Glen	Season	Anchor	Cupola	Jester
1400–1899 Tank	2500–2999 Tank	3600–3899 Tank	3000–3599 Tank	1900–2499 Tank
Tarot	Howard	Bongo	Gibbon	Lattice
3600–3899 Kite	1900–2499 Kite	3000–3599 Kite	2500–2999 Kite	1400–1899 Kite

16

> **DIRECTIONS:** This is your last practice set. Mark the location of each of the 88 addresses by writing the answer (letter) next to the question number. Do *not* look back at the boxes.

1. 3600-3899 Kite
2. 1400-1899 Mist
3. Season
4. Howard
5. 1900-2499 Tank
6. 1400-1899 Kite
7. 1900-2499 Mist
8. 2500-2999 Tank
9. Gibbon
10. Jester
11. 1400-1899 Tank
12. 3000-3599 Kite
13. 1400-1899 Mist
14. 3000-3599 Tank
15. 2500-2999 Mist
16. 1900-2499 Kite
17. Bongo
18. Anchor
19. 3600-3899 Tank
20. 3600-3899 Mist

21. 2500-2999 Kite
22. 2500-2999 Tank
23. Lattice
24. Cupola
25. Tarot
26. 3000-3599 Kite
27. 3000-3599 Mist
28. 1400-1899 Tank
29. 3000-3599 Mist
30. 3600-3899 Kite
31. 2500-2999 Mist
32. 1400-1899 Kite
33. Season
34. Glen
35. Jester
36. 1400-1899 Tank
37. 1900-2499 Tank
38. 3600-3899 Mist
39. 2500-2999 Kite
40. 2500-2999 Tank

41. Tarot
42. Lattice
43. Bongo
44. Cupola
45. 3600-3899 Tank
46. 3000-3599 Tank
47. 1400-1899 Mist
48. 1900-2499 Kite
49. Gibbon
50. Howard
51. 1900-2499 Mist
52. 3000-3599 Kite
53. Anchor
54. 1900-2499 Tank
55. 2500-2999 Kite
56. 3600-3899 Mist
57. 1400-1899 Tank
58. 2500-2999 Mist
59. 1900-2499 Kite
60. Season

61. Bongo
62. Lattice
63. 2500-2999 Tank
64. 2500-2999 Kite
65. 3600-3899 Tank
66. 3600-3899 Kite
67. Jester
68. Glen
69. 3000-3599 Kite
70. 1900-2499 Tank

71. 3600-3899 Mist
72. 1900-2499 Mist
73. Anchor
74. Cupola
75. 3000-3899 Tank
76. 1400-1899 Mist
77. 1400-1899 Kite
78. Tarot
79. Gibbon
80. 3000-3899 Mist

81. 1400-1899 Tank
82. Howard
83. 3600-3899 Mist
84. 2500-2999 Kite
85. 3600-3899 Kite
86. 2500-2999 Mist
87. Bongo
88. Lattice

Memory for Addresses

> **DIRECTIONS:** Indicate the location (A, B, C, D, or E) of each of the 88 addresses below by writing the answer (letter) next to the question number. You are *not* permitted to look at the boxes. Work from memory as quickly and as accurately as possible.

1. 3600-3899 Tank	31. 1400-1899 Mist	61. 1400-1899 Tank
2. 1900-2499 Kite	32. 1400-1899 Tank	62. 3600-3899 Tank
3. 1900-2499 Mist	33. Tarot	63. 3000-3599 Kite
4. Bongo	34. Bongo	64. 3000-3599 Mist
5. Tarot	35. 3000-3599 Tank	65. Gibbon
6. 2500-2999 Mist	36. 3600-3899 Kite	66. Glen
7. 1400-1899 Kite	37. 2500-2999 Mist	67. Cupola
8. 3000-3599 Tank	38. 3000-3599 Mist	68. 3000-3599 Tank
9. Jester	39. 3600-3899 Tank	69. 1400-1899 Kite
10. Anchor	40. Howard	70. 1900-2499 Mist
11. Glen	41. Anchor	71. 3600-3899 Mist
12. 1400-1899 Tank	42. Gibbon	72. 1900-2499 Mist
13. 2500-2999 Kite	43. 1400-1899 Kite	73. 3000-3599 Kite
14. 2500-2999 Tank	44. 2500-2999 Tank	74. Bongo
15. 3600-3899 Mist	45. 3000-3599 Kite	75. Howard
16. 3000-3599 Mist	46. Season	76. 2500-2999 Mist
17. Lattice	47. Anchor	77. 1400-1899 Kite
18. Glen	48. 1900-2499 Tank	78. 3600-3899 Tank
19. Gibbon	49. 2500-2999 Kite	79. 2500-2999 Tank
20. 1900-2499 Tank	50. 1900-2499 Kite	80. Anchor
21. 1400-1899 Mist	51. 3600-3899 Mist	81. Jester
22. 3000-3599 Kite	52. Jester	82. 3600-3899 Mist
23. Howard	53. Howard	83. 1900-2499 Mist
24. Season	54. 3600-3899 Kite	84. 1900-2499 Tank
25. Cupola	55. 2500-2999 Tank	85. Lattice
26. 2500-2999 Kite	56. 1400-1899 Mist	86. 1900-2499 Kite
27. 1900-2499 Tank	57. 2500-2999 Mist	87. Tarot
28. 3600-3899 Mist	58. Tarot	88. 3000-3599 Tank
29. Lattice	59. Lattice	
30. 1900-2499 Kite	60. Bongo	

Answers

Practice Set 1

1.	A	32.	C	63.	C
2.	D	33.	A	64.	B
3.	B	34.	E	65.	B
4.	E	35.	E	66.	C
5.	E	36.	A	67.	B
6.	C	37.	A	68.	A
7.	E	38.	E	69.	D
8.	A	39.	C	70.	E
9.	C	40.	D	71.	A
10.	A	41.	D	72.	D
11.	D	42.	B	73.	B
12.	B	43.	D	74.	C
13.	D	44.	A	75.	A
14.	D	45.	E	76.	E
15.	A	46.	D	77.	C
16.	E	47.	B	78.	D
17.	D	48.	E	79.	E
18.	C	49.	A	80.	E
19.	C	50.	A	81.	C
20.	E	51.	C	82.	A
21.	A	52.	E	83.	E
22.	B	53.	D	84.	B
23.	A	54.	C	85.	D
24.	E	55.	D	86.	B
25.	B	56.	B	87.	B
26.	D	57.	E	88.	B
27.	C	58.	A		
28.	B	59.	D		
29.	B	60.	C		
30.	B	61.	E		
31.	D	62.	A		

Practice Set 2

1.	C	31.	A	61.	E
2.	C	32.	B	62.	A
3.	E	33.	C	63.	A
4.	A	34.	A	64.	E
5.	B	35.	A	65.	A
6.	D	36.	C	66.	A
7.	B	37.	E	67.	D
8.	D	38.	C	68.	B
9.	E	39.	A	69.	D
10.	E	40.	D	70.	E
11.	E	41.	A	71.	B
12.	A	42.	C	72.	C
13.	C	43.	D	73.	B
14.	E	44.	B	74.	C
15.	D	45.	B	75.	E
16.	D	46.	E	76.	A
17.	A	47.	B	77.	D
18.	C	48.	D	78.	B
19.	B	49.	B	79.	B
20.	A	50.	C	80.	D
21.	C	51.	D	81.	E
22.	B	52.	E	82.	A
23.	D	53.	A	83.	E
24.	B	54.	D	84.	C
25.	A	55.	E	85.	B
26.	E	56.	B	86.	D
27.	D	57.	C	87.	C
28.	C	58.	C	88.	E
29.	E	59.	C		
30.	D	60.	D		

16

Practice Set 3

1.	A	31.	A	61.	C
2.	C	32.	E	62.	E
3.	B	33.	B	63.	B
4.	B	34.	A	64.	D
5.	E	35.	E	65.	C
6.	E	36.	A	66.	A
7.	D	37.	E	67.	E
8.	B	38.	B	68.	A
9.	D	39.	D	69.	C
10.	E	40.	B	70.	E
11.	A	41.	A	71.	B
12.	C	42.	E	72.	D
13.	C	43.	C	73.	C
14.	D	44.	D	74.	D
15.	A	45.	C	75.	D
16.	B	46.	D	76.	C
17.	C	47.	C	77.	E
18.	C	48.	B	78.	A
19.	C	49.	D	79.	D
20.	B	50.	B	80.	E
21.	D	51.	D	81.	A
22.	B	52.	C	82.	B
23.	E	53.	C	83.	B
24.	D	54.	E	84.	D
25.	A	55.	D	85.	A
26.	C	56.	B	86.	A
27.	E	57.	A	87.	C
28.	A	58.	A	88.	E
29.	E	59.	B		
30.	A	60.	B		

Memory for Addresses

1. C	31. C	61. A
2. B	32. A	62. C
3. D	33. A	63. C
4. C	34. C	64. E
5. A	35. D	65. D
6. A	36. A	66. A
7. E	37. A	67. D
8. D	38. E	68. D
9. E	39. C	69. E
10. C	40. B	70. D
11. A	41. C	71. B
12. A	42. D	72. D
13. D	43. E	73. C
14. B	44. B	74. C
15. B	45. C	75. B
16. E	46. B	76. A
17. E	47. C	77. E
18. A	48. E	78. C
19. D	49. D	79. B
20. E	50. B	80. C
21. C	51. B	81. E
22. C	52. E	82. B
23. B	53. B	83. D
24. B	54. A	84. E
25. D	55. B	85. E
26. D	56. C	86. B
27. E	57. A	87. A
28. B	58. A	88. D
29. E	59. E	
30. B	60. C	

The Hour in Review

1. In this hour, you took a second untimed Memory for Addresses test to reinforce the memorization techniques that you learned for these questions.

2. The practice test is intended to prepare you for the timed test that you'll take in the next hour.

3. Take this final opportunity to review weaknesses in your memorization strategies.

HOUR 17

Memory for Addresses—
Timed Test 1

What You Will Learn in This Hour

In this hour and the following two hours, you'll get the chance to take full-length Memory for Addresses practice tests under timed conditions. You'll discover how the memorization techniques that you've developed hold up under the timing constraints of the actual test. Use these timed tests as a benchmark for further study. Here are your goals for this hour:

- Learn strategies for performing well under timed conditions.
- Complete the first practice test under actual timed exam conditions.
- Check your answers, determine your raw score, and pinpoint where you need additional review.

Preparing for the Timed Practice Tests

In the following timed practice tests, concentrate on putting your memorization strategies into practice while answering questions quickly. You should see your test results improve in each successive hour, as you get more practice and become more adept at memorizing addresses in your head.

Because these practice tests simulate actual test conditions, use them to develop strategies for working under timed conditions. Follow these steps to get the best results:

1. Choose a workspace that is quiet, well-lit, and uncluttered.
2. Use a stopwatch or kitchen timer to accurately time each part of the test.
3. Start at a convenient time and proceed without stopping through the entire test, following all the specified time limits.
4. After completing the sample questions, determine if you have successfully created your memorization system or if you need more memorization time.
5. If you need additional time, "borrow" from some of the time allowed for answering the questions in Practice Set 1; otherwise, use the Practice Sets to improve your speed.
6. When answering Practice Set 1, concentrate on the boxes where the addresses are located. Don't just rush to answer as many questions as possible.
7. Use Practice Set 2 to discover gaps in your memorization of the address locations. Do your best to answer as many questions as possible.
8. Use Practice Set 3 to brush up on address locations. Remember that you don't have to answer every question.
9. After completing the entire test, check your answers in the key that immediately follows the test. Circle all wrong answers.
10. Calculate your raw score for the scored section as instructed.
11. If you have time, review Hours 6 through 8 and retake the test to see your improvement.

Remember you're not expected to answer all the questions, so don't get discouraged if you can't finish the test. Guess if you can use the process of elimination to weed out incorrect answers.

Note
On the actual test, you will answer Practice Sets 1, 2, and 3 in the test booklet, not on the separate answer sheet. They are not scored and don't count toward your final exam score; they are strictly opportunities for reinforcing and improving your memorization strategies. Therefore, you don't have to put all your effort into answering as many questions as possible in the Practice Sets, especially Practice Set 1.

Timed Test

You will have 27 minutes to complete this test.

Sample Questions

DIRECTIONS: You will have to memorize the locations (A, B, C, D, or E) of the 25 addresses in the five lettered boxes below. Indicate your answers by writing your answer (letter) next to the question number.

You now have five minutes to study the locations of the addresses. Afterwards, cover the boxes and answer the sample questions. You may look back at the boxes if you cannot yet mark the address locations from memory.

17

A	B	C	D	E
2600–3899 Hart	1400–2099 Hart	3900–4199 Hart	4200–5399 Hart	2100–2599 Hart
Linda	Ashley	Farmer	Monroe	Nolan
4200–5399 Dorp	3900–4199 Dorp	2600–3899 Dorp	2100–2599 Dorp	1400–2099 Dorp
Croft	Walton	Brendan	Orton	Gould
2100–2599 Noon	2600–3899 Noon	1400–2099 Noon	3900–4199 Noon	4200–5399 Noon

1. 3900-4199 Noon
2. 4200-5399 Dorp
3. Nolan
4. Farmer
5. 1400-2099 Hart

6. 2100-2599 Hart
7. 1400-2099 Noon
8. Monroe
9. Ashley
10. 2100-2599 Dorp

11. 2600-3899 Hart
12. 2100-2599 Noon
13. Orton
14. 2600-3899 Dorp

Answers

1. D
2. A
3. E
4. C
5. B

6. E
7. C
8. D
9. B
10. D

11. A
12. A
13. D
14. C

Practice Set 1

DIRECTIONS: The five boxes below are labeled A, B, C, D, and E. In each box are five addresses; three are street addresses with number ranges and two are unnumbered place names. You have three minutes to memorize the box location of each address. The position of an address within a box is not important. You need only remember the letter of the box in which the address is found. You will use these addresses to answer three sets of practice questions that are not scored and one actual test that is scored. If you get stuck, you may refer to the boxes during this practice exercise. If you must look at the boxes, try to memorize as you do so.

A	B	C	D	E
2600–3899 Hart	1400–2099 Hart	3900–4199 Hart	4200–5399 Hart	2100–2599 Hart
Linda	Ashley	Farmer	Monroe	Nolan
4200–5399 Dorp	3900–4199 Dorp	2600–3899 Dorp	2100–2599 Dorp	1400–2099 Dorp
Croft	Walton	Brendan	Orton	Gould
2100–2599 Noon	2600–3899 Noon	1400–2099 Noon	3900–4199 Noon	4200–5399 Noon

1. 4200-5399 Dorp
2. 3900-4199 Hart
3. 4200-5399 Noon
4. Walton
5. Monroe
6. 2100-2599 Noon
7. 1400-2199 Hart
8. Gould
9. 1400-2099 Dorp
10. 2100-2599 Dorp
11. 1400-2099 Noon
12. Linda
13. Croft
14. Brendan
15. 3900-4199 Dorp
16. 2600-3899 Noon
17. 2100-2599 Hart
18. 2600-3899 Hart

19. 1400-2099 Dorp
20. Farmer
21. Ashley
22. 3900-4199 Noon
23. 2100-2599 Dorp
24. 2100-2599 Noon
25. Nolan
26. Croft
27. 4200-5399 Dorp
28. 1400-2099 Noon
29. 4200-5399 Hart
30. Monroe
31. Gould
32. 1400-2099 Hart
33. 2600-3899 Dorp
34. 2600-3899 Noon
35. Linda
36. Walton

37. Orton
38. 3900-4199 Dorp
39. 4200-5399 Noon
40. 3900-4199 Hart
41. Brendan
42. 1400-2099 Dorp
43. 2600-3899 Noon
44. Ashley
45. 4200-5399 Hart
46. 2600-3899 Hart
47. 3900-4199 Dorp
48. Orton
49. Monroe
50. 3900-4199 Noon
51. 2100-2599 Hart
52. 4200-5399 Noon
53. 2100-2599 Noon
54. Walton

55. Farmer

56. 2600-3899 Dorp

57. 3900-4199 Hart

58. 2100-2599 Dorp

59. Gould

60. Brendan

61. 1400-2099 Hart

62. 2600-3899 Noon

63. Ashley

64. 1400-2099 Dorp

65. 4200-5399 Dorp

66. 4200-5399 Hart

67. Linda

68. Croft

69. Nolan

70. 1400-2099 Noon

71. 3900-4199 Hart

72. 2100-2599 Dorp

73. 2600-3899 Noon

74. Walton

75. 2600-3899 Dorp

76. 2600-3899 Hart

77. 4200-5399 Noon

78. Monroe

79. Ashley

80. 2100-2599 Noon

81. 2100-2599 Hart

82. 3900-4199 Hart

83. Brendan

84. Nolan

85. Croft

86. 3900-4199 Dorp

87. 2100-2599 Dorp

88. 1400-2099 Noon

17

Practice Set 2

> **DIRECTIONS:** The next 88 questions are for practice. Indicate your answers by writing in your answer (letter) next to the question number. Your time limit is three minutes. This time, however, you must not look at the boxes while answering the questions. You must rely on memory in marking the box location of each item. This practice test will not be scored.

1. 3900-4199 Hart
2. 3900-4199 Dorp
3. 2100-2599 Noon
4. Nolan
5. Orton
6. 4200-5399 Noon
7. 4200-5399 Hart
8. 1400-2099 Noon
9. Croft
10. Ashley
11. 2600-3899 Hart
12. 4200-5399 Dorp
13. 1400-2099 Dorp
14. 1400-2099 Hart
15. Farmer
16. Brendan
17. 2600-3899 Dorp
18. 2100-2599 Dorp
19. 2100-2599 Hart
20. Monroe
21. 4200-5399 Hart
22. Linda
23. 2600-3899 Noon
24. 3900-4199 Noon
25. Walton
26. Monroe
27. Ashley
28. 1400-2099 Dorp
29. 3900-4199 Hart
30. 2100-2599 Noon

31. Brendan
32. Linda
33. 2600-3899 Hart
34. 3900-4199 Dorp
35. 1400-2099 Noon
36. Nolan
37. Farmer
38. 4200-5399 Noon
39. 2100-2599 Dorp
40. 1400-2099 Hart
41. Croft
42. Walton
43. 2100-2599 Hart
44. 2600-3899 Noon
45. 2600-3899 Dorp
46. Gould
47. Orton
48. 3900-4199 Noon
49. 4200-5399 Dorp
50. 4200-5399 Hart
51. 2600-3899 Dorp
52. Linda
53. 2100-2599 Noon
54. Ashley
55. Gould
56. 4200-5399 Noon
57. 3900-4199 Noon
58. 3900-4199 Dorp
59. Nolan
60. Croft

61. 2600-3899 Hart
62. 2100-2599 Dorp
63. 3900-4199 Hart
64. Farmer
65. Orton
66. 4200-5399 Dorp
67. 1400-2099 Dorp
68. 1400-2099 Hart
69. Brendan
70. Linda
71. 1400-2099 Noon
72. 2600-3899 Noon
73. 4200-5399 Hart
74. Walton
75. Monroe
76. 3900-4199 Dorp
77. 2100-2599 Hart
78. 2100-2599 Noon
79. Ashley
80. Gould
81. Orton
82. 2600-3899 Noon
83. 1400-2099 Hart
84. 2600-3899 Dorp
85. 3900-4199 Noon
86. 2600-3899 Hart
87. Brendan
88. Croft

Practice Set 3

> **DIRECTIONS:** The same addresses from the previous set are repeated in the table below. You now have three minutes to study the locations again. Do your best to memorize the letter of the box in which each address is located; do not look back at the boxes. This is your last chance to see the table. This practice test will not be scored.

A	B	C	D	E
2600–3899 Hart	1400–2099 Hart	3900–4199 Hart	4200–5399 Hart	2100–2599 Hart
Linda	Ashley	Farmer	Monroe	Nolan
4200–5399 Dorp	3900–4199 Dorp	2600–3899 Dorp	2100–2599 Dorp	1400–2099 Dorp
Croft	Walton	Brendan	Orton	Gould
2100–2599 Noon	2600–3899 Noon	1400–2099 Noon	3900–4199 Noon	4200–5399 Noon

1. 2600-3899 Hart
2. 2600-3899 Dorp
3. 2600-3899 Noon
4. Walton
5. Nolan
6. 4200-5399 Noon
7. 2100-2599 Dorp
8. 1400-2099 Noon
9. Gould
10. Monroe
11. 3900-4199 Hart
12. 2100-2599 Hart
13. 3900-4199 Dorp
14. Brendan
15. Ashley
16. 1400-2099 Hart
17. 1400-2099 Dorp
18. 4200-5399 Dorp
19. Farmer
20. Monroe
21. Linda
22. 2100-2599 Noon

23. 3900-4199 Hart
24. 4200-5399 Hart
25. Croft
26. Ashley
27. 3900-4199 Dorp
28. 2600-3899 Noon
29. 2600-3899 Hart
30. Nolan
31. 2100-2599 Dorp
32. 4200-5399 Hart
33. 2600-3899 Noon
34. Monroe
35. Farmer
36. 3900-4199 Noon
37. 3900-4199 Dorp
38. 2600-3899 Hart
39. Nolan
40. Walton
41. 4200-5399 Dorp
42. 4200-5399 Noon
43. 1400-2099 Hart
44. Linda

45. Gould
46. 2100-2599 Hart
47. 3900-4199 Hart
48. 2600-3899 Dorp
49. Ashley
50. Croft
51. 1400-2099 Dorp
52. 1400-2099 Noon
53. 2100-2599 Noon
54. Orton
55. Brendan
56. 2600-3899 Hart
57. 3900-4199 Dorp
58. 4200-5399 Noon
59. 3900-4199 Hart
60. 1400-2099 Noon
61. Ashley
62. Brendan
63. Monroe
64. 1400-2099 Hart
65. 3900-4199 Noon
66. 4200-5399 Hart

17

67. 3900-4199 Dorp

68. Nolan

69. Walton

70. 4200-5399 Dorp

71. 1400-2099 Dorp

72. 1400-2099 Noon

73. 3900-4199 Hart

74. 2100-2599 Hart

75. Gould

76. Linda

77. Farmer

78. 2600-3899 Hart

79. 2600-3899 Noon

80. 4200-5399 Noon

81. 2600-3899 Dorp

82. 2100-2599 Dorp

83. Croft

84. Orton

85. 2100-2599 Noon

86. 3900-4199 Hart

87. 1400-2099 Dorp

88. 4200-5399 Noon

Memory for Addresses

DIRECTIONS: Indicate the location (A, B, C, D, or E) of each of the 88 addresses below by writing the answer (letter) next to the question number. You are *not* permitted to look at the boxes. Work from memory as quickly and as accurately as you can. Your time limit is five minutes.

1. Monroe
2. Walton
3. 2600-3899 Dorp
4. 2100-2599 Noon
5. 2100-2599 Hart
6. Linda
7. Gould
8. 4200-5399 Noon
9. 1400-2099 Dorp
10. 2600-3899 Hart
11. Ashley
12. Orton
13. 3900-4199 Hart
14. 1400-2099 Noon
15. 4200-5399 Dorp
16. 4200-5399 Hart
17. 2600-3899 Noon
18. 2100-2599 Dorp
19. Croft
20. Brendan
21. Nolan
22. Farmer
23. 3900-4199 Dorp
24. 3900-4199 Noon
25. 1400-3899 Hart
26. Linda
27. 2100-2599 Hart
28. 3900-4199 Hart
29. Monroe
30. 2600-3899 Dorp

31. 1400-3899 Noon
32. Brendan
33. Ashley
34. 2600-3899 Hart
35. 2100-2599 Noon
36. 1400-2099 Dorp
37. 2100-2599 Dorp
38. 4200-5399 Noon
39. Orton
40. Croft
41. 4200-5399 Hart
42. 2600-3899 Noon
43. 4200-5399 Dorp
44. Gould
45. 3900-4199 Noon
46. 2600-3899 Dorp
47. 1400-2099 Hart
48. Linda
49. Gould
50. 2100-2599 Hart
51. 2100-2599 Dorp
52. 3900-4199 Dorp
53. 2100-2599 Noon
54. Brendan
55. Farmer
56. 2600-3899 Hart
57. 4200-5399 Noon
58. 1400-2099 Dorp
59. Nolan
60. Croft

61. 4200-5399 Dorp
62. 1400-2099 Noon
63. 2600-3899 Noon
64. Monroe
65. Ashley
66. 3900-4199 Hart
67. 4200-5399 Hart
68. Orton
69. Walton
70. 2100-2599 Hart
71. 4200-5399 Dorp
72. 3900-4199 Noon
73. 2100-2599 Noon
74. 2600-3899 Dorp
75. 3900-4199 Hart
76. Croft
77. Farmer
78. 2100-2599 Hart
79. 4200-5399 Noon
80. 4200-5399 Dorp
81. Brendan
82. Monroe
83. 1400-2099 Noon
84. 3900-4199 Dorp
85. 4200-5399 Hart
86. Linda
87. Ashley
88. 1400-2099 Dorp

Answers
Practice Set 1

1.	A	31.	E	61.	B
2.	C	32.	B	62.	B
3.	E	33.	C	63.	B
4.	B	34.	B	64.	E
5.	D	35.	A	65.	A
6.	A	36.	B	66.	D
7.	B	37.	D	67.	A
8.	E	38.	B	68.	A
9.	E	39.	E	69.	E
10.	D	40.	C	70.	C
11.	C	41.	C	71.	C
12.	A	42.	E	72.	D
13.	A	43.	B	73.	B
14.	C	44.	B	74.	B
15.	B	45.	D	75.	C
16.	B	46.	A	76.	A
17.	E	47.	B	77.	E
18.	A	48.	D	78.	D
19.	E	49.	D	79.	B
20.	C	50.	D	80.	A
21.	B	51.	E	81.	E
22.	D	52.	E	82.	C
23.	D	53.	A	83.	C
24.	A	54.	B	84.	E
25.	E	55.	C	85.	A
26.	A	56.	C	86.	B
27.	A	57.	C	87.	D
28.	C	58.	D	88.	C
29.	D	59.	E		
30.	D	60.	C		

Practice Set 2

1. C	31. C	61. A
2. B	32. A	62. D
3. A	33. A	63. C
4. E	34. B	64. C
5. D	35. C	65. D
6. E	36. E	66. A
7. D	37. C	67. E
8. C	38. E	68. B
9. A	39. D	69. C
10. B	40. B	70. A
11. A	41. A	71. C
12. A	42. B	72. B
13. E	43. E	73. D
14. B	44. B	74. B
15. C	45. C	75. D
16. C	46. E	76. B
17. C	47. D	77. E
18. D	48. D	78. A
19. E	49. A	79. B
20. D	50. D	80. E
21. D	51. C	81. D
22. A	52. A	82. B
23. B	53. A	83. B
24. D	54. B	84. C
25. B	55. E	85. D
26. D	56. E	86. A
27. B	57. D	87. C
28. E	58. B	88. A
29. C	59. E	
30. A	60. A	

17

Practice Set 3

1.	A	31.	D	61.	B
2.	C	32.	D	62.	C
3.	B	33.	B	63.	D
4.	B	34.	D	64.	B
5.	E	35.	C	65.	D
6.	E	36.	D	66.	D
7.	D	37.	B	67.	B
8.	C	38.	A	68.	E
9.	E	39.	E	69.	B
10.	D	40.	B	70.	A
11.	C	41.	A	71.	E
12.	E	42.	E	72.	C
13.	B	43.	B	73.	C
14.	C	44.	A	74.	E
15.	B	45.	E	75.	E
16.	B	46.	E	76.	A
17.	E	47.	C	77.	C
18.	A	48.	C	78.	A
19.	C	49.	B	79.	B
20.	D	50.	A	80.	E
21.	A	51.	E	81.	C
22.	A	52.	C	82.	D
23.	C	53.	A	83.	A
24.	D	54.	D	84.	D
25.	A	55.	C	85.	A
26.	B	56.	A	86.	C
27.	B	57.	B	87.	E
28.	B	58.	E	88.	E
29.	A	59.	C		
30.	E	60.	C		

Memory for Addresses

1.	D	31.	C	61.	A
2.	B	32.	C	62.	C
3.	C	33.	B	63.	B
4.	A	34.	A	64.	D
5.	E	35.	A	65.	B
6.	A	36.	E	66.	C
7.	E	37.	D	67.	D
8.	E	38.	E	68.	D
9.	E	39.	D	69.	B
10.	A	40.	A	70.	E
11.	B	41.	D	71.	A
12.	D	42.	B	72.	D
13.	C	43.	A	73.	A
14.	C	44.	E	74.	C
15.	A	45.	D	75.	C
16.	D	46.	C	76.	A
17.	B	47.	B	77.	C
18.	D	48.	A	78.	E
19.	A	49.	E	79.	E
20.	C	50.	E	80.	A
21.	E	51.	D	81.	C
22.	C	52.	B	82.	D
23.	B	53.	A	83.	C
24.	D	54.	C	84.	B
25.	B	55.	C	85.	D
26.	A	56.	A	86.	A
27.	E	57.	E	87.	B
28.	C	58.	E	88.	E
29.	D	59.	E		
30.	C	60.	A		

17

Determine Your Raw Score

Your score is based on the number of questions you answered correctly minus one-fourth of the questions you answered incorrectly (number wrong divided by four):

1.   Enter number of right answers: _____

2.   Enter number of wrong answers: _____

3.   Divide number wrong by four: _____

4.   Subtract answer from number right: _____

Raw Score =   _____

Evaluate Yourself

Determine where your raw score falls on the following scale. If you scored less than Excellent, review Hours 6 through 8 and then retake the test to see if you improved your score.

IF your raw score is between	THEN your work is
75-88	Excellent
60-74	Good
45-59	Average
30-44	Fair
1-29	Poor

The Hour in Review

1.   In this hour, you took a Memory for Addresses practice test that simulates the timed conditions of Test 470.

2.   The timed test is intended to give you practice with answering Memory for Address questions accurately while working quickly.

3.   If you didn't perform your best on the test, review the Memory for Addresses lessons and retake the test for additional practice.

Hour **18**

Memory for Addresses—Timed Test 2

What You Will Learn in This Hour

In this hour, you'll take a second Memory for Addresses practice test under timed conditions to hone the memorization techniques you've already learned. This test should determine how much additional study you need. Here are your goals for this hour:

- Take the practice test under timed conditions using all the memorization strategies you learned in previous hours.

- Check your answers against the answer key and determine your raw score.

- Review the appropriate lessons in previous hours if you don't perform your best on the test.

Timed Test

You have 27 minutes to take this test.

Sample Questions

> **DIRECTIONS:** You will have to memorize the locations (A, B, C, D, or E) of the 25 addresses in the five lettered boxes below. Indicate your answers by writing your answer (letter) next to the question number.
>
> You now have five minutes to study the locations of the addresses. Then cover the boxes and answer the sample questions. You may look back at the boxes if you cannot yet mark the address locations from memory.

A	B	C	D	E
3700–4099 Rink	5200–5399 Rink	4800–5199 Rink	4100–4799 Rink	5400–5599 Rink
Chapel	Elephant	Bluff	Windmill	Quill
4800–5199 Bank	5400–5599 Bank	3700–4099 Bank	5200–5399 Bank	4100–4799 Bank
River	Package	Juggler	Thistle	Monsoon
5400–5599 Love	3700–4099 Love	4100–4799 Love	4800–5199 Love	5200–5399 Love

1. 5400-5599 Bank	6. 5400-5599 Love	11. 4800-5199 Bank
2. 4800-5199 Love	7. 5200-5399 Rink	12. 3700-4099 Love
3. 5400-5599 Rink	8. Bluff	13. Juggler
4. Windmill	9. River	14. Quill
5. Elephant	10. 4100-4799 Rink	

Answers

1. B	6. A	11. A
2. D	7. B	12. B
3. E	8. C	13. C
4. D	9. A	14. E
5. B	10. D	

Practice Set 1

> **DIRECTIONS:** The five boxes below are labeled A, B, C, D, and E. In each box are five addresses; three are street addresses with number ranges and two are unnumbered place names. You have three minutes to memorize the box locations of each address. The position of an address within a box is not important. You need only remember the letter of the box in which the address is found. You will use these addresses to answer three sets of practice questions that are not scored and one actual test that is scored.

A	B	C	D	E
3700–4099 Rink	5200–5399 Rink	4800–5199 Rink	4100–4799 Rink	5400–5599 Rink
Chapel	Elephant	Bluff	Windmill	Quill
4800–5199 Bank	5400–5599 Bank	3700–4099 Bank	5200–5399 Bank	4100–4799 Bank
River	Package	Juggler	Thistle	Monsoon
5400–5599 Love	3700–4099 Love	4100–4799 Love	4800–5199 Love	5200–5399 Love

> **DIRECTIONS:** You have three minutes to write the letter of the box for each of the following addresses. Write your answer (letter) next to the question number. Try to do this without looking at the boxes. If you get stuck, however, you may refer to the boxes during this practice exercise. If you must look at the boxes, try to memorize as you do so. This test is for practice only. It will not be scored.

18

1. 4800-5199 Rink
2. 5200-5399 Love
3. 5400-5599 Bank
4. Bluff
5. Thistle
6. 4100-4799 Love
7. 5200-5399 Bank
8. 3700-4099 Rink
9. Windmill
10. Quill
11. 5400-5599 Love
12. 3700-4099 Bank

13. 5400-5599 Rink
14. River
15. Package
16. 4100-4799 Bank
17. 4100-4799 Rink
18. 4800-5199 Love
19. Chapel
20. Monsoon
21. Thistle
22. 4100-4799 Bank
23. 3700-4099 Rink
24. 5400-5599 Love

25. 3700-4099 Bank
26. 4800-5199 Rink
27. Bluff
28. Elephant
29. 5200-5399 Love
30. 4800-5199 Love
31. 5200-5399 Rink
32. 4800-5199 Bank
33. 5400-5599 Bank
34. Chapel
35. Quill
36. 5400-5599 Rink

37. 4100-4799 Love
38. 5200-5399 Bank
39. 4100-4799 Rink
40. River
41. Package
42. 3700-4099 Love
43. Windmill
44. 3700-4099 Bank
45. 3700-4099 Rink
46. 5200-5399 Love
47. Bluff
48. Thistle
49. 4800-5199 Bank
50. 4100-4799 Rink
51. 4800-5199 Love
52. Juggler
53. Monsoon
54. 4100-4799 Love

55. 5400-5599 Bank
56. 5200-5399 Bank
57. Quill
58. Elephant
59. 5200-5399 Rink
60. 3700-4099 Rink
61. 5400-5599 Love
62. Windmill
63. Thistle
64. 3700-4099 Love
65. 4800-5199 Rink
66. 3700-4099 Bank
67. Chapel
68. Package
69. 4100-4799 Bank
70. 5400-5599 Rink
71. 5200-5399 Love
72. 5200-5399 Bank

73. Bluff
74. River
75. 3700-4099 Bank
76. 3700-4099 Love
77. 3700-4099 Rink
78. 4800-5199 Love
79. 4800-5199 Rink
80. 4800-5199 Bank
81. Package
82. Elephant
83. 4100-4799 Rink
84. 5200-5399 Rink
85. 5200-5399 Love
86. 5400-5599 Bank
87. Quill
88. Bluff

Practice Set 2

DIRECTIONS: The next 88 questions are for practice. Write your answer (letter) next to the question number. Your time limit is three minutes. This time, however, you must not look at the boxes while answering the questions. You must rely only on memory for determining the box location of each item. This practice test will not be scored.

1. 5400-5599 Rink	31. 3700-4099 Rink	61. Elephant
2. 5200-5399 Bank	32. 5400-5599 Bank	62. 4800-5199 Rink
3. 4100-4799 Love	33. 4100-4799 Love	63. 4100-4799 Bank
4. 5400-5599 Bank	34. Monsoon	64. 3700-4099 Love
5. 3700-4099 Rink	35. Thistle	65. Chapel
6. 5400-5599 Love	36. 5200-5399 Love	66. Package
7. Thistle	37. 5200-5399 Bank	67. Quill
8. Windmill	38. 4800-5199 Rink	68. 3700-4099 Rink
9. Elephant	39. Bluff	69. 5200-5399 Bank
10. 4800-5199 Rink	40. Elephant	70. 4100-4799 Love
11. 4100-4799 Bank	41. 4800-5199 Bank	71. Bluff
12. 4800-5199 Bank	42. 4100-4799 Bank	72. River
13. Quill	43. 4800-5199 Love	73. 4800-5199 Love
14. Package	44. Juggler	74. 5400-5599 Bank
15. 5200-5399 Love	45. Windmill	75. 5400-5599 Rink
16. 3700-4099 Love	46. 5400-5599 Love	76. Juggler
17. 5200-5399 Rink	47. 5200-5399 Rink	77. Quill
18. Chapel	48. 5400-5599 Rink	78. 5400-5599 Rink
19. Monsoon	49. River	79. 5200-5399 Love
20. 3700-4099 Bank	50. Package	80. 3700-4099 Bank
21. 4100-4799 Rink	51. Juggler	81. 3700-4099 Rink
22. 4800-5199 Love	52. Monsoon	82. Windmill
23. River	53. 5200-5399 Love	83. Elephant
24. Juggler	54. 4100-4799 Rink	84. 4800-5199 Rink
25. Bluff	55. 3700-4099 Bank	85. 4100-4799 Love
26. 3700-4099 Love	56. 5200-5399 Rink	86. Juggler
27. 4100-4799 Rink	57. 4800-5199 Bank	87. 5400-5599 Bank
28. 3700-4099 Bank	58. 5400-5599 Love	88. 4800-5199 Love
29. Quill	59. Windmill	
30. Chapel	60. Thistle	

18

Practice Set 3

> **DIRECTIONS:** The same addresses from the previous sets are repeated in the box below. Each address is in the same box as the original set. You now have three minutes to study the locations again. Do your best to memorize the letter of the box in which each address is located. This is your last chance to see the boxes.

A	B	C	D	E
3700–4099 Rink	5200–5399 Rink	4800–5199 Rink	4100–4799 Rink	5400–5599 Rink
Chapel	Elephant	Bluff	Windmill	Quill
4800–5199 Bank	5400–5599 Bank	3700–4099 Bank	5200–5399 Bank	4100–4799 Bank
River	Package	Juggler	Thistle	Monsoon
5400–5599 Love	3700–4099 Love	4100–4799 Love	4800–5199 Love	5200–5399 Love

> **DIRECTIONS:** This is your last practice set. Mark the location of each of the 88 addresses by writing the answer (letter) next to the question number. Your time limit is five minutes. Do not look back at the boxes. This practice test will not be scored.

1. 4800-5199 Rink
2. 5400-5599 Love
3. 5200-5399 Love
4. Chapel
5. Quill
6. 3700-4099 Bank
7. 4800-5199 Bank
8. 4100-4799 Rink
9. 5400-5599 Rink
10. Elephant
11. Bluff
12. 4800-5199 Love
13. 4100-4799 Love
14. 5200-5399 Rink
15. Windmill
16. Monsoon
17. 4100-4799 Bank

18. 5200-5399 Rink
19. 3700-4099 Rink
20. 5200-5399 Love
21. 5400-5599 Love
22. 5400-5599 Rink
23. Thistle
24. River
25. Package
26. Bluff
27. 3700-4099 Bank
28. 4800-5199 Bank
29. 4100-4799 Rink
30. 4100-4799 Love
31. 4800-5199 Love
32. Chapel
33. 5200-5399 Rink
34. Quill

35. 4100-4799 Bank
36. 3700-4099 Love
37. 3700-4099 Rink
38. Thistle
39. Windmill
40. 5200-5399 Love
41. 4100-4799 Rink
42. 5400-5599 Bank
43. 5200-5399 Bank
44. Juggler
45. Chapel
46. 4100-4799 Love
47. 3700-4099 Bank
48. 4800-5199 Love
49. Monsoon
50. Elephant
51. 4800-5199 Bank

52. 4800-5199 Rink

53. 5400-5599 Rink

54. 5400-5599 Love

55. River

56. Bluff

57. Package

58. 5200-5399 Bank

59. 3700-4099 Rink

60. 5200-5399 Love

61. 5400-5599 Rink

62. Thistle

63. Windmill

64. River

65. 3700-4099 Bank

66. 5400-5599 Love

67. 4100-4799 Rink

68. 5200-5399 Bank

69. Quill

70. Bluff

71. 5200-5399 Rink

72. 4100-4799 Love

73. 3700-4099 Love

74. Chapel

75. Monsoon

76. 4800-5199 Rink

77. 4800-5199 Bank

78. 4100-4799 Bank

79. Juggler

80. Package

81. 4800-5199 Love

82. 5200-5399 Love

83. 5400-5599 Bank

84. Elephant

85. 3700-4099 Rink

86. 5400-5599 Rink

87. 4100-4799 Love

88. Bluff

18

Memory for Addresses

DIRECTIONS: Indicate the location (A, B, C, D, or E) of each of the 88 addresses below by writing the answer (letter) next to the question number. You are not permitted to look at the boxes. Work from memory as quickly and as accurately as you can. Your time limit is five minutes.

1. 3700-4099 Love
2. 4800-5199 Rink
3. 3700-4099 Bank
4. Quill
5. Windmill
6. 5200-5399 Bank
7. 5400-5599 Rink
8. 5400-5599 Love
9. Elephant
10. Juggler
11. 4800-5199 Bank
12. 5200-5399 Rink
13. 5200-5399 Love
14. Monsoon
15. Thistle
16. 4100-4799 Love
17. 4100-4799 Rink
18. 4100-4799 Bank
19. Bluff
20. River
21. Chapel
22. 5400-5599 Bank
23. 5400-5599 Love
24. Package
25. Quill
26. 5400-5599 Rink
27. 4800-5199 Rink
28. 4800-5199 Bank
29. 5200-5399 Love
30. Thistle

31. Chapel
32. Bluff
33. 3700-4099 Bank
34. 4100-4799 Bank
35. 4100-4799 Rink
36. 4100-4799 Love
37. Windmill
38. Monsoon
39. Juggler
40. 4800-5199 Love
41. 3700-4099 Rink
42. 5200-5399 Bank
43. 5200-5399 Love
44. 4100-4799 Bank
45. 4800-5199 Rink
46. Juggler
47. Package
48. 5200-5399 Rink
49. 4100-4799 Love
50. 4800-5199 Bank
51. Quill
52. Thistle
53. 5400-5599 Bank
54. 5200-5399 Bank
55. 5400-5599 Rink
56. 3700-4099 Rink
57. Windmill
58. Bluff
59. Elephant
60. 5400-5599 Love

61. 4800-5199 Love
62. 3700-4099 Bank
63. 4100-4799 Rink
64. 3700-4099 Love
65. Monsoon
66. River
67. Chapel
68. 4100-4799 Love
69. 4800-5199 Bank
70. 5400-5599 Rink
71. 3700-4099 Rink
72. 5400-5599 Bank
73. 4100-4799 Love
74. Quill
75. Windmill
76. 5200-5399 Love
77. 4100-4799 Bank
78. 5400-5599 Rink
79. Bluff
80. Chapel
81. 4800-5199 Bank
82. 3700-4099 Love
83. 4800-5199 Love
84. 3700-4099 Bank
85. Juggler
86. Elephant
87. River
88. 4800-5199 Rink

Answers

Practice Set 1

1.	C	31.	B	61.	A
2.	E	32.	A	62.	D
3.	B	33.	B	63.	D
4.	C	34.	A	64.	B
5.	D	35.	E	65.	C
6.	C	36.	E	66.	C
7.	D	37.	C	67.	A
8.	A	38.	D	68.	B
9.	D	39.	D	69.	E
10.	E	40.	A	70.	E
11.	A	41.	B	71.	E
12.	C	42.	B	72.	D
13.	E	43.	D	73.	C
14.	A	44.	C	74.	A
15.	B	45.	A	75.	C
16.	E	46.	E	76.	B
17.	D	47.	C	77.	A
18.	D	48.	D	78.	D
19.	A	49.	A	79.	C
20.	E	50.	D	80.	A
21.	D	51.	D	81.	B
22.	E	52.	C	82.	B
23.	A	53.	E	83.	D
24.	A	54.	C	84.	B
25.	C	55.	B	85.	E
26.	C	56.	D	86.	B
27.	C	57.	E	87.	E
28.	B	58.	B	88.	C
29.	E	59.	B		
30.	D	60.	A		

18

Practice Set 2

1.	E	31.	A	61.	B		
2.	D	32.	B	62.	C		
3.	C	33.	C	63.	E		
4.	B	34.	E	64.	B		
5.	A	35.	D	65.	A		
6.	A	36.	E	66.	B		
7.	D	37.	D	67.	E		
8.	D	38.	C	68.	A		
9.	B	39.	C	69.	D		
10.	C	40.	B	70.	C		
11.	E	41.	A	71.	C		
12.	A	42.	E	72.	A		
13.	E	43.	D	73.	D		
14.	B	44.	C	74.	B		
15.	E	45.	D	75.	E		
16.	B	46.	A	76.	C		
17.	B	47.	B	77.	E		
18.	A	48.	E	78.	E		
19.	E	49.	A	79.	E		
20.	C	50.	B	80.	C		
21.	D	51.	C	81.	A		
22.	D	52.	E	82.	D		
23.	A	53.	E	83.	B		
24.	C	54.	D	84.	C		
25.	C	55.	C	85.	C		
26.	B	56.	B	86.	C		
27.	D	57.	A	87.	B		
28.	C	58.	A	88.	D		
29.	E	59.	D				
30.	A	60.	D				

Practice Set 3

1.	C	31.	D	61.	E
2.	A	32.	A	62.	D
3.	E	33.	B	63.	D
4.	A	34.	E	64.	A
5.	E	35.	E	65.	C
6.	C	36.	B	66.	A
7.	A	37.	A	67.	D
8.	D	38.	D	68.	D
9.	E	39.	D	69.	E
10.	B	40.	E	70.	C
11.	C	41.	D	71.	B
12.	D	42.	B	72.	C
13.	C	43.	D	73.	B
14.	B	44.	C	74.	A
15.	D	45.	A	75.	E
16.	E	46.	C	76.	C
17.	E	47.	C	77.	A
18.	B	48.	D	78.	E
19.	A	49.	E	79.	C
20.	E	50.	B	80.	B
21.	A	51.	A	81.	D
22.	E	52.	C	82.	E
23.	D	53.	E	83.	B
24.	A	54.	A	84.	B
25.	B	55.	A	85.	A
26.	C	56.	C	86.	E
27.	C	57.	B	87.	C
28.	A	58.	D	88.	C
29.	D	59.	A		
30.	C	60.	E		

18

Memory for Addresses

1.	B	31.	A	61.	D
2.	C	32.	C	62.	C
3.	C	33.	C	63.	D
4.	E	34.	E	64.	B
5.	D	35.	D	65.	E
6.	D	36.	C	66.	A
7.	E	37.	D	67.	A
8.	A	38.	E	68.	C
9.	B	39.	C	69.	A
10.	C	40.	D	70.	E
11.	A	41.	A	71.	A
12.	B	42.	D	72.	B
13.	E	43.	E	73.	C
14.	E	44.	E	74.	E
15.	D	45.	C	75.	D
16.	C	46.	C	76.	E
17.	D	47.	B	77.	E
18.	E	48.	B	78.	E
19.	C	49.	C	79.	C
20.	A	50.	A	80.	A
21.	A	51.	E	81.	A
22.	B	52.	D	82.	B
23.	A	53.	B	83.	D
24.	B	54.	D	84.	C
25.	E	55.	E	85.	C
26.	E	56.	A	86.	B
27.	C	57.	D	87.	A
28.	A	58.	C	88.	C
29.	E	59.	B		
30.	D	60.	A		

Determine Your Raw Score

Memory for Addresses: Your score on Memory for Addresses is based on the number of questions you answered correctly minus one-fourth of the questions you answered incorrectly (number wrong divided by four):

1.   Enter number of right answers: _____

2.   Enter number of wrong answers: _____

3.   Divide number wrong by four: _____

4.   Subtract answer from number right: _____

Raw Score =   _____

Evaluate Yourself

Determine where your raw score falls on the following scale. If you scored less than Excellent, use the remaining time in the hour to review Hours 6 through 8 and then retake the test to see if you improved your score.

IF your raw score is between	THEN your work is
75-88	Excellent
60-74	Good
45-59	Average
30-44	Fair
1-29	Poor

18

The Hour in Review

1. In this hour, you took a second timed Memory for Addresses practice test.

2. After completing this practice test, you should see improvement in your accuracy, speed, and memorization strategies.

3. Take advantage of the leftover time to review the test-taking strategies in Hours 6 through 8 and in Hours 15 through 16.

HOUR 19

Memory for Addresses—Timed Test 3

What You Will Learn in This Hour

In this hour, you'll take the last full-length Memory for Addresses timed test. Use this final test to perfect your memorization techniques and test-taking skills. Here are your goals for this hour:

- Take the practice test under actual timed conditions, focusing on the weak areas that you discovered in the previous two hours.

- Check your answers against the answer key and determine your raw score.

- Review the appropriate lessons in previous hours if necessary.

Timed Test

You will have 27 minutes to take this test.

Sample Questions

> **DIRECTIONS:** You will have to memorize the locations (A, B, C, D, or E) of the 25 addresses in the five lettered boxes below. Write your answer (letter) next to the question number.
>
> You now have five minutes to study the locations of the addresses. Then cover the boxes and answer the sample questions. You may look back at the boxes if you cannot yet mark the address locations from memory.

A	B	C	D	E
4100–4199 Plum	1000–1399 Plum	4200–4599 Plum	1400–4099 Plum	4600–5299 Plum
Bardack	Greenhouse	Flynn	Pepper	Palm
4200–4599 Ash	4600–5299 Ash	1400–4099 Ash	1000–1399 Ash	4100–4199 Ash
Lemon	Dalby	Race	Clown	Hawk
1000–1399 Neff	4100–4199 Neff	4600–5299 Neff	4200–4599 Neff	1400–4099 Neff

1. 1400-4099 Plum
2. 1000-1399 Neff
3. Lemon
4. Flynn
5. 4200-4599 Ash
6. 4600-5299 Ash
7. Palm
8. Pepper
9. 4100-4199 Plum
10. 4600-5299 Neff
11. 1000-1399 Plum
12. Clown
13. Greenhouse
14. 4100-4199 Ash

Answers

1. D
2. A
3. A
4. C
5. A
6. B
7. E
8. D
9. A
10. C
11. B
12. D
13. B
14. E

Practice Set 1

> **DIRECTIONS:** The five boxes below are labeled A, B, C, D, and E. In each box are five addresses; three are street addresses with number ranges and two are unnumbered place names. You have three minutes to memorize the box location of each address. The position of an address within a box is not important. You need only remember the letter of the box in which the address is found. You will use these addresses to answer three sets of practice questions that are not scored and one actual test that is scored.

A	B	C	D	E
4100–4199 Plum	1000–1399 Plum	4200–4599 Plum	1400–4099 Plum	4600–5299 Plum
Bardack	Greenhouse	Flynn	Pepper	Palm
4200–4599 Ash	4600–5299 Ash	1400–4099 Ash	1000–1399 Ash	4100–4199 Ash
Lemon	Dalby	Race	Clown	Hawk
1000–1399 Neff	4100–4199 Neff	4600–5299 Neff	4200–4599 Neff	1400–4099 Neff

> **DIRECTIONS:** You have three minutes to write the letter of the box for each of the following addresses next to the question numbers. Try to do this without looking at the boxes. If you get stuck, however, you may refer to the boxes during this practice exercise. If you must look at the boxes, try to memorize as you do so. This test is for practice only. It will not be scored.

1. 4600-5299 Ash	15. Hawk	29. Bardack
2. 4600-5299 Neff	16. 4100-4199 Plum	30. 4200-4599 Ash
3. 1400-4099 Plum	17. 4200-4599 Plum	31. 1400-4099 Neff
4. Palm	18. 4600-5299 Ash	32. 4600-5299 Neff
5. Bardack	19. 4200-4599 Neff	33. 1400-4099 Ash
6. 1400-4099 Neff	20. Race	34. Flynn
7. 1400-4099 Ash	21. Pepper	35. Lemon
8. 1000-1399 Plum	22. 4100-4199 Ash	36. Clown
9. Greenhouse	23. 1000-1399 Neff	37. 4100-4199 Plum
10. Lemon	24. 1000-1399 Plum	38. 1000-1399 Ash
11. 4600-5299 Plum	25. Palm	39. 4100-4199 Neff
12. 4200-4599 Ash	26. Dalby	40. Greenhouse
13. 4600-5299 Neff	27. 4600-5299 Plum	41. Hawk
14. Dalby	28. 1400-4099 Plum	42. 4600-5299 Plum

19

43. 1000-1399 Neff
44. 1400-4099 Ash
45. 4600-5299 Ash
46. Palm
47. Greenhouse
48. 1400-4099 Plum
49. 4200-4599 Neff
50. 1000-1399 Ash
51. Race
52. Flynn
53. 4600-5299 Ash
54. 4600-5299 Plum
55. 4600-5299 Neff
56. Pepper
57. Lemon
58. 1000-1399 Plum

59. 4100-4199 Plum
60. 1000-1399 Neff
61. 4100-4199 Ash
62. Bardack
63. Dalby
64. Clown
65. 4200-4599 Ash
66. 1400-4099 Ash
67. 4200-4599 Plum
68. Hawk
69. 4100-4199 Neff
70. 1400-4099 Neff
71. 1000-1399 Plum
72. Pepper
73. 1000-1399 Neff
74. 4100-4199 Ash

75. Dalby
76. Palm
77. 4100-4199 Plum
78. 1400-4099 Ash
79. 1400-4099 Plum
80. 1400-4099 Neff
81. Pepper
82. Hawk
83. 4600-5299 Ash
84. 4600-5299 Plum
85. 1000-1399 Ash
86. 1000-1399 Neff
87. Palm
88. Greenhouse

Practice Set 2

> **DIRECTIONS:** The next 88 questions are for practice. Write your answer (letter) next to the question number. Your time limit is three minutes and you must not look at the boxes while answering the questions. You must rely only on memory. This practice test will not be scored.

1. 4100-4199 Plum
2. 1400-4099 Neff
3. 1400-4099 Ash
4. Clown
5. Greenhouse
6. 4100-4199 Neff
7. 1000-1399 Ash
8. 4100-4199 Ash
9. Race
10. Flynn
11. 4600-5299 Plum
12. 1000-1399 Neff
13. 4200-4599 Ash
14. 1000-1399 Plum
15. Palm
16. Dalby
17. Pepper
18. 4600-5299 Neff
19. 4200-4599 Neff
20. 1400-4099 Plum
21. Bardack
22. Lemon
23. Hawk
24. 4200-4599 Plum
25. 4600-5299 Ash
26. 4200-4599 Plum
27. 4600-5299 Neff
28. 1400-4099 Ash
29. Lemon
30. Pepper

31. 4100-4199 Neff
32. 1400-4099 Plum
33. 4200-4599 Neff
34. Dalby
35. Flynn
36. 4200-4599 Ash
37. 4600-5299 Plum
38. 4100-4199 Plum
39. Bardack
40. Hawk
41. 1000-1399 Plum
42. 1000-1399 Neff
43. 1000-1399 Ash
44. Greenhouse
45. Clown
46. 4600-5299 Ash
47. 4100-4199 Ash
48. 1400-4099 Neff
49. Race
50. Palm
51. Flynn
52. Hawk
53. 4100-4199 Neff
54. 1000-1399 Ash
55. 4100-4199 Plum
56. 1400-4099 Plum
57. 4200-4599 Plum
58. Bardack
59. 4600-5299 Neff
60. 4200-4599 Neff

61. 4200-4599 Ash
62. Pepper
63. Clown
64. 4600-5299 Ash
65. 1000-1399 Neff
66. 1000-1399 Plum
67. Race
68. Dalby
69. 1400-4099 Ash
70. 4100-4199 Ash
71. 4600-5299 Plum
72. 4600-5299 Neff
73. Palm
74. 1400-4099 Neff
75. Greenhouse
76. 4100-4199 Plum
77. 4200-4599 Neff
78. 4200-4599 Ash
79. Clown
80. Dalby
81. 4200-4599 Plum
82. 1400-4099 Ash
83. 1000-1399 Neff
84. Pepper
85. Bardack
86. 4100-4199 Plum
87. 1400-4099 Neff
88. 4100-4199 Ash

19

Practice Set 3

DIRECTIONS: The same addresses from the previous sets are repeated in the box below, with each address in the same box as the original set. You now have three minutes to study the locations again. Do your best to memorize the letter of the box in which each address is located. This is your last chance to see the boxes.

A	B	C	D	E
4100–4199 Plum	1000–1399 Plum	4200–4599 Plum	1400–4099 Plum	4600–5299 Plum
Bardack	Greenhouse	Flynn	Pepper	Palm
4200–4599 Ash	4600–5299 Ash	1400–4099 Ash	1000–1399 Ash	4100–4199 Ash
Lemon	Dalby	Race	Clown	Hawk
1000–1399 Neff	4100–4199 Neff	4600–5299 Neff	4200–4599 Neff	1400–4099 Neff

DIRECTIONS: This is your last practice set. Mark the location for each of the 88 addresses by writing the answer (letter) next to the question number. Your time limit is five minutes. Do not look back at the boxes. This practice test will not be scored.

1. 1400-4099 Ash
2. 4600-5299 Plum
3. 1000-1399 Neff
4. Pepper
5. Greenhouse
6. 4100-4199 Plum
7. 1400-4099 Neff
8. 4600-5299 Ash
9. 1000-1399 Ash
10. Bardack
11. Lemon
12. Hawk
13. 1000-1399 Plum
14. 4200-4599 Neff
15. 4200-4599 Ash
16. 4100-4199 Ash
17. 1400-4099 Plum
18. 4100-4199 Ash
19. Clown
20. Flynn

21. 4600-5299 Ash
22. 1000-1399 Plum
23. 4200-4599 Ash
24. Lemon
25. Race
26. 4600-5299 Neff
27. 4600-5299 Plum
28. Dalby
29. Palm
30. 4200-4599 Neff
31. 1000-1399 Plum
32. 1400-4099 Ash
33. 4200-4599 Neff
34. 1400-4099 Plum
35. 4100-4199 Neff
36. Palm
37. Clown
38. Dalby
39. 4200-4599 Ash
40. 4100-4199 Ash

41. 4600-5299 Plum
42. 1000-1399 Neff
43. Greenhouse
44. Pepper
45. 4100-4199 Plum
46. 1400-4099 Neff
47. 4600-5299 Ash
48. 1000-1399 Ash
49. Clown
50. Bardack
51. Lemon
52. 4200-4599 Plum
53. 4600-5299 Neff
54. Hawk
55. Flynn
56. Race
57. 1400-4099 Plum
58. 1000-1399 Neff
59. 4100-4199 Ash
60. 1400-4099 Ash

61. 1400-4099 Plum
62. 4100-4199 Neff
63. 1400-4099 Neff
64. Hawk
65. Lemon
66. 1000-1399 Plum
67. 4100-4199 Neff
68. 4600-5299 Ash
69. Pepper
70. Dalby

71. 1000-1399 Neff
72. 4600-5299 Plum
73. 4100-4199 Ash
74. Greenhouse
75. Race
76. 4200-4599 Neff
77. 1000-1399 Ash
78. 4200-4599 Plum
79. Bardack
80. Palm

81. 4200-4599 Ash
82. 4100-4199 Plum
83. 4600-5299 Neff
84. Flynn
85. Clown
86. 1400-4099 Ash
87. 4600-5299 Plum
88. 4100-4199 Plum

19

Memory for Addresses

DIRECTIONS: Indicate the location (A, B, C, D, or E) for each of the 88 addresses below by writing the answer (letter) next to the question number. You are not permitted to look at the boxes. Work from memory as quickly and as accurately as you can. Your time limit is five minutes.

1. 1400-4099 Neff
2. 4100-4199 Plum
3. 1400-4099 Ash
4. Pepper
5. Dalby
6. 4200-4599 Plum
7. 4600-5299 Neff
8. 4100-4199 Ash
9. 4200-4599 Ash
10. Bardack
11. Hawk
12. 4600-5299 Plum
13. 1000-1399 Neff
14. 1000-1399 Ash
15. Clown
16. Flynn
17. 4600-5299 Ash
18. 1400-4099 Plum
19. 1000-1399 Plum
20. Palm
21. Race
22. Lemon
23. 4100-4199 Neff
24. Greenhouse
25. 4200-4599 Neff
26. 1000-1399 Plum
27. 1400-4099 Neff
28. 4200-4599 Ash
29. Hawk
30. Flynn

31. 4100-4199 Plum
32. 4200-4599 Neff
33. 1400-4099 Ash
34. Clown
35. Dalby
36. 4100-4199 Ash
37. 4100-4199 Neff
38. 1400-4099 Plum
39. Palm
40. Bardack
41. 1000-1399 Plum
42. 4600-5299 Neff
43. 1400-4099 Plum
44. Lemon
45. Palm
46. 4200-4599 Ash
47. 4100-4199 Ash
48. 4100-4199 Plum
49. 1000-1399 Neff
50. 4100-4199 Neff
51. Hawk
52. Greenhouse
53. Dalby
54. 1400-4099 Ash
55. 4600-5299 Ash
56. 4200-4599 Plum
57. Clown
58. Race
59. 1000-1399 Ash
60. 4600-5299 Plum

61. Bardack
62. 4200-4599 Neff
63. Flynn
64. Pepper
65. 1400-4099 Neff
66. 4100-4199 Ash
67. 4600-5299 Neff
68. 1000-1399 Plum
69. 4100-4199 Plum
70. 4600-5299 Ash
71. 4600-5299 Neff
72. Lemon
73. Pepper
74. Palm
75. 1400-4099 Ash
76. 1400-4099 Neff
77. 4100-4199 Ash
78. 4600-5299 Plum
79. Greenhouse
80. Dalby
81. 1000-1399 Plum
82. 1000-1399 Ash
83. 4100-4199 Neff
84. 4200-4599 Plum
85. Flynn
86. Clown
87. 4200-4599 Ash
88. 4100-4199 Ash

Answers

Practice Set 1

1.	B	31.	E	61.	E
2.	C	32.	C	62.	A
3.	D	33.	C	63.	B
4.	E	34.	C	64.	D
5.	A	35.	A	65.	A
6.	E	36.	D	66.	C
7.	C	37.	A	67.	C
8.	B	38.	D	68.	E
9.	B	39.	B	69.	B
10.	A	40.	B	70.	E
11.	E	41.	E	71.	B
12.	A	42.	E	72.	D
13.	C	43.	A	73.	A
14.	B	44.	C	74.	E
15.	E	45.	B	75.	B
16.	A	46.	E	76.	E
17.	C	47.	B	77.	A
18.	B	48.	D	78.	C
19.	D	49.	D	79.	D
20.	C	50.	D	80.	E
21.	D	51.	C	81.	D
22.	E	52.	C	82.	E
23.	A	53.	B	83.	B
24.	B	54.	E	84.	E
25.	E	55.	C	85.	D
26.	B	56.	D	86.	A
27.	E	57.	A	87.	E
28.	D	58.	B	88.	B
29.	A	59.	A		
30.	A	60.	A		

19

Practice Set 2

1.	A	31.	B	61.	A
2.	E	32.	D	62.	D
3.	C	33.	D	63.	D
4.	D	34.	B	64.	B
5.	B	35.	C	65.	A
6.	B	36.	A	66.	B
7.	D	37.	E	67.	C
8.	E	38.	A	68.	B
9.	C	39.	A	69.	C
10.	C	40.	E	70.	E
11.	E	41.	B	71.	E
12.	A	42.	A	72.	C
13.	A	43.	D	73.	E
14.	B	44.	B	74.	E
15.	E	45.	D	75.	B
16.	B	46.	B	76.	A
17.	D	47.	E	77.	D
18.	C	48.	E	78.	A
19.	D	49.	C	79.	D
20.	D	50.	E	80.	B
21.	A	51.	C	81.	C
22.	A	52.	E	82.	C
23.	E	53.	B	83.	A
24.	C	54.	D	84.	D
25.	B	55.	A	85.	A
26.	C	56.	D	86.	A
27.	C	57.	C	87.	E
28.	C	58.	A	88.	E
29.	A	59.	C		
30.	D	60.	D		

Practice Set 3

1.	C	31.	B	61.	D
2.	E	32.	C	62.	B
3.	A	33.	D	63.	E
4.	D	34.	D	64.	E
5.	B	35.	B	65.	A
6.	A	36.	E	66.	B
7.	E	37.	D	67.	B
8.	B	38.	B	68.	B
9.	D	39.	A	69.	D
10.	A	40.	E	70.	B
11.	A	41.	E	71.	A
12.	E	42.	A	72.	E
13.	B	43.	B	73.	E
14.	D	44.	D	74.	B
15.	A	45.	A	75.	C
16.	B	46.	E	76.	D
17.	D	47.	B	77.	D
18.	E	48.	D	78.	C
19.	D	49.	D	79.	A
20.	C	50.	A	80.	E
21.	B	51.	A	81.	A
22.	B	52.	C	82.	A
23.	A	53.	C	83.	C
24.	A	54.	E	84.	C
25.	C	55.	C	85.	D
26.	C	56.	C	86.	C
27.	E	57.	D	87.	E
28.	B	58.	A	88.	A
29.	E	59.	E		
30.	D	60.	C		

19

Memory for Addresses

1.	E	31.	A	61.	A
2.	A	32.	D	62.	D
3.	C	33.	C	63.	C
4.	D	34.	D	64.	D
5.	B	35.	B	65.	E
6.	C	36.	E	66.	E
7.	C	37.	B	67.	C
8.	E	38.	D	68.	B
9.	A	39.	E	69.	A
10.	A	40.	A	70.	B
11.	E	41.	B	71.	C
12.	E	42.	C	72.	A
13.	A	43.	D	73.	D
14.	D	44.	A	74.	E
15.	D	45.	E	75.	C
16.	C	46.	A	76.	E
17.	B	47.	E	77.	E
18.	D	48.	A	78.	E
19.	B	49.	A	79.	B
20.	E	50.	B	80.	B
21.	C	51.	E	81.	B
22.	A	52.	B	82.	D
23.	B	53.	B	83.	B
24.	B	54.	C	84.	C
25.	D	55.	B	85.	C
26.	B	56.	C	86.	D
27.	E	57.	D	87.	A
28.	A	58.	C	88.	E
29.	E	59.	D		
30.	C	60.	E		

Determine Your Raw Score

Memory for Addresses: Your score on Memory for Addresses is based on the number of questions you answered correctly minus one-fourth of the questions you answered incorrectly (number wrong divided by four):

1. Enter number of right answers: _____
2. Enter number of wrong answers: _____
3. Divide number wrong by four: _____
4. Subtract answer from number right: _____

Raw Score =   _____

Evaluate Yourself

Determine where your raw score falls on the following scale. If you scored less than Excellent, review Hours 6 through 8 and then retake the test to see if you improved your score.

IF your raw score is between	THEN your work is
75-88	Excellent
60-74	Good
45-59	Average
30-44	Fair
1-29	Poor

19

The Hour in Review

1. In this hour, you took a final timed Memory for Addresses practice test.

2. You should use this test to improve your performance on the weak areas you discovered when taking the previous two timed tests.

3. You may retake any of the timed tests as many times as you want for additional practice, but don't take more than one test in the same hour.

HOUR **20**

Number Series— Untimed Tests

What You Will Learn in This Hour

In this hour, you'll develop your skills for answering Number Series questions by completing three practice tests at your own pace. These tests are the same length as the Number Series portion of the actual Test 470. Here are your goals for this hour:

- Understand your goals for taking the untimed practice tests.

- Complete each practice test at your own pace, focusing on the techniques that you learned in Hour 9, "Number Series—1," and Hour 10, "Number Series—2."

- Review the previous lessons on answering Number Series questions if needed.

Preparing for the Untimed Practice Tests

The three practice tests that you'll take in this hour will help you get ready for the timed tests in Hour 21, "Number Series—Timed Tests." Use these tests to get comfortable with the Number Series question format and the question-answering strategies that you've already learned. The more practice you have in spotting patterns, the easier this question type becomes.

When taking the practice tests, follow these steps:

1. Complete each test in order.

2. If you need to, make notes to determine the pattern for each number series.

3. Before moving on to the next practice test, check your answers against the answer key and explanations.

4. Circle the questions that you answered incorrectly and try to see why you missed them.

5. Review the material in Hours 9 and 10 that you need more practice with.

Tip
Remember most calculations involved in Number Series questions are simple addition and subtraction and, possibly, multiplication and division. So think positively, banish any math anxiety, and trust your instincts. Above all, don't get discouraged if your first attempt at finding a pattern doesn't work; just try using a different technique. Having a flexible approach will help you achieve the highest score.

Practice Test 1

DIRECTIONS: Each question contains a series of numbers on the left that follows a definite pattern and at the right five sets of two numbers each. Look at the numbers in the series on the left and determine the order they follow. Then decide what the next two numbers in the series would be if the series were continued. Circle the letter of the correct answer.

1. 10 11 12 10 11 12 10... (A) 10 11 (B) 12 10 (C) 11 10 (D) 11 12 (E) 10 12

2. 4 6 7 4 6 7 4... (A) 6 7 (B) 4 7 (C) 7 6 (D) 7 4 (E) 6 8

3. 10 10 9 11 11 10 12... (A) 13 14 (B) 12 11 (C) 13 13 (D) 12 12 (E) 12 13

4. 3 4 10 5 6 10 7... (A) 10 8 (B) 9 8 (C) 8 14 (D) 8 9 (E) 8 10

5. 6 6 7 7 8 8 9... (A) 10 11 (B) 10 10 (C) 9 10 (D) 9 9 (E) 10 9

6. 3 8 9 4 9 10 5... (A) 6 10 (B) 10 11 (C) 9 10 (D) 11 6 (E) 10 6

7. 2 4 3 6 4 8 5... (A) 6 10 (B) 10 7 (C) 10 6 (D) 9 6 (E) 6 7

8. 11 5 9 7 7 9 5... (A) 11 3 (B) 7 9 (C) 7 11 (D) 9 7 (E) 3 7

9. 7 16 9 15 11 14 13... (A) 12 14 (B) 13 15 (C) 17 15 (D) 15 12 (E) 13 12

10. 40 42 39 44 38 46 37... (A) 48 36 (B) 37 46 (C) 36 48 (D) 43 39 (E) 46 40

11. 1 3 6 10 15 21 28 36 ... (A) 40 48 (B) 36 45 (C) 38 52 (D) 45 56 (E) 45 55

12. 1 2 3 3 4 7 5 6 11 7... (A) 8 12 (B) 9 15 (C) 8 15 (D) 6 12 (E) 8 7

13. 3 18 4 24 5 30 6 ... (A) 7 40 (B) 7 42 (C) 42 7 (D) 36 7 (E) 40 7

14. 3 3 4 8 10 30 33 132... (A) 152 158 (B) 136 680 (C) 165 500 (D) 143 560 (E) 300 900

15. 18 20 22 20 18 20 22... (A) 18 20 (B) 20 18 (C) 22 20 (D) 24 20 (E) 18 22

16. 4 8 8 16 16 32 32 ... (A) 32 64 (B) 36 40 (C) 64 64 (D) 64 128 (E) 64 82

17. 1 2 12 3 4 34 5... (A) 6 5 (B) 7 12 (C) 5 6 (D) 6 60 (E) 6 56

18. 8 16 24 32 40 48 56... (A) 64 72 (B) 60 64 (C) 70 78 (D) 62 70 (E) 64 68

19. 5 15 18 54 57 171 174... (A) 176 528 (B) 522 821 (C) 177 531 (D) 522 525 (E) 525 528

20. 25 20 24 21 23 22 22... (A) 24 20 (B) 23 21 (C) 23 24 (D) 24 21 (E) 22 23

21. 99 88 77 66 55 44 33... (A) 22 11 (B) 33 22 (C) 44 55 (D) 32 22 (E) 30 20

22. 7 5 9 7 11 9 13... (A) 9 11 (B) 11 9 (C) 7 11 (D) 9 15 (E) 11 15

23. 47 44 41 38 35 32 29... (A) 28 27 (B) 27 24 (C) 26 23 (D) 25 21 (E) 26 22

24. 99 99 99 33 33 33 11... (A) 9 7 (B) 22 33 (C) 11 0 (D) 11 33 (E) 11 11

20

Answers

1.	D	9.	B	17.	E
2.	A	10.	A	18.	A
3.	B	11.	E	19.	D
4.	E	12.	C	20.	B
5.	C	13.	D	21.	A
6.	B	14.	B	22.	E
7.	C	15.	B	23.	C
8.	A	16.	C	24.	E

Answers and Explanations

1. **(D)** The sequence 10 11 12 repeats.

2. **(A)** This series contains another repeating sequence: 4 6 7.

3. **(B)** Two sequences alternate; the first repeats, advances by 1, repeats again, and the alternating sequence simply advances by 1.

4. **(E)** The sequence consists of numbers ascending from 3, with the number 10 inserted between every two numbers.

5. **(C)** The numbers ascend from 6 by 1, with each number repeating.

6. **(B)** One series starts at 3 and ascends by 1. The alternating series consists of two numbers that ascend according to the following rule: add 1, repeat; add 1, repeat; and so on.

7. **(C)** One series ascend by 1. The alternating series ascends by 2.

8. **(A)** The first series begins with 11 and descends by 2. The alternating series begins with 5 and ascends by 2.

9. **(B)** There are two alternating series, the first ascending by 2, the other descending by 1.

10. **(A)** The first series descends by 1, while the alternating series ascends by 2.

11. **(E)** The rule for this series is add 2, add 3, add 4, add 5, add 6, add 7, add 8, add 9, and so on.

12. **(C)** The series ascends by 1, but there is a twist. After each two numbers, the sum of those numbers is inserted. Thus, the series can be read as follows: $1 + 2 = 3$; $3 + 4 = 7$; $5 + 6 = 11$; $7 + 8 = 15$; and so on.

13. **(D)** Look carefully—this is a times-6 series: $3 \times 6 = 18$; $4 \times 6 = 24$; $5 \times 6 = 30$; $6 \times 6 = 36$; and so on.

14.   **(B)** This one is not easy, but if you wrote out the steps between numbers, you should have come up with: multiply by 1, add 1; multiply by 2, add 2; multiply by 3, add 3; multiply by 4, add 4; multiply by 5, add 5; and so on.

15.   **(B)** This series is deceptively simple. The sequence 18 20 22 20 repeats.

16.   **(C)** The pattern is multiply by 2, repeat; multiply by 2, repeat; and so on. The series picks up with the second number of a repeat.

17.   **(E)** There is no mathematical formula for this series. After inspection you may see that two successive numbers are combined to form a third number: 1 2 12; 3 4 34; 5 6 56, and so on.

18.   **(A)** This is a plus 8 series.

19.   **(D)** The pattern is multiply by 3, add 3; multiply by 3, add 3; and so on.

20.   **(B)** There are two alternating series: the first begins with 25 and descends by 1; the alternating series begins with 20 and ascends by 1.

21.   **(A)** This is a simple descending series of 11.

22.   **(E)** You may see this as two alternating series, both ascending by 2. You might also interpret the series as reading subtract 2, add 4; subtract 2, add 4; and so on. Either way, you'll reach the correct answer.

23.   **(C)** This is a simple subtract 3 series.

24.   **(E)** The rule is repeat, repeat, divide by 3; repeat, repeat, divide by 3; repeat, repeat, divide by 3; and so on.

20

Practice Test 2

DIRECTIONS: Each question contains a series of numbers on the left that follows a definite pattern and at the right five sets of two numbers each. Look at the numbers in the series on the left and determine the order they follow. Then decide what the next two numbers in the series would be if the series were continued. Circle the letter of the correct answer.

1. 3 8 4 9 5 10 6…   (A) 7 11   (B) 7 8   (C) 11 8   (D) 12 7   (E) 11 7

2. 18 14 19 17 20 20 21…   (A) 22 24   (B) 14 19   (C) 24 21   (D) 21 23   (E) 23 22

3. 6 9 10 7 11 12 8…   (A) 9 10   (B) 9 13   (C) 16 14   (D) 13 14   (E) 14 15

4. 7 5 3 9 7 5 11…   (A) 13 12   (B) 7 5   (C) 9 7   (D) 13 7   (E) 9 9

5. 7 9 18 10 12 18 13…   (A) 18 14   (B) 15 18   (C) 14 15   (D) 15 14   (E) 14 18

6. 2 6 4 8 6 10 8…   (A) 12 10   (B) 6 10   (C) 10 12   (D) 12 16   (E) 6 4

7. 7 9 12 14 17 19 22…   (A) 25 27   (B) 23 24   (C) 23 25   (D) 24 27   (E) 26 27

8. 3 23 5 25 7 27 9…   (A) 10 11   (B) 27 29   (C) 29 11   (D) 11 28   (E) 28 10

9. 1 2 2 3 4 1 2 5 6 …   (A) 7 8   (B) 11 7   (C) 11 56   (D) 56 7   (E) 30 7

10. 1 2 3 6 4 5 6 6 7…   (A) 6 5   (B) 8 9   (C) 6 8   (D) 7 6   (E) 8 6

11. 1 3 40 5 7 37 9…   (A) 11 39   (B) 9 11   (C) 34 11   (D) 11 34   (E) 11 35

12. 25 27 29 31 33 35 37… (A) 39 41   (B) 38 39   (C) 37 39   (D) 37 38   (E) 39 40

13. 91 85 17 81 75 15 71… (A) 74 14   (B) 61 51   (C) 65 13   (D) 65 10   (E) 66 33

14. 41 37 46 42 51 47 56… (A) 51 70   (B) 52 61   (C) 49 60   (D) 60 43   (E) 55 65

15. 6 6 6 18 18 18 54…   (A) 54 108 (B) 54 162 (C) 108 108 (D) 108 162 (E) 54 54

16. 13 23 14 22 15 21 16… (A) 17 20   (B) 20 17   (C) 17 18   (D) 20 19   (E) 16 20

17. 52 10 48 20 44 30 40… (A) 36 50   (B) 50 36   (C) 36 40   (D) 40 36   (E) 40 40

18. 94 84 75 67 60 54 49… (A) 45 42   (B) 49 45   (C) 44 40   (D) 46 42   (E) 45 40

19. 76 38 38 48 24 24 34… (A) 34 44   (B) 34 34   (C) 17 17   (D) 34 17   (E) 17 27

20. 83 38 84 48 85 58 86… (A) 86 68   (B) 87 78   (C) 59 95   (D) 68 88   (E) 68 87

21. 19 21 21 24 24 24 28… (A) 28 31   (B) 28 33   (C) 32 36   (D) 28 28   (E) 28 32

22. 52 45 38 32 26 21 16… (A) 16 12   (B) 12 8   (C) 11 6   (D) 11 7   (E) 12 9

23. 100 81 64 49 36 25 16… (A) 12 10 (B) 8 4   (C) 8 2   (D) 9 4   (E) 9 2

24. 4 40 44 5 50 55 6…   (A) 60 66   (B) 6 60   (C) 6 66   (D) 7 70   (E) 70 77

Answers

1.	E	9.	E	17.	D
2.	E	10.	B	18.	A
3.	D	11.	D	19.	C
4.	C	12.	A	20.	E
5.	B	13.	C	21.	D
6.	A	14.	B	22.	B
7.	D	15.	E	23.	D
8.	C	16.	B	24.	A

Answers and Explanations

1. **(E)** There are two alternating series, each ascending by 1; one of them begins with 3, the other with 8.

2. **(E)** The two alternating series progress at different rates. The first, beginning with 18, moves up one number at a time. The alternating series, beginning with 14, ascends by 3.

3. **(D)** There are two alternating series, but this time two numbers of one series are inserted between the steps of the other series. Thus, one series reads 6 7 8, while the other reads 9 10 11 12 13 14.

4. **(C)** This is a series made up of a miniseries. The pattern in each miniseries is to subtract 2. Then the pattern repeats with the first number of the next miniseries two numbers higher than the first number of the preceding miniseries.

5. **(B)** The rule of this series is to add 2 and then add 1, with the number 18 inserted between the two numbers in the add 1 phase.

6. **(A)** The two series alternate, both ascending by 2.

7. **(D)** The rule is add 2, add 3; add 2, add 3; and so on.

8. **(C)** Both alternating series ascend by 2.

9. **(E)** The series is essentially 1 2 3 4 5 6 7, but after each two numbers in the series you must find the product of those two numbers: $1 \times 2 = 2$; $3 \times 4 = 12$; $5 \times 6 = 30$; and so on.

10. **(B)** The series is simply 1 2 3 4 5 6 7 8 9. After each three numbers of the series, insert the number 6.

11. **(D)** There are two series. The ascending series increases by 2. The descending series intervenes after every two steps of the ascending series in steps of 3.

20

12. (A)   Weren't you ready for an easy one? There is no catch. The series ascends by 2.

13. (C)   You may feel the rhythm of this series and spot the pattern without playing around with the numbers. If you can't solve the problem by inspection, you might see three parallel series. The first series descends by 10 (91 81 71); the second series also descends by 10 (85 75 65); the third series descends by 2 (17 15 13). You might also see a miniseries with a pattern of subtracting by 6 and then dividing by 5. Each miniseries begins with a number 10 lower than the first number of the previous miniseries.

14. (B)   The pattern is subtract 4, add 9; subtract 4, add 9; and so on. Or you might see two alternating series, both ascending by 5.

15. (E)   Each number appears three times, then is multiplied by 3.

16. (B)   There are two alternating series; one starts at 13 and ascends by 1, and the other starts at 23 and descends by 1.

17. (D)   There are two alternating series. The first series begins with 52 and descends by 4. The alternating series begins with 10 and ascends by 10.

18. (A)   The pattern is subtract 10, subtract 9, subtract 8, subtract 7, subtract 6, subtract 5, subtract 4, subtract 3, and so on.

19. (C)   The pattern is divide by 2, repeat, add 10; divide by 2, repeat, add 10; and so on.

20. (E)   You see a simple series: 83, 84, 85, 86, and so on, but following each number in the series is its mirror image. The mirror image of 83 is 38; the mirror image of 84 is 48; and so forth. You might also see a series that ascends by 1 alternating with a series that ascends by 10.

21. (D)   The pattern is add 2, repeat the number twice; add 3, repeat the number three times; add 4, repeat the number four times; and so on.

22. (B)   The pattern is subtract 7, subtract 7, subtract 6, subtract 6, subtract 5, subtract 5, subtract 4, subtract 4, and so on.

23. (D)   The series consists of the squares of the whole numbers in descending order.

24. (A)   You can probably get this one by inspection. If not, notice the group of miniseries. In each miniseries, the pattern is 10 times the first number, 11 times the first number, and so on.

Practice Test 3

DIRECTIONS: Each question contains a series of numbers on the left that follows a definite pattern and at the right five sets of two numbers each. Look at the numbers in the series on the left and determine the order they follow. Then decide what the next two numbers in the series would be if the series were continued. Circle the letter of the correct answer.

1. 8 9 9 8 10 10 8...   (A) 11 8   (B) 8 13   (C) 8 11   (D) 11 11   (E) 8 8
2. 10 10 11 11 12 12 13...   (A) 15 15   (B) 13 13   (C) 14 14   (D) 13 14   (E) 14 15
3. 6 6 10 6 6 12 6...   (A) 6 14   (B) 13 6   (C)14 6   (D) 6 13   (E) 6 6
4. 17 11 5 16 10 4 15...   (A) 13 9   (B) 13 11   (C) 8 5   (D) 9 5   (E) 9 3
5. 1 3 2 4 3 5 4...   (A) 6 8   (B) 5 6   (C) 6 5   (D) 3 4   (E) 3 5
6. 11 11 10 12 12 11 13...   (A) 12 14   (B) 14 12   (C) 14 14   (D) 13 14   (E) 13 12
7. 18 5 6 18 7 8 18...   (A) 9 9   (B) 9 10   (C) 18 9   (D) 8 9   (E) 18 7
8. 8 1 9 3 10 5 11...   (A) 7 12   (B) 6 12   (C) 12 6   (D) 7 8   (E) 6 7
9. 14 12 10 20 18 16 32 30...   (A) 60 18   (B) 32 64   (C) 27 34   (D) 28 56   (E) 28 28
10. 67 59 52 44 37 29 22...   (A) 15 7   (B) 114 8   (C) 14 7   (D) 15 8   (E) 16 11
11. 17 79 20 74 23 69 26...   (A) 64 29   (B) 65 30   (C) 29 64   (D) 23 75   (E) 26 64
12. 3 5 10 8 4 6 12 10 5...   (A) 8 16   (B) 7 14   (C) 10 20   (D) 10 5   (E) 7 9
13. 58 52 52 46 46 40 40...   (A)34 28   (B) 28 28   (C) 40 34   (D) 35 35   (E) 34 34
14. 32 37 33 33 38 34 34...   (A) 38 43   (B) 34 39   (C) 39 35   (D) 39 39   (E) 34 40
15. 15 17 19 16 18 20 17...   (A) 14 16   (B) 19 21   (C) 17 19   (D) 16 18   (E) 19 16
16. 5 15 7 21 13 39 31...   (A) 93 85   (B) 62 69   (C) 39 117   (D) 93 87   (E) 31 93
17. 84 76 70 62 56 48 42...   (A) 42 36   (B) 34 26   (C) 36 28   (D) 36 24   (E) 34 28
18. 47 23 43 27 39 31 35...   (A) 31 27   (B) 39 43   (C) 39 35   (D) 35 31   (E) 31 35
19. 14 23 31 38 44 49 53...   (A) 55 57   (B) 57 61   (C) 56 58   (D) 57 59   (E) 58 62
20. 5 6 8 8 9 11 11 12...   (A) 12 13   (B) 14 14   (C) 14 15   (D) 14 16   (E) 12 14
21. 9 18 41 41 36 72 41...   (A) 108 108   (B) 41 108   (C) 41 144   (D) 144 144 (E) 72 41
22. 13 15 17 13 15 17 13...   (A) 17 15   (B) 13 15   (C) 17 13   (D) 15 13   (E) 15 17
23. 13 92 17 89 21 86 25...   (A) 83 29   (B) 24 89   (C) 29 83   (D) 25 83   (E) 89 21
24. 10 20 23 13 26 29 19...   (A) 9 12   (B) 38 41   (C) 22 44   (D) 44 33   (E) 31 25

20

Answers

1.	D	9.	D	17.	E
2.	D	10.	C	18.	D
3.	A	11.	A	19.	C
4.	E	12.	B	20.	B
5.	C	13.	E	21.	C
6.	E	14.	C	22.	E
7.	B	15.	B	23.	A
8.	A	16.	A	24.	B

Answers and Explanations

1. **(D)**   The series consists of repeating ascending numbers. The number 8 is inserted between each pair of repeated numbers.

2. **(D)**   The numbers are repeated and ascend by 1.

3. **(A)**   The numbers 6, 6 are repeated. Between each set of 6s, the series ascends by 2.

4. **(E)**   The full sequence is a group of miniseries. Each miniseries consists of three numbers descending by 6. Each succeeding miniseries begins with a number that is one less than the previous miniseries.

5. **(C)**   Here are two alternating plus 1 series; the first series starts at 1, and the second starts at 3.

6. **(E)**   Two series alternate; the first series consists of repeating numbers that ascend by 1, and the alternating series ascends by 1 without repeating.

7. **(B)**   Here is a plus 1 series starting with 5, with the number 18 repeating between each two numbers.

8. **(A)**   The first series ascends by 1 starting with 8. The alternating series ascends by 2 starting with 1.

9. **(D)**   The pattern is subtract 2, subtract 2, multiply 2; subtract 2, subtract 2, multiply 2; and so on.

10. **(C)**   The pattern is subtract 8, subtract 7; subtract 8, subtract 7; subtract 8, subtract 7; and so on.

11. **(A)**   Two series alternate: the first series ascends by 3; and the alternating series descends by 5.

12. **(B)**   This is a tough one. The pattern is add 2, multiply by 2, subtract 2, divide by 2; add 2, multiply by 2, subtract 2, divide by 2; and so on.

13. **(E)**   The pattern is subtract 6, repeat the number; subtract 6, repeat the number; and so on.

14. **(C)**   The pattern is add 5, subtract 4, repeat the number; add 5, subtract 4, repeat the number; and so on.

15. **(B)**   The pattern is add 2, add 2, subtract 3; add 2, add 2, subtract 3; and so on.

16. **(A)**   The pattern is multiply by 3, subtract 8; multiply by 3, subtract 8; multiply by 3, subtract 8; and so on.

17. **(E)**   The pattern is subtract 8, subtract 6; subtract 8, subtract 6; subtract 8, subtract 6; and so on.

18. **(D)**   There are two alternating series; the first descends by 4 starting at 47, and the alternating series ascends by 4 starting at 23.

19. **(C)**   The pattern is add 9, add 8, add 7, add 6, add 5, add 4, add 3, add 2, add 1.

20. **(B)**   The pattern is add 1, add 2, repeat; add 1, add 2, repeat; and so on.

21. **(C)**   This is a times 2 series with the number 41 inserted twice after each two numbers in the series.

22. **(E)**   The sequence 13 15 17 is repeated.

23. **(A)**   Two series alternate: the first ascends by 4; and the other descends by 3.

24. **(B)**   The pattern is multiply by 2, add 3, subtract 10; multiply by 2, add 3, subtract 10; multiply by 2, add 3, subtract 10; and so on.

20

The Hour in Review

1. In this hour, you took three practice Number Series tests to reinforce the techniques that you learned for answering these questions.

2. These untimed practice tests are intended to prepare you for the timed tests that you'll take in the next hour.

3. Use the practice tests to pinpoint any weaknesses that you still have with these questions and then review the appropriate materials.

HOUR 21

Number Series—
Timed Tests

What You Will Learn in This Hour

In this hour, you'll take two timed Number Series tests, using the pattern-finding techniques that you've been developing. These practice tests will help you become accustomed to working under the timed conditions of the actual test. Here are your goals for this hour:

- Understand your strategies for taking the timed practice tests.
- Complete two practice Number Series tests under timed exam conditions.
- Check your answers, determine your raw score, and discover what you need to review.

Preparing for the Timed Practice Tests

This hour provides your first real chance to answer Number Series questions under the time constraints of the actual test. To get the most benefits from this practice, follow these steps:

1. Choose a workspace that is quiet, well-lit, and uncluttered.

2. Use a stopwatch or kitchen timer to accurately time each test.

3. Start the first test at a convenient time; write down the starting time and approximate ending time when you begin.

4. Keep track of time during each test and stop exactly when 20 minutes are up.

5. Give yourself at least a five-minute breather between each test. You can use this time to skim through the material in Hour 9, "Number Series—1," and Hour 10, "Number Series—2," if needed, or just take a break.

6. After completing both tests, check your answers against the keys that follow. Circle all the questions that you answered incorrectly.

7. Read the explanations for all answers, not just the ones you answered incorrectly.

8. Calculate your raw score for each test as instructed.

9. Determine where your scores fall on the self-evaluation chart; if you receive less than an Excellent score on a test, review the material from Hours 9 and 10.

10. If you have time, retake either of the tests at a convenient time to see your improvement.

Tip
There is no penalty for guessing on this part of Test 470, so remember to guess if you're stumped or can't finish the test in the time allowed.

Practice Test 1

DIRECTIONS: Each question contains a series of numbers on the left that follows a definite pattern and at the right five sets of two numbers each. Look at the numbers in the series on the left and determine the order they follow. Then decide what the next two numbers in the series would be if the series were continued. Circle the letter of the correct answer. You have 20 minutes to complete this test.

1. 19 18 12 17 16 13 15…   (A) 16 12   (B)14 14   (C) 12 14   (D) 14 12   (E) 12 16

2. 7 15 12 8 16 13 9…   (A) 17 14   (B) 17 10   (C) 14 10   (D) 14 17   (E) 10 14

3. 18 15 6 16 14 6 14…   (A) 12 6   (B) 14 13   (C) 6 12   (D) 13 12   (E) 13 6

4. 6 6 5 8 8 7 10 10…   (A) 8 12   (B) 9 12   (C) 22 12   (D) 12 9   (E) 9 9

5. 17 20 23 26 29 32 35…   (A) 37 40   (B) 41 44   (C) 38 41   (D) 38 42   (E) 36 39

6. 15 5 7 16 9 11 17…   (A) 18 13   (B) 15 17   (C) 12 19   (D) 13 15   (E) 12 13

7. 19 17 16 16 13 15 10…   (A) 14 7   (B) 12 9   (C) 14 9   (D) 7 12   (E) 10 14

8. 11 1 16 10 6 21 9…   (A) 12 26   (B) 26 8   (C) 11 26   (D) 11 8   (E) 8 11

9. 15 22 19 26 23 30 27…   (A) 28 34   (B) 27 35   (C) 31 34   (D) 29 33   (E) 34 31

10. 99 9 88 8 77 7 66 …   (A) 55 5   (B) 6 55   (C) 66 5   (D) 55 6   (E) 55 44

11. 25 29 29 33 37 37 41…   (A) 41 41   (B) 41 45   (C) 45 49   (D) 45 45   (E) 49 49

12. 81 71 61 52 43 35 27…   (A) 27 20   (B) 21 14   (C) 20 14   (D) 21 15   (E) 20 13

13. 12 14 16 48 50 52 156…   (A) 468 470   (B) 158 316   (C) 158 474   (D) 158 160   (E) 158 158

14. 47 42 38 35 30 26 23…   (A) 18 14   (B) 21 19   (C) 23 18   (D) 19 14   (E) 19 13

15. 84 84 91 91 97 97 102…   (A) 102 102   (B) 102 104   (C) 104 106   (D) 106 106   (E) 102 106

16. 66 13 62 21 58 29 54…   (A) 50 48   (B) 62 66   (C) 34 42   (D) 37 50   (E) 58 21

17. 14 12 10 10 20 18 16 16…   (A) 32 32   (B) 32 30   (C) 30 28   (D) 16 32   (E) 16 14

18. 25 30 35 30 25 30 35…   (A) 30 40   (B) 25 30   (C) 25 20   (D) 35 30   (E) 30 25

19. 19 19 19 57 57 57 171…   (A) 171 513   (B) 513 513   (C) 171 171   (D) 171 57   (E) 57 18

20. 75 69 63 57 51 45 39…   (A) 36 33   (B) 39 36   (C) 39 33   (D) 33 27   (E) 33 33

21. 6 15 23 30 36 41 45…   (A) 48 50   (B) 49 53   (C) 45 41   (D) 46 47   (E) 47 49

22. 12 58 25 51 38 44 51…   (A) 64 37   (B) 37 64   (C) 51 51   (D) 51 64   (E) 51 37

23. 1 2 4 8 16 32 64…   (A) 64 32   (B) 64 64   (C) 64 128   (D) 128 256   (E) 128 128

24. 5 86 7 81 10 77 14…   (A) 16 80   (B) 70 25   (C) 79 13   (D) 19 74   (E) 74 19

21

Practice Test 2

DIRECTIONS: Each question contains a series of numbers on the left that follows a definite pattern and at the right five sets of two numbers each. Look at the numbers in the series on the left and determine the order they follow. Then decide what the next two numbers in the series would be if the series were continued. Circle the letter of the correct answer. You have 20 minutes to complete this test.

1. 5 7 30 9 11 30 13…   (A) 15 16   (B) 15 17   (C) 14 17   (D) 15 30   (E) 30 17

2. 5 7 11 13 17 19 23…   (A) 27 29   (B) 25 29   (C) 25 27   (D) 27 31   (E) 29 31

3. 9 15 10 17 12 19 15 21 19… (A) 23 24   (B) 25 23   (C) 17 23   (D) 23 31   (E) 21 24

4. 34 37 30 33 26 29 22…   (A) 17 8   (B) 18 11   (C) 25 28   (D) 25 20   (E) 25 18

5. 10 16 12 14 14 12 16…   (A) 14 12   (B) 10 18   (C) 10 14   (D) 14 18   (E) 14 16

6. 11 12 18 11 13 19 11 14…   (A) 18 11   (B) 16 11   (C) 20 11   (D) 11 21   (E) 17 11

7. 20 9 8 19 10 9 18 11 10…   (A) 19 11   (B) 17 10   (C) 19 12   (D) 17 12   (E) 19 10

8. 28 27 26 31 30 29 34…   (A) 36 32   (B) 32 31   (C) 33 32   (D) 33 36   (E) 35 36

9. 12 24 15 30 21 42 33…   (A) 66 57   (B) 44 56   (C) 28 43   (D) 47 69   (E) 24 48

10. 46 76 51 70 56 64 61…   (A) 61 68   (B) 69 71   (C) 58 65   (D) 66 71   (E) 58 66

11. 37 28 28 19 19 10 10…   (A) 9 9   (B) 1 1   (C) 10 9   (D) 10 1   (E) 9 1

12. 1 2 3 6 4 5 6 15 7…   (A) 8 15   (B) 7 8   (C) 8 9   (D) 9 17   (E) 9 24

13. 55 51 12 56 52 12 57…   (A) 57 12   (B) 12 53   (C) 58 12   (D) 53 12   (E) 12 57

14. 75 75 8 50 50 9 25…   (A) 25 25   (B) 25 10   (C) 10 25   (D) 25 12   (E) 10 10

15. 1 2 3 4 5 5 4…   (A) 3 2   (B) 5 4   (C) 4 5   (D) 5 6   (E) 4 4

16. 3 6 9 4 7 10 5…   (A) 8 9   (B) 9 6   (C) 8 11   (D) 9 12   (E) 11 8

17. 5 7 9 18 20 22 44…   (A) 60 66   (B) 66 80   (C) 66 68   (D) 88 90   (E) 46 48

18. 94 82 72 64 58 54…   (A) 52 50   (B) 54 52   (C) 50 46   (D) 52 52   (E) 54 50

19. 85 85 86 85 86 87 85…   (A) 85 86   (B) 86 87   (C) 87 89   (D) 87 86   (E) 84 83

20. 99 89 79 69 59 49 39…   (A) 29 19   (B) 39 29   (C) 38 37   (D) 39 38   (E) 19 9

21. 33 42 41 39 48 47 45…   (A) 42 41   (B) 44 42   (C) 54 53   (D) 54 52   (E) 54 63

22. 85 89 89 84 88 88 83…   (A) 83 87   (B) 83 83   (C) 87 87   (D) 87 82   (E) 87 83

23. 1 2 3 3 4 5 5 6 7…   (A) 7 7   (B) 8 8   (C) 8 9   (D) 7 6   (E) 7 8

24. 5 10 15 15 20 15 25…   (A) 30 35   (B) 15 30   (C) 15 15   (D) 30 15   (E) 30 30

Answers

Practice Test 1

1.	B	9.	E	17.	B
2.	A	10.	B	18.	E
3.	E	11.	D	19.	C
4.	B	12.	E	20.	D
5.	C	13.	D	21.	A
6.	D	14.	A	22.	B
7.	A	15.	E	23.	D
8.	C	16.	D	24.	E

Answers and Explanations

1. **(B)**   There are two series: the first descends by 1, beginning with 19; and the second is inserted between every two numbers of the first series and ascends by 1. Thus, the series are 19 18 17 16 15 14 and 12 13 14.

2. **(A)**   The pattern is add 8, subtract 3, subtract 4; add 8, subtract 3, subtract 4; and so on.

3. **(E)**   This is a difficult problem. The first series begins with 18 and descends by 2 (18, 16, 14, and so on). The second series begins with 15 and descends by 1 (15, 14, 13, and so on). The number 6 is inserted between each pair of descending numbers.

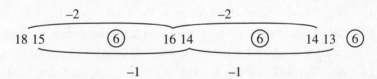

4. **(B)**   The even numbers repeat as they increase; the odd numbers simply increase by 2, alternating with the evens.

5. **(C)**   This is an add 3 series.

6. **(D)**   One series ascends by 1. The other series increases by 2. The first series is inserted between every two steps of the second series.

7. **(A)**   The first series is a subtract 3 series, and the alternating series is a subtract 1 series.

21

8. **(C)**   There are two alternating series; the first reads 11 10 9, and the second series starts at 1 and its pattern is add 15, subtract 10, add 15, subtract 10, and so on. The first series is inserted between every two steps of the second series. The solution to this problem is best seen by diagramming:

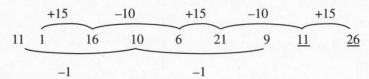

9. **(E)**   The pattern is add 7, subtract 3; add 7, subtract 3; and so on. You might see two alternating series, both increasing by 4.

10. **(B)**   You might see two series, one decreasing by 11 and the other decreasing by 1, or you might see a series of the multiples of 11, each divided by 11.

11. **(D)**   The pattern is add 4, repeat the number, add 4; add 4, repeat the number, add 4; add 4, repeat the number, add 4; and so on.

12. **(E)**   The pattern is subtract 10, subtract 10, subtract 9, subtract 9, subtract 8, subtract 8, subtract 7, subtract 7, subtract 6, subtract 6, and so on.

13. **(D)**   The pattern is add 2, add 2, multiply by 3; add 2, add 2, multiply by 3; and so on.

14. **(A)**   The pattern is subtract 5, subtract 4, subtract 3; subtract 5, subtract 4, subtract 3; and so on.

15. **(E)**   The pattern is repeat the number, add 7, repeat the number, add 6, repeat the number, add 5, repeat the number, add 4, and so on.

16. **(D)**   The first series descends by 4. The alternating series ascends by 8.

17. **(B)**   The pattern is subtract 2, subtract 2, repeat the number, multiply by 2; subtract 2, subtract 2, repeat the number, multiply by 2; and so on.

18. **(E)**   The pattern is add 5, add 5, subtract 5, subtract 5; add 5, add 5, subtract 5, subtract 5; and so on. You might see the repetition of the four numbers 25, 30, 35, 30.

19. **(C)**   The pattern is repeat the number three times, multiply by 3; repeat the number three times, multiply by 3; repeat the number three times, multiply by 3; and so on.

20. **(D)**   This is a subtract 6 series.

21. **(A)** The pattern is add 9, add 8, add 7, add 6, add 5, add 4, add 3, add 2, add 1.

22. **(B)** The first series ascends by 13. The alternating series descends by 7.

23. **(D)** This is a times 2 series.

24. **(E)** The pattern of the first series is add 2, add 3, add 4, add 5, and so on. The pattern of the alternating series is subtract 5, subtract 4, subtract 3, subtract 2, and so on.

Determine Your Raw Score

Practice Test 1: Your raw score equals the number of questions that you answered correctly:

Raw score = _____

21

Practice Test 2

1.	D	9.	A	17.	E
2.	B	10.	E	18.	D
3.	A	11.	B	19.	B
4.	E	12.	C	20.	A
5.	B	13.	D	21.	C
6.	C	14.	B	22.	C
7.	D	15.	A	23.	E
8.	C	16.	C	24.	D

Answers and Explanations

1. **(D)** The series ascends by 2. The number 30 is inserted after every two numbers in the series.

2. **(B)** The pattern is add 2, add 4; add 2, add 4; add 2, add 4; and so on.

3. **(A)** The first series begins with 9, and the rule is add 1, add 2, add 3, add 4, add 5, and so on. The alternating series begins with 15 and advances by 2.

4. **(E)** There are two alternating series, one series beginning with 34 and the other with 37. Both series descend by 4.

5. **(B)** The first series begins with 10 and ascends by 2. The alternating series begins with 16 and descends by 2.

6. **(C)** You may be able to figure out this one by reading it rhythmically. If not, consider that there are two series, one beginning with 12, the other with 18. Both series advance by 1. The number 11 in inserted before each progression of the two series.

7. **(D)** There are two series alternating at the rate of 1 to 2. The first series decreases by 1: 20, 19, 18, 17, and so on. The other series follows the rule subtract 1, add 2. It can be read like this: $9 \,^{-1}\, 8 \,^{+2}\, 10 \,^{-1}\, 9 \,^{+2}\, 11 \,^{-1}\, 10 \,^{+2}\, 12$.

8. **(C)** The pattern is subtract 1, subtract 1, add 5, repeat; subtract 1, subtract 1, add 5, repeat; and so on.

9. **(A)** The pattern is multiply by 2, subtract 9; multiply by 2, subtract 9; and so on.

10. **(E)** The first series ascends by 5, and the alternating series descends by 6.

11. **(B)** The pattern is subtract 9, repeat the number; subtract 9, repeat the number; subtract 9, repeat the number; and so on.

12. **(C)** After each set of three numbers in this add 1 series, you'll find the sum of those three numbers: $1 + 2 + 3 = 6$; $4 + 5 + 6 = 15$; $7 + 8 + 9 = 24$; and so on.

13. **(D)** The pattern is subtract 4, add 5, insert the number 12; subtract 4, add 5, insert the number 12; and so on.

14. **(B)** The first series proceeds as follows: repeat the number, subtract 25; repeat the number, subtract 25; and so on. The alternating series advances by 1.

15. **(A)** The series advances by 1 from 1 to 5, then reverses and descends by 1.

16. **(C)** You may see the following pattern: add 3, add 3, subtract 5; add 3, add 3, subtract 5; and so on. You might see a group of add 3 miniseries, with each one beginning with a number that is one higher than the beginning number of the previous miniseries.

17. **(E)** The pattern is add 2, add 2, multiply by 2; add 2, add 2, multiply by 2; and so on.

18. **(D)** The pattern is subtract 12, subtract 10, subtract 8, subtract 6, subtract 4, subtract 2, subtract 0, and so on.

19. **(B)** Each miniseries begins with 85. With each cycle the series progresses to one more number: 85; 85 86; 85 86 87; 85 86 87 88; and so on.

20. **(A)** This is a simple subtract 10 series.

21. **(C)** The pattern is add 9, subtract 1, subtract 2; add 9, subtract 1, subtract 2; and so on.

22. **(C)** The pattern is add 4, repeat the number, subtract 5; add 4, repeat the number, subtract 5; and so on. You might also notice two descending series, one beginning with 85 and descending by 1, and the other beginning with 89 and repeating before each descent.

23. **(E)** This is a deceptive series. Actually the series consists of a group of miniseries, each beginning with the last number of the previous miniseries. If you group the numbers, you can see: 1 2 3; 3 4 5; 5 6 7; 7 8 9; and so on.

24. **(D)** The series is an add 5 series with the number 15 inserted after every two numbers of the series. If you substitute X for the repeating 15, you can see that the series reads: 5 10 X 15 20 X 25 30 X.

Determine Your Raw Score

Practice Test 2: Your raw score equals the number of questions that you answered correctly:

Raw score = _____

21

Evaluate Yourself

For each practice test, determine where your raw score falls on the following scale. If you scored less than Excellent on any test, review all the appropriate study material in Hours 9 and 10, and then retake the tests where you need improvement.

IF your raw score is between	THEN your work is
25-24	Excellent
18-20	Good
14-17	Average
11-13	Fair
1-10	Poor

The Hour in Review

1. In this hour, you took two Number Series practice tests that simulate the timed conditions of the actual Test 470.

2. These timed tests are intended to give you practice with answering Number Series questions accurately while working quickly.

3. If you didn't perform your best on any of these tests, you should review the Number Series lessons and retake the tests for additional practice.

HOUR 22

Following Oral Instructions—Timed Test 1

What You Will Learn in This Hour

In this hour and the following two hours, you'll take three full-length exercises to test the techniques that you learned for answering the "Following Oral Instructions" questions. Use these timed exercises to ensure that you're prepared to tackle the actual test. Here are your goals for this hour:

- Learn how to simulate the actual test conditions as closely as possible
- Complete the first full-length timed test
- Check your answers, determine your raw score, and review as needed

Preparing for the Timed Practice Test

Because of the unique format of the Following Oral Instructions question type, simulating the actual test conditions is a bit more difficult than with the other portions of Test 470. To closely approximate testing conditions, follow these steps:

1. Before starting the test, review the reading instructions in Hour 11, "Following Oral Instructions—1." Give your reader 10 to 15 minutes to practice reading the oral instructions in a separate room to get familiar with the material, or allow at least 25 minutes for taping.

2. Choose a workspace that is quiet, well-lit, and uncluttered. Make sure that you have a comfortable sitting or standing place for your reader or free desk space for your tape recorder.

3. Start the test at a convenient time. If you're working with a reader, schedule this time in advance.

4. Proceed through the entire test without repeating any instructions.

5. After finishing the test, check your answers against the correctly completed answer grid and worksheet. Circle any incorrect answers and mistakes on your worksheet.

6. Count the number of correct answers and calculate your raw score as instructed. Remember that some lines of your answer sheet will be blank.

7. Determine where your score falls on the self-evaluation chart.

8. If you need to, review the lessons in Hours 11 and 12. You can then retake the test at a convenient time to see your improvement.

Tip
If possible, use a live reader for at least one of the timed tests and use a recording on another. When you take the actual test, the examiner may read the instructions, or they may be given on tape. Practicing with both will prepare you for either situation.

Timed Test

The answer sheet, worksheet, and oral instructions for this practice exercise are on the following pages. You will have 25 minutes to complete the test.

Answer Sheet

22

1. (A) (B) (C) (D) (E)
2. (A) (B) (C) (D) (E)
3. (A) (B) (C) (D) (E)
4. (A) (B) (C) (D) (E)
5. (A) (B) (C) (D) (E)
6. (A) (B) (C) (D) (E)
7. (A) (B) (C) (D) (E)
8. (A) (B) (C) (D) (E)
9. (A) (B) (C) (D) (E)
10. (A) (B) (C) (D) (E)
11. (A) (B) (C) (D) (E)
12. (A) (B) (C) (D) (E)
13. (A) (B) (C) (D) (E)
14. (A) (B) (C) (D) (E)
15. (A) (B) (C) (D) (E)
16. (A) (B) (C) (D) (E)
17. (A) (B) (C) (D) (E)
18. (A) (B) (C) (D) (E)
19. (A) (B) (C) (D) (E)
20. (A) (B) (C) (D) (E)
21. (A) (B) (C) (D) (E)
22. (A) (B) (C) (D) (E)

23. (A) (B) (C) (D) (E)
24. (A) (B) (C) (D) (E)
25. (A) (B) (C) (D) (E)
26. (A) (B) (C) (D) (E)
27. (A) (B) (C) (D) (E)
28. (A) (B) (C) (D) (E)
29. (A) (B) (C) (D) (E)
30. (A) (B) (C) (D) (E)
31. (A) (B) (C) (D) (E)
32. (A) (B) (C) (D) (E)
33. (A) (B) (C) (D) (E)
34. (A) (B) (C) (D) (E)
35. (A) (B) (C) (D) (E)
36. (A) (B) (C) (D) (E)
37. (A) (B) (C) (D) (E)
38. (A) (B) (C) (D) (E)
39. (A) (B) (C) (D) (E)
40. (A) (B) (C) (D) (E)
41. (A) (B) (C) (D) (E)
42. (A) (B) (C) (D) (E)
43. (A) (B) (C) (D) (E)
44. (A) (B) (C) (D) (E)

45. (A) (B) (C) (D) (E)
46. (A) (B) (C) (D) (E)
47. (A) (B) (C) (D) (E)
48. (A) (B) (C) (D) (E)
49. (A) (B) (C) (D) (E)
50. (A) (B) (C) (D) (E)
51. (A) (B) (C) (D) (E)
52. (A) (B) (C) (D) (E)
53. (A) (B) (C) (D) (E)
54. (A) (B) (C) (D) (E)
55. (A) (B) (C) (D) (E)
56. (A) (B) (C) (D) (E)
57. (A) (B) (C) (D) (E)
58. (A) (B) (C) (D) (E)
59. (A) (B) (C) (D) (E)
60. (A) (B) (C) (D) (E)
61. (A) (B) (C) (D) (E)
62. (A) (B) (C) (D) (E)
63. (A) (B) (C) (D) (E)
64. (A) (B) (C) (D) (E)
65. (A) (B) (C) (D) (E)
66. (A) (B) (C) (D) (E)

67. (A) (B) (C) (D) (E)
68. (A) (B) (C) (D) (E)
69. (A) (B) (C) (D) (E)
70. (A) (B) (C) (D) (E)
71. (A) (B) (C) (D) (E)
72. (A) (B) (C) (D) (E)
73. (A) (B) (C) (D) (E)
74. (A) (B) (C) (D) (E)
75. (A) (B) (C) (D) (E)
76. (A) (B) (C) (D) (E)
77. (A) (B) (C) (D) (E)
78. (A) (B) (C) (D) (E)
79. (A) (B) (C) (D) (E)
80. (A) (B) (C) (D) (E)
81. (A) (B) (C) (D) (E)
82. (A) (B) (C) (D) (E)
83. (A) (B) (C) (D) (E)
84. (A) (B) (C) (D) (E)
85. (A) (B) (C) (D) (E)
86. (A) (B) (C) (D) (E)
87. (A) (B) (C) (D) (E)
88. (A) (B) (C) (D) (E)

Worksheet

22

1.   6   3   13   90   45   36   12

2.

B	G	E	C	A	D
25 ___	36 ___	4 ___	17 ___	82 ___	13 ___

3.   17   4   30   25   9   41

4.

3	26
DETROIT	ST. LOUIS
HARTFORD	CLEVELAND
_____	_____

5.   27___   54___   31___   76___   18___

6.

12___   56___   87___   RED   WHITE   BLUE

7.   ___ D   ___ E   ___ A

8.   7 ___   64 ___   31 ___

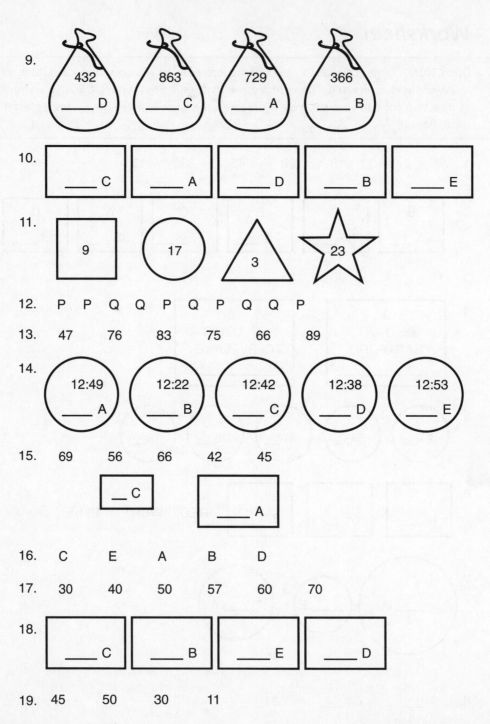

9.

432 ____D   863 ____C   729 ____A   366 ____B

10.

____ C   ____ A   ____ D   ____ B   ____ E

11.

9   17   3   23

12.   P   P   Q   Q   P   Q   P   Q   Q   P

13.   47   76   83   75   66   89

14.

12:49 ____A   12:22 ____B   12:42 ____C   12:38 ____D   12:53 ____E

15.   69   56   66   42   45

__ C   ____ A

16.   C   E   A   B   D

17.   30   40   50   57   60   70

18.

____ C   ____ B   ____ E   ____ D

19.   45   50   30   11

Directions and Sample Questions

Listening to Instructions: When you are ready to try these sample questions, give the following instructions to a friend and have the friend read them aloud to you at the rate of 80 words per minute. Do not read them to yourself. Your friend will need a watch with a second hand. Listen carefully and do exactly what your friend tells you to do with the worksheet and answer sheet. Your friend will tell you some things to do with each item on the worksheet. After each set of instructions, your friend will give you time to mark your answer by darkening a circle on the sample answer sheet. Since B and D sound very much alike, your friend will say "B as in baker" when he or she means B and "D as in dog" when he or she means D.

Before proceeding further, tear out the worksheet on pages 297 and 298. Then hand this book to your friend.

To the Person Who Is to Read the Instructions: The instructions are to be read at the rate of 80 words per minute. Do not read aloud the material that is in parentheses. Do not repeat any instructions.

Oral Instructions

Note: The words in parentheses should not be read aloud.

On the job you will have to listen to directions and then do what you have been told. In this test, I will read some instructions to you. Listen closely as I read them; I cannot repeat them. Once we begin, you may not ask any questions until the end of the test.

On the job you won't have to deal with pictures, numbers, and letters like the ones you'll find in this test, but you will have to listen to instructions and follow them. This test determines how well you can follow instructions.

You are to mark your test booklet according to the instructions I'll read to you. After each set of instructions, I'll give you time to record your answers on the separate answer sheet.

The actual test begins now.

Look at line 1 on your worksheet. (Pause slightly.) Underline the fifth number on line 1. (Pause two seconds.) Now on your answer sheet, find the number you have underlined and mark D as in dog. (Pause five seconds.)

Now look at line 2 on your worksheet. (Pause slightly.) In each box that contains a vowel, write that vowel next to the number in the box. (Pause five seconds.) Now on your answer sheet, blacken the spaces for the number-letter combinations in the box or boxes in which you just wrote. (Pause 10 seconds.)

Look at line 3 on your worksheet. (Pause slightly.) Find the smallest number on line 3 and multiply it by two. Write the number at the end of line 3. (Pause five seconds.) Now, on your answer sheet, darken space C for that number. (Pause five seconds.)

Look at line 3 again. (Pause slightly.) Divide the third number by 10 and write that number at the end of the line. (Pause two seconds.) Now on your answer sheet, darken space A for the number you just wrote. (Pause five seconds.)

Now look at line 4 on your worksheet. (Pause slightly.) Mail for Detroit and Hartford is to be put in box 3. (Pause slightly.) Mail for Cleveland and St. Louis is to be put in box 26. (Pause slightly.) Write C in the box in which you put mail for St. Louis. (Pause two seconds.) Now on your answer sheet, darken the space for the number-letter combination that is in the box you just wrote in. (Pause five seconds.)

Look at line 5 on your worksheet. (Pause slightly.) Write B as in baker on the line next to the highest number. (Pause two seconds.) Now on your answer sheet, blacken the space for the number-letter combination in the circle in which you just wrote. (Pause five seconds.)

Look at line 5 again. (Pause slightly.) Write the letter C on the line next to the lowest number. (Pause two seconds.) Now on your answer sheet, blacken the space for the number-letter combination in the circle in which you just wrote. (Pause five seconds.)

Look at the boxes and words on line 6 of your worksheet. (Pause two seconds.) In Box 1, write the first letter of the third word. (Pause five seconds.) In Box 2, write the last letter of the first word. (Pause five seconds.) In Box 3, write the last letter of the second word. (Pause five seconds.) Now, on your answer sheet, blacken spaces for the number-letter combinations in all three boxes. (Pause 15 seconds.)

Look at line 7 on your worksheet. (Pause slightly.) Write the number 33 next to the letter in the mid-size circle. (Pause two seconds.) Now on your answer sheet, darken the space for the number-letter combination in the circle in which you just wrote. (Pause five seconds.)

Look at line 8 on your worksheet. (Pause slightly.) If July comes before June, write D as in dog on the line after the second number; if not, write A on the line after the first number. (Pause 10 seconds.) Now on your answer sheet, darken the space for the number-letter combination you just wrote. (Pause five seconds.)

Look at line 9 on your worksheet. (Pause slightly.) The number on each sack represents the number of pieces of mail in that sack. Next to the letter, write the last two figures of the sack containing the most pieces of mail. (Pause two seconds.) On your answer sheet, darken the space for the number-letter combination in the sack you just wrote in. (Pause five seconds.)

Look at line 9 again. (Pause slightly.) Now write next to the letter the first two figures in the sack containing the fewest pieces of mail. (Pause two seconds.) On your answer sheet, darken the space for the number-letter combination in the sack you just wrote in. (Pause five seconds.)

Look at line 10 on your worksheet. (Pause slightly.) Answer this question: What is the sum of 8 plus 13? (Pause two seconds.) If the answer is 25, write 25 in the second box; if not, write the correct answer in the fourth box. (Pause two seconds.) Now on your answer sheet, blacken the number-letter combination in the box you just wrote in. (Pause five seconds.)

Look at line 10 again. (Pause slightly.) In the fifth box, write the number of ounces in a pound. (Pause two seconds.) Now, on your answer sheet, blacken the number-letter combination in the box you just wrote in. (Pause five seconds.)

Look at line 11 on your worksheet. (Pause slightly.) If the number in the circle is greater than the number in the star, write B as in baker in the triangle; if not, write E in the box. (Pause five seconds.) Now on your answer sheet, darken the number-letter combination in the figure you just wrote in. (Pause five seconds.)

Look at line 12 on your worksheet. (Pause slightly.) Draw one line under each P in line 12. (Pause five seconds.) Draw two lines under each Q in line 12. (Pause five seconds.) Count the number of Ps and the number of Qs. (Pause five seconds.) If there are more Ps than Qs, blacken 71A on your answer sheet; if there are not more Ps than Qs, blacken 71C on your answer sheet. (Pause five seconds.)

Look at line 13 on your worksheet. (Pause slightly.) Circle each odd number that falls between 65 and 85. (Pause 10 seconds.) Now on your answer sheet, darken space D as in dog for each number that you circled. (Pause 10 seconds.)

Look at line 13 again. (Pause slightly.) Find the number that is divisible by 6 and under-line it. (Pause two seconds.) Now, on your answer sheet, darken space A for that number. (Pause five seconds.)

Look at line 14 on your worksheet. (Pause slightly.) Each circled time represents a pickup time from a street letterbox. Find the pickup time that is farthest from noon and write the last two figures of that time on the line in the circle. (Pause two seconds.) Now on your answer sheet, darken the number-letter combination that is in the circle you just wrote in. (Pause five seconds.)

Look at line 14 again. (Pause slightly.) Find the pickup time that is closest to noon and write the last two figures of that time on the line in the circle. (Pause two seconds.) Now on your answer sheet, darken the number-letter combination that is in the circle you just wrote in. (Pause five seconds.)

Look at line 15 on your worksheet. (Pause slightly.) Write the highest number in the small box. (Pause two seconds.) Write the lowest number in the large box. (Pause two seconds.) Now on your answer sheet, darken the number-letter combinations in the boxes you just wrote in. (Pause 10 seconds.)

Look at line 16 on your worksheet. (Pause slightly.) If, in the alphabet, the fourth letter on line 16 comes before the first letter on line 16, draw a line under the fourth letter. (Pause two seconds.) If not, draw a line under the first letter on line 16. (Pause two seconds.) Now on your answer sheet, find number 39 and blacken the space for the letter you underlined. (Pause five seconds.)

Look at line 17 on your worksheet. (Pause slightly.) Find the number that does not belong on line 17 and circle that number. (Pause two seconds.) Now on your answer sheet, darken D as in dog for the number you just circled. (Pause five seconds.)

Look at line 17 again. (Pause slightly.) Find the number that is equal to 60 minus 20 and draw two lines under that number. (Pause two seconds.) Now on your answer sheet, darken space C for the number under which you just drew two lines. (Pause five seconds.)

Look at line 18 on your worksheet. (Pause slightly.) If 3 is less than 7 and 4 is more than 6, write the number 12 in the first box (pause five seconds); if not, write the number 48 in the third box. (Pause five seconds.) Now on your answer sheet, darken the space for the number-letter combination in the box you just wrote in. (Pause five seconds.)

Look at line 19 on your worksheet. (Pause slightly.) Draw a circle around the number that represents the product of 5×6. (Pause five seconds.) Now on your answer sheet, find the number that you just circled and darken space A for that number. (Pause five seconds.)

Answers

Correctly Completed Answer Sheet

1. Ⓐ Ⓑ Ⓒ Ⓓ Ⓔ	23. Ⓐ Ⓑ Ⓒ Ⓓ Ⓔ	45. Ⓐ Ⓑ Ⓒ ● Ⓔ	67. Ⓐ Ⓑ Ⓒ Ⓓ Ⓔ
2. Ⓐ Ⓑ Ⓒ Ⓓ Ⓔ	24. Ⓐ Ⓑ Ⓒ Ⓓ Ⓔ	46. Ⓐ Ⓑ Ⓒ Ⓓ Ⓔ	68. Ⓐ Ⓑ Ⓒ Ⓓ Ⓔ
3. ● Ⓑ Ⓒ Ⓓ Ⓔ	25. Ⓐ Ⓑ Ⓒ Ⓓ Ⓔ	47. Ⓐ Ⓑ Ⓒ Ⓓ Ⓔ	69. Ⓐ Ⓑ ● Ⓓ Ⓔ
4. Ⓐ Ⓑ Ⓒ Ⓓ ●	26. Ⓐ Ⓑ ● Ⓓ Ⓔ	48. Ⓐ Ⓑ Ⓒ Ⓓ ●	70. Ⓐ Ⓑ Ⓒ Ⓓ Ⓔ
5. Ⓐ Ⓑ Ⓒ Ⓓ Ⓔ	27. Ⓐ Ⓑ Ⓒ Ⓓ Ⓔ	49. Ⓐ Ⓑ Ⓒ Ⓓ Ⓔ	71. Ⓐ Ⓑ ● Ⓓ Ⓔ
6. Ⓐ Ⓑ Ⓒ Ⓓ Ⓔ	28. Ⓐ Ⓑ Ⓒ Ⓓ Ⓔ	50. Ⓐ Ⓑ Ⓒ Ⓓ Ⓔ	72. Ⓐ Ⓑ Ⓒ Ⓓ Ⓔ
7. ● Ⓑ Ⓒ Ⓓ Ⓔ	29. Ⓐ Ⓑ Ⓒ Ⓓ Ⓔ	51. Ⓐ Ⓑ Ⓒ Ⓓ Ⓔ	73. Ⓐ Ⓑ Ⓒ Ⓓ Ⓔ
8. Ⓐ Ⓑ ● Ⓓ Ⓔ	30. ● Ⓑ Ⓒ Ⓓ Ⓔ	52. Ⓐ Ⓑ Ⓒ Ⓓ Ⓔ	74. Ⓐ Ⓑ Ⓒ Ⓓ Ⓔ
9. Ⓐ Ⓑ Ⓒ Ⓓ ●	31. Ⓐ Ⓑ Ⓒ Ⓓ Ⓔ	53. Ⓐ Ⓑ Ⓒ Ⓓ ●	75. Ⓐ Ⓑ Ⓒ ● Ⓔ
10. Ⓐ Ⓑ Ⓒ Ⓓ Ⓔ	32. Ⓐ Ⓑ Ⓒ Ⓓ Ⓔ	54. Ⓐ Ⓑ Ⓒ Ⓓ Ⓔ	76. Ⓐ ● Ⓒ Ⓓ Ⓔ
11. Ⓐ Ⓑ Ⓒ Ⓓ Ⓔ	33. ● Ⓑ Ⓒ Ⓓ Ⓔ	55. Ⓐ Ⓑ Ⓒ Ⓓ Ⓔ	77. Ⓐ Ⓑ Ⓒ Ⓓ Ⓔ
12. Ⓐ ● Ⓒ Ⓓ Ⓔ	34. Ⓐ Ⓑ Ⓒ Ⓓ Ⓔ	56. Ⓐ Ⓑ Ⓒ ● Ⓔ	78. Ⓐ Ⓑ Ⓒ Ⓓ Ⓔ
13. Ⓐ Ⓑ Ⓒ Ⓓ Ⓔ	35. Ⓐ Ⓑ Ⓒ Ⓓ Ⓔ	57. Ⓐ Ⓑ Ⓒ ● Ⓔ	79. Ⓐ Ⓑ Ⓒ Ⓓ Ⓔ
14. Ⓐ Ⓑ Ⓒ Ⓓ Ⓔ	36. Ⓐ ● Ⓒ Ⓓ Ⓔ	58. Ⓐ Ⓑ Ⓒ Ⓓ Ⓔ	80. Ⓐ Ⓑ Ⓒ Ⓓ Ⓔ
15. Ⓐ Ⓑ Ⓒ Ⓓ Ⓔ	37. Ⓐ Ⓑ Ⓒ Ⓓ Ⓔ	59. Ⓐ Ⓑ Ⓒ Ⓓ Ⓔ	81. Ⓐ Ⓑ Ⓒ Ⓓ Ⓔ
16. Ⓐ Ⓑ Ⓒ Ⓓ ●	38. Ⓐ Ⓑ Ⓒ Ⓓ Ⓔ	60. Ⓐ Ⓑ Ⓒ Ⓓ Ⓔ	82. ● Ⓑ Ⓒ Ⓓ Ⓔ
17. Ⓐ Ⓑ Ⓒ Ⓓ Ⓔ	39. Ⓐ ● Ⓒ Ⓓ Ⓔ	61. Ⓐ Ⓑ Ⓒ Ⓓ Ⓔ	83. Ⓐ Ⓑ Ⓒ ● Ⓔ
18. Ⓐ Ⓑ ● Ⓓ Ⓔ	40. Ⓐ Ⓑ ● Ⓓ Ⓔ	62. Ⓐ Ⓑ Ⓒ Ⓓ Ⓔ	84. Ⓐ Ⓑ Ⓒ Ⓓ Ⓔ
19. Ⓐ Ⓑ Ⓒ Ⓓ Ⓔ	41. Ⓐ Ⓑ Ⓒ Ⓓ Ⓔ	63. Ⓐ Ⓑ ● Ⓓ Ⓔ	85. Ⓐ Ⓑ Ⓒ Ⓓ Ⓔ
20. Ⓐ Ⓑ Ⓒ Ⓓ Ⓔ	42. ● Ⓑ Ⓒ Ⓓ Ⓔ	64. Ⓐ Ⓑ Ⓒ Ⓓ Ⓔ	86. Ⓐ Ⓑ Ⓒ Ⓓ Ⓔ
21. Ⓐ ● Ⓒ Ⓓ Ⓔ	43. Ⓐ Ⓑ Ⓒ Ⓓ Ⓔ	65. Ⓐ Ⓑ Ⓒ Ⓓ Ⓔ	87. Ⓐ Ⓑ Ⓒ Ⓓ ●
22. Ⓐ ● Ⓒ Ⓓ Ⓔ	44. Ⓐ Ⓑ Ⓒ Ⓓ Ⓔ	66. ● Ⓑ Ⓒ Ⓓ Ⓔ	88. Ⓐ Ⓑ Ⓒ Ⓓ Ⓔ

Correctly Completed Worksheet

1.   6   3   13   90   <u>45</u>   36   12

2.
B	G	E	C	A	D
25 ___	36 ___	4 <u>**E**</u>	17 ___	82 <u>**A**</u>	13 ___

3.   17   4   30   25   9   41   **8**   3

4.
3 DETROIT HARTFORD _____	26 ST. LOUIS CLEVELAND <u>C</u>

5.
(27 ___)   (54 ___)   (31 ___)   (76 <u>**B**</u>)   (18 <u>C</u>)

6.
| 12 <u>B</u> | 56 <u>D</u> | 87 <u>E</u> | RED   WHITE   BLUE

7.
(___ D)   (___ E)   (<u>**33**</u> A)

8.   7 <u>**A**</u>   64 ___   31 ___

22

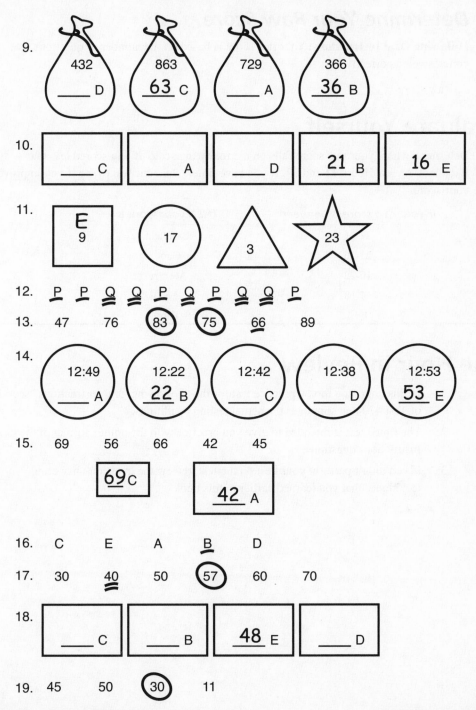

9.
432 ___ D
863 63 C
729 ___ A
366 36 B

10.
___ C
___ A
___ D
21 B
16 E

11.
E 9
17
3
23

12. P P Q Q P Q P Q Q P

13. 47   76   ⊙83   ⊙75   66   89

14.
12:49 ___ A
12:22 22 B
12:42 ___ C
12:38 ___ D
12:53 53 E

15. 69   56   66   42   45

69 C

42 A

16. C   E   A   B   D

17. 30   40   50   ⊙57   60   70

18.
___ C
___ B
48 E
___ D

19. 45   50   ⊙30   11

Determine Your Raw Score

Following Oral Instructions: Your raw score is based on the number of questions that you answered correctly:

Raw score = _____

Evaluate Yourself

Determine where your raw score falls on the following scale. If you scored less than Excellent, review Hours 11 and 12. If you have time, retake the test to see if you improved your score.

IF your raw score is between	THEN your work is
27-31	Excellent
23-26	Good
19-22	Average
14-18	Fair
1-13	Poor

The Hour in Review

1. In this hour, you took a practice test for the "Following Oral Instructions" section of Test 470 that simulates the actual testing conditions.

2. The timed test is intended to give you practice with the unique format of the Oral Instructions questions.

3. If you didn't perform your best on the test, review the question-answering techniques that you learned earlier in this book.

HOUR 23

Following Oral Instructions—Timed Test 2

What You Will Learn in This Hour

This hour provides a second chance to take a full-length, timed "Following Oral Instructions" test. By this time, you should be aware of your weaknesses when answering this question type, so concentrate on those areas. Here are your goals for this hour:

- Complete the timed test under actual testing conditions, concentrating on applying the test-taking techniques you've learned.

- Check your answers and evaluate your score.

- Pinpoint any areas that need additional study.

Timed Test

The answer sheet, worksheet, and oral instructions for this practice exercise are on the following pages. You will have 25 minutes to complete the test. Remember to simulate the actual testing conditions as instructed in Hour 22, "Following Oral Instruction—Timed Test 1."

Answer Sheet

1. Ⓐ Ⓑ Ⓒ Ⓓ Ⓔ
2. Ⓐ Ⓑ Ⓒ Ⓓ Ⓔ
3. Ⓐ Ⓑ Ⓒ Ⓓ Ⓔ
4. Ⓐ Ⓑ Ⓒ Ⓓ Ⓔ
5. Ⓐ Ⓑ Ⓒ Ⓓ Ⓔ
6. Ⓐ Ⓑ Ⓒ Ⓓ Ⓔ
7. Ⓐ Ⓑ Ⓒ Ⓓ Ⓔ
8. Ⓐ Ⓑ Ⓒ Ⓓ Ⓔ
9. Ⓐ Ⓑ Ⓒ Ⓓ Ⓔ
10. Ⓐ Ⓑ Ⓒ Ⓓ Ⓔ
11. Ⓐ Ⓑ Ⓒ Ⓓ Ⓔ
12. Ⓐ Ⓑ Ⓒ Ⓓ Ⓔ
13. Ⓐ Ⓑ Ⓒ Ⓓ Ⓔ
14. Ⓐ Ⓑ Ⓒ Ⓓ Ⓔ
15. Ⓐ Ⓑ Ⓒ Ⓓ Ⓔ
16. Ⓐ Ⓑ Ⓒ Ⓓ Ⓔ
17. Ⓐ Ⓑ Ⓒ Ⓓ Ⓔ
18. Ⓐ Ⓑ Ⓒ Ⓓ Ⓔ
19. Ⓐ Ⓑ Ⓒ Ⓓ Ⓔ
20. Ⓐ Ⓑ Ⓒ Ⓓ Ⓔ
21. Ⓐ Ⓑ Ⓒ Ⓓ Ⓔ
22. Ⓐ Ⓑ Ⓒ Ⓓ Ⓔ

23. Ⓐ Ⓑ Ⓒ Ⓓ Ⓔ
24. Ⓐ Ⓑ Ⓒ Ⓓ Ⓔ
25. Ⓐ Ⓑ Ⓒ Ⓓ Ⓔ
26. Ⓐ Ⓑ Ⓒ Ⓓ Ⓔ
27. Ⓐ Ⓑ Ⓒ Ⓓ Ⓔ
28. Ⓐ Ⓑ Ⓒ Ⓓ Ⓔ
29. Ⓐ Ⓑ Ⓒ Ⓓ Ⓔ
30. Ⓐ Ⓑ Ⓒ Ⓓ Ⓔ
31. Ⓐ Ⓑ Ⓒ Ⓓ Ⓔ
32. Ⓐ Ⓑ Ⓒ Ⓓ Ⓔ
33. Ⓐ Ⓑ Ⓒ Ⓓ Ⓔ
34. Ⓐ Ⓑ Ⓒ Ⓓ Ⓔ
35. Ⓐ Ⓑ Ⓒ Ⓓ Ⓔ
36. Ⓐ Ⓑ Ⓒ Ⓓ Ⓔ
37. Ⓐ Ⓑ Ⓒ Ⓓ Ⓔ
38. Ⓐ Ⓑ Ⓒ Ⓓ Ⓔ
39. Ⓐ Ⓑ Ⓒ Ⓓ Ⓔ
40. Ⓐ Ⓑ Ⓒ Ⓓ Ⓔ
41. Ⓐ Ⓑ Ⓒ Ⓓ Ⓔ
42. Ⓐ Ⓑ Ⓒ Ⓓ Ⓔ
43. Ⓐ Ⓑ Ⓒ Ⓓ Ⓔ
44. Ⓐ Ⓑ Ⓒ Ⓓ Ⓔ

45. Ⓐ Ⓑ Ⓒ Ⓓ Ⓔ
46. Ⓐ Ⓑ Ⓒ Ⓓ Ⓔ
47. Ⓐ Ⓑ Ⓒ Ⓓ Ⓔ
48. Ⓐ Ⓑ Ⓒ Ⓓ Ⓔ
49. Ⓐ Ⓑ Ⓒ Ⓓ Ⓔ
50. Ⓐ Ⓑ Ⓒ Ⓓ Ⓔ
51. Ⓐ Ⓑ Ⓒ Ⓓ Ⓔ
52. Ⓐ Ⓑ Ⓒ Ⓓ Ⓔ
53. Ⓐ Ⓑ Ⓒ Ⓓ Ⓔ
54. Ⓐ Ⓑ Ⓒ Ⓓ Ⓔ
55. Ⓐ Ⓑ Ⓒ Ⓓ Ⓔ
56. Ⓐ Ⓑ Ⓒ Ⓓ Ⓔ
57. Ⓐ Ⓑ Ⓒ Ⓓ Ⓔ
58. Ⓐ Ⓑ Ⓒ Ⓓ Ⓔ
59. Ⓐ Ⓑ Ⓒ Ⓓ Ⓔ
60. Ⓐ Ⓑ Ⓒ Ⓓ Ⓔ
61. Ⓐ Ⓑ Ⓒ Ⓓ Ⓔ
62. Ⓐ Ⓑ Ⓒ Ⓓ Ⓔ
63. Ⓐ Ⓑ Ⓒ Ⓓ Ⓔ
64. Ⓐ Ⓑ Ⓒ Ⓓ Ⓔ
65. Ⓐ Ⓑ Ⓒ Ⓓ Ⓔ
66. Ⓐ Ⓑ Ⓒ Ⓓ Ⓔ

67. Ⓐ Ⓑ Ⓒ Ⓓ Ⓔ
68. Ⓐ Ⓑ Ⓒ Ⓓ Ⓔ
69. Ⓐ Ⓑ Ⓒ Ⓓ Ⓔ
70. Ⓐ Ⓑ Ⓒ Ⓓ Ⓔ
71. Ⓐ Ⓑ Ⓒ Ⓓ Ⓔ
72. Ⓐ Ⓑ Ⓒ Ⓓ Ⓔ
73. Ⓐ Ⓑ Ⓒ Ⓓ Ⓔ
74. Ⓐ Ⓑ Ⓒ Ⓓ Ⓔ
75. Ⓐ Ⓑ Ⓒ Ⓓ Ⓔ
76. Ⓐ Ⓑ Ⓒ Ⓓ Ⓔ
77. Ⓐ Ⓑ Ⓒ Ⓓ Ⓔ
78. Ⓐ Ⓑ Ⓒ Ⓓ Ⓔ
79. Ⓐ Ⓑ Ⓒ Ⓓ Ⓔ
80. Ⓐ Ⓑ Ⓒ Ⓓ Ⓔ
81. Ⓐ Ⓑ Ⓒ Ⓓ Ⓔ
82. Ⓐ Ⓑ Ⓒ Ⓓ Ⓔ
83. Ⓐ Ⓑ Ⓒ Ⓓ Ⓔ
84. Ⓐ Ⓑ Ⓒ Ⓓ Ⓔ
85. Ⓐ Ⓑ Ⓒ Ⓓ Ⓔ
86. Ⓐ Ⓑ Ⓒ Ⓓ Ⓔ
87. Ⓐ Ⓑ Ⓒ Ⓓ Ⓔ
88. Ⓐ Ⓑ Ⓒ Ⓓ Ⓔ

23

Worksheet

DIRECTIONS: Listen carefully to the instructions read to you and mark each item on this worksheet as directed. Then complete each question by marking the answer sheet as directed. For each answer, you will darken the answer sheet for a number-letter combination.

23

1.   E   A   B   C   D

2.   X ☆ ☆ X X X ☆ ☆ X

3.

33 ____   56 ____   80 __   10 ____   14 ____

4.   3   38   41   7   19   28   89

5.

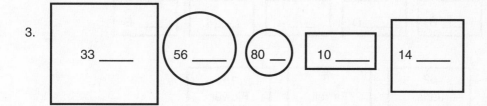

4:14 ____ A   3:28 ____ B   4:10 ____ C   3:39 ____ D   3:47 ____ E

6.

12 ____   71 ____   35 ____   66 ____   36 ____

7.   14   28   39   17   77   62   1   4

8.   BABY   CLAM   DEAR   80 ____   17 ____   51 ____

9.

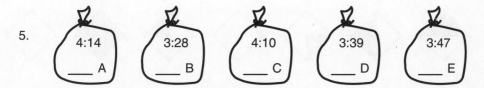

5 __   60 ____   76 __   42 __   58 __

10.   5   90   18   32   1

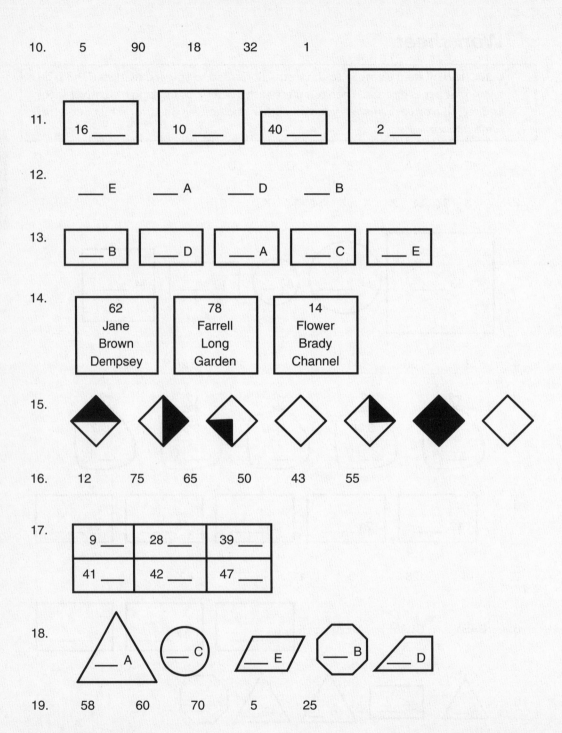

11.   16 ____   10 ____   40 ____   2 ____

12.   ___ E   ___ A   ___ D   ___ B

13.   ___ B   ___ D   ___ A   ___ C   ___ E

14.
62	78	14
Jane	Farrell	Flower
Brown	Long	Brady
Dempsey	Garden	Channel

15.

16.   12   75   65   50   43   55

17.
| 9 ___ | 28 ___ | 39 ___ |
| 41 ___ | 42 ___ | 47 ___ |

18.   ___ A   ___ C   ___ E   ___ B   ___ D

19.   58   60   70   5   25

Directions and Sample Questions

Listening to Instructions: When you are ready to try these sample questions, give the following instructions to a friend and have the friend read them aloud to you at the rate of 80 words per minute. Do not read them to yourself. Your friend will need a watch with a second hand. Listen carefully and do exactly what your friend tells you to do with the worksheet and answer sheet. Your friend will tell you some things to do with each item on the worksheet. After each set of instructions, your friend will give you time to mark your answer by darkening a circle on the sample answer sheet. Since B and D sound very much alike, your friend will say "B as in baker" when he or she means B and "D as in dog" when he or she means D.

Before proceeding further, tear out the worksheet on pages 311 and 312. Then hand this book to your friend.

To the Person Who Is to Read the Instructions: The instructions are to be read at the rate of 80 words per minute. Do not read aloud the material that is in parentheses. Do not repeat any instructions.

Oral Instructions

(Note: The words in parentheses should *not* be read aloud.)

On the job you will have to listen to directions and then do what you have been told. Listen closely as I read the directions; I cannot repeat them. Once we begin, you may not ask any questions until the end of the test.

On the job you won't have to deal with pictures, numbers, and letters like those in the test, but you will have to listen to instructions and follow them. We are using this test to see how well you can follow instructions.

You are to mark your test booklet according to the instructions that I'll read to you. After each set of instructions, I'll give you time to record your answers on the separate answer sheet.

The actual test begins now.

Look at line 1 on your worksheet. (Pause slightly.) Draw a line under the fourth letter in the line. (Pause two seconds.) Now, on your answer sheet, find number 21 and darken the space for the letter under which you drew a line. (Pause five seconds.)

Now look at line 2 on your worksheet. (Pause slightly.) Draw a line under each star on line 2. (Pause five seconds.) Count the number of lines you have drawn and write that number at the end of line 2. (Pause five seconds.) Now, on your answer sheet, find that number and darken space A. (Pause five seconds.)

Look at line 3 on your worksheet. (Pause slightly.) Find the largest circle and write the letter D as in dog on the line in the circle. (Pause two seconds.) Now, on your answer sheet, find the number that is in the circle and darken the number-letter combination that is in that circle. (Pause five seconds.)

Look at line 3 again. (Pause slightly.) Find the largest square. (Pause two seconds.) Draw a line through the number in the square, subtract 4 from that number, and write your answer on the line beside the number. (Pause five seconds.) Now, on your answer sheet, darken space E for the number that you wrote in the box. (Pause five seconds.)

Look at line 4 on your worksheet. (Pause slightly.) Draw two lines under the fifth number on line 4. (Pause two seconds.) If the number under which you drew the two lines is an even number, darken space B as in baker for that number on your answer sheet. If the number under which you drew the two lines is an odd number, darken space A. (Pause 10 seconds.)

Look at line 4 again. (Pause slightly.) Circle the middle number in the line. (Pause two seconds.) Now, on your answer sheet, darken space B as in baker for the number you circled. (Pause five seconds.)

Look at line 5 on your worksheet. (Pause slightly.) Five mail sacks are on line 5 with a time printed on each sack. The train carrying the mail leaves the station promptly at 4:00 p.m., so mail must be on the platform before that time. Find the mail sack with the latest possible time for arrival at the station, and write the last two digits of the time on the line in the mail sack. (Pause five seconds.) Now, on your answer sheet, find the number you wrote and darken the space for the number-letter combination in the mail sack. (Pause five seconds.)

Look at line 6 on your worksheet. (Pause slightly.) If the number 35 is divisible by two, write the letter C in the third box. If not, write the letter D as in dog in the fifth box. (Pause five seconds.) Now, on your answer sheet, darken the space for the number-letter combination in the box. (Pause five seconds.)

Look at line 6 again. (Pause slightly.) Find the box with the highest number and write the letter A on the line in that box. (Pause two seconds.) Now, on your answer sheet, darken the space for the number-letter combination in that box. (Pause five seconds.)

Look at line 7 on your worksheet. (Pause slightly.) Count up the number of even numbers on line 7 and write that number at the end of the line. (Pause five seconds.) If the number you wrote is greater than 3, circle the fourth number on the line. If the number you wrote is less than 3, circle the fifth number on line 7. (Pause five seconds.) Now, on your answer sheet, darken space B as in baker for the number that you circled. (Pause five seconds.)

Look at line 8 on your worksheet. (Pause slightly.) There are three words and three boxes with numbers on the line. Write the second letter of the third word in the first box. (Pause five seconds.) Write the first letter of the second word in the third box. (Pause five seconds.) Now, on your answer sheet, darken the spaces for the number-letter combinations in both boxes. (Pause 10 seconds.)

Look at line 8 again. (Pause slightly.) Find the letter of the alphabet that appears more than two times in the three words and circle that letter in each word. (Pause two seconds.) Now, on your answer sheet, darken that letter for space 13. (Pause five seconds.)

Look at line 9 on your worksheet. (Pause slightly.) If Monday comes before Wednesday and if 11 is greater than 7, write the letter B as in baker in the second triangle. Otherwise, write the letter D as in dog in the square. (Pause 10 seconds.) Now, on your answer sheet, darken the space for the number-letter combination you just wrote. (Pause five seconds.)

Look at line 9 again. (Pause slightly.) Write the letter C in the figure with the most sides. (Pause two seconds.) Now add the number 10 to the number in the figure in which you just wrote the letter C and darken the space for that number-letter combination on your answer sheet. (Pause 10 seconds.)

Look at line 10 on your worksheet. (Pause slightly.) Draw one line under the third even number on line 10. (Pause two seconds.) Now, on your answer sheet, darken space D as in dog for the number under which you just drew one line. (Pause five seconds.)

Look at line 10 again. (Pause slightly.) Draw two lines under the first number in the line. (Pause two seconds.) Multiply that number by five and write the number at the end of line 10. (Pause two seconds.) Now, on your answer sheet, darken space A for the number you wrote at the end of the line. (Pause five seconds.)

Look at line 11 on your worksheet. (Pause slightly.) If the number in the smallest box is smaller than the number in the first box, write the letter C in the smallest box. If not, write the letter E in the largest box. (Pause five seconds.) Now, on your answer sheet, darken the space for the number-letter combination in the box you just wrote in. (Pause five seconds.)

Look at line 12 on your worksheet. (Pause slightly.) Write the number of days in the month of February not in a leap year next to the fourth letter on line 12. (Pause two seconds.) Now, on your answer sheet, darken the space for that number-letter combination. (Pause five seconds.)

Look at line 13 on your worksheet. (Pause slightly.) In the fourth box, write the answer to this question: Which of the following is the largest number: 72, 12, 85, 51, or 67? (Pause two seconds.) Now, on your answer sheet, darken the space for the number-letter combination in the box you just wrote in. (Pause five seconds.)

Look at line 13 again. (Pause slightly.) If the number of minutes in an hour is equal to the number of seconds in a minute, write the number 24 in the middle box. If not, write the number 60 in the first box. (Pause five seconds.) Now, on your answer sheet, darken the space for the number-letter combination in the box you just wrote in. (Pause five seconds.)

Look at line 14 on your worksheet. (Pause slightly.) Mail for individual carrier routes is sorted into individual boxes as indicated by the names in the boxes. The numbers on the boxes are the numbers of the carrier routes. Write the letter E in the box for the carrier route to which mail for Dempsey is assigned. (Pause two seconds.) Now, on your answer sheet, darken the space for the number-letter combination in the box you just wrote in. (Pause five seconds.)

Look at line 15 on your worksheet. (Pause slightly.) Count the number of diamonds that are partially shaded, multiply that number by 4, and write the new number in the first unshaded diamond. (Pause two seconds.) Now, on your answer sheet, darken space B as in baker for the number you wrote in the first unshaded diamond. (Pause five seconds.)

Look at line 15 again. (Pause slightly.) If more diamonds are fully shaded than fully unshaded, write the number 79 in the first diamond. If not, write the number 10 in the last diamond. Now, on your answer sheet, darken space D as in dog for the number you just wrote. (Pause five seconds.)

Look at line 16 on your worksheet. (Pause slightly.) Draw a line under every number that is 55 or greater but less than 75. (Pause five seconds.) Now, on your answer sheet, darken the letter C for every number under which you drew a line. (Pause 10 seconds.)

Look at line 17 on your worksheet. (Pause slightly.) Write the letter A in the middle square in the bottom row of mailboxes. (Pause two seconds.) Now, on your answer sheet, darken the space for the number-letter combination in the mailbox you just wrote in. (Pause five seconds.)

Look at line 17 again. (Pause slightly.) If the sum of 5 plus 3 is 8 and the sum of 7 plus 2 is 9, write B as in baker in the upper right-hand mailbox. Otherwise, write C in the lower right-hand mailbox. (Pause five seconds.) Now, on your answer sheet, darken the space for the number-letter combination in the mailbox you just wrote in. (Pause five seconds.)

Look at line 18 on your worksheet. (Pause slightly.) Find the figure with the greatest number of corners. Add 70 to the number of corners and write the sum on the line in the figure. (Pause five seconds.) Now, on your answer sheet, darken the space for the number-letter combination in the figure you just wrote in. (Pause five seconds.)

Look at line 18 again. (Pause slightly.) If the second figure is larger than the first figure, write the number 40 on the line in the second figure. (Pause two seconds.) Otherwise, write the number 40 on the line in the fifth figure. (Pause two seconds.) Now, on your answer sheet, darken the space for the number-letter combination in the figure you just wrote in. (Pause five seconds.)

Look at line 19 on your worksheet. (Pause slightly.) Draw a circle around each number on line 19 that is a multiple of 10. (Pause five seconds.) Now, on your answer sheet, darken the letter E for each number around which you drew a circle. (Pause 10 seconds.)

Answers

Correctly Completed Answer Sheet

1. Ⓐ Ⓑ Ⓒ Ⓓ Ⓔ   23. Ⓐ Ⓑ Ⓒ Ⓓ Ⓔ   45. Ⓐ Ⓑ Ⓒ Ⓓ Ⓔ   67. Ⓐ Ⓑ Ⓒ Ⓓ Ⓔ
2. Ⓐ Ⓑ Ⓒ Ⓓ ●   24. ● Ⓑ Ⓒ Ⓓ Ⓔ   46. Ⓐ Ⓑ Ⓒ Ⓓ Ⓔ   68. Ⓐ Ⓑ ● Ⓓ Ⓔ
3. Ⓐ Ⓑ Ⓒ Ⓓ Ⓔ   25. ● Ⓑ Ⓒ Ⓓ Ⓔ   47. Ⓐ Ⓑ Ⓒ Ⓓ ●   69. Ⓐ Ⓑ Ⓒ Ⓓ Ⓔ
4. ● Ⓑ Ⓒ Ⓓ Ⓔ   26. Ⓐ Ⓑ Ⓒ Ⓓ Ⓔ   48. Ⓐ Ⓑ Ⓒ Ⓓ Ⓔ   70. Ⓐ Ⓑ Ⓒ Ⓓ ●
5. Ⓐ Ⓑ Ⓒ Ⓓ Ⓔ   27. Ⓐ Ⓑ Ⓒ Ⓓ Ⓔ   49. Ⓐ Ⓑ Ⓒ Ⓓ Ⓔ   71. ● Ⓑ Ⓒ Ⓓ Ⓔ
6. Ⓐ Ⓑ Ⓒ Ⓓ Ⓔ   28. Ⓐ ● Ⓒ Ⓓ Ⓔ   50. Ⓐ Ⓑ Ⓒ Ⓓ Ⓔ   72. Ⓐ Ⓑ Ⓒ Ⓓ Ⓔ
7. Ⓐ ● Ⓒ Ⓓ Ⓔ   29. Ⓐ Ⓑ Ⓒ Ⓓ ●   51. Ⓐ Ⓑ ● Ⓓ Ⓔ   73. Ⓐ Ⓑ Ⓒ Ⓓ Ⓔ
8. Ⓐ Ⓑ Ⓒ Ⓓ Ⓔ   30. Ⓐ Ⓑ Ⓒ Ⓓ Ⓔ   52. Ⓐ Ⓑ Ⓒ Ⓓ Ⓔ   74. Ⓐ Ⓑ Ⓒ Ⓓ Ⓔ
9. Ⓐ Ⓑ Ⓒ Ⓓ Ⓔ   31. Ⓐ Ⓑ Ⓒ Ⓓ Ⓔ   53. Ⓐ Ⓑ Ⓒ Ⓓ Ⓔ   75. Ⓐ Ⓑ Ⓒ Ⓓ Ⓔ
10. Ⓐ Ⓑ Ⓒ ● Ⓔ   32. Ⓐ Ⓑ Ⓒ ● Ⓔ   54. Ⓐ Ⓑ Ⓒ Ⓓ Ⓔ   76. Ⓐ ● Ⓒ Ⓓ Ⓔ
11. Ⓐ Ⓑ Ⓒ Ⓓ Ⓔ   33. Ⓐ Ⓑ Ⓒ Ⓓ Ⓔ   55. Ⓐ Ⓑ ● Ⓓ Ⓔ   77. Ⓐ Ⓑ Ⓒ Ⓓ Ⓔ
12. Ⓐ Ⓑ Ⓒ Ⓓ Ⓔ   34. Ⓐ Ⓑ Ⓒ Ⓓ Ⓔ   56. Ⓐ Ⓑ Ⓒ ● Ⓔ   78. Ⓐ ● Ⓒ Ⓓ Ⓔ
13. ● Ⓑ Ⓒ Ⓓ Ⓔ   35. Ⓐ Ⓑ Ⓒ Ⓓ Ⓔ   57. Ⓐ Ⓑ Ⓒ Ⓓ Ⓔ   79. Ⓐ Ⓑ Ⓒ Ⓓ Ⓔ
14. Ⓐ Ⓑ Ⓒ Ⓓ Ⓔ   36. Ⓐ Ⓑ Ⓒ ● Ⓔ   58. Ⓐ Ⓑ Ⓒ Ⓓ Ⓔ   80. Ⓐ Ⓑ Ⓒ Ⓓ ●
15. Ⓐ Ⓑ Ⓒ Ⓓ Ⓔ   37. Ⓐ Ⓑ Ⓒ Ⓓ Ⓔ   59. Ⓐ Ⓑ Ⓒ Ⓓ Ⓔ   81. Ⓐ Ⓑ Ⓒ Ⓓ Ⓔ
16. Ⓐ ● Ⓒ Ⓓ Ⓔ   38. Ⓐ Ⓑ Ⓒ Ⓓ Ⓔ   60. Ⓐ Ⓑ Ⓒ Ⓓ ●   82. Ⓐ Ⓑ Ⓒ Ⓓ Ⓔ
17. Ⓐ ● Ⓒ Ⓓ Ⓔ   39. Ⓐ ● Ⓒ Ⓓ Ⓔ   61. Ⓐ Ⓑ Ⓒ Ⓓ Ⓔ   83. Ⓐ Ⓑ Ⓒ Ⓓ Ⓔ
18. Ⓐ Ⓑ Ⓒ Ⓓ Ⓔ   40. Ⓐ Ⓑ Ⓒ ● Ⓔ   62. Ⓐ Ⓑ Ⓒ Ⓓ ●   84. Ⓐ Ⓑ Ⓒ Ⓓ Ⓔ
19. ● Ⓑ Ⓒ Ⓓ Ⓔ   41. Ⓐ Ⓑ Ⓒ Ⓓ Ⓔ   63. Ⓐ Ⓑ Ⓒ Ⓓ Ⓔ   85. Ⓐ Ⓑ ● Ⓓ Ⓔ
20. Ⓐ Ⓑ Ⓒ Ⓓ Ⓔ   42. ● Ⓑ Ⓒ Ⓓ Ⓔ   64. Ⓐ Ⓑ Ⓒ Ⓓ Ⓔ   86. Ⓐ Ⓑ Ⓒ Ⓓ Ⓔ
21. Ⓐ Ⓑ ● Ⓓ Ⓔ   43. Ⓐ Ⓑ Ⓒ Ⓓ Ⓔ   65. Ⓐ Ⓑ ● Ⓓ Ⓔ   87. Ⓐ Ⓑ Ⓒ Ⓓ Ⓔ
22. Ⓐ Ⓑ Ⓒ Ⓓ Ⓔ   44. Ⓐ Ⓑ Ⓒ Ⓓ Ⓔ   66. Ⓐ Ⓑ Ⓒ Ⓓ Ⓔ   88. Ⓐ Ⓑ Ⓒ Ⓓ Ⓔ

Correctly Completed Worksheet

1.   E   A   B   C̲   D

2.   X ☆ ☆ X X X ☆ ☆ X **4**

3.   [⬚28 **29**]   (56 **D**)   (80 ___)   [10 _____]   [14 _____]

4.   3   38   41   ⑦   1̲9̲   28   89

5.   🗑 4:14 ___ A   🗑 3:28 ___ B   🗑 4:10 ___ C   🗑 3:39 ___ D   🗑 3:47 **47̲** E

6.   [12 ____]   [71 **A**]   [35 ____]   [66 ____]   [36 **D**]

7.   14   28   39   ⑰   77   62   1   4   **4**

8.   ⊘BABY   ⊘CLAM   ⊘DEAR   [80 **E**]   [17 _____]   [51 **C**]

9.   △ 5 __   [60 ___]   △ 76 **B**   △ 42 __   ⬡ 58 **C̲**

23

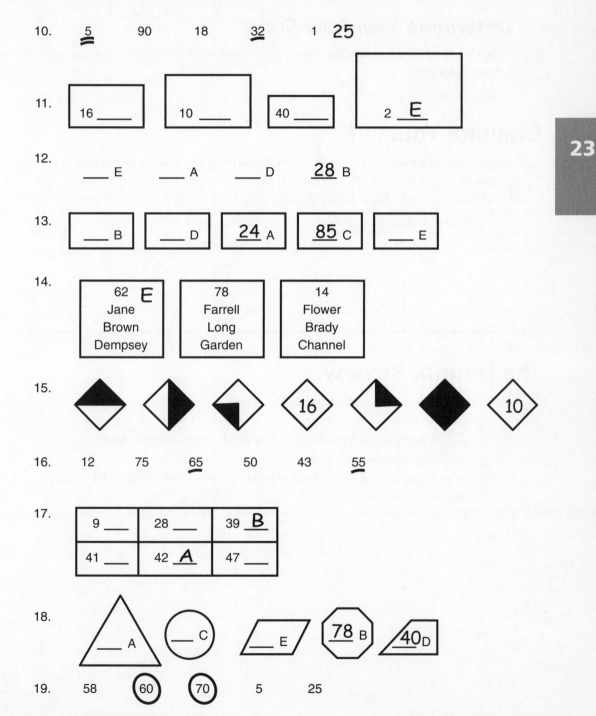

10.   5   90   18   32   1   **25**

11. | 16 ___ | | 10 ___ | | 40 ___ | 2 _E_ |

12.   ___ E   ___ A   ___ D   **28** B

13.   ___ B   ___ D   **24** A   **85** C   ___ E

14. | 62 E
Jane
Brown
Dempsey | | 78
Farrell
Long
Garden | | 14
Flower
Brady
Channel |

15.

16.   12   75   65   50   43   55

17. | 9 ___ | 28 ___ | 39 **B** |
      | 41 ___ | 42 **A** | 47 ___ |

18.   ___ A   ___ C   ___ E   **78** B   **40** D

19.   58   (60)   (70)   5   25

Determine Your Raw Score

Following Oral Instructions: Your raw score is based on the number of questions that you answered correctly:

Raw score = _____

Evaluate Yourself

Determine where your raw score falls on the following scale. If you scored less than Excellent, review Hour 11, "Following Oral Instructions—1," and Hour 12, "Following Oral Instructions—2." If you have time, retake the test to see if your score improves.

IF your raw score is between	THEN your work is
27-31	Excellent
23-26	Good
19-22	Average
14-18	Fair
1-13	Poor

The Hour in Review

1. In this hour, you completed a second, timed "Following Oral Instructions" practice test.

2. After completing this practice test, you should see an improvement in your score and your test-taking strategies.

3. If you have time, review the techniques in Hours 11 and 12 with which you're still having trouble.

Hour **24**

Following Oral Instructions—Timed Test 3

What You Will Learn in This Hour

In this hour, you'll take the last full-length "Following Oral Instructions" timed test. Use this final test to perfect all the question-answering techniques that you learned in previous hours. Here are your goals for this hour:

- Complete the test under actual timed conditions, focusing on the weak areas that you discovered in the previous two hours.
- Check your answers against the answer key and determine your raw score.
- Review the appropriate lessons in previous hours if necessary.

Timed Test

The answer sheet, worksheet, and oral instructions for this practice exercise are on the following pages. You have 25 minutes to complete it. Remember to simulate the actual testing conditions as instructed in Hour 22, "Following Oral Instruction—Timed Test 1."

Answer Sheet

1. Ⓐ Ⓑ Ⓒ Ⓓ Ⓔ   23. Ⓐ Ⓑ Ⓒ Ⓓ Ⓔ   45. Ⓐ Ⓑ Ⓒ Ⓓ Ⓔ   67. Ⓐ Ⓑ Ⓒ Ⓓ Ⓔ

2. Ⓐ Ⓑ Ⓒ Ⓓ Ⓔ   24. Ⓐ Ⓑ Ⓒ Ⓓ Ⓔ   46. Ⓐ Ⓑ Ⓒ Ⓓ Ⓔ   68. Ⓐ Ⓑ Ⓒ Ⓓ Ⓔ

3. Ⓐ Ⓑ Ⓒ Ⓓ Ⓔ   25. Ⓐ Ⓑ Ⓒ Ⓓ Ⓔ   47. Ⓐ Ⓑ Ⓒ Ⓓ Ⓔ   69. Ⓐ Ⓑ Ⓒ Ⓓ Ⓔ

4. Ⓐ Ⓑ Ⓒ Ⓓ Ⓔ   26. Ⓐ Ⓑ Ⓒ Ⓓ Ⓔ   48. Ⓐ Ⓑ Ⓒ Ⓓ Ⓔ   70. Ⓐ Ⓑ Ⓒ Ⓓ Ⓔ

5. Ⓐ Ⓑ Ⓒ Ⓓ Ⓔ   27. Ⓐ Ⓑ Ⓒ Ⓓ Ⓔ   49. Ⓐ Ⓑ Ⓒ Ⓓ Ⓔ   71. Ⓐ Ⓑ Ⓒ Ⓓ Ⓔ

6. Ⓐ Ⓑ Ⓒ Ⓓ Ⓔ   28. Ⓐ Ⓑ Ⓒ Ⓓ Ⓔ   50. Ⓐ Ⓑ Ⓒ Ⓓ Ⓔ   72. Ⓐ Ⓑ Ⓒ Ⓓ Ⓔ

7. Ⓐ Ⓑ Ⓒ Ⓓ Ⓔ   29. Ⓐ Ⓑ Ⓒ Ⓓ Ⓔ   51. Ⓐ Ⓑ Ⓒ Ⓓ Ⓔ   73. Ⓐ Ⓑ Ⓒ Ⓓ Ⓔ

8. Ⓐ Ⓑ Ⓒ Ⓓ Ⓔ   30. Ⓐ Ⓑ Ⓒ Ⓓ Ⓔ   52. Ⓐ Ⓑ Ⓒ Ⓓ Ⓔ   74. Ⓐ Ⓑ Ⓒ Ⓓ Ⓔ

9. Ⓐ Ⓑ Ⓒ Ⓓ Ⓔ   31. Ⓐ Ⓑ Ⓒ Ⓓ Ⓔ   53. Ⓐ Ⓑ Ⓒ Ⓓ Ⓔ   75. Ⓐ Ⓑ Ⓒ Ⓓ Ⓔ

10. Ⓐ Ⓑ Ⓒ Ⓓ Ⓔ   32. Ⓐ Ⓑ Ⓒ Ⓓ Ⓔ   54. Ⓐ Ⓑ Ⓒ Ⓓ Ⓔ   76. Ⓐ Ⓑ Ⓒ Ⓓ Ⓔ

11. Ⓐ Ⓑ Ⓒ Ⓓ Ⓔ   33. Ⓐ Ⓑ Ⓒ Ⓓ Ⓔ   55. Ⓐ Ⓑ Ⓒ Ⓓ Ⓔ   77. Ⓐ Ⓑ Ⓒ Ⓓ Ⓔ

12. Ⓐ Ⓑ Ⓒ Ⓓ Ⓔ   34. Ⓐ Ⓑ Ⓒ Ⓓ Ⓔ   56. Ⓐ Ⓑ Ⓒ Ⓓ Ⓔ   78. Ⓐ Ⓑ Ⓒ Ⓓ Ⓔ

13. Ⓐ Ⓑ Ⓒ Ⓓ Ⓔ   35. Ⓐ Ⓑ Ⓒ Ⓓ Ⓔ   57. Ⓐ Ⓑ Ⓒ Ⓓ Ⓔ   79. Ⓐ Ⓑ Ⓒ Ⓓ Ⓔ

14. Ⓐ Ⓑ Ⓒ Ⓓ Ⓔ   36. Ⓐ Ⓑ Ⓒ Ⓓ Ⓔ   58. Ⓐ Ⓑ Ⓒ Ⓓ Ⓔ   80. Ⓐ Ⓑ Ⓒ Ⓓ Ⓔ

15. Ⓐ Ⓑ Ⓒ Ⓓ Ⓔ   37. Ⓐ Ⓑ Ⓒ Ⓓ Ⓔ   59. Ⓐ Ⓑ Ⓒ Ⓓ Ⓔ   81. Ⓐ Ⓑ Ⓒ Ⓓ Ⓔ

16. Ⓐ Ⓑ Ⓒ Ⓓ Ⓔ   38. Ⓐ Ⓑ Ⓒ Ⓓ Ⓔ   60. Ⓐ Ⓑ Ⓒ Ⓓ Ⓔ   82. Ⓐ Ⓑ Ⓒ Ⓓ Ⓔ

17. Ⓐ Ⓑ Ⓒ Ⓓ Ⓔ   39. Ⓐ Ⓑ Ⓒ Ⓓ Ⓔ   61. Ⓐ Ⓑ Ⓒ Ⓓ Ⓔ   83. Ⓐ Ⓑ Ⓒ Ⓓ Ⓔ

18. Ⓐ Ⓑ Ⓒ Ⓓ Ⓔ   40. Ⓐ Ⓑ Ⓒ Ⓓ Ⓔ   62. Ⓐ Ⓑ Ⓒ Ⓓ Ⓔ   84. Ⓐ Ⓑ Ⓒ Ⓓ Ⓔ

19. Ⓐ Ⓑ Ⓒ Ⓓ Ⓔ   41. Ⓐ Ⓑ Ⓒ Ⓓ Ⓔ   63. Ⓐ Ⓑ Ⓒ Ⓓ Ⓔ   85. Ⓐ Ⓑ Ⓒ Ⓓ Ⓔ

20. Ⓐ Ⓑ Ⓒ Ⓓ Ⓔ   42. Ⓐ Ⓑ Ⓒ Ⓓ Ⓔ   64. Ⓐ Ⓑ Ⓒ Ⓓ Ⓔ   86. Ⓐ Ⓑ Ⓒ Ⓓ Ⓔ

21. Ⓐ Ⓑ Ⓒ Ⓓ Ⓔ   43. Ⓐ Ⓑ Ⓒ Ⓓ Ⓔ   65. Ⓐ Ⓑ Ⓒ Ⓓ Ⓔ   87. Ⓐ Ⓑ Ⓒ Ⓓ Ⓔ

22. Ⓐ Ⓑ Ⓒ Ⓓ Ⓔ   44. Ⓐ Ⓑ Ⓒ Ⓓ Ⓔ   66. Ⓐ Ⓑ Ⓒ Ⓓ Ⓔ   88. Ⓐ Ⓑ Ⓒ Ⓓ Ⓔ

24

Worksheet

> **DIRECTIONS:** Listen carefully to the instructions read to you and mark each item on this worksheet as directed. Then complete each question by marking the answer sheet as directed. For each answer, darken the answer sheet with the number-letter combination.

1.   16   88   3   51   46   71   24

2.   C   A   E   D   B

3.
| ___ B | ___ D | ___ C | ___ A | ___ E |

4.

(56 ___) (13 ___) (85 ___) (37 ___) (44 ___) (32 ___) (41 ___)

5.
| B | C | E |
| $9.00 | $42.00 | $19.00 |

6.   87 ____   27 ____   64 ____   PLANE   TRAIN   BUS

7.   46   35   39   43   42   38

8.   G   D   P   F   E   C   L   J

9.

△ 2   ☆ 20   ○ 11   ▢ 5

24

10.   74   21   53   57   42   51

11.

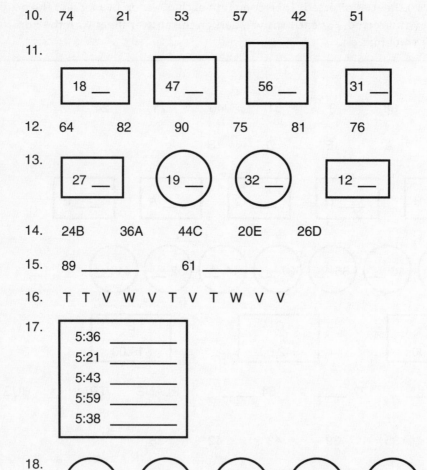

18 __   47 __   56 __   31 __

12.   64   82   90   75   81   76

13.

27 __   19 __   32 __   12 __

14.   24B   36A   44C   20E   26D

15.   89 _____   61 _____

16.   T   T   V   W   V   T   V   T   W   V   V

17.

5:36   _____
5:21   _____
5:43   _____
5:59   _____
5:38   _____

18.   __ E   __ D   __ A   __ B   __ C

19.   __ C   __ A   __ B   __ E

Directions and Sample Questions

Listening to Instructions: When you are ready to try these sample questions, give the following instructions to a friend and have the friend read them aloud to you at the rate of 80 words per minute. Do not read them to yourself. Your friend will need a watch with a second hand. Listen carefully and do exactly what your friend tells you to do with the worksheet and answer sheet. Your friend will tell you some things to do with each item on the worksheet. After each set of instructions, your friend will give you time to mark your answer by darkening a circle on the sample answer sheet. Since B and D sound very much alike, your friend will say "B as in baker" when he or she means B and "D as in dog" when he or she means D.

Before proceeding further, tear out the worksheet on pages 325 and 326. Then hand this book to your friend.

To the Person Who Is to Read the Instructions: The instructions are to be read at the rate of 80 words per minute. Do not read aloud the material that is in parentheses. Do not repeat any instructions.

Oral Instructions

(Note: The words in parentheses should not be read aloud.)

On the job you will have to listen to directions and then do what you have been told. In this test, I will read the instructions to you. Listen closely as I read them; I cannot repeat them. Once we begin, you may not ask any questions until the end of the test.

On the job you won't have to deal with pictures, numbers, and letters like those in the test, but you will have to listen to instructions and follow them. We are using this test to see how well you can follow instructions.

You are to mark your test booklet according to the instructions that I'll read to you. After each set of instructions, I'll give you time to record your answers on the separate answer sheet.

The actual test begins now.

Look at line 1 on your worksheet. (Pause slightly.) Draw a line under the sixth number in line 1. (Pause two seconds.) Now, on your answer sheet, darken space E for the number under which you just drew a line. (Pause five seconds.)

Look at line 1 again. (Pause slightly.) Draw two lines under the third number on the line. (Pause two seconds.) Now, on your answer sheet, darken space B as in baker for the number under which you drew two lines. (Pause five seconds.)

Look at line 2 on your worksheet. (Pause slightly.) Find the letter that is fifth in the alphabet and circle it. (Pause two seconds.) Now darken that letter for number 77 on your answer sheet. (Pause five seconds.)

Look at line 3 on your worksheet. (Pause slightly.) Write the number 17 in the third box. (Pause two seconds.) Now, on your answer sheet, darken the number-letter combination that is in the box you just wrote in. (Pause five seconds.)

Look at line 3 again. (Pause slightly.) In the fourth box, write the number of hours in a day. (Pause two seconds.) Now, on your answer sheet, darken the number-letter combination that is in the box you just wrote in. (Pause five seconds.)

Look at line 4 on your worksheet. (Pause slightly.) Write D as in dog in the circle containing the second-lowest number. (Pause five seconds.) Now, on your answer sheet, darken the space for the number-letter combination in the circle you just wrote in. (Pause five seconds.)

Look at line 4 again. (Pause slightly.) Write the letter C on the line in the middle circle. (Pause two seconds.) Now, on your answer sheet, darken the space for the number-letter combination in the circle you just wrote in. (Pause five seconds.)

Look at line 5 on your worksheet. Each box represents a letter carrier and the amount of money that he or she collected on the route in one day. (Pause slightly.) Find the carrier who collected the smallest amount of money that day and circle his or her letter. (Pause two seconds.) On your answer sheet, darken the number-letter combination in the box in which you circled a letter. (Pause five seconds.)

Look at line 6 on your worksheet. (Pause slightly.) Write the first letter of the third means of transportation on the second line. (Pause eight seconds.) Write the last letter of the first means of transportation on the first line. (Pause eight seconds.) Write the middle letter of the middle means of transportation on the last line. (Pause eight seconds.) Now, on your answer sheet, darken the number-letter combinations on the three lines. (Pause 15 seconds.)

Look at line 7 on your worksheet. (Pause slightly.) Reading right to left, find the first number that is higher than the number 39 and draw a box around the number. (Pause five seconds.) Now, on your answer sheet, darken D as in dog for the number around which you just drew a box. (Pause five seconds.)

Look at line 8 on your worksheet. (Pause slightly.) Select the letter contained on line 8 that appears first in the alphabet and underline that letter. (Pause five seconds.) Now, on your answer sheet, darken that letter for space number 1. (Pause five seconds.)

Look at line 9 on your worksheet. (Pause slightly.) In the figure with the least number of points, write the letter A. (Pause two seconds.) In the figure with the greatest number of points, write the letter E. (Pause two seconds.) Now, on your answer sheet, darken the number-letter combinations in the two figures you just wrote in. (Pause 10 seconds.)

Look at line 10 on your worksheet. (Pause slightly.) If the third number in line 10 should, in normal counting, appear before the fourth number in line 10, write the letter B as in baker above the third number; if not, write the letter A above the fourth number. (Pause five seconds.) Now, on your answer sheet, darken the number-letter combination of the number you just wrote in. (Pause five seconds.)

Look at line 11 on your worksheet. (Pause slightly.) Write the letter A in the second box. (Pause two seconds.) Now, on your answer sheet, darken the number-letter combination in the box you just wrote in. (Pause five seconds.)

Look at line 11 again. (Pause slightly.) If the number in the smallest box is greater than the number in the first box, write the letter C in the largest box (pause five seconds); if not, write the letter D as in dog in the largest box. (Pause two seconds.) Now, on your answer sheet, darken the number-letter combination in the box you just wrote in. (Pause five seconds.)

Look at line 12 on your worksheet. (Pause slightly.) Draw one line under each number that falls between 75 and 90 and is even. (Pause eight seconds.) Now, on your answer sheet, blacken space D as in dog for each number under which you drew one line. (Pause 10 seconds.)

Look at line 12 again. (Pause slightly.) Draw two lines under each number that falls between 75 and 90 and is odd. (Pause eight seconds.) Now, on your answer sheet, darken space E for each number under which you drew two lines. (Pause five seconds.)

Look at line 13 on your worksheet. (Pause slightly.) Write the letter A in the left-hand circle. (Pause two seconds.) Now, on your answer sheet, darken the space for the number-letter combination in the figure you just wrote in. (Pause five seconds.)

Look at line 13 again. (Pause slightly.) Write the letter B as in baker in the right-hand square. (Pause two seconds.) Now, on your answer sheet, darken the space for the number-letter combination in the figure in which you just wrote. (Pause five seconds.)

Look at line 14 on your worksheet. (Pause slightly.) Write the answer to this multiplication problem at the end of line 14: 22 × 2. (Pause two seconds.) Find the answer that you wrote among the numbers on line 14 (pause two seconds) and darken that number-letter combination on your answer sheet. (Pause five seconds.)

Look at line 15 on your worksheet. (Pause slightly.) If 3 is less than 5 and more than 7, write the letter E next to number 89 (pause five seconds); if not, write the letter E next to number 61. (Pause two seconds.) Now, on your answer sheet, darken the number-letter combination of the line you just wrote on. (Pause five seconds.)

24

Look at line 16 on your worksheet. (Pause slightly.) Count the number of Vs on line 16 and write the number at the end of the line. (Pause two seconds.) Now, add 11 to that number and, on your answer sheet, darken space D as in dog for the number of Vs plus 11. (Pause 10 seconds.)

Look at line 17 on your worksheet. (Pause slightly.) Each time represents the scheduled A.M. arrival time of a mail truck. Write the letter A on the line beside the earliest scheduled time. (Pause two seconds.) Write the letter C next to the latest scheduled time. (Pause two seconds.) Now, on your answer sheet, darken the number-letter combinations of the last two digits of the times beside which you wrote the letters. (Pause 10 seconds.)

Look at line 18 on your worksheet. (Pause slightly.) If in one day there are more hours before noon than after noon, write the number 47 in the second circle (pause two seconds); if not, write the number 38 in the first circle. (Pause two seconds.) Now, on your answer sheet, blacken the space for the number-letter combination in the circle in which you just wrote. (Pause five seconds.)

Look at line 18 again. (Pause slightly.) Write the number 69 in the second circle from the right. (Pause two seconds.) Now, on your answer sheet, darken the space for the number-letter combination in the circle in which you just wrote. (Pause five seconds.)

Look at line 19 on your worksheet. (Pause slightly.) Write the smallest of these numbers in the first box: 84, 35, 73. (Pause five seconds.) Now, on your answer sheet, darken the space for the number-letter combination in the figure in which you just wrote. (Pause five seconds.)

Answers

Correctly Completed Answer Sheet

1. Ⓐ Ⓑ ● Ⓓ Ⓔ	23. Ⓐ Ⓑ Ⓒ Ⓓ Ⓔ	45. Ⓐ Ⓑ Ⓒ Ⓓ Ⓔ	67. Ⓐ Ⓑ Ⓒ Ⓓ Ⓔ
2. Ⓐ Ⓑ Ⓒ Ⓓ Ⓔ	24. ● Ⓑ Ⓒ Ⓓ Ⓔ	46. Ⓐ Ⓑ Ⓒ Ⓓ Ⓔ	68. Ⓐ Ⓑ Ⓒ Ⓓ Ⓔ
3. Ⓐ ● Ⓒ Ⓓ Ⓔ	25. Ⓐ Ⓑ Ⓒ Ⓓ Ⓔ	47. ● Ⓑ Ⓒ Ⓓ Ⓔ	69. Ⓐ ● Ⓒ Ⓓ Ⓔ
4. Ⓐ Ⓑ Ⓒ Ⓓ Ⓔ	26. Ⓐ Ⓑ Ⓒ Ⓓ Ⓔ	48. Ⓐ Ⓑ Ⓒ Ⓓ Ⓔ	70. Ⓐ Ⓑ Ⓒ Ⓓ Ⓔ
5. Ⓐ Ⓑ Ⓒ Ⓓ Ⓔ	27. Ⓐ ● Ⓒ Ⓓ Ⓔ	49. Ⓐ Ⓑ Ⓒ Ⓓ Ⓔ	71. Ⓐ Ⓑ Ⓒ Ⓓ ●
6. Ⓐ Ⓑ Ⓒ Ⓓ Ⓔ	28. Ⓐ Ⓑ Ⓒ Ⓓ Ⓔ	50. Ⓐ Ⓑ Ⓒ Ⓓ Ⓔ	72. Ⓐ Ⓑ Ⓒ Ⓓ Ⓔ
7. Ⓐ Ⓑ Ⓒ Ⓓ Ⓔ	29. Ⓐ Ⓑ Ⓒ Ⓓ Ⓔ	51. Ⓐ Ⓑ Ⓒ Ⓓ Ⓔ	73. Ⓐ Ⓑ Ⓒ Ⓓ Ⓔ
8. Ⓐ Ⓑ Ⓒ Ⓓ Ⓔ	30. Ⓐ Ⓑ Ⓒ Ⓓ Ⓔ	52. Ⓐ Ⓑ Ⓒ Ⓓ Ⓔ	74. Ⓐ Ⓑ Ⓒ Ⓓ Ⓔ
9. Ⓐ ● Ⓒ Ⓓ Ⓔ	31. Ⓐ Ⓑ Ⓒ Ⓓ Ⓔ	53. Ⓐ ● Ⓒ Ⓓ Ⓔ	75. Ⓐ Ⓑ Ⓒ Ⓓ Ⓔ
10. Ⓐ Ⓑ Ⓒ Ⓓ Ⓔ	32. Ⓐ Ⓑ Ⓒ ● Ⓔ	54. Ⓐ Ⓑ Ⓒ Ⓓ Ⓔ	76. Ⓐ Ⓑ Ⓒ ● Ⓔ
11. ● Ⓑ Ⓒ Ⓓ Ⓔ	33. Ⓐ Ⓑ Ⓒ Ⓓ Ⓔ	55. Ⓐ Ⓑ Ⓒ Ⓓ Ⓔ	77. Ⓐ Ⓑ Ⓒ Ⓓ ●
12. Ⓐ ● Ⓒ Ⓓ Ⓔ	34. Ⓐ Ⓑ Ⓒ Ⓓ Ⓔ	56. Ⓐ Ⓑ ● Ⓓ Ⓔ	78. Ⓐ Ⓑ Ⓒ Ⓓ Ⓔ
13. Ⓐ Ⓑ Ⓒ Ⓓ Ⓔ	35. ● Ⓑ Ⓒ Ⓓ Ⓔ	57. Ⓐ Ⓑ Ⓒ Ⓓ Ⓔ	79. Ⓐ Ⓑ Ⓒ Ⓓ Ⓔ
14. Ⓐ Ⓑ Ⓒ Ⓓ Ⓔ	36. Ⓐ Ⓑ Ⓒ Ⓓ Ⓔ	58. Ⓐ Ⓑ Ⓒ Ⓓ Ⓔ	80. Ⓐ Ⓑ Ⓒ Ⓓ Ⓔ
15. Ⓐ Ⓑ Ⓒ Ⓓ Ⓔ	37. Ⓐ Ⓑ ● Ⓓ Ⓔ	59. Ⓐ Ⓑ ● Ⓓ Ⓔ	81. Ⓐ Ⓑ Ⓒ Ⓓ ●
16. Ⓐ Ⓑ Ⓒ ● Ⓔ	38. Ⓐ Ⓑ Ⓒ Ⓓ ●	60. Ⓐ Ⓑ Ⓒ Ⓓ Ⓔ	82. Ⓐ Ⓑ Ⓒ ● Ⓔ
17. Ⓐ Ⓑ ● Ⓓ Ⓔ	39. Ⓐ Ⓑ Ⓒ Ⓓ Ⓔ	61. Ⓐ Ⓑ Ⓒ Ⓓ ●	83. Ⓐ Ⓑ Ⓒ Ⓓ Ⓔ
18. Ⓐ Ⓑ Ⓒ Ⓓ Ⓔ	40. Ⓐ Ⓑ Ⓒ Ⓓ Ⓔ	62. Ⓐ Ⓑ Ⓒ Ⓓ Ⓔ	84. Ⓐ Ⓑ Ⓒ Ⓓ Ⓔ
19. ● Ⓑ Ⓒ Ⓓ Ⓔ	41. Ⓐ Ⓑ Ⓒ Ⓓ Ⓔ	63. Ⓐ Ⓑ Ⓒ Ⓓ Ⓔ	85. Ⓐ Ⓑ Ⓒ Ⓓ Ⓔ
20. Ⓐ Ⓑ Ⓒ Ⓓ ●	42. Ⓐ Ⓑ Ⓒ ● Ⓔ	64. ● Ⓑ Ⓒ Ⓓ Ⓔ	86. Ⓐ Ⓑ Ⓒ Ⓓ Ⓔ
21. ● Ⓑ Ⓒ Ⓓ Ⓔ	43. Ⓐ Ⓑ Ⓒ Ⓓ Ⓔ	65. Ⓐ Ⓑ Ⓒ Ⓓ Ⓔ	87. Ⓐ Ⓑ Ⓒ Ⓓ ●
22. Ⓐ Ⓑ Ⓒ Ⓓ Ⓔ	44. Ⓐ Ⓑ ● Ⓓ Ⓔ	66. Ⓐ Ⓑ Ⓒ Ⓓ Ⓔ	88. Ⓐ Ⓑ Ⓒ Ⓓ Ⓔ

24

Correctly Completed Worksheet

1.   16   88   <u>3</u>   51   46   <u>71</u>   24

2.   C   A   Ⓔ   D   B

3.
| ___ B | ___ D | <u>17</u> C | <u>24</u> A | ___ E |

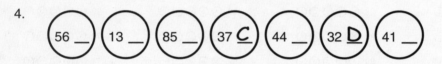

4.
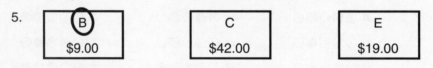

(56 __) (13 __) (85 __) (37 <u>C</u>) (44 __) (32 <u>D</u>) (41 __)

5.
| Ⓑ | C | E |
| $9.00 | $42.00 | $19.00 |

6.   87 <u>E</u>   27 <u>B</u>   64 <u>A</u>   PLANE   TRAIN   BUS

7.   46   35   39   43   [42]   38

8.   G   D   P   F   E   <u>C</u>   L   J

9.   △ 2   ☆ E 20   Ⓐ 11   ☐ 5

10.   74   21   **B**   57   42   51
                          53

11.

    [18 __]   [47 **A**]   [56 **C**]   [31 __]

12.   64   **82**   90   75   **81**   **76**

13.

    [27 __]   (19 **A**)   (32 __)   [12 **B**]

14.   24B   36A   44C   20E   26D   **44**

15.   89 _____   61 __**E**__

16.   T   T   V   W   V   T   V   T   W   V   V   **5**

17.

    5:36 _____
    5:21 __**A**__
    5:43 _____
    5:59 __**C**__
    5:38 _____

18.

    (**38** E)   (__ D)   (__ A)   (**69** B)   (__ C)

19.

    (__ C)   [**35** A]   [__ B]   (__ E)

Determine Your Raw Score

Following Oral Instructions: Your raw score is based on the number of questions that you answered correctly:

Raw score = _____

Evaluate Yourself

Determine where your raw score falls on the following scale. If you scored less than Excellent, review Hour 11, "Following Oral Instructions—1," and Hour 12, "Following Oral Instructions—2." If you have time, retake the test to see if you improved your score.

IF your raw score is between	THEN your work is
27-31	Excellent
23-26	Good
19-22	Average
14-18	Fair
1-13	Poor

The Hour in Review

1. In this hour, you took a final, timed "Following Oral Instructions" practice test.

2. You should use this test to improve your performance on the weak areas that you discovered when taking the previous two timed tests.

3. You can retake any of the timed tests as many times as you want for additional practice.

BONUS HOUR

Full-Length Practice Test

What You Will Learn in This Hour

In this special Bonus Hour, you'll take a full-length practice test to prepare
you for the actual Test 470 battery. Answer keys, a scoring sheet, and a self-
evaluation chart are provided after the test so you can assess your performance
on the full-length test. Treat this test as an actual exam; use it to gauge your
strengths and weaknesses and to determine where you need further review
before taking the actual test. Here are your goals for this hour:

- Prepare for the full-length practice test.

- Complete the full-length test in one sitting.

- Check your answers and determine your raw score on the entire test.

- Evaluate your performance on each part of the test and determine where
  you need further study.

Preparing for the Practice Test

To get the most benefit from this practice test, follow these steps when taking the test:

1. Schedule the practice test for a convenient time. Allow yourself 90 minutes to complete the test.

2. Arrange for a friend or family member to read the oral instructions for Part D. If you can't find a reader, tape the instructions in advance.

3. Choose a workspace that is quiet, well-lit, clean, and uncluttered.

4. Have the right equipment at hand: a stopwatch or kitchen timer and several sharp number-two pencils with good erasers.

5. Tear out the answer sheets and place them beside your book.

6. Proceed through the entire test in the order indicated. Do not allow interruptions once you've started the test.

7. Time yourself accurately for all test parts, including the sample questions.

8. For all test parts, stop as soon as time is up.

9. After finishing the entire test, check your answers against the keys at the end of the hour. Circle all incorrect answers so that you can easily locate them when you analyze your errors.

10. Calculate your raw score for each part of the test as instructed.

11. Determine where your scores fall on the self-evaluation chart.

12. If you receive less than an Excellent score on any test section, review the appropriate study hours and retake as many practice exercises as you have time to complete.

Practice Test

Answer Sheet

Part A: Address Checking

1. Ⓐ Ⓑ	20. Ⓐ Ⓑ	39. Ⓐ Ⓑ	58. Ⓐ Ⓑ	77. Ⓐ Ⓑ
2. Ⓐ Ⓑ	21. Ⓐ Ⓑ	40. Ⓐ Ⓑ	59. Ⓐ Ⓑ	78. Ⓐ Ⓑ
3. Ⓐ Ⓑ	22. Ⓐ Ⓑ	41. Ⓐ Ⓑ	60. Ⓐ Ⓑ	79. Ⓐ Ⓑ
4. Ⓐ Ⓑ	23. Ⓐ Ⓑ	42. Ⓐ Ⓑ	61. Ⓐ Ⓑ	80. Ⓐ Ⓑ
5. Ⓐ Ⓑ	24. Ⓐ Ⓑ	43. Ⓐ Ⓑ	62. Ⓐ Ⓑ	81. Ⓐ Ⓑ
6. Ⓐ Ⓑ	25. Ⓐ Ⓑ	44. Ⓐ Ⓑ	63. Ⓐ Ⓑ	82. Ⓐ Ⓑ
7. Ⓐ Ⓑ	26. Ⓐ Ⓑ	45. Ⓐ Ⓑ	64. Ⓐ Ⓑ	83. Ⓐ Ⓑ
8. Ⓐ Ⓑ	27. Ⓐ Ⓑ	46. Ⓐ Ⓑ	65. Ⓐ Ⓑ	84. Ⓐ Ⓑ
9. Ⓐ Ⓑ	28. Ⓐ Ⓑ	47. Ⓐ Ⓑ	66. Ⓐ Ⓑ	85. Ⓐ Ⓑ
10. Ⓐ Ⓑ	29. Ⓐ Ⓑ	48. Ⓐ Ⓑ	67. Ⓐ Ⓑ	86. Ⓐ Ⓑ
11. Ⓐ Ⓑ	30. Ⓐ Ⓑ	49. Ⓐ Ⓑ	68. Ⓐ Ⓑ	87. Ⓐ Ⓑ
12. Ⓐ Ⓑ	31. Ⓐ Ⓑ	50. Ⓐ Ⓑ	69. Ⓐ Ⓑ	88. Ⓐ Ⓑ
13. Ⓐ Ⓑ	32. Ⓐ Ⓑ	51. Ⓐ Ⓑ	70. Ⓐ Ⓑ	89. Ⓐ Ⓑ
14. Ⓐ Ⓑ	33. Ⓐ Ⓑ	52. Ⓐ Ⓑ	71. Ⓐ Ⓑ	90. Ⓐ Ⓑ
15. Ⓐ Ⓑ	34. Ⓐ Ⓑ	53. Ⓐ Ⓑ	72. Ⓐ Ⓑ	91. Ⓐ Ⓑ
16. Ⓐ Ⓑ	35. Ⓐ Ⓑ	54. Ⓐ Ⓑ	73. Ⓐ Ⓑ	92. Ⓐ Ⓑ
17. Ⓐ Ⓑ	36. Ⓐ Ⓑ	55. Ⓐ Ⓑ	74. Ⓐ Ⓑ	93. Ⓐ Ⓑ
18. Ⓐ Ⓑ	37. Ⓐ Ⓑ	56. Ⓐ Ⓑ	75. Ⓐ Ⓑ	94. Ⓐ Ⓑ
19. Ⓐ Ⓑ	38. Ⓐ Ⓑ	57. Ⓐ Ⓑ	76. Ⓐ Ⓑ	95. Ⓐ Ⓑ

25

Part B: Memory for Addresses—Practice Set 1

1. Ⓐ Ⓑ Ⓒ Ⓓ Ⓔ
2. Ⓐ Ⓑ Ⓒ Ⓓ Ⓔ
3. Ⓐ Ⓑ Ⓒ Ⓓ Ⓔ
4. Ⓐ Ⓑ Ⓒ Ⓓ Ⓔ
5. Ⓐ Ⓑ Ⓒ Ⓓ Ⓔ
6. Ⓐ Ⓑ Ⓒ Ⓓ Ⓔ
7. Ⓐ Ⓑ Ⓒ Ⓓ Ⓔ
8. Ⓐ Ⓑ Ⓒ Ⓓ Ⓔ
9. Ⓐ Ⓑ Ⓒ Ⓓ Ⓔ
10. Ⓐ Ⓑ Ⓒ Ⓓ Ⓔ
11. Ⓐ Ⓑ Ⓒ Ⓓ Ⓔ
12. Ⓐ Ⓑ Ⓒ Ⓓ Ⓔ
13. Ⓐ Ⓑ Ⓒ Ⓓ Ⓔ
14. Ⓐ Ⓑ Ⓒ Ⓓ Ⓔ
15. Ⓐ Ⓑ Ⓒ Ⓓ Ⓔ
16. Ⓐ Ⓑ Ⓒ Ⓓ Ⓔ
17. Ⓐ Ⓑ Ⓒ Ⓓ Ⓔ
18. Ⓐ Ⓑ Ⓒ Ⓓ Ⓔ
19. Ⓐ Ⓑ Ⓒ Ⓓ Ⓔ
20. Ⓐ Ⓑ Ⓒ Ⓓ Ⓔ
21. Ⓐ Ⓑ Ⓒ Ⓓ Ⓔ
22. Ⓐ Ⓑ Ⓒ Ⓓ Ⓔ

23. Ⓐ Ⓑ Ⓒ Ⓓ Ⓔ
24. Ⓐ Ⓑ Ⓒ Ⓓ Ⓔ
25. Ⓐ Ⓑ Ⓒ Ⓓ Ⓔ
26. Ⓐ Ⓑ Ⓒ Ⓓ Ⓔ
27. Ⓐ Ⓑ Ⓒ Ⓓ Ⓔ
28. Ⓐ Ⓑ Ⓒ Ⓓ Ⓔ
29. Ⓐ Ⓑ Ⓒ Ⓓ Ⓔ
30. Ⓐ Ⓑ Ⓒ Ⓓ Ⓔ
31. Ⓐ Ⓑ Ⓒ Ⓓ Ⓔ
32. Ⓐ Ⓑ Ⓒ Ⓓ Ⓔ
33. Ⓐ Ⓑ Ⓒ Ⓓ Ⓔ
34. Ⓐ Ⓑ Ⓒ Ⓓ Ⓔ
35. Ⓐ Ⓑ Ⓒ Ⓓ Ⓔ
36. Ⓐ Ⓑ Ⓒ Ⓓ Ⓔ
37. Ⓐ Ⓑ Ⓒ Ⓓ Ⓔ
38. Ⓐ Ⓑ Ⓒ Ⓓ Ⓔ
39. Ⓐ Ⓑ Ⓒ Ⓓ Ⓔ
40. Ⓐ Ⓑ Ⓒ Ⓓ Ⓔ
41. Ⓐ Ⓑ Ⓒ Ⓓ Ⓔ
42. Ⓐ Ⓑ Ⓒ Ⓓ Ⓔ
43. Ⓐ Ⓑ Ⓒ Ⓓ Ⓔ
44. Ⓐ Ⓑ Ⓒ Ⓓ Ⓔ

45. Ⓐ Ⓑ Ⓒ Ⓓ Ⓔ
46. Ⓐ Ⓑ Ⓒ Ⓓ Ⓔ
47. Ⓐ Ⓑ Ⓒ Ⓓ Ⓔ
48. Ⓐ Ⓑ Ⓒ Ⓓ Ⓔ
49. Ⓐ Ⓑ Ⓒ Ⓓ Ⓔ
50. Ⓐ Ⓑ Ⓒ Ⓓ Ⓔ
51. Ⓐ Ⓑ Ⓒ Ⓓ Ⓔ
52. Ⓐ Ⓑ Ⓒ Ⓓ Ⓔ
53. Ⓐ Ⓑ Ⓒ Ⓓ Ⓔ
54. Ⓐ Ⓑ Ⓒ Ⓓ Ⓔ
55. Ⓐ Ⓑ Ⓒ Ⓓ Ⓔ
56. Ⓐ Ⓑ Ⓒ Ⓓ Ⓔ
57. Ⓐ Ⓑ Ⓒ Ⓓ Ⓔ
58. Ⓐ Ⓑ Ⓒ Ⓓ Ⓔ
59. Ⓐ Ⓑ Ⓒ Ⓓ Ⓔ
60. Ⓐ Ⓑ Ⓒ Ⓓ Ⓔ
61. Ⓐ Ⓑ Ⓒ Ⓓ Ⓔ
62. Ⓐ Ⓑ Ⓒ Ⓓ Ⓔ
63. Ⓐ Ⓑ Ⓒ Ⓓ Ⓔ
64. Ⓐ Ⓑ Ⓒ Ⓓ Ⓔ
65. Ⓐ Ⓑ Ⓒ Ⓓ Ⓔ
66. Ⓐ Ⓑ Ⓒ Ⓓ Ⓔ

67. Ⓐ Ⓑ Ⓒ Ⓓ Ⓔ
68. Ⓐ Ⓑ Ⓒ Ⓓ Ⓔ
69. Ⓐ Ⓑ Ⓒ Ⓓ Ⓔ
70. Ⓐ Ⓑ Ⓒ Ⓓ Ⓔ
71. Ⓐ Ⓑ Ⓒ Ⓓ Ⓔ
72. Ⓐ Ⓑ Ⓒ Ⓓ Ⓔ
73. Ⓐ Ⓑ Ⓒ Ⓓ Ⓔ
74. Ⓐ Ⓑ Ⓒ Ⓓ Ⓔ
75. Ⓐ Ⓑ Ⓒ Ⓓ Ⓔ
76. Ⓐ Ⓑ Ⓒ Ⓓ Ⓔ
77. Ⓐ Ⓑ Ⓒ Ⓓ Ⓔ
78. Ⓐ Ⓑ Ⓒ Ⓓ Ⓔ
79. Ⓐ Ⓑ Ⓒ Ⓓ Ⓔ
80. Ⓐ Ⓑ Ⓒ Ⓓ Ⓔ
81. Ⓐ Ⓑ Ⓒ Ⓓ Ⓔ
82. Ⓐ Ⓑ Ⓒ Ⓓ Ⓔ
83. Ⓐ Ⓑ Ⓒ Ⓓ Ⓔ
84. Ⓐ Ⓑ Ⓒ Ⓓ Ⓔ
85. Ⓐ Ⓑ Ⓒ Ⓓ Ⓔ
86. Ⓐ Ⓑ Ⓒ Ⓓ Ⓔ
87. Ⓐ Ⓑ Ⓒ Ⓓ Ⓔ
88. Ⓐ Ⓑ Ⓒ Ⓓ Ⓔ

Part B: Memory for Addresses—Practice Set 2

1. Ⓐ Ⓑ Ⓒ Ⓓ Ⓔ   23. Ⓐ Ⓑ Ⓒ Ⓓ Ⓔ   45. Ⓐ Ⓑ Ⓒ Ⓓ Ⓔ   67. Ⓐ Ⓑ Ⓒ Ⓓ Ⓔ

2. Ⓐ Ⓑ Ⓒ Ⓓ Ⓔ   24. Ⓐ Ⓑ Ⓒ Ⓓ Ⓔ   46. Ⓐ Ⓑ Ⓒ Ⓓ Ⓔ   68. Ⓐ Ⓑ Ⓒ Ⓓ Ⓔ

3. Ⓐ Ⓑ Ⓒ Ⓓ Ⓔ   25. Ⓐ Ⓑ Ⓒ Ⓓ Ⓔ   47. Ⓐ Ⓑ Ⓒ Ⓓ Ⓔ   69. Ⓐ Ⓑ Ⓒ Ⓓ Ⓔ

4. Ⓐ Ⓑ Ⓒ Ⓓ Ⓔ   26. Ⓐ Ⓑ Ⓒ Ⓓ Ⓔ   48. Ⓐ Ⓑ Ⓒ Ⓓ Ⓔ   70. Ⓐ Ⓑ Ⓒ Ⓓ Ⓔ

5. Ⓐ Ⓑ Ⓒ Ⓓ Ⓔ   27. Ⓐ Ⓑ Ⓒ Ⓓ Ⓔ   49. Ⓐ Ⓑ Ⓒ Ⓓ Ⓔ   71. Ⓐ Ⓑ Ⓒ Ⓓ Ⓔ

6. Ⓐ Ⓑ Ⓒ Ⓓ Ⓔ   28. Ⓐ Ⓑ Ⓒ Ⓓ Ⓔ   50. Ⓐ Ⓑ Ⓒ Ⓓ Ⓔ   72. Ⓐ Ⓑ Ⓒ Ⓓ Ⓔ

7. Ⓐ Ⓑ Ⓒ Ⓓ Ⓔ   29. Ⓐ Ⓑ Ⓒ Ⓓ Ⓔ   51. Ⓐ Ⓑ Ⓒ Ⓓ Ⓔ   73. Ⓐ Ⓑ Ⓒ Ⓓ Ⓔ

8. Ⓐ Ⓑ Ⓒ Ⓓ Ⓔ   30. Ⓐ Ⓑ Ⓒ Ⓓ Ⓔ   52. Ⓐ Ⓑ Ⓒ Ⓓ Ⓔ   74. Ⓐ Ⓑ Ⓒ Ⓓ Ⓔ

9. Ⓐ Ⓑ Ⓒ Ⓓ Ⓔ   31. Ⓐ Ⓑ Ⓒ Ⓓ Ⓔ   53. Ⓐ Ⓑ Ⓒ Ⓓ Ⓔ   75. Ⓐ Ⓑ Ⓒ Ⓓ Ⓔ

10. Ⓐ Ⓑ Ⓒ Ⓓ Ⓔ   32. Ⓐ Ⓑ Ⓒ Ⓓ Ⓔ   54. Ⓐ Ⓑ Ⓒ Ⓓ Ⓔ   76. Ⓐ Ⓑ Ⓒ Ⓓ Ⓔ

11. Ⓐ Ⓑ Ⓒ Ⓓ Ⓔ   33. Ⓐ Ⓑ Ⓒ Ⓓ Ⓔ   55. Ⓐ Ⓑ Ⓒ Ⓓ Ⓔ   77. Ⓐ Ⓑ Ⓒ Ⓓ Ⓔ

12. Ⓐ Ⓑ Ⓒ Ⓓ Ⓔ   34. Ⓐ Ⓑ Ⓒ Ⓓ Ⓔ   56. Ⓐ Ⓑ Ⓒ Ⓓ Ⓔ   78. Ⓐ Ⓑ Ⓒ Ⓓ Ⓔ

13. Ⓐ Ⓑ Ⓒ Ⓓ Ⓔ   35. Ⓐ Ⓑ Ⓒ Ⓓ Ⓔ   57. Ⓐ Ⓑ Ⓒ Ⓓ Ⓔ   79. Ⓐ Ⓑ Ⓒ Ⓓ Ⓔ

14. Ⓐ Ⓑ Ⓒ Ⓓ Ⓔ   36. Ⓐ Ⓑ Ⓒ Ⓓ Ⓔ   58. Ⓐ Ⓑ Ⓒ Ⓓ Ⓔ   80. Ⓐ Ⓑ Ⓒ Ⓓ Ⓔ

15. Ⓐ Ⓑ Ⓒ Ⓓ Ⓔ   37. Ⓐ Ⓑ Ⓒ Ⓓ Ⓔ   59. Ⓐ Ⓑ Ⓒ Ⓓ Ⓔ   81. Ⓐ Ⓑ Ⓒ Ⓓ Ⓔ

16. Ⓐ Ⓑ Ⓒ Ⓓ Ⓔ   38. Ⓐ Ⓑ Ⓒ Ⓓ Ⓔ   60. Ⓐ Ⓑ Ⓒ Ⓓ Ⓔ   82. Ⓐ Ⓑ Ⓒ Ⓓ Ⓔ

17. Ⓐ Ⓑ Ⓒ Ⓓ Ⓔ   39. Ⓐ Ⓑ Ⓒ Ⓓ Ⓔ   61. Ⓐ Ⓑ Ⓒ Ⓓ Ⓔ   83. Ⓐ Ⓑ Ⓒ Ⓓ Ⓔ

18. Ⓐ Ⓑ Ⓒ Ⓓ Ⓔ   40. Ⓐ Ⓑ Ⓒ Ⓓ Ⓔ   62. Ⓐ Ⓑ Ⓒ Ⓓ Ⓔ   84. Ⓐ Ⓑ Ⓒ Ⓓ Ⓔ

19. Ⓐ Ⓑ Ⓒ Ⓓ Ⓔ   41. Ⓐ Ⓑ Ⓒ Ⓓ Ⓔ   63. Ⓐ Ⓑ Ⓒ Ⓓ Ⓔ   85. Ⓐ Ⓑ Ⓒ Ⓓ Ⓔ

20. Ⓐ Ⓑ Ⓒ Ⓓ Ⓔ   42. Ⓐ Ⓑ Ⓒ Ⓓ Ⓔ   64. Ⓐ Ⓑ Ⓒ Ⓓ Ⓔ   86. Ⓐ Ⓑ Ⓒ Ⓓ Ⓔ

21. Ⓐ Ⓑ Ⓒ Ⓓ Ⓔ   43. Ⓐ Ⓑ Ⓒ Ⓓ Ⓔ   65. Ⓐ Ⓑ Ⓒ Ⓓ Ⓔ   87. Ⓐ Ⓑ Ⓒ Ⓓ Ⓔ

22. Ⓐ Ⓑ Ⓒ Ⓓ Ⓔ   44. Ⓐ Ⓑ Ⓒ Ⓓ Ⓔ   66. Ⓐ Ⓑ Ⓒ Ⓓ Ⓔ   88. Ⓐ Ⓑ Ⓒ Ⓓ Ⓔ

25

Part B: Memory for Address—Practice Set 3

1. Ⓐ Ⓑ Ⓒ Ⓓ Ⓔ
2. Ⓐ Ⓑ Ⓒ Ⓓ Ⓔ
3. Ⓐ Ⓑ Ⓒ Ⓓ Ⓔ
4. Ⓐ Ⓑ Ⓒ Ⓓ Ⓔ
5. Ⓐ Ⓑ Ⓒ Ⓓ Ⓔ
6. Ⓐ Ⓑ Ⓒ Ⓓ Ⓔ
7. Ⓐ Ⓑ Ⓒ Ⓓ Ⓔ
8. Ⓐ Ⓑ Ⓒ Ⓓ Ⓔ
9. Ⓐ Ⓑ Ⓒ Ⓓ Ⓔ
10. Ⓐ Ⓑ Ⓒ Ⓓ Ⓔ
11. Ⓐ Ⓑ Ⓒ Ⓓ Ⓔ
12. Ⓐ Ⓑ Ⓒ Ⓓ Ⓔ
13. Ⓐ Ⓑ Ⓒ Ⓓ Ⓔ
14. Ⓐ Ⓑ Ⓒ Ⓓ Ⓔ
15. Ⓐ Ⓑ Ⓒ Ⓓ Ⓔ
16. Ⓐ Ⓑ Ⓒ Ⓓ Ⓔ
17. Ⓐ Ⓑ Ⓒ Ⓓ Ⓔ
18. Ⓐ Ⓑ Ⓒ Ⓓ Ⓔ
19. Ⓐ Ⓑ Ⓒ Ⓓ Ⓔ
20. Ⓐ Ⓑ Ⓒ Ⓓ Ⓔ
21. Ⓐ Ⓑ Ⓒ Ⓓ Ⓔ
22. Ⓐ Ⓑ Ⓒ Ⓓ Ⓔ

23. Ⓐ Ⓑ Ⓒ Ⓓ Ⓔ
24. Ⓐ Ⓑ Ⓒ Ⓓ Ⓔ
25. Ⓐ Ⓑ Ⓒ Ⓓ Ⓔ
26. Ⓐ Ⓑ Ⓒ Ⓓ Ⓔ
27. Ⓐ Ⓑ Ⓒ Ⓓ Ⓔ
28. Ⓐ Ⓑ Ⓒ Ⓓ Ⓔ
29. Ⓐ Ⓑ Ⓒ Ⓓ Ⓔ
30. Ⓐ Ⓑ Ⓒ Ⓓ Ⓔ
31. Ⓐ Ⓑ Ⓒ Ⓓ Ⓔ
32. Ⓐ Ⓑ Ⓒ Ⓓ Ⓔ
33. Ⓐ Ⓑ Ⓒ Ⓓ Ⓔ
34. Ⓐ Ⓑ Ⓒ Ⓓ Ⓔ
35. Ⓐ Ⓑ Ⓒ Ⓓ Ⓔ
36. Ⓐ Ⓑ Ⓒ Ⓓ Ⓔ
37. Ⓐ Ⓑ Ⓒ Ⓓ Ⓔ
38. Ⓐ Ⓑ Ⓒ Ⓓ Ⓔ
39. Ⓐ Ⓑ Ⓒ Ⓓ Ⓔ
40. Ⓐ Ⓑ Ⓒ Ⓓ Ⓔ
41. Ⓐ Ⓑ Ⓒ Ⓓ Ⓔ
42. Ⓐ Ⓑ Ⓒ Ⓓ Ⓔ
43. Ⓐ Ⓑ Ⓒ Ⓓ Ⓔ
44. Ⓐ Ⓑ Ⓒ Ⓓ Ⓔ

45. Ⓐ Ⓑ Ⓒ Ⓓ Ⓔ
46. Ⓐ Ⓑ Ⓒ Ⓓ Ⓔ
47. Ⓐ Ⓑ Ⓒ Ⓓ Ⓔ
48. Ⓐ Ⓑ Ⓒ Ⓓ Ⓔ
49. Ⓐ Ⓑ Ⓒ Ⓓ Ⓔ
50. Ⓐ Ⓑ Ⓒ Ⓓ Ⓔ
51. Ⓐ Ⓑ Ⓒ Ⓓ Ⓔ
52. Ⓐ Ⓑ Ⓒ Ⓓ Ⓔ
53. Ⓐ Ⓑ Ⓒ Ⓓ Ⓔ
54. Ⓐ Ⓑ Ⓒ Ⓓ Ⓔ
55. Ⓐ Ⓑ Ⓒ Ⓓ Ⓔ
56. Ⓐ Ⓑ Ⓒ Ⓓ Ⓔ
57. Ⓐ Ⓑ Ⓒ Ⓓ Ⓔ
58. Ⓐ Ⓑ Ⓒ Ⓓ Ⓔ
59. Ⓐ Ⓑ Ⓒ Ⓓ Ⓔ
60. Ⓐ Ⓑ Ⓒ Ⓓ Ⓔ
61. Ⓐ Ⓑ Ⓒ Ⓓ Ⓔ
62. Ⓐ Ⓑ Ⓒ Ⓓ Ⓔ
63. Ⓐ Ⓑ Ⓒ Ⓓ Ⓔ
64. Ⓐ Ⓑ Ⓒ Ⓓ Ⓔ
65. Ⓐ Ⓑ Ⓒ Ⓓ Ⓔ
66. Ⓐ Ⓑ Ⓒ Ⓓ Ⓔ

67. Ⓐ Ⓑ Ⓒ Ⓓ Ⓔ
68. Ⓐ Ⓑ Ⓒ Ⓓ Ⓔ
69. Ⓐ Ⓑ Ⓒ Ⓓ Ⓔ
70. Ⓐ Ⓑ Ⓒ Ⓓ Ⓔ
71. Ⓐ Ⓑ Ⓒ Ⓓ Ⓔ
72. Ⓐ Ⓑ Ⓒ Ⓓ Ⓔ
73. Ⓐ Ⓑ Ⓒ Ⓓ Ⓔ
74. Ⓐ Ⓑ Ⓒ Ⓓ Ⓔ
75. Ⓐ Ⓑ Ⓒ Ⓓ Ⓔ
76. Ⓐ Ⓑ Ⓒ Ⓓ Ⓔ
77. Ⓐ Ⓑ Ⓒ Ⓓ Ⓔ
78. Ⓐ Ⓑ Ⓒ Ⓓ Ⓔ
79. Ⓐ Ⓑ Ⓒ Ⓓ Ⓔ
80. Ⓐ Ⓑ Ⓒ Ⓓ Ⓔ
81. Ⓐ Ⓑ Ⓒ Ⓓ Ⓔ
82. Ⓐ Ⓑ Ⓒ Ⓓ Ⓔ
83. Ⓐ Ⓑ Ⓒ Ⓓ Ⓔ
84. Ⓐ Ⓑ Ⓒ Ⓓ Ⓔ
85. Ⓐ Ⓑ Ⓒ Ⓓ Ⓔ
86. Ⓐ Ⓑ Ⓒ Ⓓ Ⓔ
87. Ⓐ Ⓑ Ⓒ Ⓓ Ⓔ
88. Ⓐ Ⓑ Ⓒ Ⓓ Ⓔ

Part B: Memory for Addresses

1. Ⓐ Ⓑ Ⓒ Ⓓ Ⓔ   23. Ⓐ Ⓑ Ⓒ Ⓓ Ⓔ   45. Ⓐ Ⓑ Ⓒ Ⓓ Ⓔ   67. Ⓐ Ⓑ Ⓒ Ⓓ Ⓔ

2. Ⓐ Ⓑ Ⓒ Ⓓ Ⓔ   24. Ⓐ Ⓑ Ⓒ Ⓓ Ⓔ   46. Ⓐ Ⓑ Ⓒ Ⓓ Ⓔ   68. Ⓐ Ⓑ Ⓒ Ⓓ Ⓔ

3. Ⓐ Ⓑ Ⓒ Ⓓ Ⓔ   25. Ⓐ Ⓑ Ⓒ Ⓓ Ⓔ   47. Ⓐ Ⓑ Ⓒ Ⓓ Ⓔ   69. Ⓐ Ⓑ Ⓒ Ⓓ Ⓔ

4. Ⓐ Ⓑ Ⓒ Ⓓ Ⓔ   26. Ⓐ Ⓑ Ⓒ Ⓓ Ⓔ   48. Ⓐ Ⓑ Ⓒ Ⓓ Ⓔ   70. Ⓐ Ⓑ Ⓒ Ⓓ Ⓔ

5. Ⓐ Ⓑ Ⓒ Ⓓ Ⓔ   27. Ⓐ Ⓑ Ⓒ Ⓓ Ⓔ   49. Ⓐ Ⓑ Ⓒ Ⓓ Ⓔ   71. Ⓐ Ⓑ Ⓒ Ⓓ Ⓔ

6. Ⓐ Ⓑ Ⓒ Ⓓ Ⓔ   28. Ⓐ Ⓑ Ⓒ Ⓓ Ⓔ   50. Ⓐ Ⓑ Ⓒ Ⓓ Ⓔ   72. Ⓐ Ⓑ Ⓒ Ⓓ Ⓔ

7. Ⓐ Ⓑ Ⓒ Ⓓ Ⓔ   29. Ⓐ Ⓑ Ⓒ Ⓓ Ⓔ   51. Ⓐ Ⓑ Ⓒ Ⓓ Ⓔ   73. Ⓐ Ⓑ Ⓒ Ⓓ Ⓔ

8. Ⓐ Ⓑ Ⓒ Ⓓ Ⓔ   30. Ⓐ Ⓑ Ⓒ Ⓓ Ⓔ   52. Ⓐ Ⓑ Ⓒ Ⓓ Ⓔ   74. Ⓐ Ⓑ Ⓒ Ⓓ Ⓔ

9. Ⓐ Ⓑ Ⓒ Ⓓ Ⓔ   31. Ⓐ Ⓑ Ⓒ Ⓓ Ⓔ   53. Ⓐ Ⓑ Ⓒ Ⓓ Ⓔ   75. Ⓐ Ⓑ Ⓒ Ⓓ Ⓔ

10. Ⓐ Ⓑ Ⓒ Ⓓ Ⓔ   32. Ⓐ Ⓑ Ⓒ Ⓓ Ⓔ   54. Ⓐ Ⓑ Ⓒ Ⓓ Ⓔ   76. Ⓐ Ⓑ Ⓒ Ⓓ Ⓔ

11. Ⓐ Ⓑ Ⓒ Ⓓ Ⓔ   33. Ⓐ Ⓑ Ⓒ Ⓓ Ⓔ   55. Ⓐ Ⓑ Ⓒ Ⓓ Ⓔ   77. Ⓐ Ⓑ Ⓒ Ⓓ Ⓔ

12. Ⓐ Ⓑ Ⓒ Ⓓ Ⓔ   34. Ⓐ Ⓑ Ⓒ Ⓓ Ⓔ   56. Ⓐ Ⓑ Ⓒ Ⓓ Ⓔ   78. Ⓐ Ⓑ Ⓒ Ⓓ Ⓔ

13. Ⓐ Ⓑ Ⓒ Ⓓ Ⓔ   35. Ⓐ Ⓑ Ⓒ Ⓓ Ⓔ   57. Ⓐ Ⓑ Ⓒ Ⓓ Ⓔ   79. Ⓐ Ⓑ Ⓒ Ⓓ Ⓔ

14. Ⓐ Ⓑ Ⓒ Ⓓ Ⓔ   36. Ⓐ Ⓑ Ⓒ Ⓓ Ⓔ   58. Ⓐ Ⓑ Ⓒ Ⓓ Ⓔ   80. Ⓐ Ⓑ Ⓒ Ⓓ Ⓔ

15. Ⓐ Ⓑ Ⓒ Ⓓ Ⓔ   37. Ⓐ Ⓑ Ⓒ Ⓓ Ⓔ   59. Ⓐ Ⓑ Ⓒ Ⓓ Ⓔ   81. Ⓐ Ⓑ Ⓒ Ⓓ Ⓔ

16. Ⓐ Ⓑ Ⓒ Ⓓ Ⓔ   38. Ⓐ Ⓑ Ⓒ Ⓓ Ⓔ   60. Ⓐ Ⓑ Ⓒ Ⓓ Ⓔ   82. Ⓐ Ⓑ Ⓒ Ⓓ Ⓔ

17. Ⓐ Ⓑ Ⓒ Ⓓ Ⓔ   39. Ⓐ Ⓑ Ⓒ Ⓓ Ⓔ   61. Ⓐ Ⓑ Ⓒ Ⓓ Ⓔ   83. Ⓐ Ⓑ Ⓒ Ⓓ Ⓔ

18. Ⓐ Ⓑ Ⓒ Ⓓ Ⓔ   40. Ⓐ Ⓑ Ⓒ Ⓓ Ⓔ   62. Ⓐ Ⓑ Ⓒ Ⓓ Ⓔ   84. Ⓐ Ⓑ Ⓒ Ⓓ Ⓔ

19. Ⓐ Ⓑ Ⓒ Ⓓ Ⓔ   41. Ⓐ Ⓑ Ⓒ Ⓓ Ⓔ   63. Ⓐ Ⓑ Ⓒ Ⓓ Ⓔ   85. Ⓐ Ⓑ Ⓒ Ⓓ Ⓔ

20. Ⓐ Ⓑ Ⓒ Ⓓ Ⓔ   42. Ⓐ Ⓑ Ⓒ Ⓓ Ⓔ   64. Ⓐ Ⓑ Ⓒ Ⓓ Ⓔ   86. Ⓐ Ⓑ Ⓒ Ⓓ Ⓔ

21. Ⓐ Ⓑ Ⓒ Ⓓ Ⓔ   43. Ⓐ Ⓑ Ⓒ Ⓓ Ⓔ   65. Ⓐ Ⓑ Ⓒ Ⓓ Ⓔ   87. Ⓐ Ⓑ Ⓒ Ⓓ Ⓔ

22. Ⓐ Ⓑ Ⓒ Ⓓ Ⓔ   44. Ⓐ Ⓑ Ⓒ Ⓓ Ⓔ   66. Ⓐ Ⓑ Ⓒ Ⓓ Ⓔ   88. Ⓐ Ⓑ Ⓒ Ⓓ Ⓔ

25

Part C: Number Series

1. Ⓐ Ⓑ Ⓒ Ⓓ Ⓔ
2. Ⓐ Ⓑ Ⓒ Ⓓ Ⓔ
3. Ⓐ Ⓑ Ⓒ Ⓓ Ⓔ
4. Ⓐ Ⓑ Ⓒ Ⓓ Ⓔ
5. Ⓐ Ⓑ Ⓒ Ⓓ Ⓔ
6. Ⓐ Ⓑ Ⓒ Ⓓ Ⓔ

7. Ⓐ Ⓑ Ⓒ Ⓓ Ⓔ
8. Ⓐ Ⓑ Ⓒ Ⓓ Ⓔ
9. Ⓐ Ⓑ Ⓒ Ⓓ Ⓔ
10. Ⓐ Ⓑ Ⓒ Ⓓ Ⓔ
11. Ⓐ Ⓑ Ⓒ Ⓓ Ⓔ
12. Ⓐ Ⓑ Ⓒ Ⓓ Ⓔ

13. Ⓐ Ⓑ Ⓒ Ⓓ Ⓔ
14. Ⓐ Ⓑ Ⓒ Ⓓ Ⓔ
15. Ⓐ Ⓑ Ⓒ Ⓓ Ⓔ
16. Ⓐ Ⓑ Ⓒ Ⓓ Ⓔ
17. Ⓐ Ⓑ Ⓒ Ⓓ Ⓔ
18. Ⓐ Ⓑ Ⓒ Ⓓ Ⓔ

19. Ⓐ Ⓑ Ⓒ Ⓓ Ⓔ
20. Ⓐ Ⓑ Ⓒ Ⓓ Ⓔ
21. Ⓐ Ⓑ Ⓒ Ⓓ Ⓔ
22. Ⓐ Ⓑ Ⓒ Ⓓ Ⓔ
23. Ⓐ Ⓑ Ⓒ Ⓓ Ⓔ
24. Ⓐ Ⓑ Ⓒ Ⓓ Ⓔ

Part D: Following Oral Instructions

1. Ⓐ Ⓑ Ⓒ Ⓓ Ⓔ   23. Ⓐ Ⓑ Ⓒ Ⓓ Ⓔ   45. Ⓐ Ⓑ Ⓒ Ⓓ Ⓔ   67. Ⓐ Ⓑ Ⓒ Ⓓ Ⓔ

2. Ⓐ Ⓑ Ⓒ Ⓓ Ⓔ   24. Ⓐ Ⓑ Ⓒ Ⓓ Ⓔ   46. Ⓐ Ⓑ Ⓒ Ⓓ Ⓔ   68. Ⓐ Ⓑ Ⓒ Ⓓ Ⓔ

3. Ⓐ Ⓑ Ⓒ Ⓓ Ⓔ   25. Ⓐ Ⓑ Ⓒ Ⓓ Ⓔ   47. Ⓐ Ⓑ Ⓒ Ⓓ Ⓔ   69. Ⓐ Ⓑ Ⓒ Ⓓ Ⓔ

4. Ⓐ Ⓑ Ⓒ Ⓓ Ⓔ   26. Ⓐ Ⓑ Ⓒ Ⓓ Ⓔ   48. Ⓐ Ⓑ Ⓒ Ⓓ Ⓔ   70. Ⓐ Ⓑ Ⓒ Ⓓ Ⓔ

5. Ⓐ Ⓑ Ⓒ Ⓓ Ⓔ   27. Ⓐ Ⓑ Ⓒ Ⓓ Ⓔ   49. Ⓐ Ⓑ Ⓒ Ⓓ Ⓔ   71. Ⓐ Ⓑ Ⓒ Ⓓ Ⓔ

6. Ⓐ Ⓑ Ⓒ Ⓓ Ⓔ   28. Ⓐ Ⓑ Ⓒ Ⓓ Ⓔ   50. Ⓐ Ⓑ Ⓒ Ⓓ Ⓔ   72. Ⓐ Ⓑ Ⓒ Ⓓ Ⓔ

7. Ⓐ Ⓑ Ⓒ Ⓓ Ⓔ   29. Ⓐ Ⓑ Ⓒ Ⓓ Ⓔ   51. Ⓐ Ⓑ Ⓒ Ⓓ Ⓔ   73. Ⓐ Ⓑ Ⓒ Ⓓ Ⓔ

8. Ⓐ Ⓑ Ⓒ Ⓓ Ⓔ   30. Ⓐ Ⓑ Ⓒ Ⓓ Ⓔ   52. Ⓐ Ⓑ Ⓒ Ⓓ Ⓔ   74. Ⓐ Ⓑ Ⓒ Ⓓ Ⓔ

9. Ⓐ Ⓑ Ⓒ Ⓓ Ⓔ   31. Ⓐ Ⓑ Ⓒ Ⓓ Ⓔ   53. Ⓐ Ⓑ Ⓒ Ⓓ Ⓔ   75. Ⓐ Ⓑ Ⓒ Ⓓ Ⓔ

10. Ⓐ Ⓑ Ⓒ Ⓓ Ⓔ   32. Ⓐ Ⓑ Ⓒ Ⓓ Ⓔ   54. Ⓐ Ⓑ Ⓒ Ⓓ Ⓔ   76. Ⓐ Ⓑ Ⓒ Ⓓ Ⓔ

11. Ⓐ Ⓑ Ⓒ Ⓓ Ⓔ   33. Ⓐ Ⓑ Ⓒ Ⓓ Ⓔ   55. Ⓐ Ⓑ Ⓒ Ⓓ Ⓔ   77. Ⓐ Ⓑ Ⓒ Ⓓ Ⓔ

12. Ⓐ Ⓑ Ⓒ Ⓓ Ⓔ   34. Ⓐ Ⓑ Ⓒ Ⓓ Ⓔ   56. Ⓐ Ⓑ Ⓒ Ⓓ Ⓔ   78. Ⓐ Ⓑ Ⓒ Ⓓ Ⓔ

13. Ⓐ Ⓑ Ⓒ Ⓓ Ⓔ   35. Ⓐ Ⓑ Ⓒ Ⓓ Ⓔ   57. Ⓐ Ⓑ Ⓒ Ⓓ Ⓔ   79. Ⓐ Ⓑ Ⓒ Ⓓ Ⓔ

14. Ⓐ Ⓑ Ⓒ Ⓓ Ⓔ   36. Ⓐ Ⓑ Ⓒ Ⓓ Ⓔ   58. Ⓐ Ⓑ Ⓒ Ⓓ Ⓔ   80. Ⓐ Ⓑ Ⓒ Ⓓ Ⓔ

15. Ⓐ Ⓑ Ⓒ Ⓓ Ⓔ   37. Ⓐ Ⓑ Ⓒ Ⓓ Ⓔ   59. Ⓐ Ⓑ Ⓒ Ⓓ Ⓔ   81. Ⓐ Ⓑ Ⓒ Ⓓ Ⓔ

16. Ⓐ Ⓑ Ⓒ Ⓓ Ⓔ   38. Ⓐ Ⓑ Ⓒ Ⓓ Ⓔ   60. Ⓐ Ⓑ Ⓒ Ⓓ Ⓔ   82. Ⓐ Ⓑ Ⓒ Ⓓ Ⓔ

17. Ⓐ Ⓑ Ⓒ Ⓓ Ⓔ   39. Ⓐ Ⓑ Ⓒ Ⓓ Ⓔ   61. Ⓐ Ⓑ Ⓒ Ⓓ Ⓔ   83. Ⓐ Ⓑ Ⓒ Ⓓ Ⓔ

18. Ⓐ Ⓑ Ⓒ Ⓓ Ⓔ   40. Ⓐ Ⓑ Ⓒ Ⓓ Ⓔ   62. Ⓐ Ⓑ Ⓒ Ⓓ Ⓔ   84. Ⓐ Ⓑ Ⓒ Ⓓ Ⓔ

19. Ⓐ Ⓑ Ⓒ Ⓓ Ⓔ   41. Ⓐ Ⓑ Ⓒ Ⓓ Ⓔ   63. Ⓐ Ⓑ Ⓒ Ⓓ Ⓔ   85. Ⓐ Ⓑ Ⓒ Ⓓ Ⓔ

20. Ⓐ Ⓑ Ⓒ Ⓓ Ⓔ   42. Ⓐ Ⓑ Ⓒ Ⓓ Ⓔ   64. Ⓐ Ⓑ Ⓒ Ⓓ Ⓔ   86. Ⓐ Ⓑ Ⓒ Ⓓ Ⓔ

21. Ⓐ Ⓑ Ⓒ Ⓓ Ⓔ   43. Ⓐ Ⓑ Ⓒ Ⓓ Ⓔ   65. Ⓐ Ⓑ Ⓒ Ⓓ Ⓔ   87. Ⓐ Ⓑ Ⓒ Ⓓ Ⓔ

22. Ⓐ Ⓑ Ⓒ Ⓓ Ⓔ   44. Ⓐ Ⓑ Ⓒ Ⓓ Ⓔ   66. Ⓐ Ⓑ Ⓒ Ⓓ Ⓔ   88. Ⓐ Ⓑ Ⓒ Ⓓ Ⓔ

25

Part A: Address Checking

Sample Questions

DIRECTIONS: For each question, compare the address in the left column with the address in the right column. If the two addresses are alike in every way, write A next to the question number. If the two addresses are different in any way, write D next to the question number. You have three minutes to mark your answers to the sample questions on the sample answer sheet below.

1 …3380 Federal Street	3380 S Federal Street
2 …1618 Highland Way	1816 Highland Way
3 …Greenvale NY 11548	Greenvale NY 11548
4 …Ft. Collins CO 80523	Ft. Collings CO 80523
5 …7214 NW 83rd St	7214 NW 83rd St

SAMPLE ANSWER SHEET		CORRECT ANSWERS	
1. Ⓐ Ⓓ	4. Ⓐ Ⓓ	1. Ⓐ ●	4. Ⓐ ●
2. Ⓐ Ⓓ	5. Ⓐ Ⓓ	2. Ⓐ ●	5. ● Ⓓ
3. Ⓐ Ⓓ		3. ● Ⓓ	

25

Address Checking

DIRECTIONS: For each question, compare the address in the left column with the address in the right column. If the two addresses are *alike* in every way, blacken space A on your answer sheet. If the two addresses are *different* in any way, blacken space D on your answer sheet. You have six minutes to complete Part A of the test.

1.	…12310 Claire Pl	12310 Claire Pl
2.	…24038 Johnson Rd	24038 Johnston Rd
3.	…578 Abraham Kazan Blvd	578 Abraham Kazan Blvd
4.	…11390 W Dogwood Rd	111390 E Dogwood Rd
5.	…11000 West Plaza Cir	11000 West Plaza Cir
6.	…Canadiqua NY 14424	Canadiqua NY 14424
7.	…13450 Montgomery Park	13450 Montegomery Park
8.	…16235 Zimbrich Dr	16235 Zimbrench Dr
9.	…43961 Remmington Ave	43961 Remmington Ave
10.	…11236 Shorewood La	11236 Sherwood La
11.	…16002 Dalewood Gardens	1602 Dalewood Gardens
12.	…11335 Yarkerdale Dr	11335 Yorkerdale Dr
13.	…12305 NE Teutonia Ave	12305 NW Teutonia Ave
14.	…1508 Duanesburg Rd	1508 Duanesburg Rd
15.	…Wachapregue VA 23480	Wachapergue Rd 23480
16.	…34001 E Atkinson Cir	34001 E Atkinson Cir
17.	…43872 E Tottenham Rd	43873 E Tottenham Rd
18.	…13531 Briar Ave NE	13531 Briar Ave NW
19.	…22633 N Abingdon Pl	22336 N Abingdon Pl
20.	…14615 Leni Lenape Way	14615 Leni Lenape Way
21.	…15609 Seaside Ter	15609 Seaside Park
22.	…10001 N Magee Ave	10001 N McGee Ave
23.	…14617 Quattara Blvd	14716 Quattara Blvd
24.	…89 South Timberland Rd	89 South Timberland Rd
25.	…18619 Boca Largo Park	18619 Boca Largo Pky
26.	…29888 Abbey View Way	29888 Abbey View Way
27.	…16567 Handle Rd	16567 Handel Rd
28.	…18900 W Passaic Ave	18900 S Passaic Ave

29.	...9092 E Trelawne Dr	9092 E Treelawne Dr
30.	...8202 NE Morrisville St	8201 NE Morrisville St
31.	...Emancipation PR 00802	Emancipation PR 00802
32.	...11925 Fairfield Cir	11925 Fairfield Dr
33.	...41011 Livingston Park A	41011 Livingston Park B
34.	...15789 Kearny Rd	157879 Kearny St
35.	...31991 Springvale Rd	31991 Springville Rd
36.	...14201 W Galbraith Ave	14201 W Galbraith Ave
37.	...21235 Laureldale La	21235 Laureldell La
38.	...11235 N Coletown Ave	11235 N Coaltown Ave
39.	...21003 NE Cronwell Blvd	21003 NE Cromwell Blvd
40.	...47989 S Bloomfield Dr	49789 S Bloomfield Dr
41.	...22122 Roebling Rd	22122 Rowbeling Rd
42.	...4434 N Glenorchard Ln	4434 N Glenorchard Ln
43.	...12087 Neyartnell Pky	12087 Neyartell Pky
44.	...31756 Falconbridge Dr	31756 Falconbridge Dr
45.	...Stambaugh MI 49964	Stanbaugh MI 49964
46.	...16735 Haledon Ln	16735 Haledom Ln
47.	...133288 La Torneau Ave	133288 La Torneau Ave
48.	...10154 Ottercreek Rd	10154 Ottercreek Rd
49.	...4867 NE Kellerman Ct	4867 NE Kellerman Ct
50.	...15089 Brookhavenn Cir	15089 Brookhaven Dr
51.	...12196 SW Westminster Pl	12196 SW Westminster Pl
52.	...7800 SE Grantham Way	7800 SE Grantham Way
53.	...20697 Indianbluff Dr	20997 Indianbluff Dr
54.	...4400 Amberacres Rd	4400 Amberacres Rd
55.	...5801 Paulmeadows Dr	5801 Paulmeadows Dr
56.	...5101 Pinehurst Ln	5101 Pinehorst Ln
57.	...8966 Verona Ct NE	8966 Verona Cir NE
58.	...1399 Valhalla Ave NE	1399 Valhalla Ave SE
59.	...12397 Reicosky Ln NW	12397 Reikosky Ln NW
60.	...3600 Palmetto Ave SE	3600 Palmetto Ave SE
61.	...5260 Gettysburg W	5260 Gettysburg W
62.	...4563 Terrahaute Dr NW	4563 Terrahaute Dr NW
63.	...2190 Glastonbury Dr SE	2190 Glastonberry Dr SE

25

64.	...2207 Hazleton Cir	2207 Hazelton Cir
65.	...11300 North Central Ave	11300 North Center Ave
66.	...21205 Canadensis Cir	21205 Canadenses Cir
67.	...4499 Mt. Carmel Ave	4499 Mt. Carmel St.
68.	...4056 Maplewood Ln NW	4056 Mapplewood Ln SW
69.	...Tamaqua OH 45624	Tamaqua OH 45624
70.	...1257 Zesiger Ave	1257 Zesinger Ave
71.	...2697 Remington Ave NW	2697 Remington Ave NW
72.	...5409 East Tremont Rd	5409 East Tremont Rd
73.	...901 Airymeadows Ln	901 Airymeadows Ln
74.	...1795 NE Second Ave	1795 NW Second Ave
75.	...PO Box 46972	PO Box 46792
76.	...11299 Wolverine Ct SE	11929 Wolverine Ct Se
77.	...2000 Bloomnigdale Ave NW	2000 Bloomingdale St NW
78.	...3989 Phillipsburg Pl NW	3989 Phillipsberg Pl NW
79.	...5700 Inverness Pky SE	5700 Inverness Pky SE
80.	...899 Mount Graymore Ave NE	899 Mount Greymore Ave NE
81.	...1166 Crockett Ave SE	1166 Crockett Ave SE
82.	...89001 Flathollow Trl	89001 Flathollow Trl
83.	...Fort Steilacoon WA 98494	Fort Stielacoon WA 98494
84.	...2255 Parkridge Cir NW	2255 Partridge Cir NW
85.	...5477 Westbury Ave NE	5477 Westbury St NE
86.	...35501 Gambrinus Ct SE	3501 Gambrinus Ct SE
87.	...11089 Stanhaus St NW	11909 Stanhaus St NW
88.	...7700 Cherryhill Dr NW	7700 Cherryhill Cir NW
89.	...3303 Allendale Pl SE	3303 Allendale Pl NE
90.	...22449 Tatamy Trl	22449 Tatamy Trl
91.	...8803 Lawrence Rd S	8803 Lawrence Rd S
92.	...12468 Deer Run Ave	12486 Deer Run Ave
93.	...Kitatinny AK 99681	Kitatinny AR 99681
94.	...700 Equinunk Falls Rd	700 Equinank Falls Rd
95.	...297 Montville Valley Ct NW	297 Montville Valley St NW

Part B: Memory for Addresses

Sample Questions

DIRECTIONS: In this part of the test, you will have to memorize the locations (A, B, C, D, or E) of the 25 addresses in the five lettered boxes below. Your task is to mark on your answer sheet the letter of the box in which each address belongs.

You will now have five minutes to study the locations of the addresses. Then cover the boxes and answer the questions. You may look back at the boxes if you cannot yet mark the address locations from memory.

The exam provides three practice sessions before the actual test in addition to these sample questions. Practice Set 1 and Practice Set 3 supply you with the boxes and permit you to refer to them if necessary. Practice Set II and the actual Memory for Addresses test do not permit you to look at the boxes.

A	B	C	D	E
2300–3499 Main	3500–3999 Main	4000–4299 Main	1200–2199 Main	2200–2299 Main
Liberty	Willow	Hopper	Magnet	Carrot
4000–4299 Oak	2200–2299 Oak	1200–2199 Oak	3500–3999 Oak	2300–3499 Oak
Iron	Boulder	Window	Press	Forest
1200–2199 Post	2300–3499 Post	3500–3999 Post	2200–2299 Post	4000–4299 Post

1. Willow
2. 2200-2299 Oak
3. 1200-2199 Post
4. 4000-4299 Main
5. Press
6. Carrot
7. 2200-2299 Post

8. 2200-2299 Main
9. 4000-4299 Oak
10. 3500-3999 Main
11. Boulder
12. Forest
13. 1200-2199 Oak
14. 2300-3499 Post

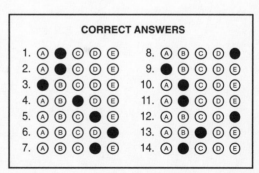

SAMPLE ANSWER SHEET

1. Ⓐ Ⓑ Ⓒ Ⓓ Ⓔ   8. Ⓐ Ⓑ Ⓒ Ⓓ Ⓔ
2. Ⓐ Ⓑ Ⓒ Ⓓ Ⓔ   9. Ⓐ Ⓑ Ⓒ Ⓓ Ⓔ
3. Ⓐ Ⓑ Ⓒ Ⓓ Ⓔ   10. Ⓐ Ⓑ Ⓒ Ⓓ Ⓔ
4. Ⓐ Ⓑ Ⓒ Ⓓ Ⓔ   11. Ⓐ Ⓑ Ⓒ Ⓓ Ⓔ
5. Ⓐ Ⓑ Ⓒ Ⓓ Ⓔ   12. Ⓐ Ⓑ Ⓒ Ⓓ Ⓔ
6. Ⓐ Ⓑ Ⓒ Ⓓ Ⓔ   13. Ⓐ Ⓑ Ⓒ Ⓓ Ⓔ
7. Ⓐ Ⓑ Ⓒ Ⓓ Ⓔ   14. Ⓐ Ⓑ Ⓒ Ⓓ Ⓔ

CORRECT ANSWERS

1. Ⓐ ● Ⓒ Ⓓ Ⓔ   8. Ⓐ Ⓑ Ⓒ Ⓓ ●
2. Ⓐ ● Ⓒ Ⓓ Ⓔ   9. ● Ⓑ Ⓒ Ⓓ Ⓔ
3. ● Ⓑ Ⓒ Ⓓ Ⓔ   10. Ⓐ ● Ⓒ Ⓓ Ⓔ
4. Ⓐ Ⓑ ● Ⓓ Ⓔ   11. Ⓐ ● Ⓒ Ⓓ Ⓔ
5. Ⓐ Ⓑ Ⓒ ● Ⓔ   12. Ⓐ Ⓑ Ⓒ Ⓓ ●
6. Ⓐ Ⓑ Ⓒ Ⓓ ●   13. Ⓐ Ⓑ ● Ⓓ Ⓔ
7. Ⓐ Ⓑ Ⓒ ● Ⓔ   14. Ⓐ ● Ⓒ Ⓓ Ⓔ

25

Practice for Memory for Addresses

DIRECTIONS: The five boxes below are labeled A, B, C, D, and E. In each box are five addresses; three are street addresses with number ranges and two are unnumbered place names. You have three minutes to memorize the box location of each address. The position of an address within a box is not important. You need only remember the letter of the box in which the address is found. You will use these addresses to answer three sets of practice questions that are not scored and one actual test that is scored.

A	B	C	D	E
2300–3499 Main	3500–3999 Main	4000–4299 Main	1200–2199 Main	2200–2299 Main
Liberty	Willow	Hopper	Magnet	Carrot
4000–4299 Oak	2200–2299 Oak	1200–2199 Oak	3500–3999 Oak	2300–3499 Oak
Iron	Boulder	Window	Press	Forest
1200–2199 Post	2300–3499 Post	3500–3999 Post	2200–2299 Post	4000–4299 Post

Practice Set 1

DIRECTIONS: You have three minutes to complete this exercise by marking the letter of the box for each of the following addresses found on your answer sheet. Try to do this without looking at the boxes. However, if you get stuck, you may refer to the boxes during this practice exercise. If you must look at the boxes, try to memorize as you do so. This test is for practice only. It will not be scored.

1. 3500-3999 Oak
2. 2300-3499 Post
3. Iron
4. Forest
5. 4000-4299 Main
6. 2300-3299 Oak
7. 3500-3999 Post
8. 2300-3499 Main
9. Magnet
10. Carrot
11. 2200-2299 Post
12. 3500-3999 Main
13. 2200-2299 Main
14. 4000-4299 Oak
15. Liberty
16. Willow
17. 1200-2199 Oak
18. 1200-2199 Main
19. Window
20. Press
21. 2300-3499 Post
22. 4000-4299 Oak
23. 4000-4299 Post
24. 3500-3999 Oak
25. Magnet
26. Boulder
27. Willow
28. 4000-4299 Main
29. 2300-3499 Main
30. 3500-3999 Post

31. 1200-2199 Post
32. Liberty
33. Carrot
34. 2200-2299 Oak
35. 2300-3499 Oak
36. Hopper
37. Iron
38. 2200-2299 Post
39. 3500-3999 Main
40. 2200-2299 Main
41. Forest
42. Window
43. 3500-3999 Oak
44. 2300-3499 Post
45. 2300-3499 Main
46. 2200-2299 Oak
47. 3500-3999 Post
48. 3500-3999 Oak
49. 2200-2299 Main
50. Magnet
51. Window
52. Willow
53. 4000-4299 Post
54. Press
55. 1200-2199 Oak
56. Boulder
57. 1200-2199 Post
58. 4000-4299 Oak
59. 2300-3499 Oak

60. 4000-4299 Main
61. Carrot
62. Forest
63. 1200-2199 Main
64. 3500-3999 Main
65. 2300-3499 Post
66. Liberty
67. Hopper
68. 2200-2299 Post
69. Iron
70. 1200-2199 Oak
71. 3500-3999 Post
72. Boulder
73. 2200-2299 Main
74. 1200-2199 Post
75. Press
76. Carrot
77. 4000-4299 Post
78. 4000-4299 Oak
79. 2300-3499 Main
80. 3500-3999 Oak
81. Window
82. Hopper
83. Boulder
84. 1200-2199 Oak
85. 1200-2199 Main
86. 2300-3499 Post
87. Willow
88. Liberty

25

Practice Set 2

DIRECTIONS: The next 88 questions are for practice. Mark your answers on the Practice II answer sheet. Again, your time limit is three minutes. This time, however, you must not look at the boxes while answering the questions. You must rely on your memory for marking the box location of each item. This practice test will not be scored.

1.	2300-3499 Oak	31.	4000-4299 Main	61.	4000-4299 Post
2.	2200-2299 Post	32.	2300-3499 Main	62.	Carrot
3.	3500-3999 Main	33.	4000-4299 Oak	63.	Liberty
4.	1200-2199 Post	34.	2300-3499 Post	64.	3500-3999 Oak
5.	Hopper	35.	Boulder	65.	2300-3499 Main
6.	Carrot	36.	Liberty	66.	3500-3999 Main
7.	4000-4299 Main	37.	Forest	67.	Willow
8.	1200-2199 Oak	38.	2200-2299 Oak	68.	Boulder
9.	2300-3499 Post	39.	4000-4299 Post	69.	1200-2199 Post
10.	Forest	40.	3500-3999 Oak	70.	Magnet
11.	Boulder	41.	Willow	71.	Window
12.	4000-4299 Oak	42.	Carrot	72.	4000-4299 Main
13.	2200-2299 Main	43.	3500-3999 Post	73.	3500-3999 Post
14.	1200-2199 Post	44.	2200-2299 Main	74.	2200-2299 Main
15.	3500-3999 Oak	45.	3500-3999 Main	75.	4000-4299 Post
16.	Magnet	46.	Iron	76.	2300-3499 Main
17.	Willow	47.	1200-2199 Main	77.	3500-3999 Oak
18.	Liberty	48.	4000-4299 Oak	78.	2200-2299 Oak
19.	3500-3999 Post	49.	2200-2299 Post	79.	Willow
20.	1200-2199 Main	50.	Press	80.	Hopper
21.	2300-3499 Main	51.	Forest	81.	1200-2199 Oak
22.	2200-2299 Oak	52.	2200-2299 Main	82.	1200-2199 Post
23.	Iron	53.	1200-2199 Oak	83.	2200-2299 Main
24.	Press	54.	2300-3499 Post	84.	Carrot
25.	Window	55.	3500-3999 Post	85.	Iron
26.	1200-2199 Main	56.	Hopper	86.	Liberty
27.	1200-2199 Oak	57.	Iron	87.	3500-3999 Main
28.	2200-2299 Post	58.	4000-4299 Main	88.	2200-2299 Post
29.	Hopper	59.	2200-2299 Oak		
30.	Magnet	60.	2300-3499 Oak		

Practice Set 3

> **DIRECTIONS:** The same addresses from the previous practice sets are repeated in the box below. You have five minutes to study the locations again. Do your best to memorize the letter of the box in which each address is located. This is your last chance to see the boxes.

A	B	C	D	E
2300–3499 Main Liberty 4000–4299 Oak Iron 1200–2199 Post	3500–3999 Main Willow 2200–2299 Oak Boulder 2300–3499 Post	4000–4299 Main Hopper 1200–2199 Oak Window 3500–3999 Post	1200–2199 Main Magnet 3500–3999 Oak Press 2200–2299 Post	2200–2299 Main Carrot 2300–3499 Oak Forest 4000–4299 Post

> **DIRECTIONS:** This is your last practice test. Mark the location of each of the 88 addresses on the Practice III answer sheet. You will have five minutes to answer these questions. Do not look back at the boxes. This practice test will not be scored.

1. Willow
2. Window
3. 1200-2199 Main
4. 3500-3999 Post
5. 4000-4299 Oak
6. 2300-3499 Oak
7. 2200-2299 Post
8. Liberty
9. Carrot
10. Magnet
11. 2300-3499 Main
12. 4000-4299 Main
13. 1200-2199 Oak
14. 2200-2299 Oak
15. Hopper
16. 3500-3999 Main
17. 3500-3999 Oak
18. 2300-3499 Post
19. Press
20. Boulder

21. 4000-4299 Main
22. 1200-2100 Post
23. 2300-3499 Oak
24. Iron
25. Forest
26. 4000-4299 Oak
27. 2300-3499 Main
28. 2200-2299 Post
29. 4000-4299 Post
30. Willow
31. 1200-2199 Oak
32. 3500-3999 Main
33. 2200-2299 Post
34. Forest
35. Magnet
36. 2300-3499 Post
37. 4000-4299 Main
38. 1200-2199 Main
39. Carrot
40. Press

41. 2300-3499 Oak
42. 4000-4299 Oak
43. 3500-3999 Post
44. 4000-4299 Post
45. Liberty
46. Boulder
47. Hopper
48. 2300-3499 Main
49. 2200-2299 Main
50. 3500-3999 Oak
51. Window
52. Willow
53. 2200-2299 Oak
54. 1200-2199 Post
55. 2200-2299 Oak
56. Iron
57. 1200-2199 Main
58. 2300-3499 Oak
59. 4000-4299 Main
60. 4000-4299 Oak

25

61. 3500-3999 Main
62. 2200-2299 Post
63. 2300-3499 Post
64. 2200-2299 Oak
65. Boulder
66. Willow
67. 1200-2199 Oak
68. 2200-2299 Main
69. 1200-2199 Post
70. 4000-4299 Post

71. Magnet
72. Hopper
73. Carrot
74. 2200-2299 Oak
75. 2300-3499 Oak
76. 2300-3499 Main
77. 4000-4299 Main
78. Forest
79. Press
80. Iron

81. 3500-3999 Post
82. 3500-3999 Oak
83. 1200-2199 Main
84. Liberty
85. Window
86. 1200-2199 Oak
87. 1200-2199 Post
88. 2200-2299 Main

Memory for Addresses

> **DIRECTIONS:** Mark your answer sheet to indicate the location (A, B, C, D, or E) of each of the 88 addresses below. This test will be scored. You are not permitted to look at the boxes. Work from memory as quickly and as accurately as you can. You have five minutes to complete Part B of the test.

1.	2300-3499 Main	31.	Forest	61.	2200-2299 Oak
2.	1200-2199 Oak	32.	1200-2199 Post	62.	2200-2299 Post
3.	4000-4299 Post	33.	1200-2199 Oak	63.	3500-3999 Main
4.	2200-2299 Main	34.	4000-4299 Main	64.	3500-3999 Oak
5.	1200-2199 Post	35.	Hopper	65.	Boulder
6.	Iron	36.	Carrot	66.	Magnet
7.	Boulder	37.	2300-3499 Main	67.	1200-2199 Oak
8.	Magnet	38.	2300-3499 Oak	68.	2200-2299 Main
9.	2300-3499 Oak	39.	2200-2299 Oak	69.	Press
10.	4000-4299 Oak	40.	Liberty	70.	1200-2199 Post
11.	3500-3999 Post	41.	Magnet	71.	4000-4299 Oak
12.	4000-4299 Main	42.	3500-3999 Main	72.	2200-2299 Post
13.	Carrot	43.	3500-3999 Post	73.	3500-3999 Main
14.	Forest	44.	4000-4299 Post	74.	Liberty
15.	Window	45.	4000-4299 Oak	75.	4000-4299 Post
16.	3500-3999 Main	46.	2200-2299 Main	76.	2300-3499 Main
17.	3500-3999 Post	47.	Hopper	77.	Window
18.	2300-3499 Post	48.	Willow	78.	Magnet
19.	3500-3999 Oak	49.	2300-3499 Main	79.	1200-2199 Oak
20.	Press	50.	Window	80.	2300-3499 Oak
21.	Liberty	51.	2300-3499 Main	81.	1200-2199 Main
22.	4000-4299 Oak	52.	Window	82.	2300-3499 Post
23.	3500-3999 Post	53.	Liberty	83.	Hopper
24.	1200-2199 Main	54.	Iron	84.	Press
25.	Window	55.	1200-2199 Oak	85.	2200-2299 Oak
26.	Iron	56.	2300-3499 Oak	86.	4000-4299 Main
27.	2200-2299 Main	57.	4000-4299 Main	87.	3500-3999 Post
28.	3500-3999 Oak	58.	1200-2199 Post	88.	Forest
29.	2300-3499 Post	59.	Carrot		
30.	Willow	60.	Forest		

25

Part C: Number Series

Sample Questions

> **DIRECTIONS:** The following sample questions show you the type of question that will be used in Part C. You will have three minutes to answer the sample questions and study the explanations.
>
> For each question below, there is at the left a series of numbers that follows some definite pattern and at the right five sets of two numbers each. Look at the numbers in the series at the left and find out the pattern they follow. Then decide what the next two numbers in the series would be if the pattern continued. Mark your answers on your answer sheet.

1. 42 40 38 35 32 28 24...   (A) 20 18 (B) 18 14(C) 19 14 (D) 20 16 (E) 19 15

   If you write the steps between the numbers, you will find this pattern emerging: subtract 2, subtract 2, subtract 3, subtract 3, subtract 4, subtract 4.... Because it appears that after each two numbers the number being subtracted increases, it is logical to choose answer (C) because $24 - 5 = 19$ and $19 - 5 = 14$.

2. 2 2 4 2 6 2 8...   (A) 8 2   (B) 2 8 (C) 2 10 (D) 10 2 (E) 10 12

   The series progresses by a factor of 2: 2 4 6 8 10. After each number of the advancing series, we find the number 2. The answer is (C).

3. 88 88 82 82 76 76 70...   (A) 70 70 (B) 70 65(C) 64 64 (D) 70 64 (E) 64 48

   The pattern in this series is a simple one: repeat the number, subtract 6; repeat the number, subtract 6; and so on. To complete the series, repeat the number 70 and subtract 6 to yield 64. The answer is (D).

4. 35 46 39 43 43 40 47...   (A) 47 43 (B) 51 40(C) 43 51 (D) 70 64 (E) 37 51

   This is a more complicated problem. Here are two series that alternate. The first series begins with 35 and ascends by 4: 35 39 43 47 51. The alternating series begins with 4 and descends by 3: 46 43 40 37. The number 43 is not repeated; the two series pass each other at that point. In answering a question of this type, you must be careful to maintain alternating the series. The answer is (E) because 37 continues the descending series and 51 continues the ascending one.

5. 8 10 13 17 22 28 35...   (A) 43 52 (B) 40 45(C) 35 42 (D) 42 50 (E) 44 53

   The pattern is add 2, add 3, add 4, add 5, add 6, add 7, and so on. Continue the series with: $35 + 8 = 43 + 9 = 52$ to choose (A) as the correct answer.

```
┌─────────────────────────────┐   ┌─────────────────────────────┐
│   SAMPLE ANSWER SHEET       │   │      CORRECT ANSWERS        │
│   1. Ⓐ Ⓑ Ⓒ Ⓓ Ⓔ           │   │   1. Ⓐ Ⓑ ● Ⓓ Ⓔ           │
│   2. Ⓐ Ⓑ Ⓒ Ⓓ Ⓔ           │   │   2. Ⓐ Ⓑ ● Ⓓ Ⓔ           │
│   3. Ⓐ Ⓑ Ⓒ Ⓓ Ⓔ           │   │   3. Ⓐ Ⓑ Ⓒ ● Ⓔ           │
│   4. Ⓐ Ⓑ Ⓒ Ⓓ Ⓔ           │   │   4. Ⓐ Ⓑ Ⓒ Ⓓ ●           │
│   5. Ⓐ Ⓑ Ⓒ Ⓓ Ⓔ           │   │   5. ● Ⓑ Ⓒ Ⓓ Ⓔ           │
└─────────────────────────────┘   └─────────────────────────────┘
```

Number Series

DIRECTIONS: For each question below, there is at the left a series of numbers that follows some definite pattern and at the right five sets of two numbers each. Look at the numbers in the series at the left and determine its pattern. Then decide what the next two numbers in the series would be if the order were continued. Mark your answers on your answer sheet. You have 20 minutes to complete Part C of the test.

1. 13 12 8 11 10 8 9   (A) 8 7   (B) 6 8   (C) 8 6   (D) 8 8   (E) 7 8

2. 13 18 13 17 13 16 13   (A) 15 13 (B) 13 14 (C) 13 15 (D) 14 15 (E) 15 14

3. 13 13 10 12 12 10 11   (A) 10 10 (B) 10 9   (C) 11 9   (D) 9 11   (E) 11 10

4. 6 5 4 6 5 4 6   (A) 4 6   (B) 6 4   (C) 5 4   (D) 5 6   (E) 4 5

5. 10 10 9 8 8 7 6   (A) 5 5   (B) 5 4   (C) 6 5   (D) 6 4   (E) 5 3

6. 20 16 18 14 16 12 14   (A) 16 12 (B) 10 12 (C) 16 18 (D) 12 12 (E) 12 10

7. 7 12 8 11 9 10 10   (A) 11 9   (B) 9 8   (C) 9 11   (D) 10 11 (E) 9 10

8. 13 13 12 15 15 14 17   (A) 17 16 (B) 14 17 (C) 16 19 (D) 19 19 (E) 16 16

9. 65 59 53 51 49 43 37 35 (A) 29 27 (B) 33 29 (C) 27 24 (D) 33 27 (E) 32 25

10. 73 65 65 58 58 52 52   (A) 52 46 (B) 52 47 (C) 47 47 (D) 46 46 (E) 45 45

11. 6 4 8 5 15 13 26 23   (A) 69 67 (B) 37 33 (C) 29 44 (D) 75 78 (E) 46 49

12. 19 16 21 18 23 20 25   (A) 30 33 (B) 22 27 (C) 28 22 (D) 22 24 (E) 30 27

13. 35 40 5 45 50 5 55   (A) 55 5   (B) 60 5   (C) 5 60   (D) 5 55   (E) 60 65

14. 22 20 18 18 16 14 14   (A) 14 12 (B) 12 12 (C) 14 10 (D) 14 16 (E) 12 10

15. 11 22 23 13 26 27 17   (A) 7 8   (B) 18 36 (C) 18 8   (D) 7 14   (E) 34 35

16. 9 1 10 1 11 1 12   (A) 13 14 (B) 13 1   (C) 1 13   (D) 12 1   (E) 12 13

17. 48 10 46 17 44 24 42   (A) 31 40 (B) 27 28 (C) 40 38 (D) 28 38 (E) 30 40

18. 8 8 17 26 26 35 44   (A) 53 53 (B) 44 53 (C) 44 44 (D) 44 55 (E) 44 54

25

19.   71 68 62 59 53 50 44   (A) 40 32   (B) 38 35   (C) 41 38   (D) 41 35   (E) 41 33

20.   1 7 8 2 7 8 3   (A) 4 7   (B) 7 8   (C) 4 5   (D) 7 4   (E) 2 8

21.   1 2 2 1 1 2 2   (A) 1 1   (B) 1 2   (C) 2 1   (D) 2 2   (E) 1 3

22.   14 25 37 48 60 71 83   (A) 92 100   (B) 96 110   (C) 89 98   (D) 95 105   (E) 94 106

23.   35 43 45 53 55 63 65   (A) 65 68   (B) 75 83   (C) 73 75   (D) 65 73   (E) 73 83

24.   3 6 12 12 24 48 48   (A) 48 96   (B) 96 96   (C) 60 96   (D) 96 192   (E) 60 60

Part D: Following Oral Instructions

Sample Worksheet

> **DIRECTIONS:** Listen carefully to the instructions read to you and mark each item on this worksheet as directed. Then complete each question by marking the sample answer sheet as directed. For each answer, you will darken the answer sheet for a number-letter combination.

1.

| 4 __ | 20 __ | 11 __ | 7 __ | 9 __ |

2.

    3 __   12 __   22 __   18 __   1 __

3.

    __ E   __ C   __ A   __ E   __ D

4.   X O X X X X O O X O X O X X O X

25

Sample Answer Sheet

1. Ⓐ Ⓑ Ⓒ Ⓓ Ⓔ	6. Ⓐ Ⓑ Ⓒ Ⓓ Ⓔ	11. Ⓐ Ⓑ Ⓒ Ⓓ Ⓔ
2. Ⓐ Ⓑ Ⓒ Ⓓ Ⓔ	7. Ⓐ Ⓑ Ⓒ Ⓓ Ⓔ	12. Ⓐ Ⓑ Ⓒ Ⓓ Ⓔ
3. Ⓐ Ⓑ Ⓒ Ⓓ Ⓔ	8. Ⓐ Ⓑ Ⓒ Ⓓ Ⓔ	13. Ⓐ Ⓑ Ⓒ Ⓓ Ⓔ
4. Ⓐ Ⓑ Ⓒ Ⓓ Ⓔ	9. Ⓐ Ⓑ Ⓒ Ⓓ Ⓔ	14. Ⓐ Ⓑ Ⓒ Ⓓ Ⓔ
5. Ⓐ Ⓑ Ⓒ Ⓓ Ⓔ	10. Ⓐ Ⓑ Ⓒ Ⓓ Ⓔ	15. Ⓐ Ⓑ Ⓒ Ⓓ Ⓔ

Sample Oral Instructions

(Note: The words in parentheses should not be read aloud.)

You are to follow the instructions that I shall read to you. I cannot repeat them.

Look at line 1 on your worksheet. (Pause slightly). Write a C in the third box. (Pause two seconds). Now on your answer sheet, find the number in that box and darken space C for that number. (Pause five seconds.)

Look at line 2 on your worksheet. (Pause slightly). The number in each circle is the number of employees in a post office. In the circle for the post office holding more than 10 employees but less than 15, write the letter E next to the number. (Pause five seconds.) Now, on your answer sheet, darken the space for the number-letter combination that is in the circle you just wrote in. (Pause five seconds).

Look at the circles on line 3 of your worksheet. (Pause slightly.) In the second circle, write the answer to this question: Which of the following numbers is smallest: 9, 21, 16, 17, 23? (Pause five seconds.) In the third circle, write the answer to this question: How many days are there in a week? (Pause two seconds.) Now, on your answer sheet, darken the number-letter combinations that are in the circles you wrote in. (Pause 10 seconds.)

Look at line 4 on your worksheet. (Pause slightly.) Count the number of O's in the line. (Pause five seconds.) subtract 2 from the number you have counted, and darken the space for the letter B as in baker on your answer sheet next to that number. (Pause 10 seconds.)

```
┌─────────────────────────────────────────────────────────┐
│           CORRECT ANSWERS TO SAMPLE QUESTIONS             │
│                                                           │
│  1. Ⓐ Ⓑ Ⓒ Ⓓ Ⓔ    6. Ⓐ Ⓑ Ⓒ Ⓓ Ⓔ    11. Ⓐ Ⓑ ● Ⓓ Ⓔ     │
│  2. Ⓐ Ⓑ Ⓒ Ⓓ Ⓔ    7. ● Ⓑ Ⓒ Ⓓ Ⓔ    12. Ⓐ Ⓑ Ⓒ Ⓓ ●     │
│  3. Ⓐ Ⓑ Ⓒ Ⓓ Ⓔ    8. Ⓐ Ⓑ Ⓒ Ⓓ Ⓔ    13. Ⓐ Ⓑ Ⓒ Ⓓ Ⓔ     │
│  4. Ⓐ ● Ⓒ Ⓓ Ⓔ    9. Ⓐ Ⓑ ● Ⓓ Ⓔ    14. Ⓐ Ⓑ Ⓒ Ⓓ Ⓔ     │
│  5. Ⓐ Ⓑ Ⓒ Ⓓ Ⓔ   10. Ⓐ Ⓑ Ⓒ Ⓓ Ⓔ    15. Ⓐ Ⓑ Ⓒ Ⓓ Ⓔ     │
└─────────────────────────────────────────────────────────┘
```

Correctly Completed Worksheet

1.

| 4 __ | 20 __ | 11 _C_ | 7 __ | 9 __ |

2.

(3 __)   (12 _E_)   (22 __)   (18 __)   (1 __)

3.

(__ E)   (_9_ C)   (_7_ A)   (__ E)   (__ D)

4.   X O X X X X O O X O X O X X O X

Worksheet

DIRECTIONS: Listen carefully to the instructions read to you and mark each item on this worksheet as directed. Then complete each question by marking the answer sheet as directed. For each answer, you will darken the answer sheet for a number-letter combination. You will have approximately 25 minutes to complete Part D of the exam.

1.   59   35   62   58   8

2.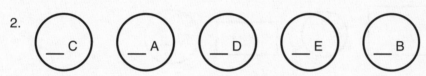

3.   15 _____   20 _____

4.
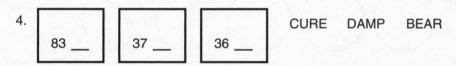
CURE   DAMP   BEAR

5.   A   C   B   A   B   D   C   E   D

6.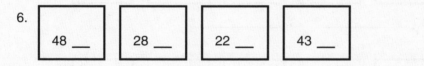

7.   51 _____   69 _____   50 _____

8.

25

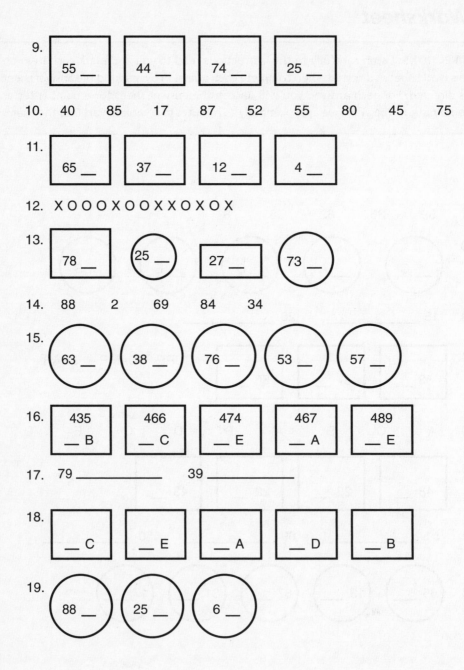

9. | 55 __ | 44 __ | 74 __ | 25 __ |

10.   40   85   17   87   52   55   80   45   75

11. | 65 __ | 37 __ | 12 __ | 4 __ |

12. X O O O X O O X X O X O X

13. | 78 __ | (25 __) | 27 __ | (73 __)

14.   88   2   69   84   34

15. (63 __) (38 __) (76 __) (53 __) (57 __)

16. | 435 __ B | 466 __ C | 474 __ E | 467 __ A | 489 __ E |

17.   79 _____   39 _____

18. | __ C | __ E | __ A | __ D | __ B |

19. (88 __) (25 __) (6 __)

Oral Instructions

(Note: The words in parentheses should not be read aloud.)

On the job you will have to listen to instructions and then do what you have been told. In this test, I will read some instructions to you. Listen closely as I read them; I cannot repeat them. Once we begin, you may not ask any questions until the end of the test.

On the job you won't have to deal with pictures, numbers, and letters like those on this test, but you will have to listen to instructions and follow them. We are using this test to see how well you can follow instructions.

You are to mark your worksheet according to the instructions that I'll read to you. After each set of instructions, I'll give you time to record your answers on the separate answer sheet.

The actual test begins now.

Look on line 1 of your worksheet. (Pause slightly.) Draw a line under the largest number in the line. (Pause two seconds.) Now, on your answer sheet, find the number under which you just drew a line and darken box D as in dog for that number. (Pause five seconds.)

Look at line 1 on your worksheet again. (Pause slightly.) Draw two lines under the smallest number in the line. (Pause two seconds.) Now on your answer sheet, find the number under which you just drew two lines and darken box E. (Pause five seconds.)

Look at the circles in line 2 on your worksheet. (Pause slightly.) In the second circle, write the answer to this question: How much is 6 plus 4? (Pause eight seconds.) In the third circle, write the answer to this question: Which of the following numbers is largest: 67, 48, 15, 73, 61? (Pause five seconds.) In the fourth circle, write the answer to this question: How many months are there in a year? (Pause two seconds.) Now, on your answer sheet, darken the letter-number combinations that are in the circles you wrote in. (Pause 10 seconds.)

Now look at line 3 of your worksheet. (Pause slightly.) Write the letter C on the blank next to the right-hand number. (Pause two seconds.) Now, on your answer sheet, find the space for the number beside which you wrote and darken box C. (Pause five seconds.)

Now look at line 3 of your worksheet again. (Pause slightly.) Write the letter B as in baker on the blank next to the left-hand number. (Pause two seconds.) Now, on your answer sheet, find the space for the number you just wrote beside and darken box B as in baker. (Pause five seconds.)

Look at the boxes and words in line 4 on your worksheet. (Pause slightly.) Write the first letter of the second word in the third box. (Pause two seconds.) Write the last letter of the

25

first word in the second box. (Pause two seconds.) Write the first letter of the third word in the first box. (Pause two seconds.) Now, on your answer sheet, darken the space for the letter-number combinations that are in the three boxes you just wrote in. (Pause 10 seconds.)

Look at the letters on line 5 on your worksheet. (Pause slightly.) Draw a line under the fifth letter in the line. (Pause two seconds.) Now, on your answer sheet, find the number 56 (pause two seconds) and darken the space for the letter under which you drew a line. (Pause five seconds.)

Look at the letters on line 5 on your worksheet again. (Pause slightly.) Draw two lines under the fourth letter in the line. (Pause two seconds.) Now, on your answer sheet, find the number 66 (pause two seconds) and darken the space for the letter under which you drew two lines. (Pause five seconds.)

Look at the drawings on line 6 on your worksheet. (Pause slightly.) The four boxes indicate the number of buildings in four different carrier routes. In the box for the route with the fewest number of buildings, write an A. (Pause two seconds.) Now, on your answer sheet, darken the space for the number-letter combination that is in the box you just wrote in. (Pause five seconds.)

Now look at line 7 on your worksheet. (Pause slightly.) If fall comes before summer, write the letter B as in baker on the line next to the middle number. (Pause slightly.) Otherwise write an E on the blank next to the left-hand number. (Pause five seconds.) Now, on your answer sheet, darken the space for the number-letter combination that you have just written. (Pause five seconds.)

Now look at line 8 on your worksheet. (Pause slightly.) Write D as in dog in the circle with the lowest number. (Pause two seconds.) Now, on your answer sheet, darken the space for the number-letter combination that is in the circle you just wrote in.

Look at the drawings in line 9 on your worksheet. The four boxes are planes for carrying mail. (Pause slightly.) The plane with the highest number is to be loaded first. Write an E in the box with the highest number. (Pause two seconds.) Now, on your answer sheet, darken the space for the number-letter combination that is in the box you just wrote in. (Pause five seconds.)

Look at line 10 on your worksheet. (Pause slightly.) Draw a line under every number that is more than 35 but less than 55. (Pause 12 seconds.) Now, on your answer sheet, for each line that you drew a box under, darken box A. (Pause 25 seconds.)

Look at line 10 on your worksheet again. (Pause slightly.) Draw two lines under every number that is more than 55 and less than 80. (Pause 12 seconds.) Now, on your answer sheet, for each number that you drew two lines under, darken box C. (Pause 25 seconds.)

Look at line 11 on your worksheet. (Pause slightly.) Write an E in the last box. (Pause two seconds.) Now, on your answer sheet, find the number in that box and darken box E for that number. (Pause five seconds.)

Look at line 12 on your worksheet. (Pause slightly.) Draw a line under every X in the line. (Pause five seconds.) Count the number of lines that you have drawn, add 3, and write that number at the end of the line. (Pause five seconds.) Now, on your answer sheet, find that number and darken space E for that number. (Pause five seconds.)

Look at line 13 on your worksheet. (Pause slightly.) If the number in the right-hand box is larger than the number in the left-hand circle, add 4 to the number in the left-hand circle, and change the number in the circle to this number. (Pause eight seconds.) Then write C next to the new number. (Pause slightly.) Otherwise, write A next to the number in the smaller box. (Pause three seconds.) Now, on your answer sheet, darken the space for the number-letter combination that is in the box or circle you just wrote in. (Pause five seconds.)

Now look at line 14 on your worksheet. (Pause slightly.) Draw a line under the middle number in the line. (Pause two seconds.) Now, on your answer sheet, find the number under which you just drew the line and darken box D as in dog for that number. (Pause five seconds.)

Now look at line 15 on your worksheet. (Pause slightly.) Write a B as in baker in the third circle. (Pause two seconds.) Now, on your answer sheet, find the number in that circle and darken box B as in baker for that number. (Pause five seconds.)

Now look at line 15 again. (Pause slightly.) Write a C in the last circle. (Pause two seconds.) Now, on your answer sheet, find the number in that circle and darken box C for that number. (Pause five seconds.)

Look at the drawings on line 16 on your worksheet. The number in each box is the number of employees in a post office. (Pause slightly.) In the box for the post office with the smallest number of employees, write the last two figures of the number of employees on the line. (Pause five seconds.) Now, on your answer sheet, darken the space for the number-letter combination that is in the box you just wrote in. (Pause five seconds.)

Now look at line 17 on your worksheet. (Pause slightly.) Write an A next to the right-hand number. (Pause two seconds.) Now, on your answer sheet, find the space for the number next to which you just wrote and darken box A. (Pause five seconds.)

Now look at line 18 on your worksheet. (Pause slightly.) In the fourth box, write the answer to this question: How many feet are in a yard? (Pause two seconds.) Now, on your answer sheet, darken the space for the number-letter combination that is in the box you just wrote in. (Pause five seconds.)

25

Look at line 18 again. (Pause slightly.) In the second box, write the number 32. (Pause two seconds.) Now, on your answer sheet, find the number-letter combination that is in the box you just wrote in. (Pause five seconds.)

Look at line 19 on your worksheet. (Pause slightly.) In the circle with the highest number, write the second letter that I will read to you: B as in baker, D as in dog, A as in apple. (Pause five seconds.) Now, on your answer sheet, darken the space for the number-letter combination in the circle you just wrote in. (Pause five seconds.)

Answers

Part A: Address Checking

1.	A	33.	D	65.	D
2.	D	34.	D	66.	D
3.	A	35.	D	67.	D
4.	D	36.	D	68.	D
5.	A	37.	D	69.	A
6.	A	38.	D	70.	D
7.	D	39.	D	71.	A
8.	D	40.	D	72.	A
9.	A	41.	D	73.	A
10.	D	42.	A	74.	D
11.	D	43.	D	75.	D
12.	D	44.	A	76.	D
13.	D	45.	D	77.	D
14.	A	46.	D	78.	D
15.	D	47.	A	79.	A
16.	A	48.	A	80.	D
17.	D	49.	A	81.	A
18.	D	50.	D	82.	A
19.	D	51.	A	83.	D
20.	A	52.	A	84.	D
21.	D	53.	D	85.	D
22.	D	54.	A	86.	D
23.	D	55.	A	87.	D
24.	A	56.	A	88.	D
25.	D	57.	D	89.	D
26.	A	58.	D	90.	A
27.	D	59.	D	91.	A
28.	A	60.	A	92.	D
29.	D	61.	A	93.	D
30.	D	62.	A	94.	D
31.	A	63.	D	95.	D
32.	D	64.	D		

25

Part B: Memory for Addresses
Practice Set 1

1.	D	31.	A	61.	E
2.	B	32.	A	62.	E
3.	A	33.	E	63.	D
4.	E	34.	B	64.	B
5.	C	35.	E	65.	B
6.	E	36.	C	66.	A
7.	C	37.	A	67.	C
8.	A	38.	D	68.	D
9.	D	39.	B	69.	A
10.	E	40.	E	70.	C
11.	D	41.	E	71.	C
12.	B	42.	C	72.	B
13.	E	43.	D	73.	E
14.	A	44.	B	74.	A
15.	A	45.	A	75.	D
16.	B	46.	B	76.	E
17.	C	47.	C	77.	E
18.	D	48.	D	78.	A
19.	C	49.	E	79.	A
20.	D	50.	D	80.	D
21.	B	51.	C	81.	C
22.	A	52.	B	82.	C
23.	E	53.	E	83.	B
24.	D	54.	D	84.	C
25.	D	55.	C	85.	D
26.	B	56.	B	86.	B
27.	B	57.	A	87.	B
28.	C	58.	A	88.	A
29.	A	59.	E		
30.	C	60.	C		

Practice Set 2

1.	E	32.	A	63.	A
2.	D	33.	A	64.	D
3.	B	34.	B	65.	A
4.	A	35.	B	66.	B
5.	C	36.	A	67.	B
6.	E	37.	E	68.	B
7.	C	38.	B	69.	A
8.	C	39.	E	70.	D
9.	B	40.	D	71.	C
10.	E	41.	B	72.	C
11.	B	42.	E	73.	C
12.	A	43.	C	74.	E
13.	E	44.	E	75.	E
14.	A	45.	B	76.	A
15.	D	46.	A	77.	D
16.	D	47.	D	78.	B
17.	B	48.	A	79.	B
18.	A	49.	D	80.	C
19.	C	50.	D	81.	C
20.	D	51.	E	82.	A
21.	A	52.	E	83.	E
22.	B	53.	C	84.	E
23.	A	54.	B	85.	A
24.	D	55.	C	86.	A
25.	C	56.	C	87.	B
26.	D	57.	A	88.	D
27.	C	58.	C		
28.	D	59.	B		
29.	C	60.	E		
30.	D	61.	E		
31.	C	62.	E		

25

Practice Set 3

1.	B	32.	B	63.	B
2.	C	33.	D	64.	B
3.	D	34.	E	65.	B
4.	C	35.	D	66.	B
5.	A	36.	B	67.	C
6.	E	37.	C	68.	E
7.	D	38.	D	69.	A
8.	A	39.	E	70.	E
9.	E	40.	D	71.	D
10.	D	41.	E	72.	C
11.	A	42.	A	73.	E
12.	C	43.	C	74.	B
13.	C	44.	E	75.	E
14.	B	45.	A	76.	A
15.	C	46.	B	77.	C
16.	B	47.	C	78.	E
17.	D	48.	A	79.	D
18.	B	49.	E	80.	A
19.	D	50.	D	81.	C
20.	B	51.	C	82.	D
21.	C	52.	B	83.	D
22.	A	53.	B	84.	A
23.	E	54.	A	85.	C
24.	A	55.	B	86.	C
25.	E	56.	A	87.	A
26.	A	57.	D	88.	E
27.	A	58.	E		
28.	D	59.	C		
29.	E	60.	A		
30.	B	61.	B		
31.	C	62.	D		

Memory for Addresses

1.	A	32.	A	63.	B
2.	C	33.	C	64.	D
3.	E	34.	C	65.	B
4.	E	35.	C	66.	D
5.	A	36.	E	67.	C
6.	A	37.	A	68.	E
7.	B	38.	E	69.	D
8.	D	39.	B	70.	A
9.	E	40.	A	71.	A
10.	A	41.	D	72.	D
11.	C	42.	B	73.	B
12.	C	43.	C	74.	A
13.	E	44.	E	75.	E
14.	E	45.	A	76.	A
15.	C	46.	E	77.	C
16.	B	47.	C	78.	D
17.	C	48.	B	79.	C
18.	B	49.	A	80.	E
19.	D	50.	C	81.	D
20.	D	51.	A	82.	B
21.	A	52.	C	83.	C
22.	A	53.	A	84.	D
23.	C	54.	A	85.	B
24.	D	55.	C	86.	C
25.	C	56.	E	87.	C
26.	A	57.	C	88.	E
27.	E	58.	A		
28.	D	59.	E		
29.	B	60.	E		
30.	B	61.	B		
31.	E	62.	D		

25

Part C: Number Series

Answers

1.	D	9.	D	17.	A
2.	A	10.	C	18.	B
3.	E	11.	A	19.	D
4.	C	12.	B	20.	B
5.	C	13.	B	21.	A
6.	B	14.	E	22.	E
7.	C	15.	E	23.	C
8.	A	16.	C	24.	D

Answers and Explanations

1. **(D)** The series descends 13 12 11 10 9 8, with the number 8 appearing between each set of two numbers.

2. **(A)** Again the series descends by one. This time the number 13 appears between all numbers.

3. **(E)** This time the number is repeated before descending. The number 10 appears between each set of descending numbers.

4. **(C)** The three-number series is repeated.

5. **(C)** The series descends. The even numbers repeat.

6. **(B)** Mark the differences between numbers. The pattern that emerges is: subtract 4, add 2; subtract 4, add 2; and so on.

7. **(C)** There are two alternating series. The first series begins with 7 and ascends by 1. The alternating series begins with 12 and descends one number at a time.

8. **(A)** One series, the odd numbers, repeats and ascends by 2. The alternating series, the even numbers, also ascends by 2, but does not repeat.

9. **(D)** The pattern is subtract 6, subtract 6, subtract 2, subtract 2; subtract 6, subtract 6, subtract 2, subtract 2; and so on.

10. **(C)** The pattern is subtract 8, repeat the number; subtract 7, repeat the number; subtract 6, repeat the number; subtract 5, repeat the number; and so on.

11. **(A)** The pattern is subtract 2, multiply by 2, subtract 3, multiply by 3; subtract 2, multiply by 2, subtract 3, multiply by 3; subtract 2, multiply by 2, subtract 3, multiply by 3; and so on.

12. **(B)** The easiest way to see this pattern is to mark it as follows: subtract 3, add 5; subtract 3, add 5; and so on. If, however, you see two alternating series both ascending by 2, you will also get the correct answer.

13. **(B)** This is a plus 5 series with the number 5 inserted after every two numbers in the series.

14. **(E)** The pattern is subtract 2, subtract 2, repeat the number; subtract 2, subtract 2, repeat the number; and so on.

15. **(E)** The pattern is multiply by 2, add 1, subtract 10; mulitply by 2, add 1, subtract 10; multiply by 2, add 1, subtract 10; and so on.

16. **(C)** The series is simply 9 10 11 12 13… with the number 1 inserted between each step of the series.

17. **(A)** There are two alternating series. The first series starts with 48 and descends by 2. The alternating series starts with 10 and ascends by 7.

25

18. **(B)** The pattern is repeat the number, add 9, add 9; repeat the number, add 9, add 9; and so on.

19. **(D)** The pattern is subtract 3, subtract 6; subtract 3, subtract 6; and so on.

20. **(B)** The pattern is 1 2 3… with the numbers 7 and 8 inserted between each number of the series.

21. **(A)** The series is a repetition of the sequence 1 2 2 1, or, if you see it otherwise, repetitions of 1 1; 2 2; 1 1; 2 2; 1 1; beginning with the repetitions of 1s.

22. **(E)** The pattern is add 11, add 12; add 11, add 12; and so on.

23. **(C)** The pattern is add 8, add 2; add 8, add 2; and so on.

24. **(D)** The pattern is multiply by 2, multiply by 2, repeat the number; multiply by 2, multiply by 2, repeat the number; and so on.

Part D: Following Oral Instructions

Correctly Completed Answer Sheet

1. Ⓐ Ⓑ Ⓒ Ⓓ Ⓔ	23. Ⓐ Ⓑ Ⓒ Ⓓ Ⓔ	45. ● Ⓑ Ⓒ Ⓓ Ⓔ	67. Ⓐ Ⓑ Ⓒ Ⓓ Ⓔ
2. Ⓐ Ⓑ Ⓒ Ⓓ Ⓔ	24. Ⓐ Ⓑ Ⓒ Ⓓ Ⓔ	46. Ⓐ Ⓑ Ⓒ Ⓓ Ⓔ	68. Ⓐ Ⓑ Ⓒ Ⓓ Ⓔ
3. Ⓐ Ⓑ Ⓒ ● Ⓔ	25. Ⓐ Ⓑ Ⓒ Ⓓ Ⓔ	47. Ⓐ Ⓑ Ⓒ Ⓓ Ⓔ	69. Ⓐ Ⓑ Ⓒ ● Ⓔ
4. Ⓐ Ⓑ Ⓒ Ⓓ ●	26. Ⓐ Ⓑ Ⓒ Ⓓ Ⓔ	48. Ⓐ Ⓑ Ⓒ Ⓓ Ⓔ	70. Ⓐ Ⓑ Ⓒ Ⓓ Ⓔ
5. Ⓐ Ⓑ Ⓒ Ⓓ Ⓔ	27. Ⓐ Ⓑ Ⓒ Ⓓ Ⓔ	49. Ⓐ Ⓑ Ⓒ Ⓓ Ⓔ	71. Ⓐ Ⓑ Ⓒ Ⓓ Ⓔ
6. Ⓐ Ⓑ Ⓒ Ⓓ Ⓔ	28. Ⓐ Ⓑ Ⓒ Ⓓ Ⓔ	50. Ⓐ Ⓑ Ⓒ Ⓓ Ⓔ	72. Ⓐ Ⓑ Ⓒ Ⓓ Ⓔ
7. Ⓐ Ⓑ Ⓒ Ⓓ Ⓔ	29. Ⓐ Ⓑ ● Ⓓ Ⓔ	51. Ⓐ Ⓑ Ⓒ Ⓓ ●	73. Ⓐ Ⓑ Ⓒ ● Ⓔ
8. Ⓐ Ⓑ Ⓒ Ⓓ ●	30. Ⓐ Ⓑ Ⓒ Ⓓ Ⓔ	52. ● Ⓑ Ⓒ Ⓓ Ⓔ	74. Ⓐ Ⓑ Ⓒ Ⓓ ●
9. Ⓐ Ⓑ Ⓒ Ⓓ ●	31. Ⓐ Ⓑ Ⓒ Ⓓ Ⓔ	53. Ⓐ Ⓑ Ⓒ Ⓓ Ⓔ	75. Ⓐ Ⓑ ● Ⓓ Ⓔ
10. ● Ⓑ Ⓒ Ⓓ Ⓔ	32. Ⓐ Ⓑ Ⓒ Ⓓ ●	54. Ⓐ Ⓑ Ⓒ Ⓓ Ⓔ	76. Ⓐ ● Ⓒ Ⓓ Ⓔ
11. Ⓐ Ⓑ Ⓒ Ⓓ Ⓔ	33. Ⓐ Ⓑ Ⓒ Ⓓ Ⓔ	55. Ⓐ Ⓑ Ⓒ Ⓓ Ⓔ	77. Ⓐ Ⓑ Ⓒ Ⓓ Ⓔ
12. Ⓐ Ⓑ Ⓒ Ⓓ ●	34. Ⓐ Ⓑ Ⓒ Ⓓ Ⓔ	56. Ⓐ ● Ⓒ Ⓓ Ⓔ	78. Ⓐ Ⓑ Ⓒ Ⓓ Ⓔ
13. Ⓐ Ⓑ Ⓒ ● Ⓔ	35. Ⓐ ● Ⓒ Ⓓ Ⓔ	57. Ⓐ Ⓑ ● Ⓓ Ⓔ	79. Ⓐ Ⓑ Ⓒ Ⓓ Ⓔ
14. Ⓐ Ⓑ Ⓒ Ⓓ Ⓔ	36. Ⓐ Ⓑ Ⓒ ● Ⓔ	58. Ⓐ Ⓑ Ⓒ Ⓓ Ⓔ	80. Ⓐ Ⓑ Ⓒ Ⓓ Ⓔ
15. Ⓐ ● Ⓒ Ⓓ Ⓔ	37. Ⓐ Ⓑ Ⓒ Ⓓ ●	59. Ⓐ Ⓑ Ⓒ Ⓓ Ⓔ	81. Ⓐ Ⓑ Ⓒ Ⓓ Ⓔ
16. Ⓐ Ⓑ Ⓒ Ⓓ Ⓔ	38. Ⓐ Ⓑ Ⓒ Ⓓ Ⓔ	60. Ⓐ Ⓑ Ⓒ Ⓓ Ⓔ	82. Ⓐ Ⓑ Ⓒ Ⓓ Ⓔ
17. Ⓐ Ⓑ Ⓒ Ⓓ Ⓔ	39. ● Ⓑ Ⓒ Ⓓ Ⓔ	61. Ⓐ Ⓑ Ⓒ Ⓓ Ⓔ	83. Ⓐ ● Ⓒ Ⓓ Ⓔ
18. Ⓐ Ⓑ Ⓒ Ⓓ Ⓔ	40. ● Ⓑ Ⓒ Ⓓ Ⓔ	62. Ⓐ Ⓑ Ⓒ ● Ⓔ	84. Ⓐ Ⓑ Ⓒ Ⓓ Ⓔ
19. Ⓐ Ⓑ Ⓒ Ⓓ Ⓔ	41. Ⓐ Ⓑ Ⓒ Ⓓ Ⓔ	63. Ⓐ Ⓑ Ⓒ Ⓓ Ⓔ	85. Ⓐ Ⓑ Ⓒ Ⓓ Ⓔ
20. Ⓐ Ⓑ ● Ⓓ Ⓔ	42. Ⓐ Ⓑ Ⓒ Ⓓ Ⓔ	64. Ⓐ Ⓑ Ⓒ Ⓓ Ⓔ	86. Ⓐ Ⓑ Ⓒ Ⓓ Ⓔ
21. Ⓐ Ⓑ Ⓒ Ⓓ Ⓔ	43. Ⓐ Ⓑ Ⓒ Ⓓ Ⓔ	65. Ⓐ Ⓑ Ⓒ Ⓓ Ⓔ	87. Ⓐ Ⓑ Ⓒ Ⓓ Ⓔ
22. ● Ⓑ Ⓒ Ⓓ Ⓔ	44. Ⓐ Ⓑ Ⓒ Ⓓ Ⓔ	66. ● Ⓑ Ⓒ Ⓓ Ⓔ	88. Ⓐ Ⓑ Ⓒ ● Ⓔ

25

Correctly Completed Worksheet

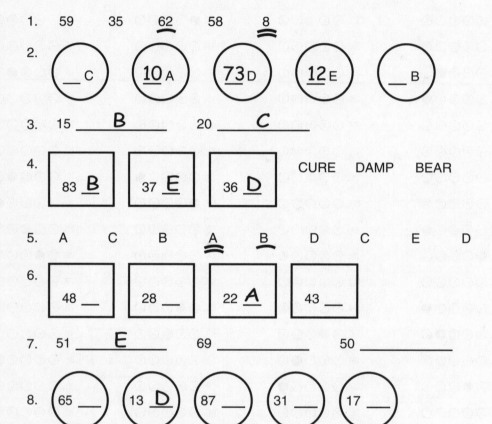

1.   59   35   62   58   8

2.

__ C   10 A   73 D   12 E   __ B

3.   15 ___B___   20 ___C___

4.   83 B   37 E   36 D   CURE   DAMP   BEAR

5.   A   C   B   A   B   D   C   E   D

6.   48 __   28 __   22 A   43 __

7.   51 ___E___   69 _____   50 _____

8.   65 __   13 D   87 __   31 __   17 __

9.
| 55 __ | 44 __ | 74 **E** | 25 __ |

10.   <u>40</u>   85   17   87   <u>52</u>   55   80   <u>45</u>   <u>75</u>

11.
| 65 __ | 37 __ | 12 __ | 4 <u>**E**</u> |

12.   X O O O <u>X</u> O O <u>X</u> <u>X</u> O <u>X</u> O <u>X</u>   **9**

13.
| 78 __ | 29 / 25 **C** | 27 __ | 73 __ |

14.   88   2   <u>69</u>   84   34

15.
| 63 __ | 38 __ | 76 <u>**B**</u> | 53 __ | 57 <u>**C**</u> |

16.
| 435 <u>35</u> B | 466 __ C | 474 __ E | 467 __ A | 489 __ E |

17.   79 _____   39 _____ **A** _____

18.
| __ C | <u>32</u> E | __ A | <u>3</u> D | __ B |

19.
| 88 **D** | 25 __ | 6 __ |

Evaluate Yourself

First, determine your raw score for each part of the exam. Then assess each score according to the evaluation chart. Remember that Parts A and B have a scoring penalty.

Determine Your Raw Score

When determining your raw scores, don't count any questions that you left blank. You're not penalized for unanswered questions.

Part A: Address Checking

Your score on Address Checking is based on the number of questions you answered correctly minus the number of questions you missed:

1. Enter number of right answers: _____
2. Enter number of wrong answers: _____
3. Subtract number wrong from number right: _____

                                         Raw Score =   _____

Part B: Memory for Addresses

Your score on Memory for Addresses is based on the number of questions you answered correctly minus one-fourth of the questions you answered incorrectly (number wrong divided by four):

1. Number of right answers: _____
2. Number of wrong answers: _____
3. Divide number wrong by 4:   _____
4. Subtract answer from number right: _____

                                         Raw Score =   _____

Part C: Number Series

Your score is based on the number of questions answered correctly:

                                         Raw Score =   _____

Part D: Following Oral Instructions

Your score is based on the number of questions answered correctly:

Raw Score = _____

Total Score

To find your total raw score, add the raw scores for each section of the exam:

Address Checking: _____

Memory for Addresses: _____

Number Series: _____

Following Oral Instructions: _____

Total Raw Score =   _____

25

Evaluate Your Score

Determine where your raw scores on each part of the test fall on the scale from Poor to Excellent in the following table. Lightly shade in the boxes in which your scores fall.

Part	Excellent	Good	Average	Fair	Poor
Address Checking	80-95	65-79	50-64	35-49	1-34
Memory for Addresses	75-88	60-74	45-59	30-44	1-29
Number Series	21-24	18-20	14-17	11-13	1-10
Following Oral Instructions	27-31	23-26	19-22	14-18	1-13

Determine Where You Need Review

If you scored less than Excellent on any part of the exam, review the appropriate lessons and retake the appropriate practice tests as indicated in the following table:

Part	Lessons to Review	Practice Tests to Retake
Address Checking	Hours 4–5	Hours 13–14
Memory for Addresses	Hours 6–8	Hours 15–19
Number Series	Hours 9–10	Hours 20–21
Following Oral Instructions	Hours 11–12	Hours 22–24

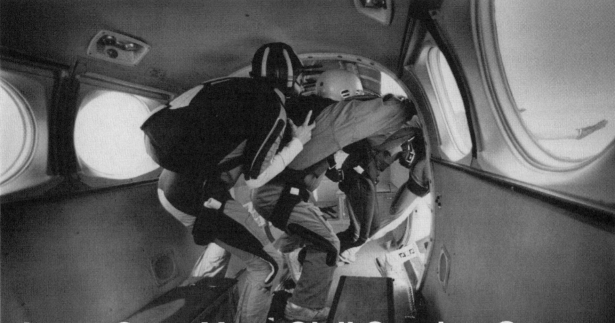